IF GOD LOVES ME
WHY CAN'T I
GET MY LOCKER OPEN?

Billy Frank

IF GOD LOVES ME
WHY CAN'T I
GET MY LOCKER OPEN?

LORRAINE PETERSON

BETHANY HOUSE PUBLISHERS

Minneapolis, Minnesota

If God Loves Me, Why Can't I Get My Locker Open?
Copyright © 2006
Lorraine Peterson

Cover design by Josh Madison

Published by Bethany House Publishers
11400 Hampshire Avenue South
Bloomington, Minnesota 55438

Bethany House Publishers is a division of
Baker Publishing Group, Grand Rapids, Michigan.

Printed in the United States of America

ISBN   978-0-7642-0189-9

Library of Congress Cataloging-in-Publication Data

Peterson, Lorraine.
    If God loves me, why can't I get my locker open? : the yearbook / Lorraine Peterson.
        p.   cm.
    Summary: "This 365-day devotional 'yearbook' for teens offers biblical advice and guidance on topics such as faith, family, school, dating, and friendship"—Provided by publisher.
    ISBN 0-7642-0189-1 (pbk.)
    1. Youth—Prayer-books and devotions—English. 2. Devotional calendars—Juvenile literature. I. Title.
    BV4850.P46   2006
    242'.63—dc22   2006013762

For all the teenagers I've
worked with in the past and
those I'm working with now.

LORRAINE PETERSON has written several bestselling devotional books for teens. She received her BA in history from North Park College in Chicago and has taken summer courses from the University of Minnesota and the University of Mexico in Mexico City. Lorraine has taught high school and junior high, has been an advisor to nondenominational Christian clubs in Minneapolis public schools, has taught teenage Bible studies, and continues to work with young people. She currently makes her home in Cuidad Juarez, Mexico.

Also by Lorraine Peterson: *God's an Artist and You're a Masterpiece: The Mind-Boggling Science of an Awesome Creator.*

Contents

Tiffany glanced at herself in the mirror one last time. She had spent an hour putting on makeup and doing her hair. Her dress was the most expensive she had ever worn. Although she wished she could instantly lose fifteen pounds, she had done the best she could to make herself attractive. Being invited to Jewell's party meant instant membership into Central High's VIP club. It was her chance to shake off the "boring and born-again" label. Besides, Todd, the strikingly handsome captain of the basketball team, was sure to be there, and Tiffany wanted to prove to him that she was more on the ball than his present girlfriend.

Ignoring the small voice warning her against hypocrisy, jealousy, and compromise, she flitted out the door, starring in her own version of the perfect saturday night. By the time she arrived, she had cast herself into the role of a vivacious but slightly sophisticated "go-along-with-the-crowd" celebrity. She pretended not to notice that Jewell's parents weren't home and accepted the drinks she was offered. Downing one drink after another as if they were Coca-Cola, she became dizzy and sick to her stomach. The reflection she saw in the bathroom mirror bore no resemblance to the pretty girl who had left the house three hours before.

If Tiffany had listened to that still, small voice, she might have thought of this passage:

> So then, just as you received Christ Jesus as Lord, continue to live in him, rooted and built up in him, strengthened in the faith as you were taught, and overflowing with thankfulness. See to it that no one takes you captive through hollow and deceptive philosophy, which depends on human tradition and the basic principles of this world rather than on Christ. For in Christ all the fullness of the Deity lives in bodily form, and you have been given fullness in Christ. Colossians 2:6–10

You don't have to learn this lesson the hard way, as Tiffany did. All you have to do is believe God's Word and live by it.

Day 2

Unmasking the "Nobody's-Going-to-Tell-Me-What-to-Do" Thief

Rocky felt his muscles stiffen, and he mentally prepared his defensive strategy. He was nearly eighteen years old, and he didn't appreciate anyone else trying to run his life.

"Rocky," his mother said, "you're gifted intellectually, and there's no excuse for bringing home Cs on your report card. Your senior grades are important for getting into a good college. You're about to blow everything. And you show the same irresponsibility around the house."

"Besides," his father went on, "you could show your parents a little respect. I suppose that 'please' and 'thank you' and 'I'd be glad to help' are too old-fashioned to show up in your vocabulary."

Rocky's face flushed as he snapped back, "After seven more months I'll move out forever and the house will become a paradise! It's time you realized that I'm grown up and you can't treat me like a little kid anymore!" With that he left the house and drove away in his car.

Do you hate having someone boss you around? If so, you need to listen to something God says in His Word:

> *But the wisdom that comes from heaven is first of all pure; then peace-loving, considerate, submissive, full of mercy and good fruit, impartial and sincere.*
> James 3:17

Because true wisdom is submissive, there's no place in a Christian for the "nobody's-going-to-tell-me-what-to-do" attitude. The devil tempts all young people to destroy the personality Jesus planned for them by having an unteachable spirit. God didn't make us to be self-sufficient beings. He created us to depend on Him and on the body of Christ. One of the easiest ways to ruin your life is to refuse to take advice from your parents, teachers, pastors, and other Christians. Helping you maintain a bad attitude is one of the devil's most effective methods for robbing you of God's blessings and keeping you from seeing His fantastic design for your personality. Unmask the nobody's-going-to-tell-me-what-to-do thief, and don't let him take anything from you.

Day 3

Donna was on the youth planning team at her church. When Dave interrupted her idea with, "Only a dumb blonde could think that's a good idea," it was like a knife going through her. Later, when he asked if he had offended her, she said everything was okay. It was a lie, but she didn't know how to say, "Yes, your remark hurt me."

Months later, when Dave was giving orders to everyone, she came out with a snippy "*Heil* Hitler!"

Most of us suffer the consequences of dishonesty in some area of life. Lying to avoid hurting someone's feelings or to keep the peace is still breaking one of God's Ten Commandments. Saying, "No, nothing's bothering me," instead of "I really can't talk about it now," is just another lie.

Some people are so defensive they have an automatic reflex that blames the weather, the person in authority, the dog, or the traffic when anything might be their fault. Others live a lie either by exaggerating to get attention or telling some stories to make themselves look good.

Rather, we have renounced secret and shameful ways; we do not use deception. 2 Corinthians 4:2

Jesus offers us freedom from our imagined need to hide the truth. But first we must realize that fear of rejection often springs the dishonesty trap. We are afraid that rejection will follow the revelation of weakness. Anxiety reasons, "Nobody will want to listen to me if I don't spice up my weekend a little bit." Insecurity screams, "You can't take the blame yourself or stop bragging, because you've got to prove yourself to be superior if anybody is going to respect you."

Bring your need for acceptance to Jesus. Receive His love and power. Your prayer should be something like this: "Dear God, help me to be able to say, 'I'm sorry; it's my fault,' when I'm guilty, instead of transferring the blame. I know you love me even if I'm not perfect. Put the spotlight on any dishonesty in my life. I don't want lack of integrity to keep me from being the person you created me to be."

Day 4

Measuring Up

Tracy felt like a slave working for many masters: teachers, parents, bosses, and peers. She worked for hours each week to write a paper that would get an A from Miss Johnson. Chemistry was worse. No matter what she did, she couldn't get above a B. And for Tracy, that big B on her otherwise straight-A report card said, "Tracy, you're not good enough."

For Tracy, being a member of the girls' volleyball team was anything but relaxing. If she made any mistakes it was a major disaster. Precise and demanding, Tracy's father often corrected her. Tracy's goal was to do everything right the first time so that her father would be pleased with her, but she seldom succeeded. As a scooper at the local ice-cream shop, she attempted to be accurate and efficient, but the manager noticed her only when she did something wrong.

Then one Sunday morning the pastor's words shocked her. "Do you really know what God expects of you? Or have you been making up your own standards? Well, God tells us what He wants from us. Micah 6:8 reads, 'And what does the Lord require of you? To act justly and to love mercy and to walk humbly with your God.'

"Notice," the pastor continued, "that God says nothing about winning, being the best, or receiving high ratings from your supervisors. God asks you to 'act justly.' That means that you please God only—you work hard, you're fair, your motives are pure, and you don't permit false earthly standards to be the measure of your value. You show compassion, you think about others, and you keep the spotlight off yourself. And you 'walk humbly with your God.' You spend quality time with Jesus. Because you realize that He is all-powerful and all-knowing, you submit yourself totally to Him. This is the only way you can become the person God saved you to be."

That morning Tracy made a discovery: The Lord always noticed her good work. Tracy realized that she could stop trying so hard and relax in the presence of Jesus. Maybe you, like Tracy, have been trying to measure up to the wrong standard. If so, determine right now that prayerful study of the Scriptures will free you to live by God's yardstick.

Eric sat in the dugout with his teammates, unable to believe his ears. The coach was benching him for two weeks.

The guy must have rocks in his head! thought Eric. *I have nearly as many RBIs as the rest of the team combined. I'm the star of the team.* He tuned in to the coach's speech: "We all know that Eric is the most talented player to come through Park High in years. But this is a team—not a one-man show. Instead of staying in center field, he's all over the outfield and tries to make spectacular catches in the second baseman's territory. Learning that the world doesn't revolve around one person is an important lesson that I want to teach all of you. Eric, you're not playing until you learn that you're judged on teamwork, not on individual performance."

Have you ever tried to be the star on God's team? God created you with gifts and abilities to function in the body of Christ. He purposely made you unable to do everything so you'd *have* to work with other Christians and depend on them. The Bible says:

> But in fact God has arranged the parts in the body, every one of them, just as he wanted them to be. . . . The eye cannot say to the hand, "I don't need you!" And the head cannot say to the feet, "I don't need you!" 1 Corinthians 12:18, 21

As a Christian, you depend on God for your sense of competence, and you're part of a team. There are many things God does not expect you to do. Eyes should not try to be hands, and feet should not feel discouraged because they're not heads. God will give you the power to be or do anything that is necessary to communicate the new life Jesus offers to the world—and that does not require bowling 250, getting straight A's, or being voted Personality Plus by the senior class.

Pray and ask God what He has called you to do. Believe that He will equip you for the work He wants you to do—but don't expect to excel in every area. Too many have already tried to be one-man shows and failed. Don't join the casualty list.

Day 6

Turn on the Faucet—Full Blast

Marcy broke into tears. Life was a pressure cooker, one of those nightmares in which a person gets worn out trying to reach the top of the mountain but never makes any progress. Only Marcy never woke up to discover it was just a bad dream.

She knew she was supposed to love her enemies, share Jesus with those who didn't know Him, and be respectful and obedient. But she felt like a failure. So many non-Christians she knew seemed so happy-go-lucky that at times she even envied them.

There is a way out of this kind of dilemma. If you attempt to live up to the ideals of Jesus in your own strength, you can feel much less competent than a non-Christian who chooses to live by some human yardstick. (People who don't know Jesus often assume that it's perfectly legitimate to get by as easily as possible.)

The ability to live a Jesus-style life comes from the power of the Holy Spirit. If you try to live a supernatural life in human strength, failure is inevitable. The Holy Spirit comes to make His home in you when you are born again—that miracle that occurs when you invite Jesus to take over your whole life. In fact, the Bible states:

Don't you know that you yourselves are God's temple and that God's Spirit lives in you? 1 Corinthians 3:16

When you put your faith in Jesus, the question isn't "How much of the Holy Spirit do you have?" It's "How much of *you* does the Holy Spirit possess?"

The Bible teaches that you are to "Be filled with the Spirit" (Ephesians 5:18). Let the Holy Spirit be himself in you. Search the Scriptures to discover what the Holy Spirit wants to accomplish in your life. Surrender your rights to direct your own life. Step out of that box you've been living in and expect new and miraculous workings of the Holy Spirit in *your* life. Turn on the faucet to experience Jesus' promise:

Whoever believes in me, as the Scripture has said, streams of living water will flow from within him. John 7:38

Day 7

Give Jesus More Than a Piece of Your Mind

Kevin wished he could wake up from the nightmare—but he wasn't dreaming. He still had to play the second half of the game. As a well-trained athlete who was voted Most Valuable Player by the Jefferson High basketball team, Kevin knew that concentration was everything. Tonight, however, he had lost it completely.

Not only had Amy broken up with him, but she was sitting in the front row with her new boyfriend. To top it off, the fans from Lakeview were making a concentrated effort to heckle Kevin about his over-sized nose. He'd missed six free throws in a row, he fumbled the ball, and he had scored only two points.

Even when things are tough, as a Christian, you know that you can join Isaiah in telling God:

You will keep in perfect peace him whose mind is steadfast, because he trusts in you. Isaiah 26:3

Because the devil so cleverly uses our weaknesses to undermine us, every honest Christian must admit to the type of defeat Kevin experienced on the basketball court. Maybe you sang your solo while you were wrapped up in what other people were thinking, rather than singing to offer praise to God. Because Jesus' opinion was not your only concern, you were devastated when the friend you tried talking to about Jesus made fun of you. Perhaps you fell apart when you saw that big red C on your chemistry test because your standards for yourself are more important to you than those Jesus has for you.

Self-consciousness, fear of what others will think, and slavery to the expectations of others are chains we must permit God to break. Then we can receive the sense of confidence and competence He wants to give us.

Live by God's expectations—not yours or others'. Getting rid of unreasonable goals will take off a lot of pressure. Admit that you took your eyes off Jesus, then purpose in your heart not to let it happen again. Practice keeping your thoughts on Jesus by meditating on Scripture. When your mind wants to wander, firmly bring it back to thinking about Him.

What's on *your* mind? Is it Jesus? Give Him more than a piece of your mind.

Day 8

Confidence Comes on Crutches!

Jamil knew that not only was the conference championship at stake with this game, but so was the possibility of his getting a college football scholarship. After sustained drives, he threw a completed pass for one touchdown and carried the ball for another. Nearing the end zone for the third time, Jamil dropped back to pass. Out of nowhere, North High's middle linebacker tackled him so hard he lost the ball. Sharp pain shot through his ankle as he lay on the twenty-yard line. An emergency room visit left Jamil with crutches—and doctor's orders to stay on the bench for the rest of the season. Slowly, Jamil realized that stardom had caused him to substitute trusting God with a misplaced confidence in himself. Like Jamil, all of us face situations that prove we need supernatural help.

The Bible clearly teaches that confidence in what you can do by yourself is misplaced. Jesus said, "Apart from me you can do nothing" (John 15:5). So often the areas of great natural abilities become a person's trap. A thrifty person becomes a Scrooge, an easygoing guy ends up a bum, or a brilliant girl falls into egotism. Any strength or talent used in the wrong way turns into a weakness.

However, the Bible has a lot to say about confidence in what God can do *through* you.

We have confidence in the Lord that you are doing and will continue to do the things we command. 2 Thessalonians 3:4

Not that we are competent in ourselves to claim anything for ourselves, but our competence comes from God. 2 Corinthians 3:5

To be really confident, you do need crutches—and the only support system that will work is God.

Day 9

Vanessa wished that life were like a television set and she could just switch channels. Her father was going into the hospital for a cancer operation. Although she knew that her all-powerful God was in control of the situation, the fear of losing her dad kept coming back. Her boyfriend, Ted, was leaving for college in New York; California and New York were so far apart that he might as well be moving to China. Besides all this, her name had appeared on the list of students who would be bussed to another school in order to equalize student population in the two buildings.

Wasn't there anything she could depend on?

There is a love that won't ever let you down. The apostle Paul tells the Romans:

> *For I am convinced that neither death nor life, neither angels nor demons, neither the present nor the future, nor any powers, neither height nor depth, nor anything else in all creation, will be able to separate us from the love of God that is in Christ Jesus our Lord.* Romans 8:38–39

If you make a fool of yourself, you can count on the love of God. Your bad breath, nervous cough, or stammering tongue will not alienate you from God's love. Giving wrong answers, fumbling the ball, or coming late won't affect God's great love for you one bit. And you can't run away from God's love or turn it off if you try.

You can merely accept this fact and enjoy it. It's a little bit like the weather—you can simply live through it, or you can stop to appreciate it. The snow glittering in the sunshine, the refreshing soft spring breeze, and the spectacular show put on by a thunderstorm. In the same way, you can revel in God's love. You can run into His arms after an especially hard day, drawing strength from His presence.

Do you treat God's love with indifference, or do you enjoy every minute of it? Do you own a heart-shaped umbrella that deflects all those love showers, or have you thrown it away so you can soak it all in?

Day 10

Fifteen Tons of Pure Smush

When Tina saw her two-year-old nephew for the first time, she squealed with delight. Jacob was the cutest little boy she'd ever seen. When Tina's sister gave Jacob a swat for taking his grandmother's china out of the cupboard, Tina thought she was cruel. It almost broke her heart to see Jacob cry. Tina thought she loved her little nephew too much to ever spank him.

One afternoon, Tina volunteered to baby-sit Jacob when her sister went to have lunch with her girl friends. When Tina took him out into the yard to play, the first thing he did was run out into the street. Tina ran after him, picked him up, gave him a hug, and sweetly said, "Jacob, you can't play in the street. It's dangerous." There were two or three repeat performances.

Then the telephone rang, and Tina ran in to answer it. Returning a minute later, she saw Jacob lying in the street. He had been hit by a car!

At the hospital she told her mother the whole story. "But Tina," her mother scolded, "don't you love Jacob enough to discipline him and keep him from danger?"

"I guess I never thought of it that way," replied Tina.

What's your idea of love—fifteen pounds of pure smush? Does it include restraint, discipline, and commands? Do you understand that because God loves you, He'll give you rules to live by?

God disciplines us for our good, that we may share in his holiness. No discipline seems pleasant at the time, but painful. Later on, however, it produces a harvest of righteousness and peace for those who have been trained by it.
Hebrews 12:10–11

Aren't you glad that God loves you enough to see that you receive the discipline you need? Isn't it neat that God won't let your rough edges go unattended? The new you deep inside has to break those bad habits, wrong thought patterns, and old reactions. God's scolding isn't the result of His having had a bad day! In love He gives warnings that will save you from heartbreak and failure. Learn to appreciate the purpose of His discipline.

Focused on her June wedding for the Saturday after graduation, Joy was so much in love that she didn't even notice other people existed—much less consider their advice. She married Chuck against her parents' wishes and contrary to the counsel of all her trusted Christian friends.

Six months after the wedding, she found herself in a small apartment in the city with a husband who was out of work. Whenever she'd mention that he might look for a job, he'd laugh, take her in his arms, and tell her how much he loved her. "Nothing matters as long as we're together," he'd say.

Joy turned to her Bible.

If you love me, you will obey what I command. . . . If anyone loves me, he will obey my teaching. My father will love him, and we will come to him and make our home with him. John 14:15, 23

Joy had treated Jesus the same way Chuck was treating her. She had told Him she loved Him, and then disobeyed His commandments. Joy knew she'd have to face some dreadful consequences because of her rebellion, but she also knew that she could come back to Jesus and receive forgiveness. From now on, she would show Jesus she loved Him *by her actions,* not just by what she said.

God's love is all action—God shows His love to you in rays of sunshine and fuzzy kittens, but most of all in allowing Jesus to take the punishment that you deserve because of your sin. You respond by accepting this free gift of salvation and obeying His commandments. God comes back by putting His Spirit within you to give you love and joy and power as you obey, and you reply by carrying out His wishes.

This love cycle is very satisfying. Christ living in you and you in Him involves a relationship deeper than any expression of human love. It produces a continuous action of loving and being loved. When you give yourself to Jesus with total abandon, you just want to obey more and more commands, because giving and receiving of love is exciting and fulfilling.

There's nothing quite like putting "I love you" into practice.

Day 12

Loving Enemies and Other Difficult People

Brenna showed up at school dressed in clothes from the last decade, and she didn't even bring a notebook. She never smiled or said hi to anyone. After four months at Roosevelt High, Brenna didn't even have one friend. Melody began to pray for her. She gave Brenna some of her own clothes and invited her over for dinner. Brenna began to open up and share some of her problems.

When Brenna asked if she could borrow twenty dollars, something inside Melody told her this wasn't wise. But Mel pushed it aside and said, "Of course I'll give money to someone I love."

Soon Melody realized that Brenna had no intention of paying it back—but she got enough love from Jesus to forgive her friend completely. Gradually she realized that Brenna was becoming more and more distant. Mel knew something was wrong. A week later, she saw Brenna at the mall with the purse Mel couldn't find!

Mel was really discouraged. She had prayed for and helped a really difficult person. Why did it have to end up like this?

Has anyone ever taken advantage of your love? The solution is not to stop loving. It's learning how to love with Jesus' love.

And this is my prayer: that your love may abound more and more in knowledge and depth of insight, so that you may be able to discern what is best.
Philippians 1:9–10

If the love you give away comes from what is stored up inside, you'll soon burn out. You'll grow to resent the "love leeches" that congregate around you. You must consciously reach out to God to receive more of His love. Then you'll find that He showers you with so much understanding and mercy and affection that it just overflows. And there'll even be enough leftover for enemies and difficult people.

After receiving *God's* love for a person, pray for wisdom. Sometimes love must be tough, sometimes cautious, and sometimes demonstrative.

Daring to love is exciting—and dangerous. If you use God's love *and* His wisdom, God will reach out to His world through you.

Day 13

Join the Exterminators!

Lizette received her schedule during homeroom on the first day of school. Apprehensively, she checked the names of her teachers. Sure enough, there it was—third-hour science with Jerome Crabtree!

Nearly ready to retire, Mr. Crabtree had become a living legend—the toughest, meanest teacher in the whole district. In fact, Lizette's uncle had flunked his science course and still recounted science room horror stories.

At 10:05 Lizette headed for room 205, commonly referred to as "Jerry's Jail." Mr. Crabtree's beginning-of-the-year speech fulfilled all her expectations.

Soon Lizette dreaded third hour and felt that Mr. Crabtree had singled her out as the object of his anger. Even in her dreams she could hear, "Why don't you speak up so everyone can hear?" One day when she burst into tears, he ridiculed her in front of the class. Lizette had a very hard time receiving faith for the situation in science class.

One evening, as she was reading 1 John, five words caught her eye: "Perfect love drives out fear" (1 John 4:18).

Lizette was always afraid of what would happen next. She couldn't imagine loving Mr. Crabtree, and she didn't even know what perfect love was.

As she prayed for wisdom, she realized that the only perfect love was God's love, and she asked Him to provide her with love for Mr. Crabtree.

The first thing God showed her was that she should pray for him daily. As God put His love in her heart for her science teacher, the fear began to leave. Lizette kept asking God for more love, and there was less and less fear. When Mr. Crabtree read the riot act, she'd ask God to give her love for him—and it kept the fear away. Even when Mr. Crabtree criticized her report in front of the whole class, she didn't fall apart. (She'd stored up some extra love just for the occasion.)

Fear is the symptom that tells you there is lack of love. The Bible teaches that love and fear are opposites; the two can't exist side by side. Keep receiving God's never-ending supply of love, and join the exterminators who do away with fear and doubt.

Day 14
Don't Be a Turkey

A man stole an egg from an eagle's nest and put it among the eggs of a turkey he was raising. When the eggs hatched, the other turkeys thought that a rather ugly member of their species had emerged. His wings were different from those of the turkeys, but no one taught him how to fly. Because he knew no other way to act, the eagle was scratching on the ground with all the turkeys.

One day an eagle flew overhead. How the baby eagle wished to fly, effortlessly, like that soaring bird! The others laughed and said, "You're a turkey and turkeys can't fly." But his desire became even stronger. Deep inside, he knew he was missing out on something, and it made him miserable.

Do you sympathize with the eagle who lived like a turkey?

Those who hope in the Lord will renew their strength. They will soar on wings like eagles; they will run and not grow weary, they will walk and not be faint. Isaiah 40:31

When you gave your life to Jesus, you became new on the *inside*. You now have new desires and new capacities. The only problem is that these are not visible to the naked eye. You still look the same. You live in the same environment. And your mental and emotional patterns appear to be fairly well established. If you don't concentrate on God's definition of a new creation in Christ, it's pretty easy for you to live like that eagle among the turkeys, experiencing constant defeat, discouragement, and frustration—all because you are unaware of who you really are in Christ. Instead of becoming a reality, the victorious life is only some longing deep in your heart.

But this doesn't have to be your biography. Someone once quipped, "It's difficult to soar with the eagles when you live all day among the turkeys." But that person didn't take into account the dynamite power of the Holy Spirit in the life of new creatures in Christ. You need to know that you are no longer a turkey but an eagle with the supernatural energy to rise in joy and victory. When you fail, the devil's sarcastic, "You turkey!" may echo someplace back in your mind. Yet you must stand firm.

Day 15

Have you ever watched trapeze artists perform? Balancing seventy feet above a cheering crowd must be completely mind-blowing. But there are qualities to admire in these circus performers: They realize the full potential of human life in one small area, and they have learned to put their minds and bodies under the discipline required to achieve a higher goal.

In order to live the abundant life Jesus promised, you must discover how to discipline your mind and body so that it becomes a help rather than a hindrance to living for Jesus. Although you may feel like a Dr. Jekyll/Mr. Hyde combination, you're not. The Bible says that you are a "co-heir with Christ" (Romans 8:17), "the salt of the earth" (Matthew 5:13), and part of a "chosen people, a royal priesthood, a holy nation" (1 Peter 2:9).

Paul concludes his discussion of good vs. evil this way:

For in my inner being I delight in God's law; but I see another law at work in the members of my body, waging war against the law of my mind and making me a prisoner of the law of sin at work within my members. Romans 7:22–23

In other words, the new you is capable of living free from the grip of sin through the power of the Holy Spirit. However, your flesh—the part of you that isn't eternal and is used to sinning—will protest. The devil with all his lies will try to convince you that the new you wants to sin. Because your undisciplined mind would rather think about cute guys or beautiful girls than about Jesus, the devil will taunt, "See—you're not a new creature. You don't really love Jesus one bit, and maybe you're not a Christian."

What are you going to do about these attacks?

First, keep searching the Scriptures and meditating on God's Word to know who you are in Christ. Second, discipline your mind and body. Paul urges, "Be transformed by the renewing of your mind" (Romans 12:2). Fill your mind with God's truth to contradict Satan's lies and break old patterns. Don't let an unrenewed mind and an undisciplined body prevent you from expressing your spiritual self.

Day 16

"But I Just Can't Change"

Katie's father was an alcoholic and her mother was a nervous wreck. Because Katie couldn't stand any more hurt and disappointment, she became hard and indifferent. She kept her distance from most people. "That's the way I am," she told herself. "I can't change."

Can you identify with Katie? Do you wonder if your personality will ever change? It's true that a nervous breakdown or a tragedy can alter someone drastically. Yet if you're a natural scatterbrain and have seriously tried to become cool, calm, and sophisticated, you've probably been very disappointed with the results. Without new circumstances, it's pretty hard to change—that is, unless you plug into God's power system.

For you have been born again, not of perishable seed, but of imperishable, through the living and enduring word of God. 1 Peter 1:23

When you're tempted to moan in desperation, "I've tried and tried but I just can't change," remember some important things. First, deeper than the personality trait you don't like is the life of the Holy Spirit. First John 3:9 declares that a Christian will change his or her actions because "God's seed remains in him."

Second, don't condemn yourself. Romans 8:1 declares, "There is now no condemnation for those who are in Christ Jesus"—even if you have some unlovable characteristics.

Third, ask God to show you if there is sin, lack of self-discipline, or unteachableness on your part. Proverbs 28:13 teaches that when we confess our sin, we find mercy.

Fourth, ask God to heal the scars from the past that interfere with change in your personality. Psalm 147:3 is especially for you: "He heals the brokenhearted and binds up their wounds."

Last, pray constantly that God will "strengthen you with power through his Spirit in your inner being" (Ephesians 3:16). Receive God's power—yours just isn't good enough.

How about basing your life on Scripture and continuing in prayer so the new you shows up in your personality?

Day 17
Wishy-Washy Wishes vs. Deepest Desires

After a mini-concert by the praise band, the youth speaker gave a stirring pep talk on Luke 9:24: "Whoever loses his life for me will save it."

To Debbie it sounded as though she would have to give up everything she enjoyed to follow Jesus. Debbie pictured herself in the middle of Swaziland, hundreds of miles from the nearest pizza parlor, working among a tribe that considered it a disgrace for a woman to wear blue jeans.

On Sunday morning, her pastor preached on Psalm 37:4: "Delight yourself in the Lord and he will give you the desires of your heart." Now Debbie was ready to pray for a red sports car with Dolby Surround sound.

Have you, like Debbie, had problems reconciling "deny yourself" verses with "delight yourself" verses? Maybe you're confusing the deep longing of the new you with the temporary desires influenced by fads and peers. Sorting out what the real you wants and then acting on it isn't easy.

The apostle Paul struggled with this. He writes, "For I have the desire to do what is good, but I cannot carry it out. . . . The evil I do not want to do—this I keep on doing" (Romans 7:18-19). Two kinds of desires fight within you: those of your physical human existence and those of your new life in Christ. A part of you feels like taking the easy way out, substituting chocolate for veggies, getting even and bragging, while there is a deeper desire for the ability to genuinely love everyone, power to truly forgive, purity of life, and strength to obey God when no one else is.

The quality of the supernatural life of Jesus in you, which is described as the working of "the law of the Spirit of life" (Romans 8:2), can drive out harmful and temporary desires. When you find that you really want something, it's a good idea to ask God, "Is this a temporary desire of my flesh, or is it a real desire of my new life?" Give it some time. God wants to fulfill all the desires of the new you, as you delight in Him. He won't ask you to go against the true personality He put inside you. But you need His help in discerning the difference between wishy-washy wishes that aren't good for you and the deepest desires of the new nature He gave you.

Day 18

"Just Accept Me—Don't Try to Change Me"

A competitor at heart, Bob gave everything he had—but in a friendly ski race, instead of carving around the gate, he hit ice and veered into the trees on the side of the mountain. A stately Norway pine stopped him. Major ouch.

Suppose that at the hospital, a doctor approached him and said, "Bob, I want you to know that I accept you just the way you are. Don't be embarrassed about skiing into a tree and breaking your leg. Here there is nothing but total acceptance." And then he left the room.

Does this sound weird? The doctor had the capacity to change the situation for the better, so we expect more than acceptance from him. God, too, has the power not only to accept you, but to change you. God's acceptance of you includes not only love, mercy, and forgiveness, but also surgery to remove hatred, stitches to mend a broken heart, and out-patient therapy to teach you patience. *God completely accepts you in order to change you!*

Most correction we receive from other people is not really intended to help us but to eliminate behavior they find bothersome. Our bosses nag us about laziness because they want the present task completed. The teacher lectures about illegible handwriting because she's had a bad week. Because so many people try to scold us out of selfish motives, we tend to equate correction with lack of acceptance. Jesus loves us just the way we are, but He loves us too much to leave us just the way we are.

[Jesus said], "Go, sell everything you have and give to the poor, and you will have treasure in heaven. Then come, follow me." At this the man's face fell. He went away sad, because he had great wealth. Mark 10:21-22

When we realize we aren't living as God intended, we, like the rich young man, often feel rejected by God too. But God, like a good doctor, lovingly accepts His patients just as they are while using His power to transform them. God accepts you and understands you totally, He just doesn't want you to go through life handicapped by a quick temper, a feeling of resentment, or a bad conscience. God accepts you just as you are; God wants to change you. Both statements are equally true.

Don't ever tell God, "Accept me but don't try to change me." Receive the acceptance of Jesus, and then let Him completely transform you.

In 1929, Roy Riegels, a college football player who was much too nervous to be playing in the Rose Bowl, picked up a fumble and headed for the end zone—in the wrong direction! A teammate chased him for sixty-five yards and tackled him just before the goal line. One play later, the other team scored a two-point safety.

Riegels' coach did not give him a big lecture during halftime, and there were no changes in the lineup. That coach showed acceptance and demonstrated that he believed in Roy Riegels—no matter what.

God is like that coach. He has confidence in His children. He has no other plans.

You did not choose me, but I chose you and appointed you to go and bear fruit—fruit that will last. Then the Father will give you whatever you ask in my name. John 15:16

Not only does God show His confidence in us by entrusting us with the responsibility to tell the world about the new life available in Jesus, but He forgets about the sins and errors we confess to Him. Read Hebrews 11, the faith hall of fame chapter. God doesn't even mention the unbelief of Abraham and Sarah, the instability of Jacob, the murder that Moses committed, or the complaints of the Israelites. God chose to record the final results—the victories and not the blunders that were part of the struggle.

Maybe you wish that someone would believe in you instead of constantly pointing out your faults. You may long for a second chance to prove yourself in the eyes of a person who has already labeled you a failure. Perhaps you've said, "I just wish someone would accept me for what I am." God is that person. Not only does He believe in you, but He offers you the unlimited power of the Holy Spirit—supernatural energy—so that the potential He sees in you can become a reality.

Somebody believes in you. And that Somebody is God.

Day 20

Dateless, Deprived, and Dejected

Stacey was depressed. For the third year in a row, she'd be going to the church youth banquet without a date.

Although she knew there'd be a lot of other unaccompanied girls attending, she longed for a guy to ask her out for this special occasion. But it wasn't only that. She couldn't remember the last time that one of her girl friends called to invite her to do something. She had to initiate activities with her friends and keep her ears open so she could tag along for shopping trips and basketball games.

Do you sometimes feel like Stacey? If you do, you need to know that God has picked you for something extremely important.

In him we were also chosen, having been predestined according to the plan of him who works out everything in conformity with the purpose of his will, in order that we, who were the first to hope in Christ, might be for the praise of his glory. Ephesians 1:11–12

God chose you to show off to the world how wonderful He is. His plan is to give you His love, joy, and peace so that you can pass it on to others.

Because God is God, He has the capacity to shower all His love and attention on you, His chosen one. You can be the center of His attention just as if no other person existed on this planet. And He can do the same for all His children. The Bible refers to the church—all who have completely given their lives to Jesus—as the bride of Christ. Jesus has the capacity to give the tender caring of a bridegroom to each Christian.

All the acceptance and love in the world is there for the taking. How will you respond? Just as the new wife can decide to reject the love of her husband and become cold and indifferent, you can keep your distance from God. You can create a world in which you are truly deprived and dejected—and maybe dateless besides. But it's an unwise choice because you *can* learn to receive from God all He has planned to give you.

Try a "date" with Jesus. Take your Bible and go to a quiet place, and as you read John 14–17, bask in the love and acceptance of God. Ask Him to fill that hole deep down inside that comes from feeling left out.

Day 21

All of us have become like one who is unclean, and all our righteous acts are like filthy rags. Isaiah 64:6

You came to God as a sinner, unable to save yourself. How do you square that with the fact that God created you to be something special, so you should accept yourself? You can thank God that you have knobby knees, red hair, and freckles, and at the same time confess to Him that your motives are selfish and need to be changed by Him—if you're willing to accept God's definition of who you are.

My car is a good little car—it runs well, doesn't have any big dents, and requires very little repair. However, when an incredibly heavy rainfall turned every low area in the city into a lake and my car came to waist-deep water, it was totally helpless, as were all the other cars. One driver thought his car should be able to double as a boat and went full speed into that deep water. Of course, his car stopped because the entire engine was drowned.

What if that poor car, nearly covered by water, began thinking, *I'm a total failure because here I am in all this water and I can't do a thing*? We'd think it was pretty dumb for a car to be depressed because it couldn't also function as a boat.

Jesus enters our lives and changes us from the inside out. When you get discouraged because you are not naturally good, you are like the car trying to be a boat. Just as the car could be thankful that it was painted red and had a leather interior, so you should be thankful for the way God made you—for the unique qualities and talents you have and for the special ways you can be of service to God. But you can't measure up to God's standards. Make David's prayer your own.

Remember, O Lord, your great mercy and love, for they are from of old. Remember not the sins of my youth and my rebellious ways; according to your love remember me, for you are good, O Lord. Psalm 25:6–7

God loves you very much. That's why He sent Jesus to save you. But your natural "goodness" does not impress God, and you can't save yourself. Even after you become a Christian, you can't live the Christian life in your own strength—you need to depend on Jesus' power.

Day 22

God Loves You—Pimples and All

If you possessed the power to change anything about the way you look, would you use that power? Would you like to have a shorter nose, thinner legs, thicker hair, or smaller feet? Most people would answer yes to this question, but in answering yes, they are forgetting some important things. Why do so many people wish to be cast in the Mr. or Ms. America role? It's because right now, that is the world's definition of "beautiful" or "sexy." However, popular standards of beauty change; a woman with a tan was once considered ugly, and the somewhat hefty Statue of Liberty was once considered the ideal feminine form!

God wants you to accept His definition of "beautiful," and He wants to make you beautiful from the *inside* out. God made you just the way you are so you could best reflect His beauty. A problem with wanting to remake yourself is that you're actually telling God He did a bad job when He created you. You don't like it when people tell you your painting or cake is the worst they've ever seen; the Master Designer of the universe doesn't exactly appreciate nasty comments from you either.

You'll enjoy a great sense of relaxation and peace when you accept yourself the way God made you. After you have done this, ask God what things you can do to look your best with what He gave you. A diet, more exercise, or a change of hairstyle may be in God's plan for you. Accepting the way God made you, and thanking Him for it, will save you from one of two extremes: not caring about your appearance because you think you're so ugly it won't help, or spending too much time and money trying to look acceptable.

For you created my inmost being; you knit me together in my mother's womb. I praise you because I am fearfully and wonderfully made; your works are wonderful, I know that full well. My frame was not hidden from you when I was made in the secret place. When I was woven together in the depths of the earth, your eyes saw my unformed body. All the days ordained for me were written in your book before one of them came to be. Psalm 139:13–16

Do you ever feel worthless? Do zits, greasy hair, and a lack of poise get you down? Do you dwell on the fact that you are uncoordinated or a poor student or not particularly popular? You need this truth from the Bible:

The Lord does not look at the things man looks at. Man looks at the outward appearance, but the Lord looks at the heart. 1 Samuel 16:7

Getting out of the low self-image syndrome involves deciding who is important to you and who is going to shape your image of yourself. If you let society do it, you will always come out a loser because no one can be good-looking, witty, successful, intelligent, athletic, musical, and well informed all at the same time. TV commercials warn that you are lacking in some way. You could let your friends shape your self-image, but conforming to the crowd has its dangers. Besides, your friends could let you down.

You may think you would feel good about yourself if you fell in love and a special person believed in you. However, married people usually seem just as insecure as those who are single, and sweethearts can turn into people who compete with each other and tear each other down. You may be able to see that your family loves you most when you're simply doing what is expected of you. Or maybe you don't even look for acceptance within your family.

If you decide that God is going to be so important in your life that nothing else matters, you'll sense God's love and comfort when no one else understands. The God who made the universe, controls the galaxies, and presides over history loves you—warts and all—with a constant love. In the light of this great fact, should what other people think of you be that important? If God is really first in your life, the opinions of others will never ruin your self-image.

Yet I am always with you; you hold me by my right hand. You guide me with your counsel, and afterward you will take me into glory. Whom have I in heaven but you? And earth has nothing I desire besides you. My flesh and my heart may fail, but God is the strength of my heart and my portion forever.
Psalm 73:23–26

Day 24
Self-Consciousness

One definition of self-consciousness is "thinking about yourself." How much time do you waste worrying about how you look, wondering if others have a good impression of you, or trying to analyze why your feelings are hurt? Self-consciousness can keep a talented pianist from ever performing in front of a group, prevent a guy from giving a word of encouragement or affection, or stop someone from learning to ski. Every time we start thinking only about ourselves, we spend time in self-pity, which can only hurt us.

You may agree that self-consciousness is bad, and you'd love to forget about how you look to others; you really want to ignore ridicule, and you would like to try new things that you may not be able to do well. The question you have is, "How can I live above self-consciousness?"

There's a man in the Bible who had self-consciousness licked. Sure, some people made fun of him. After all, camel's-hair T-shirts weren't high fashion, and the Roman emperor didn't eat locusts and wild honey for breakfast. Living in the desert wasn't the thing to do either. But John the Baptist had something, and his preaching was worth listening to—even worth going out to the desert to hear. The fact that he was losing all his disciples to Jesus didn't bother him either. He had learned to replace self-consciousness with Christ-consciousness.

It is impossible to really concentrate on two things at once. If you are only aware of serving Christ and living for Him, self-consciousness will disappear. John the Baptist thought so much of Jesus that he described Him as One "whose sandals I am not fit to carry" (Matthew 3:11).

When self-consciousness comes to haunt you, always ask the question, "Who am I living for anyway—God or myself?"

"Ah, Sovereign Lord," I said, "I do not know how to speak; I am only a child." But the Lord said to me, "Do not say, 'I am only a child.' You must go to everyone I send you to and say whatever I command you. Do not be afraid of them, for I am with you and will rescue you," declares the Lord. . . . "Get yourself ready! Stand up and say to them whatever I command you."
Jeremiah 1:6–8, 17

Day 25

Paul's situation in Rome was "the pits"—and then some. He was in prison, and his only "crime" was preaching the good news of Jesus Christ. Almost all of his friends had deserted him, and at his trial no one defended him. Even though he had not been fed to the lions this time, a shortage of criminals to execute at the next Coliseum show could affect the outcome of a future court hearing. He didn't even have his coat and his books.

Most people in a situation like this would have written, "Everything I've ever lived for is gone. I'm a miserable failure and there is no one to cheer me up." Instead, Paul wrote that he had fought a good fight, he had kept the faith, and he was praising the Lord. Paul knew that success was obeying God, regardless of how things turn out.

> *For I am already being poured out like a drink offering, and the time has come for my departure. I have fought the good fight, I have finished the race, I have kept the faith. Now there is in store for me the crown of righteousness, which the Lord, the righteous Judge, will award to me on that day—and not only to me, but also to all who have longed for his appearing.* 2 Timothy 4:6–8

A lot of frustration comes from your deciding you're a failure because you didn't measure up to your own goals or the expectations someone else made for you. How about learning a lesson from Paul? How about measuring success and failure by God's standards? If you are disobeying God, you may look very successful, but you are still a failure. If you are wholeheartedly obeying God, you are a success—even if all your report card grades are below C-level.

Day 26

The Right Frame for the Picture

Once you decide to let Jesus be the Lord of your life, you can develop a strategy for coping with feelings of inadequacy and inferiority. The most important consideration is what Jesus thinks and what He wants. That makes you like a picture frame; the beautiful and valuable painting is Jesus within you.

People don't go to art galleries to admire frames. However, it is important that the frame blends with the picture to complement its beauty. God had a plan for you before you were born. Your looks and your personality were especially designed to complement the life of Jesus within you. To the person who puts Jesus first, there is no higher purpose than displaying Him. If someone says of you, "If a person like that can be a Christian, I can too," your whole life will be worthwhile.

But how does this relate to feeling like a failure because you struck out again, or feeling self-conscious because everyone else dressed up and you didn't? If Jesus is first in your life, these other things will not be important enough to ruin your day. Constantly carry on a little conversation with Jesus, saying things like, "Well, Lord, if you think I look great, that's good enough for me"; or "Lord, now that everyone is mad at me for causing the team to lose, I know more about the rejection you faced on earth."

Of course, there's nothing especially spiritual about being a bad baseball player or dressing out of place, but how we look or perform is not terribly important. God's "picture frames" should remember that most of all, we want to help people see the picture inside the frame—Jesus.

All you have made will praise you, O Lord; your saints will extol you. They will tell of the glory of your kingdom and speak of your might, so that all men may know of your mighty acts and the glorious splendor of your kingdom. Psalm 145:10–12

And whatever you do, whether in word or deed, do it all in the name of the Lord Jesus, giving thanks to God the Father through him. Colossians 3:17

Marching with the high school band in a big parade can be exciting and enjoyable—unless you're in the front row marching out of step and you're wearing the last available hat, which would have fit Humpty Dumpty but won't stay on your head even with two newspapers stuffed in it. That happened to Anja when she moved to a new high school. After one practice, Anja was stuck in a parade. The tuba player kept retrieving her hat, and she marched out of step for a mile and a half. Anja cried all the way home, thinking she had ruined the whole parade. She never even suspected the glaring pride involved in her self-evaluation.

We don't recognize that it's pride that makes us so afraid of making fools out of ourselves. It's pride that wants everyone to think you're graceful, smooth, and cool; that's why you nearly die when you mess up on something simple. It's pride that wants everyone to recognize your great intelligence; that's why you're crushed when you say something dumb and everyone laughs. It's pride that keeps you in front of the mirror for an hour a day and makes your world cave in when you get a bad haircut.

Pride can easily become your jailer. Pride rattles its chains when you have to give an oral report in science, when only the most expensive clothes will make you look acceptable, or when you don't want anyone to see you play tennis. Pride demands that you be Superman or Wonder Woman. Confess your pride as sin and come into the freedom Jesus wants to give you to be yourself. The truth is, you make a perfect you.

Pride goes before destruction, a haughty spirit before a fall. Proverbs 16:18

"The pride of your heart has deceived you, you who live in the clefts of the rocks and make your home on the heights, you who say to yourself, 'Who can bring me down to the ground?' Though you soar like the eagle and make your nest among the stars, from there I will bring you down," declares the Lord. Obadiah 1:3–4

Day 28

Who Tells You What to Do?

Someone once said, "Do what you like and pretty soon you won't like what you do." That philosophy is likely to get you into a lot of trouble. Saying exactly what you think will not endear you to your sister and may incur the anger of your parents and teachers. Doing whatever you wish, whenever you wish, may even acquaint you with policemen and a judge.

Since the "real you" seems to be such a monster, you've probably allowed others to dictate your behavior. You congratulate the homecoming queen and say you're glad she won—even if you think she's the worst possible choice. You feel obligated to pretend you like eating pizza and drinking Coke, because everyone else at the wrap party is. When people ask how you are, you answer "Fine," even if you're on the verge of tears. The hypocrisy of it all is frightening, and the thought of being a "carbon-copy teen" doesn't give you any sense of individuality or importance.

What's the way out? Only your Creator can transform the "real you" into a totally authentic "new you." If you give your life to Jesus and determine to obey Him, He'll bring out your true personality. If you ask Him to show you the reason you were put on this earth, He will.

> Woe to him who quarrels with his Maker, to him who is but a potsherd among the potsherds on the ground. Does the clay say to the potter, "What are you making?" . . . This is what the Lord says—the Holy One of Israel, and its Maker: Concerning things to come, do you question me about my children, or give me orders about the work of my hands? It is I who made the earth and created mankind upon it. My own hands stretched out the heavens; I marshaled their starry hosts. Isaiah 45:9, 11–12

> And now the Lord says—he who formed me in the womb to be his servant to bring Jacob back to him and gather Israel to himself . . . I will also make you a light for the Gentiles. Isaiah 49:5–6

God put great thought and love into designing you. How about following His instructions?

Day 29

Are you being yourself, or are you constantly trying to impress people? For many people, life is more like acting than living. Putting on a good front is something our society teaches us to do. When some girl talks about all the exciting places her new boyfriend has taken her, then asks her friend where her dates have been lately, an honest, "I haven't been on a date for a year" would be hard to admit. And it's embarrassing to reveal that you've never even heard of the book everyone is reading. Not exaggerating about your weekend is equally difficult. Saying, "I studied for the chemistry test and I failed it" takes a lot of guts.

Besides trying to make people think we've done great things, we try to impress people by what we wear and what we own. Worse than this, Christians often want to appear more "spiritual" than they actually are. A guy once remarked, "I don't want to take my new Bible to church. The people will think I never read it."

> *Be careful not to do your "acts of righteousness" before men, to be seen by them. If you do, you will have no reward from your Father in heaven. So when you give to the needy, do not announce it with trumpets, as the hypocrites do in the synagogues and on the streets, to be honored by men. I tell you the truth, they have received their reward in full. But when you give to the needy, do not let your left hand know what your right hand is doing, so that your giving may be in secret. Then your Father, who sees what is done in secret, will reward you.* Matthew 6:1–4

God sees and judges you exactly for what you are. He isn't impressed with a holiness act. Any pretense you make in any area of life blocks communication with God. Besides, acting is hard work. Jesus wants us to be completely honest and be ourselves. As soon as you stop pretending to be what you're not, the strain goes away.

Day 30

About That Log in Your Eye

If you don't thank God for the way you look, the abilities you have, and the things that happen to you, you're certain to get a "log" in your eye that will keep you from seeing anything clearly. That log is jealousy. Jealousy always comes from lack of trust in God—you don't trust that God has a reason for your lack of dates right now, so you're jealous of the person with a girlfriend or a boyfriend. You don't thank God for your straight brown hair, so you're jealous of the beautiful blonde with lots of curls. You don't appreciate the clothes you have, so you're jealous of the doctor's kid's wardrobe. You aren't thankful for the talents God has given you, so you're jealous of the best player on the team.

Look what happened when Saul was not thankful for what God had given him:

> When the men were returning home after David had killed the Philistine, the women came out from all the towns of Israel to meet King Saul with singing and dancing, with joyful songs and with tambourines and lutes. As they danced, they sang: "Saul has slain his thousands, and David his tens of thousands." . . . And from that time on Saul kept a jealous eye on David. 1 Samuel 18:6–7, 9

Every time jealousy raises its ugly head, confess it as sin and determine to be satisfied with what God has given you—and even thank Him for it. Why don't you start with these two practical suggestions: If you find you are jealous of someone right now, decide to pray for that person every day for the next month. This will give you a chance to experience one of God's miracles—a complete attitude change. Second, make a list of all the things you've never thanked God for, then tell God how much you appreciate Him and the things He has given you. Thanklessness is a sin that opens the door to jealousy.

> For where you have envy and selfish ambition, there you find disorder and every evil practice. James 3:16

The school auditorium is packed with students, parents, relatives, and people from the community. The graduates march in. Except for the fact that you lost your mortarboard on the way in and your gown is shocking pink while everyone else's is navy blue, it is an exciting evening and a great way to end your illustrious high school career. Then the principal says in a booming voice, "We are pleased to present the Personality Minus Award for this year's graduating class." He calls out your name and the band plays off-key.

You wake up from your nightmare, wondering if that's what everyone thinks of you.

Although you should accept yourself as God made you, there are times that you should not feel good about yourself. You're *not* okay if you are not dependable—you can change that. Saying, "I won't worry about my laziness because that's just the way I am," is just like stating, "I can ignore God's Word, and I don't believe God has the power to change me." Don't just accept the fact that you are always late—*decide* to start being on time.

God has a lot to say about character development, especially in the book of Proverbs. Every teenager should read Proverbs several times, and follow the advice found there. Ask the Holy Spirit to show specific steps necessary to reach the goal. In tenth grade I read a book called *How to Improve Your Personality*. I remember thinking, "This book doesn't say one thing that a person who reads the Bible doesn't already know."

And we, who with unveiled faces all reflect the Lord's glory, are being transformed into his likeness with ever-increasing glory, which comes from the Lord, who is the Spirit. 2 Corinthians 3:18

Don't use accepting yourself as an excuse for the wrong attitudes and undesirable actions that God would give you the power to change. You're not okay, and neither am I. We're God's works in progress.

Day 32

Who Do You Look Like?

You may be a rugged individualist, determined to be your own person and not like anyone else. But it can't really be done. It's a fact that most people are a lot like their parents, and often they most resemble the parent they're determined *not* to copy. A husband and wife often think very much alike. A teenager reflects the values of the friends he or she has.

In the final analysis there are only two molds: you can either be like Jesus or be like the world. Jesus and the world are opposites, so it's an either-or proposition. Being like the world is easy. You absorb the latest trends of the media, such as the "new" morality, freedom to do your own thing, and pleasure at any price. Behind these trends is the overriding emphasis of the world—you are the center of the universe and everything should revolve around you.

The basic premise of the world—that individuals are the focal point of everything—always has and always will remain the same. However, the expressions of it will change so fast that in twenty years, you'll be the older generation. You will have some choice as to what part of the world to follow and which people will mold your thinking, but you will not be "yourself."

The alternative is to be conformed to the image of Jesus—to not only pattern yourself after Him but also to allow the living Holy Spirit to produce the attitudes and actions of Jesus in you. When that happens, you may not be the most popular person in school—but so what? Being God's friend has eternal rewards!

Do not conform any longer to the pattern of this world, but be transformed by the renewing of your mind. Then you will be able to test and approve what God's will is—his good, pleasing and perfect will. Romans 12:2

We have not received the spirit of the world but the Spirit who is from God, that we may understand what God has freely given us. 1 Corinthians 2:12

You adulterous people, don't you know that friendship with the world is hatred toward God? Anyone who chooses to be a friend of the world becomes an enemy of God. James 4:4

Do you resemble Jesus?

Maybe answering yes to that question seems impossible to you. Well, the Bible says that God planned long ago for each of us to be like Jesus. God isn't like the people who make all kinds of plans and dreams that they can't possibly fulfill. God has the means and the power to work out His plans.

The Holy Spirit has put within you the characteristics of Jesus, just as a child has within him the characteristics of his parents. However, if a two-week-old baby could leave his or her parents forever, most likely little more than the physical resemblances would show up. Most children spend hours imitating their parents—and are extremely successful. They spend so much time with their parents that they are bound to pick up character traits.

The traits of Jesus placed within you by the Holy Spirit at your conversion will never show through unless you strive to be like Jesus. This means you have a willingness to deny the thinking of the world in order to follow His teachings. It means spending time—a lot of time—with Jesus. The more time you spend with Him, the more you will think, act, and talk like Him.

A student is not above his teacher, but everyone who is fully trained will be like his teacher. Luke 6:40

Follow my example, as I follow the example of Christ. 1 Corinthians 11:1

Whoever claims to live in him must walk as Jesus did. 1 John 2:6

Day 34
The Treasure Inside You

With only a dime in your pocket, you can be as careless and haphazard as you wish. However, if you were carrying a million dollars in cash to deposit in the bank, your whole attitude would be different. The importance of your mission, and the value of the treasure, would make you a lot more careful.

In Solomon's time, God's presence was in a beautiful temple made of stone, but today God has made our hearts the place where He lives!

Do you not know that your body is a temple of the Holy Spirit, who is in you, whom you have received from God? You are not your own; you were bought at a price. Therefore honor God with your body. 1 Corinthians 6:19-20

If you have been born again of the Spirit of God, you carry God in your heart! This should instill in you a sense of awe and respect. *You are the temple of God.* When it dawns on you that you are indeed the house God lives in, you can do nothing but surrender yourself totally to Him.

Since your heart is Christ's home, He should have control over every part of His house. You no longer have the right to think anything you want to; Jesus has a right to dominate your thoughts. What God's temple looks like on the outside is no longer determined by your taste and your sense of style; what you wear must be acceptable to Jesus. God's temple can't be as lazy as it wants to be; God gets to reform the work habits of His temple. Live so others will notice Jesus, the treasure inside you.

Consequently, you are no longer foreigners and aliens, but fellow citizens with God's people and members of God's household, built on the foundation of the apostles and prophets, with Christ Jesus himself as the chief cornerstone. In him the whole building is joined together and rises to become a holy temple in the Lord. And in him you too are being built together to become a dwelling in which God lives by his Spirit. Ephesians 2:19-22

Day 35

Who Do You Think You Are?

Rafael looked forward to school. He got good grades and excelled in athletics. He was ashamed, though, of his poor family and junky yard. His Mexican parents didn't catch on to American ways or learn much English. He determined that he would be different.

In his sophomore year, Rafael joined the Christian club at the high school and became active in a local church. By working long hours after school and in the summer, he had saved enough money to buy a car and nicer clothes. Soon, no one suspected the kind of immigrant home he came from.

Early in the spring, Rafael went to the bus depot to pick Amber up after she visited a friend in another city. As he picked up her suitcase, he nearly did a double-take. There were his poorly dressed uncle and cousin, claiming the battered box they'd brought with them from Mexico!

He turned away and hoped they hadn't seen him. But it was too late.

"Rafael!" yelled his uncle.

Rafael grabbed Amber's arm and pushed her rapidly toward the parking lot. But Rafael's cousin caught up with them. "Rafael! Why you walk away when we call to you?"

Amber was upset with him. "You turned your back on them, didn't you? If you don't take them with you, I'm not going."

The four of them rode together in complete silence.

Haughty eyes and a proud heart . . . are sin! Proverbs 21:4

Do not be proud, but be willing to associate with people of low position. Do not be conceited. Romans 12:16

Accept yourself just the way you are, with all the *unchangeables*—your physical appearance, family background, and mental ability. The pridethat makes you pretend to be somebody you're not is a sin. It hurts you *and* others. Failure to see that God has a purpose for each unchangeable feature of your life—and those of other people—will result in the pride that covers something up or looks down on another.

Day 36

Nobody Loves Me

Have you ever wondered if God *really* loves you? Maybe you've talked to someone who has serious doubts about God's love for him. A friend of mine received a call from a nurse at a local hospital. She was afraid that an eighteen-year-old patient of hers might die because he had absolutely no desire to live.

A talk with the boy revealed that he had suffered a crippling disease as a child, but had, through constant exercise and work, not only learned to walk again, but run and excel in athletics. He was now in the hospital as a result of a terrible automobile accident that had killed everyone else in his family. He had suffered severe injuries, but the doctors told him if he worked hard he had a chance of walking again. This young man would not believe that God loved him.

My friend took his Bible and read to him the story of the trial and crucifixion of Jesus.

Then the governor's soldiers took Jesus into the Praetorium and gathered the whole company of soldiers around him. They stripped him and put a scarlet robe on him, and then twisted together a crown of thorns and set it on his head. They put a staff in his right hand and knelt in front of him and mocked him. "Hail, king of the Jews!" they said. They spit on him, and took the staff and struck him on the head again and again. After they had mocked him, they took off the robe and put his own clothes on him. Then they led him away to crucify him. Matthew 27:27–31*

After he finished he asked gently, "Don't you think the God who sent Jesus to suffer and die for you really does love you?" The young man agreed.

You may not understand anything that has happened to you, what you are going through now, or what the future will hold, but the crown of thorns, the spear in His side, and the nails in His hands forever say, "I love you."

This is how God showed his love among us: He sent his one and only Son into the world that we might live through him. 1 John 4:9

The Bible speaks often about God's "steadfast love." Steadfast love is *forever* love. It never changes. It is always the same. Your sister might not have loved you for a few hours after you broke her clay figurine she made in art class. Your boyfriend or girlfriend may have loved you less after you disappointed him or her. Your employer may not have loved you at all the day you overslept and left the restaurant short-handed.

But God will always love you. Jesus came to earth to offer visible proof of God's eternal love. Although Jesus knew that the "rich young ruler" would not give up his wealth to follow Him, the Bible says, "Jesus looked at him and loved him" (Mark 10:21). After Peter had denied Jesus three times, the Lord turned and looked at him. That look of love caused the tough fisherman to run out and cry. Jesus loved the woman with the bad reputation who put perfume on His feet at a dinner party, and He made her feel comfortable among the critical guests. Jesus loved Thomas the doubter and did everything possible to help him believe.

Jesus loves you and will demonstrate His love to you—if you let Him. A person can accept love only from someone trustworthy. You can trust Jesus and depend on Him for never-ending love.

The Lord is compassionate and gracious, slow to anger, abounding in love. He will not always accuse, nor will he harbor his anger forever; he does not treat us as our sins deserve or repay us according to our iniquities. For as high as the heavens are above the earth, so great is his love for those who fear him; as far as the east is from the west, so far has he removed our transgressions from us. As a father has compassion on his children, so the Lord has compassion on those who fear him; for he knows how we are formed, he remembers that we are dust. Psalm 103:8–14

Day 38

But You Can't Hug God!

The guy tells the girl that he loves her and will do anything for her, and she responds with the same words. This is the theme for a million stories, movies, and song lyrics. Something within us longs for someone who will give him or herself totally for us. Although we know that "happily ever after" in children's storybooks is a myth, there's something about a total commitment to another person that we all want to experience.

The apostle Paul says that marriage is a picture of the love between Christ and the church. The beautiful thing is that Jesus has given himself *totally* for you. He left heaven for you. He was born in a manger for you. He put up with the Pharisees for you. He allowed Roman soldiers to put nails in His hands for you. He rose again for you. He is now in heaven praying for you.

Jesus can, and will, do everything for you. The more you think about all that Jesus has done, the more you'll want to respond to Him with a total surrender of your life. It isn't such a tough thing. It's a natural response to give to someone who has given everything for you. And even if you can't hug God, you'll discover that the relationship you can have with Him is deeper than anything you could experience with another human being.

> *Praise be to the God and Father of our Lord Jesus Christ, who has blessed us in the heavenly realms with every spiritual blessing in Christ. For he chose us in him before the creation of the world to be holy and blameless in his sight. In love he predestined us to be adopted as his sons through Jesus Christ, in accordance with his pleasure and will—to the praise of his glorious grace, which he has freely given us in the One he loves.* Ephesians 1:3-6

> *This is love: not that we loved God, but that he loved us and sent his Son as an atoning sacrifice for our sins.* 1 John 4:10

God has enough love to satisfy you completely. Most people are unable to receive all of God's love because they have not given themselves totally to Him. If you really love someone, pleasing that person is more important to you than your own desires. Is pleasing Jesus the most important thing in your life? True love gives without counting the cost. Will you give up everything for Jesus because of all He means to you?

A man from India lost all he had when he became a Christian. His wife and children left him and his friends became his enemies. His comment was, "People always ask me what I gave up to become a Christian, but nobody asks me what I gained." He believed that what he had acquired was well worth the price he paid. That man knew that the more he gave in love to Jesus, the more of His love he would experience in return.

Since you're human, you may respond to God's love imperfectly; but determine to give yourself totally to God, and you will have a beautiful relationship with Him.

Some time later God tested Abraham. He said to him, "Abraham!" "Here I am," he replied. Then God said, "Take your son, your only son, Isaac, whom you love, and go to the region of Moriah. Sacrifice him there as a burnt offering on one of the mountains I will tell you about." . . . The angel of the Lord called to Abraham from heaven a second time and said, "I swear by myself, declares the Lord, that because you have done this and have not withheld your son, your only son, I will surely bless you and make your descendants as numerous as the stars in the sky and as the sand on the seashore. Your descendants will take possession of the cities of their enemies, and through your offspring all nations on earth will be blessed, because you have obeyed me." Genesis 22:1-2, 15–18

Whoever has my commands and obeys them, he is the one who loves me. He who loves me will be loved by my Father, and I too will love him and show myself to him. John 14:21

Day 40

How to Get Enough Water in Your Bucket

Can you imagine a game in which the object is to get your bucket full of water by begging, borrowing, or stealing from someone else's half-full pail? Since the other players also want full buckets, the game doesn't tend to produce friendships.

Most people playing such a game are playing for keeps. Worst of all, the scarce "water" they're fighting for is *love*. Everyone needs love and tries to obtain it from other people, but people just don't have enough to give very generously. Some people completely give of themselves until they reach a certain point, and then they call a sudden halt. Others give only when their love is sure to be returned. Some have been hurt and they become loners rather than risk more heartbreak. Others have no love to give and become leeches, trying to get love and attention wherever they can find it.

Obviously, what's needed is a never-ending supply of "water"—or love—from an outside source. God is a never-ending supply of love. In fact, He *is* love. He loves you now. He has loved you all your life and will love you forever—no matter what. God can give you so much love that you can spend your life giving love to others.

How priceless is your unfailing love! Both high and low among men find refuge in the shadow of your wings. Psalm 36:7

By day the Lord directs his love, at night his song is with me—a prayer to the God of my life. Psalm 42:8

It is good to praise the Lord and make music to your name, O Most High, to proclaim your love in the morning and your faithfulness at night. Psalm 92:1–2

Day 41

If God Loves Me, Why Can't I Get My Locker Open?

A three-year-old's definition of love would be something like this: "If Mommy really loved me, she'd let me eat all the candy I want."

An eight-year-old's definition of love might sound like this: "If our teacher loved us, she'd let us spend four hours on the playground each day."

As we grow older, our definitions don't get much better. We often feel that if God really loved us, He'd let us have our own way, give us the possessions we want, always let us get our lockers open on the first try, and keep trouble away from our lives. We forget that since God *is* love, He is the One who understands love.

Love is not just giving a person whatever he or she wants; God does not love you by satisfying your every whim and fancy, and you don't love others that way either. Genuine love always stays within the boundaries of God's commandments. Real love is sometimes tough—it's not always what we want. A God who really loves us will not fulfill our every desire.

We can enjoy God's love only if we accept the fact that He knows how to run His universe. If you're a cat lover, you know that some kittens can be lovingly petted on your lap and their purr will nearly drown out the TV set, but with the same loving intentions, you can pick up another cat and it will spit and scratch and bristle. The difference is only a matter of the cats' attitudes. In the same way, you can choose to accept God's love or reject it. Are you a purrer or a spitter?

Dear friends, let us love one another, for love comes from God. Everyone who loves has been born of God and knows God. Whoever does not love does not know God, because God is love. . . . And we have seen and testify that the Father has sent his Son to be the Savior of the world. . . . In this way, love is made complete among us so that we will have confidence on the day of judgment, because in this world we are like him. There is no fear in love. But perfect love drives out fear, because fear has to do with punishment. The one who fears is not made perfect in love. 1 John 4:7–8, 14, 17–18

Day 42

Nothing Else Matters

Jesus warned that if we love anyone or anything more than we love Him, we are not worthy of Him. Jesus is to be more important to us than anything else.

One can be so taken up with the beauty of the countryside that looking for landmarks or remembering the way back becomes irrelevant. Sweethearts can forget the time of day and even skip a meal. Have you ever loved Jesus so much that nothing else mattered or seemed the least bit important? Seeing Jesus like this will take away your sense of self-sufficiency. You will not dare to depend on yourself to serve God. The hard times that prove you are nothing in yourself will not throw you, because you realize that each time you become dependent on God in a given area, you find the real life God has for you. You will also be willing to do anything God asks—even something you would normally dislike.

Losing your life for Jesus involves giving unselfishly. There is a plaque that says, "Cooking, like love, must be entered into with utter abandon, or not at all." When a person really loves someone, the gift isn't too expensive, the effort to please isn't too great, and the self-sacrifice necessary to do what the other person wants isn't too big a price to pay. Everyone else might say, "What a waste," but the person in love could care less. Do you love Jesus so much that you'll do what He wants even if everyone thinks it's ridiculous?

Wholeheartedly loving Jesus means doing everything for Him and not for other people. If you do good deeds for the poor, help the sick, or comfort the people who hurt, you'll soon feel that these people are taking advantage of you. However, if you do all for Jesus and you love these people because Jesus loves them, it won't matter, because you're doing it only to please Jesus—and He's worth any sacrifice. Nothing else matters.

Anyone who loves his father or mother more than me is not worthy of me; anyone who loves his son or daughter more than me is not worthy of me.
Matthew 10:37

If Your Best Friend Doesn't Tell You, Your Enemies Might

Jesus was a friend of sinful people, and to some, that was dreadful. He ate with men who collected the taxes for the hated Roman Empire. He was a close friend to those who did not possess spotless reputations. He even allowed a prostitute to pour a bottle of perfume on His feet. The Pharisees argued that a good person would choose a better caliber of friends. But Jesus brought these sinful people up to His level and never condescended to theirs. For instance, Matthew, a tax collector, became an apostle.

The Pharisees complained that, instead of fasting, Jesus was enjoying the dinner parties He attended. And they accused Him of breaking the Sabbath.

The beauty of Jesus' life was its *balance*. In spite of His purity, He had great compassion for the worst sinners. He cared for them in a real and human way. Although He was serious and devout, He showed us by example how to enjoy the good things God gives in life. He got at the heart of God's commandments and discarded the legalistic baloney.

Jesus' enemies had to hire false witnesses to make accusations at His trial. But the false witnesses couldn't agree, Herod wouldn't condemn Him, and Pilate declared Jesus innocent as he washed his hands before the mob. The dying thief said, "This man has done nothing wrong," and the Roman centurion, who stood by the cross, exclaimed, "Truly this was the Son of God." It was very hard to find something bad to say about Jesus.

For those of us who follow Jesus, the challenge always remains—to so live that those who are looking for our faults will have a hard time finding them. It's good to make sure that your enemies have no ammunition.

Live such good lives among the pagans that, though they accuse you of doing wrong, they may see your good deeds and glorify God on the day he visits us.
1 Peter 2:12

[Keep] a clear conscience, so that those who speak maliciously against your good behavior in Christ may be ashamed of their slander. 1 Peter 3:16

Day 44
Do As I Say, Not As I Do

Bruchko, the story of Bruce Olson, is the autobiography of a man whom many would consider a spiritual giant. It tells of a nineteen-year-old who obeyed God's call to bring His Word to the Motilone Indians, a fierce jungle tribe of Colombia. He left the U.S. with seventy dollars in his pocket. Once in Colombia, he had to learn two languages before he even approached the Motilones. When he did, they tried to kill him. He got tapeworms and suffered other health problems from eating unsanitary food. But he willingly gave up everything to follow Jesus.

In spite of all this, he was keenly aware of his failures. He recognized the sin in his life. When discouraged, he thought of the missionaries he had been critical of. Sometimes he found the Bible boring, and he doubted his calling. Those who live close to God—people who others consider saints—sense their sin and guilt and failure more strongly than others.

Jesus was different. He felt no need to confess any sin. The New Testament describes the temptations He faced, and He didn't yield to any of them. But He did see the sin in others. His disciples were sinners, and they sinned toward other people, so He taught them to pray, "Forgive us our debts, as we also have forgiven our debtors" (Matthew 6:12). But in His prayer to His Father, Jesus said, "I have brought you glory on earth by completing the work you gave me to do" (John 17:4).

Everyone hates a "do-as-I-say, not-as-I-do" teacher, but Jesus could say, "Do as I do," because He was perfect. As we learn more about God and get closer to Him, He shows us our shortcomings. This should not upset us. The brighter the light, the more clearly the imperfections show up. This is the process of becoming more like Jesus. We simply confess the sin as we become aware of it, then stop doing it. The Holy Spirit will give us power to keep from deliberately rebelling against God.

But if we walk in the light, as he is in the light, we have fellowship with one another, and the blood of Jesus, his Son, purifies us from all sin. 1 John 1:7

Day 45

Love Is Not That Queasy Feeling in Your Stomach

After watching a romantic comedy or reading romantic novels, one can view love as a great sensation that suddenly overwhelms a person. A thousand television commercials a day declare that you must be physically attractive so someone will fall in love with you. It would be a shame to miss it all because you're using the wrong toothpaste!

We treat love like an emotion that is either absent or present. Common tests for love include questions like: Do you get butterflies in your stomach every time you see that "special someone"? Do you think about this person so much you have trouble studying? Is he or she your "perfect" ideal? When you ask how to recognize this unparalleled unpredictable emotion, many answer, "You'll just know."

But then, people fall out of love for the most amazing reasons. Liz cut her hair, so Harry doesn't love her anymore. Jim decided to play baseball three nights a week, so Jennifer broke up with him. When a good-looking football player asked Sue out, she forgot all about Sergio.

These misconceptions our society forces on people locks them into a treadmill of falling in and out of love, marrying, divorcing, remarrying, and divorcing. People think that if their heart skips a beat, they'd better marry the person who caused this great feeling. Don't fall into that trap. It comes straight from the pit. It is not the kind of love God wants between a man and a woman.

Because this whole maze of guy-girl relationships can become such a sticky mess, you desperately need God's guidance in choosing the person to date. He or she may not even put one butterfly in your stomach—but you can count on God to give you *the very best!*

For the Lord gives wisdom, and from his mouth come knowledge and understanding. . . . Discretion will protect you, and understanding will guard you. Proverbs 2:6, 11

For these commands are a lamp, this teaching is a light, and the corrections of discipline are the way to life, keeping you from the immoral woman, from the smooth tongue of the wayward wife. Do not lust in your heart after her beauty or let her captivate you with her eyes. Proverbs 6:23–25

Day 46

Thirsty Camels and Prince Charming

The Bible defines love as an *act of the will*. It *commands* all people to love God, followers of Jesus to love their enemies, and husbands to love their wives. Because real love isn't based on emotions, a Bible love story is very different from most novels you've read. It starts with obedience to God and prayer.

Abraham obeyed God by determining not to let his son Isaac marry an idol-worshiper, even though he had to send a servant to a far country to choose a wife for his son. Imagine the faith involved in this decision! The servant prayed that God would send the right girl to the well and that she'd offer water for his camels. Sure enough, Rebekah came and volunteered to water his camels. When Rebekah's father and brother heard the story, they answered, "This is from the Lord; we can say nothing to you one way or the other. Here is Rebekah; take her and go, and let her become the wife of your master's son, as the Lord has directed," (Genesis 24:50–51). It was a marriage based on God's will.

> He [Isaac] went out to the field one evening to meditate, and as he looked up, he saw camels approaching. Rebekah also looked up and saw Isaac. She got down from her camel and asked the servant, "Who is that man in the field coming to meet us?" "He is my master," the servant answered. So she took her veil and covered herself. Then the servant told Isaac all he had done. Isaac brought her into the tent of his mother Sarah, and he married Rebekah.
> Genesis 24:63–67

Maybe this kind of arranged marriage doesn't sound very romantic, but after Isaac and Rebekah had been married forty years, we read, "Abimelech king of the Philistines looked down from a window and saw Isaac caressing his wife Rebekah" (Genesis 26:8).

Love based solely on emotions changes if the other person does something we don't like. Love based first on God's will and then on our willingness to love that other person—no matter what—is the kind that lasts. That relationship will even be more romantic in the long run. Your first step toward getting in on the kind of romance God has in store is letting *God* decide whom you should or shouldn't date.

Day 47

The True Love Exam

Skiing at top speed down your favorite slope through crisp, sparkling snow. Scoring the winning touchdown in a championship game. Strolling down lovers' lane on a moonlit night. These can be enjoyable experiences. Yet breaking a leg, dropping the ball, or starting an argument could turn these same activities into pure misery. It's not very logical to build a lifetime commitment on emotions. But because emotions can be gripping and real, it's all too easy to base everything on them.

When you're experiencing that feeling of falling in love, pray a lot. Ask God to sort out your emotions. You can *choose* to follow God no matter how you feel. Keep in mind that the Bible not only defines love as an act of the will, but it also declares that love can be tested by certain attitudes found in a person. Here is the Bible's "true love exam":

Love is patient, love is kind. It does not envy, it does not boast, it is not proud. It is not rude, it is not self-seeking, it is not easily angered, it keeps no record of wrongs. Love does not delight in evil but rejoices with the truth. It always protects, always trusts, always hopes, always perseveres. 1 Corinthians 13:4–7

In light of these verses, check the statements that are tests of genuine love.

_____ I just *have* to be with him/her all the time.

_____ I'm so jealous when he/she pays attention to someone else.

_____ I wish he/she would give me a really nice birthday present.

_____ When he/she is on vacation, I miss him/her so much I get crabby.

_____ He/she is so understanding, and he/she is the only one who makes me feel good about myself.

_____ He/she had better not be dating someone else.

_____ We love each other so much we've decided to move in together.

If you checked even one of the statements, you'd better reread the verses. Every statement is *false*. The way God tests true love and the way the world tests love are very different.

Think of someone that you're interested in. Take each quality of true love listed in the above Bible verses and write down how you could show that quality of love. (Example: If I really loved him, I'd be *patient* about his lack of organization and inability to plan ahead.) That's the real test.

Day 48

The Bible Talks About Figs, Not Dates

"He's not a Christian, but he's the nicest guy I know—a lot nicer than the *Christian* guys I know. Besides, *the Bible doesn't say anything about dating.*" You can't get through life without hearing that a few times. It is true that dating, as we know it, was nonexistent in Bible times, so the Bible doesn't mention it. However, this does not mean that the Bible has nothing to say on the subject.

What the Bible says about friendships and life attitudes applies to dating. For example, the Bible states:

Bad company corrupts good character. 1 Corinthians 15:33

Dating a non-Christian automatically initiates some strong desires. You want your relationship to work out, so you defend that person before your Christian friends. You also want to please that person, so you're tempted to compromise your morals. Wanting something that's wrong opens the way for the devil to deceive you. You may want the person to be a Christian so much that you convince yourself he or she is a Christian. It's easy to close your eyes to all the faults of that person. If you raise an immediate defense every time someone questions your actions, you'd better talk to God and ask Him to sort out your desires.

Another thing that you do by dating a non-Christian is encourage in him or her a false interest in the Bible or church. If the subtle deceit gets this far, then it might not be long before you realize that the person is "faking it" in other areas too, such as drinking or lying. If a person keeps acting a certain way just to please you, that person will begin to resent you for being his or her conscience. The only thing left will be for the two of you to break up—or for you to lower your standards. Giving God the control of your desires will keep you from hurting yourself and other people.

Hope deferred [postponed] makes the heart sick, but a longing fulfilled is a tree of life. Proverbs 13:12

Day 49
I Don't Need Any Advice

When your father starts out with, "When I was a boy," or "I've lived a long time and I know," it's easy to snap back, "But I don't need any advice!" The truth is, all of us accept advice from someone. The girl who thinks her mother's ideas are old-fashioned will constantly ask her girl friends to help her pick out clothes. The guy who won't get a haircut to please his parents will do so immediately if he finds out his girlfriend likes short hair.

From whom will you take advice? When will you refuse to listen? These are important choices. The Bible talks about taking advice:

Blessed is the man who does not walk in the counsel of the wicked or stand in the way of sinners or sit in the seat of mockers. But his delight is in the law of the Lord, and on his law he meditates day and night. Psalm 1:1–2

For lack of guidance a nation falls, but many advisers make victory sure. Proverbs 11:14

The plans of the righteous are just, but the advice of the wicked is deceitful. Proverbs 12:5

Pride only breeds quarrels, but wisdom is found in those who take advice. Proverbs 13:10

A person who is secure in doing the right thing listens to advice from many people without becoming defensive. The Bible teaches that we are to obey those in authority unless their orders are contrary to God's will. If you're constantly on the defensive and can't stand any questions from your parents, your youth director, or Christian friends about the person you date or how you use your money or how you spend your time, something is wrong. Unwillingness to take advice from other Christians is dangerous.

If you don't have Christian parents, and even if you do, find a mature Christian to advise you. Ask that person to pray for you. Godly advice is a valuable aid to right living.

Day 50
Your Responsibility in Dating

The responsibility you have toward the person you date is greater than the responsibility you have toward other Christians because of your closeness and the importance of the other person's opinion. The number one responsibility in a relationship is to *help the other person be the very best Christian he or she can be.* This obviously includes helping that person keep the highest moral standards. Do some advance thinking, so when you plan a date, consider these kinds of questions: Would seeing this movie bring us closer to Christ? Would sitting around talking for a long time in the moonlight invite unnecessary temptation? Would wearing this outfit make it harder for my date to keep his or her thoughts pure?

How can a young man keep his way pure? By living according to your word. I seek you with all my heart; do not let me stray from your commands. I have hidden your word in my heart that I might not sin against you. Praise be to you, O Lord; teach me your decrees. Psalm 119:9–12

Because you are Christians, your purpose in life—and on every date— is to glorify God. It is your responsibility to pray for the person you date and encourage that person in Bible study. Be willing to give up some time spent with each other so each of you can serve Christ—maybe another friend needs some of your time. Encourage the person you date to put love for Jesus above love for you.

An important responsibility you have toward those of the opposite sex is giving them a healthy self-image. If one girl tells another she has a lousy figure, the remark, although inexcusable, can be forgotten. But if a guy says, "Well, if the fat, flat look were in, you'd make Hollywood," that girl will remember it until she's ninety.

If a girl tells a guy, "You are the clumsiest thing on two feet," that will help ruin his self-image.

Flattery is wrong, but carefully worded encouragement can be invaluable in building up another Christian. Dating is a good place to practice showing consideration, kindness, and acceptance.

Day 51

I'd Rather Lie Than Hurt His Feelings

After your dating relationship ends, the person you dated will either be closer to Christ or farther away because of you. Consider that. Be careful not to hurt the other person unnecessarily; judge your actions according to the effect they will have on him or her. Don't just consider what *you* mean but also what the other person *thinks* you mean.

Keep me from deceitful ways; be gracious to me through your law. Psalm 119:29

Instead, speaking the truth in love, we will in all things grow up into him who is the Head, that is, Christ. Ephesians 4:15

Girls, you have no right to flirt with a shy fellow just because you need a New Year's Eve date, and then suddenly become "busy" for the next five months. The woman who leaves a string of broken hearts behind her certainly isn't heeding Jesus' command to "love one another."

Guys, realize that girls are dreamers who make mental memory books out of all your words and actions. Don't say "I love you" unless you really mean it—she may start planning the wedding! Girls sometimes interpret an outward display of affection more deeply than you intended, so guys need to be careful. It isn't fair to set another person up for a big letdown.

Covering up true feelings by pretending that you are going to date the person indefinitely, and then dropping him or her like a hot potato, has no place in Christian dating. If you habitually pray together, you'll find it much easier to be honest and open with each other. Besides, you need God's help. Because prayer knits hearts together, it's wise to pray by telephone or in a public place to avoid sexual temptation afterward. Books on marriage seem to agree that lack of communication is the number one problem in marriage. If you think being honest would ruin your relationship, it should be ruined, because it has no future.

Day 52

Broken, Bleeding Hearts and Puppy Love

"You'll get over it."

"You're too young to understand—it's just puppy love."

"There are other fish in the sea."

When breaking up was not your idea, none of these comments is very comforting. But you can bring your aching heart to Jesus. "He heals the brokenhearted and binds up their wounds" (Psalm 147:3).

First, confess any bitterness or resentment you feel. Bitterness and resentment are sin and are like dirt that keeps a wound from healing. A broken heart is bad enough. You don't need to get it full of infection.

Second, you must *want* Jesus to heal you. This may sound strange, but we enjoy self-pity. But indulging in self-pity is wrong and must be confessed. No matter how much you were wronged or how deceitful the other person was, you must reject self-pity and treat it as sin.

Finally, Jesus can't heal your broken heart if you decide to act tough and let your heart harden. Don't join those who keep their distance from others because they're afraid to love and forgive. Jesus wants to heal your heart. He understands heartaches; He's been there.

He grew up before him like a tender shoot, and like a root out of dry ground. He had no beauty or majesty to attract us to him, nothing in his appearance that we should desire him. He was despised and rejected by men, a man of sorrows, and familiar with suffering. Like one from whom men hide their faces he was despised, and we esteemed him not. Surely he took up our infirmities and carried our sorrows, yet we considered him stricken by God, smitten by him, and afflicted. Isaiah 53:2–4

You cannot heal your own broken heart—it takes a miracle that only Jesus can do. Be honest with Him. In faith, ask Him to heal your broken heart and *expect* Him to act. Hearts don't always heal instantly, so keep trusting Him, even if the hurt is still there after you've prayed. Let Jesus use the experience to draw you closer to Him.

Jesus, the Heart Healer

You may feel like a Humpty Dumpty—not only all the king's horses and all the king's men, but the whole U.S. Army and all of medical science can't put you back together again. Your heart is broken into so many pieces that it's not even recognizable. The girl who is depressed because her boyfriend broke up with her might seem like "kid stuff" to you. Maybe you've given in to sexual temptation, and it resulted in shattering heartbreak. Maybe your home is in constant turmoil and you feel as if no one has ever cared about you. Perhaps you are part of a vicious circle: no one has really loved you, so you are afraid to or don't know how to love anyone else; therefore, no one finds you easy to love.

God's love and forgiveness offer a way out. God will forgive you and make you a new person—no matter what you've done.

The Spirit of the Sovereign Lord is on me, because the Lord has anointed me to preach good news to the poor. He has sent me to bind up the broken-hearted, to proclaim freedom for the captives and release from darkness for the prisoners. Isaiah 61:1

Receive His forgiveness and then receive His healing for your broken heart. As you give each hurt to Him, ask Jesus to heal your heartaches. Jesus can take you out of the vicious circle and put you into the winner's circle where you can receive love from God and give it to other people.

I will praise the Lord, who counsels me; even at night my heart instructs me. I have set the Lord always before me. Because he is at my right hand, I will not be shaken. . . . You have made known to me the path of life; you will fill me with joy in your presence, with eternal pleasures at your right hand. Psalm 16:7–8, 11

Day 54
But Everybody's Doing It!

"The only people I know of who think sex before marriage is wrong are Queen Victoria and my grandmother." You may have heard statements like that. There's a virtual epidemic of people living together before marriage. Because the couples living together include everyone from your girlfriend's mother and her boyfriend to college students who grew up in your church, you may wonder if it can really be so bad.

When it comes to moral standards, whether or not others are doing it is completely irrelevant. The point is, *what does God think about it?* Older people in our country were accustomed to a society in which a majority of people supported Christian moral standards. When they were young, the Christian didn't have to be "different" to have high morals. But all that has changed. If you follow God's moral standards now, you are in the minority. But there is no room in the life of a Christian for justifying sex before marriage.

Although God has very important psychological and physical reasons for prohibiting sex outside of marriage, the proponents of sex before marriage can make their arguments sound very good. In this area of life, as in every other, we obey what God says because our Creator is smarter than we are, He loves us, and He knows what is best for us. What other people are doing and what may seem logical must be disregarded if it is contrary to the Bible.

> The body is not meant for sexual immorality, but for the Lord, and the Lord for the body. . . . Do you not know that your bodies are members of Christ himself? 1 Corinthians 6:13, 15

> It is God's will that you should be sanctified: that you should avoid sexual immorality; that each of you should learn to control his own body in a way that is holy and honorable, not in passionate lust like the heathen, who do not know God. 1 Thessalonians 4:3–5

If you have been involved in sexual immorality, God offers complete forgiveness and a new life.

If you've ever made a model airplane, decorated a cake, rebuilt an engine, or painted a picture, you took extremely good care of your creation. God made you, and His rules about sex are designed to take the very best care of you. He created sex, and He knows that within marriage, you will receive the maximum enjoyment from sex.

Marriage should be honored by all, and the marriage bed kept pure.
Hebrews 13:4

This does mean, of course, that you will have to give up momentary pleasure for the more lasting satisfaction. If you are given a choice between a hamburger at McDonald's now and a steak dinner at the best restaurant in town three hours from now, you would have to deny your stomach instant food in order to enjoy the steak. The steak dinner will taste all the better because you didn't have the hamburger.

God's rule is, "You shall not commit adultery" (Exodus 20:14). Someone has observed that God gave ten *commandments,* not ten *suggestions!* His laws are based on the fact that people have willpower and are responsible for their actions. He doesn't talk in terms of "accidents" or people who "just can't help themselves." If you have a good enough reason for not doing something, you'll refrain from it. If you knew that your every move would be televised on the major networks, you'd find it very possible to exercise a lot of self-control. In the movie *The Truman Show,* the main character doesn't know that his whole life is a television program watched by millions. If he found out, he'd change a lot of things. Remember, God sees everything—even if others don't.

But you've got an even better reason for doing right: God's rules are safeguards for us. God gives them not to punish us when we mess up, but for the sake of our well-being. Instead of looking on God's commandments as unwelcome restrictions, learn to say like the psalmist:

Your statues are my delight; they are my counselors. Psalm 119:24

Day 56

Are You Running a Reform School?

A radio drama program began with, "I married a beautiful Christian girl and she was determined to reform me, but it just didn't work out." That day I gained new insight on the issue of trying to use one's influence to reform another person—something that happens all the time.

Bekah was convinced she couldn't stop dating her non-Christian boyfriend because he "needed" her good influence. She thought, *If I drop him, who will win him to Christ?*

Trying to reform any person by charm and influence is not only hopeless, it's clearly wrong. When I listened to that radio program, I saw it. Since only Jesus can redeem a soul, only Jesus can reform a life, and only He can meet every human need, our input is never indispensable. When trying to help a person spiritually, any time we make that person depend on us instead of on God, we are doing something terribly wrong.

"O house of Israel, can I not do with you as this potter does?" declares the Lord. "Like clay in the hand of the potter, so are you in my hand." Jeremiah 18:6

The reason that it's so easy to fall for Satan's lie at this point is that our "need to be needed" is so great. This is God's answer: In Jesus we can find everything we need, so we won't need a certain person around to make us feel secure. Also, we are wanted and loved by Jesus. The old poem that begins, "He has no hands but our hands to do His work today" is true. God could have been self-sufficient, but He designed the world so that He would need us to cooperate with Him in doing His work. *That* should make you feel needed!

Also realize that if Jesus can supply our every need, He can do the same for everyone else. You can drop your non-Christian boyfriend, and God will take *better care* of him than you ever could. God loves him much more than you do. If you really want to help him, pray for him! There's no room for the kind of pride that says, "I can do something that God cannot do." All of us sooner or later need to realize that God is the only One who can change people from the inside out. Then we will stop trying to reform people ourselves and start praying that God will work in their lives.

"I just can't stand that woman."

"That guy gives me the creeps."

"He'd do the human race a favor by evaporating!"

Have you ever said or thought things like that? People show great lack of love toward others for a thousand reasons: they use the wrong deodorant, they sing off-key, they talk too much, or they slurp their soup. Sometimes we try to sound "good" by saying, "I love her, but I don't like her," or "I usually love her, but I don't today," or "I'd love him if he'd change."

Jesus, however, commands us to love one another unconditionally— "My command is this: Love each other as I have loved you" (John 15:12). Jesus loved us enough to die for us when we deserved nothing from Him.

> *If you love those who love you, what credit is that to you? Even "sinners" love those who love them. And if you do good to those who are good to you, what credit is that to you? Even "sinners" do that. . . . But love your enemies, do good to them, and lend to them without expecting to get anything back. Then your reward will be great, and you will be sons of the Most High, because he is kind to the ungrateful and wicked. Be merciful, just as your Father is merciful.* Luke 6:32–33, 35–36

If Trisha hates Karissa, but God says she should love her, Trisha can't just *say* she loves Karissa; that would make her a hypocrite. If Jesus commands us to love everyone, He'll give us the power to do it. If Trisha has ever done anything wrong to Karissa, she should apologize—even if Karissa has hurt Trisha ten times. "Will you forgive me?" can work wonders.

Trisha can also do nice things for Karissa, such as help her with homework or invite her to dinner with some friends. Without knowing God's love, Trisha could be whispering under her breath, "I'm going to love Karissa if it kills me," but rather, she prays, "Jesus, what I'm doing for Karissa, I'm doing for you, and I'm asking you for the love I don't have." If you obey God's command to show love, sooner or later the right emotions will come tagging along behind.

Day 58

Love Can Melt Enemies

Maybe it's the kid at school who constantly calls you names, shoots rubber bands at you, and spreads false rumors about you; perhaps it's the person who was terribly unkind and unfair to your mother; maybe it's the teacher who constantly scoffs at "Bible-believing fanatics"; or it could even be another Christian that you have trouble getting along with. Somebody is bound to give you the opportunity to demonstrate God's dynamite weapon against enemies. *Prayer!*

God commands us to pray for our enemies. If you sincerely and constantly pray for your enemies, some exciting things will happen. For instance, you can't hate and pray at the same time. If you continue to pray, God will miraculously give you love for those who have wronged you. Also, God will work in *their* lives, and they will begin to notice that in spite of what they've done, you love them. Now, the other person will not necessarily stop hating you. In fact, the person may feel so guilty that he or she will treat you even worse. But God will use your actions to advertise Christianity.

You have heard that it was said, "Love your neighbor and hate your enemy." But I tell you: Love your enemies and pray for those who persecute you, that you may be sons of your Father in heaven. He causes his sun to rise on the evil and the good, and sends rain on the righteous and the unrighteous. If you love those who love you, what reward will you get? Are not even the tax collectors doing that? And if you greet only your brothers, what are you doing more than others? Do not even pagans do that? Be perfect, therefore, as your heavenly Father is perfect. Matthew 5:43–48

If Christians don't love their enemies, they're no different from the world. God has made "love your enemies" love available to all of us. Maybe you'd better start by making a "Those Who Don't Like Me Very Much" prayer list, and pray for those people every day.

Day 59

Adriana was ashamed of her house and her parents. Her mom was always dressed out of style, and her dad treated her like he was a general in the army and she was the lowest of soldiers. They were so strict with her that she felt like she never had any fun. They didn't want her to go out with friends or wear the latest clothes. They just didn't understand that times were changing, and they had to stop living in the nineteenth century

The devil is a master deceiver. He has successfully hoodwinked generations of teenagers into thinking they know more than their parents, and that they are perfectly within their "rights" to disobey "old-fashioned" rules and ideas. Society considers this normal. But disobeying God's command to honor one's parents is not par for the course, and it's not to be excused by saying, "Times have changed." *It is sin.* What the Bible has to say hasn't changed:

> *Listen to your father, who gave you life, and do not despise your mother when she is old. Buy the truth and do not sell it; get wisdom, discipline and understanding. The father of a righteous man has great joy; he who has a wise son delights in him. May your father and mother be glad; may she who gave you birth rejoice!* Proverbs 23:22–25

What would your home be like if your parents were suddenly transformed into full-fledged teenagers? You'd probably do almost anything to turn them back into their reliable, consistent, older generation selves! A car needs both an engine and brakes. At your house, most likely you are the engine and your parents are the brakes. Respect them and honor them for their position—and *love* them, even when it seems they unnecessarily pull the emergency brake.

Learning to love your parents despite their failures is the best preparation for life. Do everything possible to make them happy. If you decide to really work at loving and serving your parents, you're investing in changing your family for the better.

Day 60

Postscript to a Practical Joke

If boredom were a fatal disease, Mr. Niznik's class would be dead.

"I'll go crazy," Joe declared, "if we can't lighten up third hour."

"I've got an idea," Zane replied. "We could pull off the ultimate April Fool's joke. I'll bring my dad's big van to school and park it so that it blocks Mr. Niznik's view of his car. Al, you distract him while I hide his keys. Then Joe, you come in tardy and tell him his car is gone. He'll go nuts!"

At 10:23 on April 1, Al asked Mr. Niznik for homework help while Zane snuck up to his cluttered desk to swipe his keys. Just then, Joe sauntered in with a tardy pass. "Mr. Niznik," he said, "did you park your car where you always do? It's not there!"

Mr. Niznik peered out the window, and not seeing his car, he began frantically searching for his keys. It suddenly dawned on him that his car may have been stolen. A look of panic crossed his face, and he grabbed for his chair. Moaning in agony, he collapsed to the floor, suffering a major panic attack. One of the girls used her cell phone to call 9-1-1.

Like a madman shooting firebrands or deadly arrows is a man who deceives his neighbor and says, "I was only joking!" Proverbs 26:18–19

If you're serious about obeying God, there are some laughs you are going to have to live without. Practical jokes are an American institution—but they're *wrong* if they involve lying or exposing the other person to treatment you yourself would not like.

So in everything, do to others what you would have them do to you, for this sums up the Law and the Prophets. Matthew 7:12

It's easy to do things without thinking. What if the kid you throw into the pool can't swim or is wearing an expensive non-waterproof watch? What if your prank call gives Ms. Westfield several sleepless nights?

Everybody likes to do crazy, fun things—and God doesn't want you to be straight-laced, somber, and sad. But your teasing *must* stay within the limits of God's Word. When you're uncertain whether your practical joke will be well received, you'd better stop short. If in doubt, *don't.*

Dorian had always been taught to stick up for his rights. He didn't have to wear his "Don't Push Me Around" T-shirt for people to notice him. He was the first to complain about the soggy French fries and demand his money back. He let his teachers know when he was dissatisfied with the grading system. Taking the best seat or butting into line didn't bother him in the least. After all, it was the "survival of the fittest," and he was determined to be on top.

Dorian decided to use the only techniques he knew to win Maria's affection. He bragged about his plans to become a lawyer, showed her pictures of his parents' luxurious home, and even invited her to the fanciest restaurant in town. But Maria said she had a date with Tom. Dorian couldn't believe it. He thought of Tom as sickeningly polite, overly responsible, and one who always let other people run all over him.

"Maria," he couldn't resist asking, "what do you *see* in Tom?"

Maria replied, "He loves his enemies. He puts the interests of others above his own. He's a great guy." For once Dorian had nothing to say.

Let another praise you, and not your own mouth; someone else, and not your own lips. Proverbs 27:2

Honor one another above yourselves. Romans 12:10

One who personifies self-advancement doesn't make a good friend or a good citizen. But it's important to see why so many people are bummed-out on being good. Those who haven't plugged into God's supernatural power (and Christians who haven't turned on the switch!) will feel like constant losers in the struggle with selfishness.

Only love that comes from Jesus gives us the will to genuinely want to put others above ourselves. Only the security of knowing that an all-powerful God is protecting us makes it unnecessary to defend ourselves. Only knowing that God considers us so valuable that He sent His Son to die for us can remove the temptation to tell everyone how great we are. There's all the difference in the world between playing Mr. Good Guy or Miss Good Gal when convenient and letting Jesus live His selfless life of love and compassion through you.

Day 62

How Can So Many People Be So Wrong?

It was a sultry summer afternoon, and Erica was thoroughly bored. She flipped on the TV only to find talk-show after boring talk-show.

She turned off the TV and picked up one of her mother's magazines. The feature article was called "Sex Is a Basic Need." It went on to list all the psychological problems you could have if you don't express your sexuality. Her mom had a lot of boyfriends, and although they never discussed it, Erica suspected that her mom had affairs with quite a few men.

Six months before, Erica had accepted Jesus as her Savior. She'd gone to club meetings and teen Bible studies where she learned that sex outside of marriage is a sin, and it would spoil the beautiful plan God had for her life. Because it was in the Bible, she'd believed it, but now she wondered how the small group of Christians at her school could be so sure they were right?

Let's set it straight—the basic need you have is for love, not sex. God wants to meet your love requirement through himself and many different people. Close friendships are God-ordained, and healthy Christian relationships with both guys and girls can keep you from being so starved for attention that you easily fall into any trap.

A friend loves at all times. Proverbs 17:17

There is a friend who sticks closer than a brother. Proverbs 18:24

And the pleasantness of one's friend springs from his earnest counsel. Proverbs 27:9

Because the God who created us loves us, He made rules for our happiness. "It is God's will that you should ... avoid sexual immorality" (1 Thessalonians 4:3). This is *the* reason for guarding your purity. However, the consequences of immorality—STDs, AIDS, pregnancy, abortion, inability to trust a marriage partner, and untold heartache—should also make a person think twice before entering an illicit relationship.

Because Lincoln was overcrowded, some students were assigned to attend East High. Eddie was one of them, and that meant being separated from all his closest friends.

At first, Eddie felt out of place in the new school. His new friends weren't like his Christian friends. Their jokes were off-color, and they made fun of everyone. Riley distributed the questions to Ms. MacCarthy's English test, and Lane shared the answers for the pop science quizzes. "Never rat on a member of the group" became like the eleventh commandment.

One day one of the guys brought a few frogs, which he let loose in the lasagna pan as he passed through the lunch line. Omar got blamed for it. Although Omar was suspended for a day, Eddie was afraid to tell the truth. The "eleventh commandment" had kicked in.

Eddie was bothered by the explicit lyrics of their music at first, but he got used to it. Eventually the provocative posters in the guys' bedrooms were just something else to look at. At least Eddie had friends.

One day Darren invited the guys to his house after school. "I'm getting bored," he announced. "It's time we experiment a little. My uncle accidentally left this cocaine. You're not chicken, are you?"

Eddie had a huge decision to make.

He who walks with the wise grows wise, but a companion of fools suffers harm. Proverbs 13:20

The fear of the Lord is the beginning of knowledge. Proverbs 1:7

You can see that God's will is for you to be careful about who your close friends are. Of course you will have casual friends who don't know Christ, but if they are influencing you instead of being influenced by you, something has to change. Don't hang out with people just so you can feel like you fit in. Are your friends really the ones who will help you choose what honors God?

Think about who you hang out with. It's now or never.

Day 64

The Syndrome of Self

Jared was the only child of parents whose professions absorbed almost all their time. Because they felt guilty for not spending more time with their son, his parents mostly let Jared have his own way. Jared played all the latest video games for hours at a stretch and got anything he wanted at home. What he enjoyed most was chess. He was a member of the chess club at school, and he had won several championships.

But Jared was lonely and not good at making friends. Then Phil, a guy from church, invited Jared home for dinner. Jared enjoyed sitting around the table with a family, and the food tasted so much better than his microwave meals.

After that, Jared kept showing up at Phil's house just in time to eat. Finally Phil's father told him straight out, "Our rule is that you never go to someone's house at mealtime unless you're invited."

Jared felt hurt. He started avoiding Phil and turned his attention to Craig, whose father was one of the richest men in the city. Because Craig wanted to learn how to play chess, he welcomed Jared's friendship. He drove Jared around in his new truck and took him to eat in expensive restaurants. But one day, after an argument, he told Jared where to get off.

"You don't care about me. You just like my money."

You need God's help to learn how to sense the needs of others and to think of your friends' happiness first. If you're spoiled, a loner, or from a family with serious problems, you probably have some handicaps in the area of knowing how to be a friend. But by recognizing unhealthy behavior patterns and asking God for wisdom and power, you can change.

Better is open rebuke than hidden love. Wounds from a friend can be trusted, but an enemy multiplies kisses. Proverbs 27:5–6

As iron sharpens iron, so one man sharpens another. Proverbs 27:17

We all need close friends. Pay attention when others point out your faults. If you're self-centered, you're not a good friend—no matter how charming and witty you may appear. Wanting all the attention or calling all the shots will only destroy true friendship.

Amanda had lent her English book to Jessica, who then lost it. Jess didn't seem the least bit concerned that Amanda had to walk a half mile to Melanie's house to do her assignments until she could get a new book. And Jess didn't offer to pay the sixteen dollars to replace it either.

Although they'd been friends since seventh grade, Amanda didn't really want to forgive Jess. She knew that Jessica's parents were unbelievers who were careless about paying debts and returning borrowed things, but Amanda wasn't ready to excuse Jess on that account. Jessica was gone for the weekend on a ski trip, so Amanda had until Monday to make her decision. She thought she'd just stop speaking to Jessica altogether.

At nine-thirty on Sunday evening, the phone rang. It was Jessica. "Amanda, I'm so glad you're home. We're stuck on the freeway and I ran out of gas. Could you bring me a couple gallons?"

Inside, Amanda was fuming. That was just like Jess—irresponsible and asking for help. Amanda was studying for her first-hour Spanish test, and she didn't feel like bailing Jessica out. But Amanda knew that this was the perfect opportunity to show that Jesus lived inside her.

Learning how to forgive is basic to Christian living. If you decide not to pardon those who wrong you, you'll have very few friends.

He who covers an offense promotes love, but whoever repeats the matter separates close friends. Proverbs 17:9

Cover over an offense with forgiveness and don't keep bringing it up again and again. This verse does not recommend sweeping everything under the rug. Deal with the situation *once,* and then forgive and forget.

Don't make excuses if you don't feel like forgiving. Unwillingness to forgive causes disastrous results. But when you're *willing* to forgive, God will supply the grace you need. And don't worry about your emotions. They'll catch up with your will sooner or later.

If your idea of friendship is fifty-fifty, forget it. Going the extra mile, turning the other cheek, paying more than your share—that's what Jesus taught. It's just that if the motivation, the willingness, and the power don't come from the Author of this type of lifestyle, it won't work.

Day 66

The Story That Grew

Ray was the best-looking guy in the youth group. Athletic, outgoing, and considerate, he was the favorite of the girls. Marji had a crush on him. When Ray started dating Lori, Marji was heartbroken. She knew that God's will might be different from hers, yet she had a hard time seeing Ray and Lori together.

One Friday night, Marji went out for ice cream with her friend Hannah. It was a little past ten as they drove by a big downtown hotel where they saw Ray and Lori walking into the lobby. "What on earth are Ray and Lori doing at a hotel?" Marji wondered out loud.

"Maybe they're going out to eat," Hannah answered.

"I wonder," Marji said with a hint of suspicion.

A couple weeks later, Marji got a call from a girl in her church class. "Did you know that Ray and Lori spent a night at the Ambassador Hotel?"

"Who told you that? And how do you know it's true?" Marji asked.

"My cousin works there, and he checked them in."

Before Saturday's youth meeting, Ray's best friend called Marji aside. "Everyone says that you've been spying on Ray and Lori, and that you're trying to break them up by saying they spent the night in a hotel."

"That's not true," Marji replied angrily.

Soon the youth group was divided in half—one half defended Ray and Lori, and the other thought they were sleeping together.

Without wood a fire goes out; without gossip a quarrel dies down. Proverbs 26:20

A perverse man stirs up dissension, and a gossip separates close friends. Proverbs 16:28

Gossip is a leading cause of destroyed friendships, and losing a Christian friend is a tragedy. A few do it on purpose, but most simply pass on information or opinions without carefully checking the facts.

Be very careful about what information you give others. Remember, you can even share a prayer request for a person without passing on all the details. God already knows what the problem is.

One Saturday morning Jewell called. She was my co-worker in Christian youth work. She sounded discouraged. The club president was unreliable and hardly anyone was attending the Bible study groups.

I finally said, "Hold on. I remember reading a verse this morning: 'Preach the Word; be prepared in season and out of season' (2 Timothy 4:2). I guess it must be the 'out of season' time right now." Encouragement from God's Word came to our rescue.

If you try to reach the world for Jesus, the devil will be there with an arsenal of automatic weapons. If you are planning to rely on your own enthusiasm, he will shoot you down. If you're not getting your power from the Holy Spirit, Christian work will be exhausting and discouraging.

The real reason we should share our faith is because Jesus told us to, not because people need us. If our main goal is just to help people, it's too easy to be overly concerned with their responses. We will become discouraged when things go wrong or people don't like what we say.

Jesus' love should keep us from discouragement. The person who really loves us will eat our burned toast with a smile or appreciate that we stopped to buy flowers even if the shop had none left. Jesus totally loves us and is pleased with us regardless of how others respond to our witness.

Therefore we do not lose heart. Though outwardly we are wasting away, yet inwardly we are being renewed day by day. For our light and momentary troubles are achieving for us an eternal glory that far outweighs them all. So we fix our eyes not on what is seen, but on what is unseen. For what is seen is temporary, but what is unseen is eternal. 2 Corinthians 4:16–18

We must look to the Holy Spirit for the power, joy, and love that we need. His supply is limitless, so there is no need for discouragement—no need to be hostages in the dungeon of despair. If we descend into "the pits," it's only because we have cut off our supply of love, power, joy, and peace by looking only at ourselves or at the work we are doing.

Day 68

Pearls, Pigs, and Perishing

Deception (believing what is not true) comes from unwillingness to accept God's truth. Therefore, you must beware of people involved in cults and false teachings. Their power comes from Satan, and he is very dangerous. Pray for the deceived person who is about to become one of the guru's assistants. Warn an individual who is willing to listen. However, if the person wants to argue, don't keep talking. God will give special grace and protection in handling such people with whom you must associate, but in situations where you are sharing Christ, be careful of those who want to destroy Christians.

Jesus himself cautioned us:

> *Do not give dogs what is sacred; do not throw your pearls to pigs. If you do, they may trample them under their feet, and then turn and tear you to pieces.* Matthew 7:6

Deceived, godless people will turn and attack you. Don't be guilty of the pride that says, "I'm so strong in my beliefs that nothing anyone could do or say will hurt me." That's not true. Satan is working through many people, and he is very strong. Let God guide you, and don't foolishly and recklessly decide that with your great Bible knowledge you can convert the cult leader. Obey Jesus' warning. Use great caution and much prayer.

> *But avoid foolish controversies and genealogies and arguments and quarrels about the law, because these are unprofitable and useless. Warn a divisive person once, and then warn him a second time. After that, have nothing to do with him. You may be sure that such a man is warped and sinful; he is self-condemned.* Titus 3:9–11

Stay away from religious arguments. You will never argue anyone into the kingdom of God. If you're a good debater, you may enjoy the challenge, but this isn't doing God's work. If your discussion is unreasonable, if neither of you is listening and trying to understand the other person's viewpoint, change the subject and don't cast your pearls before pigs.

One of the devil's chief tactics is making people so busy that they have no time for *God's* priorities: Bible study, prayer, helping lonely people, and encouraging other Christians. Your life is most likely too busy already. If you look around, you can see how easy it is to be so occupied with life that God's priorities have to be sandwiched in here and there.

Is Jesus your *number one* priority? You may be able to say yes and mean it, but everyday tasks will decide whether or not you'll spend a lot of time with Jesus. Many couples have gotten so engrossed in planning a wedding, building a house, or getting ahead in their careers that they have nearly forgotten one another. And it isn't because they don't love each other.

If spending time with Jesus and doing the things He considers most important are to be first in your life, you must rearrange your whole schedule. For example, don't skip devotions and church to study for the biology test; put Jesus first and let Him take care of everything else. Doing what He wants should be your top priority. Perhaps you'll miss a day of skiing with your friends in order to do something that will mean a lot to your mom. Maybe you'll cancel a date to spend extra time with the friend whose father just died. (If you're dating the right kind of person, he or she will understand.)

> *But seek first his kingdom and his righteousness, and all these things will be given to you as well.* Matthew 6:33

> *Offer right sacrifices and trust in the Lord.* Psalm 4:5

Working for Jesus may mean working fewer hours and getting by on less money, dropping out of a sport for a while, or giving up your favorite TV programs so you can be part of an evangelistic team.

Telling other people about Jesus is greater than getting straight A's, making money so you can have a car, or having the right clothes or the perfect haircut. Let Jesus decide what your priorities should be.

Day 70

Penetrating Pride and Prejudice

As you listen to the news, you hear of tension between races, nations, and economic groups. So much suspicion and lack of understanding among people of different backgrounds makes peace and even common-sense decisions seem impossible.

Jesus came to give you genuine love and understanding for all people. Individuals from all races, languages, and cultures belong to the body of Christ. People who love the same Lord and belong to the same body have *everything* in common.

God can use you as a living advertisement to show His love, which can build bridges over the chasms of pride and prejudice. Ask Him for a close friendship that will be an example to the rest of the world. Maybe He wants you to be a helpful friend to a senior citizen and show the world that with Jesus, there is no generation gap. Maybe a person with a disability needs a friend with extra patience. The Lord might lead you to a person of another race or ethnic background. Maybe He wants you to befriend someone from the poorest part of town. Be willing to go beyond the comfortable clique of kids who are just like you.

My brothers, as believers in our glorious Lord Jesus Christ, don't show favoritism. Suppose a man comes into your meeting wearing a gold ring and fine clothes, and a poor man in shabby clothes also comes in. If you show special attention to the man wearing fine clothes and say, "Here's a good seat for you," but say to the poor man, "You stand there" or "Sit on the floor by my feet," have you not discriminated among yourselves and become judges with evil thoughts? James 2:1–4

In order to demonstrate the love of God, love and pray for the people in your church who seem to be prejudiced or narrow-minded. Jesus loves people even when they are wrong. Prejudiced people don't need more information; only Jesus can change inner attitudes. But if they can see the love of Jesus in another person, their walls of prejudice might come tumbling down.

Medical science has made great strides, but no one is yet proposing head transplants! The body without the head is useless because the brain controls most of our body functions.

The Bible says, "Christ is the head of the church, his body, of which he is the Savior" (Ephesians 5:23). This means that Jesus is the authority of the church and that we are to receive our directions from Him. If we really did that, things would be a lot different.

Jesus didn't say one thing about whether the church should have modern or traditional music, but He did pray:

My prayer is not for them alone. I pray also for those who will believe in me through their message, that all of them may be one, Father, just as you are in me and I am in you. May they also be in us so that the world may believe that you have sent me. John 17:20–21

Jesus didn't tell us His views on bowling on Sunday or dress codes for church, but He did say:

My command is this: Love each other as I have loved you. John 15:12

Jesus didn't mention what time church should start in the summer or whether youth groups should sponsor all-night parties, but He did state:

By this all men will know that you are my disciples, if you love one another. John 13:35

Before you reenact Custer's Last Stand as you insist that your youth group spend the car wash money on a ski weekend, remember what happened to Custer. Instead of wisely retreating, he and his men tried to hold the line in the wrong place at the wrong time and were wiped out. Don't invest your time and energy fighting unless you're defending a clear biblical principle, so you know God is on your side. Remember that your enemy's strategy is "divide and conquer." And more important, recognize that following Jesus' command to love other Christians is more significant than getting the "right" things done or expressing your opinion.

Day 72

So What If You're a Kidney?

"She's so talented it's sickening!"

"I wish I could play the piano the way he does."

"If I could meet people as easily as Hector does, I wouldn't be such a dweeb."

Feelings of jealousy or inferiority that often plague Christians would melt away if all of us really understood the meaning of "the body of Christ." God tells us in the Bible that all true Christians are part of His body. He is the Head, and just as impulses from the brain direct the actions in our human bodies, so Jesus is to direct the actions of Christians.

God made you with exactly the right kind of personality and abilities to best fit into Christ's body. No one can fill the place you have as well as you can. Ask God how you can best be used in each situation.

In a body, it would seem that the teeth, eyes, and hair, which are constantly seen and often admired, would be the most important. But the truth is that we could live without any of those things; however, we could not survive without some of the *unseen* parts of our bodies, like the kidneys or lungs.

It's foolish to be jealous of someone else's ability to speak or play the guitar, and thus hurt the whole body of Christ by not recognizing or praying about how to use your own gift for encouraging people. The people who hold churches together are not the leaders. They are people who are completely dedicated to Jesus and are quietly and obediently carrying out their functions in the body regardless of what others are doing.

> *And if the ear should say, "Because I am not an eye, I do not belong to the body," it would not for that reason cease to be part of the body. If the whole body were an eye, where would the sense of hearing be? If the whole body were an ear, where would the sense of smell be? . . . The eye cannot say to the hand, "I don't need you!" And the head cannot say to the feet, "I don't need you!"* 1 Corinthians 12:16–17, 21

Nothing will make you feel more defeated than comparing yourself with others. Follow Jesus. Do the work for Him that only you can do, then relax. You don't have to be a carbon-copy Christian.

Day 73
Pigpens and Peace

Jill and Kyisha had been close friends for two years. Then it happened. Jill and Dan started dating exclusively. Since Kyisha had really liked Dan, she felt that her best friend had betrayed her by stealing "her" guy. Kyisha wouldn't even talk to Jill, and Jill didn't try to straighten things out, since she felt she had done nothing wrong. They both sang "We are one in the Spirit" in the same choir. They repeated, "Forgive us our debts as we forgive our debtors" while sitting in the same row, but they weren't on speaking terms.

Have you ever been a Jill or a Kyisha? What do you do in a situation like that? The first step is to meditate on Scripture, and remember that you are one in Christ with the Christian you're having trouble getting along with.

Let us therefore make every effort to do what leads to peace and to mutual edification. Romans 14:19

You are responsible to work hard for Christian unity—whether or not the fault was yours. First go to the person to humbly ask forgiveness. Or if you don't know what you've done, ask the person how you've offended him or her. If the person refuses to forgive you, pray for that person every day. Ask God what extra special thing you can do for that person to demonstrate your love and concern.

If you have a clear title to one hundred acres of beautiful wooded shoreline property, it's yours. You have a right to enjoy all that fresh air, inspiring scenery, the peace and quiet. If squatters come in and erect tar paper shacks, and another person tries to fence in a piece of your land to pasture hogs, you can fight for your legal rights.

In the spiritual realm it's no different. Jesus has already bought a clear title for peace among Christians, paying for it with His blood. Don't allow the devil to set up his pigpen on your property.

As strange as it may seem, Christians must fight to keep the unity that Jesus purchased for them. If there is strain between you and another Christian, it's your responsibility to do everything possible to resolve it.

Day 74

Saved, Sanctified—and Petrified

When the biology teacher explained that a big explosion had caused the universe, Rosa raised her hand and asked, "Mr. Jones, where did the materials for the big bang come from, and what caused the explosion?"

The teacher glared at her. "Rosa, you certainly don't believe the Genesis fairy tale, with Adam and Eve and the snake, do you?"

"I sure do," replied Rosa.

Everyone stared at Rosa. Janelle smiled and rushed to her side after class, explaining that she too was a Christian. They became friends, but soon problems developed. Rosa believed things that Janelle's church taught were wrong. And Janelle had trouble accepting some things Rosa believed.

Has the fact that all of God's children don't always think alike ever bothered you? Since all true Christians are part of the body of Christ, we need to seek biblical solutions when differences of opinion threaten to divide us. We should take Ephesians 4:3 seriously: Make every effort to keep the unity of the Spirit through the bond of peace.

Notice Jesus doesn't say that we all have to believe exactly the same thing. When we get to heaven, we'll all discover that we've had some wrong ideas; however, God's supernatural love is available so we can truly appreciate each other. It's wonderful to experience a love so strong that the differences no longer matter.

It wasn't a system of belief in outline form that Jesus gave us when He left for heaven, but a promise:

But when he, the Spirit of truth, comes, he will guide you into all truth.
John 16:13

The Holy Spirit will tell us what the Bible means—not modern science or current public opinion.

Rosa and Janelle could learn a great deal if they went to their church leaders and asked for the Bible verses to support church beliefs; then they could ask the Holy Spirit to give them light. Both girls could change if their beliefs were not supported by God's Word, and their love for each other could increase in spite of differences that still remained.

We all must be willing to learn from other Christians. Saints who consider themselves "saved, sanctified, and petrified" are missing out on a whole lot.

Day 75
Part of the Package Deal

Miss Burns was young, a lot of fun, and as good a speech teacher as anyone could ask for. Juanita was one of four Christian students in the class. All of them were working together to try to win Miss Burns to Jesus. They took advantage of speech topics like "The Best Thing I Ever Did Was" to talk to the class about their faith in Jesus. Juanita asked Miss Burns to come to church with her, and afterward she invited her teacher home for dinner. Miss Burns expressed interest in studying the Bible.

Then it happened. Dustyn was caught using a cheat sheet on the semester exam. Miss Burns exploded. "I thought Christians were supposed to do what's right. I'm an atheist, but at least I'm honest. From now on any speeches on religion receive an automatic F."

Juanita was furious. How could Dustyn have done such a thing?

Every Christian encounters the problem Juanita faced. What do *you* do when the sin of another Christian messes things up for you?

First of all, you must remember that the person who sinned is still part of the body of Christ, and your primary obligation is to forgive him or her. Next, just let God be God. Pray that He will repair the unfair damage. Pray that He will provide another opportunity for the non-Christian to see that Jesus really does manufacture new creations. Psalm 37:6 is a promise:

He will make your righteousness shine like the dawn, the justice of your cause like the noonday sun.

It all starts with forgiveness. Don't let the devil convince you that you're justified in not forgiving a Christian whose sin has caused great harm to others in the body. "Forgiving each other, just as in Christ God forgave you" (Ephesians 4:32) is the way the body operates. Forgiving others isn't just an optional extra—it's part of the package deal along with everlasting love, purpose for living, and pardon for all your sins.

Loretta looked around uneasily as she entered the small church. She sat near the back. No one greeted her and several people stared. After a couple of songs and Scripture readings, the leader up front asked people to go to their classes. Loretta didn't know where the senior high class met, but she spotted a girl she had noticed in her English class and followed her.

The teacher greeted Loretta formally and asked for her name, but no one seemed genuinely glad to see her. Loretta was African-American, and because of her father's job, her family had moved to a mostly white community. She had expected a cool reception at school, but it hurt her deeply that fellow Christians refused to fully accept her.

Unfortunately, Loretta's situation isn't unique. Many Christians feel rejected and left out for various reasons. Being a different color, speaking with an accent, not dressing as well as the others, and having different interests are some of those reasons. How can you deal with disapproval from other Christians? You always start with the fact of Scripture:

> *You have taken off your old self with its practices and have put on the new self, which is being renewed in knowledge in the image of its Creator. Here there is no Greek or Jew, circumcised or uncircumcised, barbarian, Scythian, slave or free, but Christ is all, and is in all.* Colossians 3:9–11

The fact is that as a true Christian, you've taken off the old self that allows others to make you feel inferior, and you've put on a new self that is as important in the body of Christ as anybody else. It's just that you have to constantly adopt God's mindset to remember truth and reject icy stares, lack of consideration, unkind words, and unfair judgments.

God can use you to bring other Christians to the realization that those who know Jesus are meant to be one big happy family, in which there is overflowing love for one another. In God's family it doesn't matter if you are black or white, rich or poor, best-all-around, Ordinary Oscar, Cesar the Brain, or Macho Matt. Love is contagious. If you allow God to give you love to display to those who reject you, they'll catch some of it too. Wouldn't you like to be the one who started the love epidemic?

Day 77

Everybody Needs One Body!

Steve's parents had just had another fight.

Predictable as a TV rerun, it began when Steve's mother announced that she had called an interior decorator to get an estimate for completely redoing the living room. Steve's father had exploded and decreed that his hard-earned money would not be spent so frivolously. His mother announced that she was leaving, and she went to the bedroom to pack. Steve's father mumbled, "Well, it sure would cut down on living expenses." Then he sat down in his favorite chair and turned on the TV.

After giving his father time to calm down, Steve took advantage of a commercial. "Dad," he began, "I've saved all the money I need. Please let me go on the youth retreat this weekend."

His father used his "this-is-the-last-word" tone of voice: "I don't want you mixed up with religious fanatics. The answer is *no*."

Steve had accepted Christ, but his parents did everything possible to prevent him from having Christian friends. The only thing his parents seemed to agree on was that there was no God, and Christians were ignorant and weak.

Have you ever felt like Steve? You're not alone. You're part of the body of Christ. An army of people really do care for you and want to help.

Don't let pride or timidity keep you away from other Christians. The Bible commands us:

> *Carry each other's burdens, and in this way you will fulfill the law of Christ.*
> Galatians 6:2

This means that Christians are to share their problems with each other.

Because humans make mistakes, your complete confidence must always be in Jesus—not in any person. But God intended for a Christian to put loving arms around you when you're hurting. He planned for you to hear soothing words from a member of God's family. He has arranged that a group of Christian friends would come to your aid in time of crisis. Everybody needs one body!

"Why did I say that?"

Who hasn't despairingly made that remark? All of us need discretion—the ability to say the right thing at the right time.

Living the Christian life is like operating in enemy territory—sin is everywhere and we must be on the lookout. For that reason the psalmist prayed, "Set a guard over my mouth, O Lord" (Psalm 141:3).

But it isn't true that if a statement is accurate, a Christian automatically has the right to say it. The person who is discreet relies on God for *every* word. This shouldn't be a self-conscious fear of opening your mouth, but instead like the confidence a child has that he won't get lost as long as he holds his mother's hand. It's the child that goes off who gets into trouble, and it's the Christian who tries to run the show alone who falls.

When words are many, sin is not absent, but he who holds his tongue is wise.
Proverbs 10:19

Do not be quick with your mouth, do not be hasty in your heart to utter anything before God. God is in heaven and you are on earth, so let your words be few. Ecclesiastes 5:2

An old saying goes, "What exists in the well of the thoughts will soon come up in the bucket of the speech." Guarding your speech starts with guarding your heart. Jealousy can quickly cause an unkind word. Trying to protect your selfish interests can cause you to lash out at someone else. Unwillingness to see your own faults can make you defensive.

Discretion has its root in self-knowledge. We know we're sinful and must depend on God. Any pride or cockiness on our part means we don't know what's in the human heart. Jeremiah asks about the human heart, "Who can know it?" The answer, of course, is that only God knows, and He says it's sinful. But if we exercise faith, God will give us true discretion. We best learn discretion by being silent rather than by talking all the time. But that doesn't mean you should put your tongue in jail and be afraid to say anything. True discretion balks at rashness but is quick to encourage and speak positively.

Day 79

Please Erase the Remark I Just Made

A woman went to see her pastor. "I've been guilty of spreading false rumors and now I want to undo all the damage."

The pastor told her to come with him. He bought some goose feathers and they climbed to the top of the church's bell tower. The pastor then asked the lady to drop the goose feathers. The wind quickly scattered them. "Now," the pastor ordered, "go down and gather the feathers."

"But Pastor," protested the woman, "that would be impossible."

"I know," he replied, "just as impossible as taking back all the words you've spoken."

Words just don't disappear. An inner recording keeps playing back certain words someone has said to you. Maybe it's your exasperated father roaring, "If you don't like it here, leave—and don't bother to come back!" or a teacher, at wit's end, exploding, "You're hopeless. You'll never learn algebra!"

Words like these sometimes affect us for a long time—even if the person who said them didn't really mean them.

No man can tame the tongue. It is a restless evil, full of deadly poison. With the tongue we praise our Lord and Father, and with it we curse men, who have been made in God's likeness. Out of the same mouth come praise and cursing. My brothers, this should not be. James 3:8–10

But I tell you that men will have to give account on the day of judgment for every careless word they have spoken. Matthew 12:36

Talking is one of the most dangerous things we do. Words can't be erased or obliterated, so think how your words will affect the other person before you say them. People who recognize that they don't have the right to say whatever they want can get help from Jesus just by asking for it.

One of the constant temptations Christians face is the temptation to lie. We can do it in so many ways. "It wasn't my fault," or "I didn't do anything!" slip out before we even think.

The truth, however, would sound more like this: "We were playing catch too close to the window and I missed the ball," or "Yes, I did cheat on the test." Do you lie when you want to avoid punishment?

Then there's exaggeration: "All the other kids (all six of them) are going on the camping trip, and I'm the only one (along with four others) whose parents won't let me go," or "I have to have a new outfit because my old one is ragged and faded and has ink spots, glue splotches, and mustard on it."

Then there are lies to make us look just a little better: "I knew the answer, but I just didn't say it," or "I thought the program started at eight, so that's why I am late," or "Didn't you say the assignment was due on Monday instead of Friday?"

Truthful lips endure forever, but a lying tongue lasts only a moment. Proverbs 12:19

The Lord detests lying lips, but he delights in men who are truthful. Proverbs 12:22

A false witness will not go unpunished, and he who pours out lies will not go free. Proverbs 19:5

We tend to think that everybody stretches the truth a little, so it's no big deal. But God thinks lying is so bad that He included it in the Ten Commandments. Don't excuse yourself for lying. Confess it as sin so you can receive God's forgiveness.

Take Jesus with you through every day as your own personal Lie Detector. He will teach you how to tell the truth in every situation.

Day 81

You Mean Complaining Is a Sin?

Sometimes when you read the Old Testament you think there's nothing there that applies to you. Yet people who keep on reading the Old Testament find many verses that almost jump off the pages and tell them how to live. One such verse is Numbers 11:1:

Now the people complained about their hardships in the hearing of the Lord, and when he heard them his anger was aroused.

God hates complaining! In fact, He sent a terrible fire to burn some of the tents of the Israelites as punishment for their complaints. Another time He sent poisonous snakes. He parted the Red Sea so they could safely escape slavery and drowned Pharaoh's army in the same sea. He was giving them bread from heaven to eat every day. Yet they complained.

But look what God has done for us. He has saved us from sin. We have Christian friends and family who care about us. We have enough food—so much, in fact, that many of us must see that we don't overeat. And we have so many clothes that we have difficulty deciding what to wear.

Adults complain about high taxes, the cost of living, presidents, and the weather. Teenagers complain about the food in the lunchroom, parents who don't understand them, mean teachers, and the price of pizza.

I'll bet even you spend some time every day complaining! But complaining is a sin, and God hates it. This is hard to face because most of us would have to admit that we're terrible sinners. Complaining is wrong and it must stop. Complaining is a lack of trust in God and a slap in the face of our heavenly Father, who has done so much for us.

Do everything without complaining or arguing, so that you may become blameless and pure, children of God without fault in a crooked and depraved generation, in which you shine like stars in the universe. Philippians 2:14–15

Complaining ruins your personality. Everyone tries to avoid a chronic complainer. Ask God to help you hate complaining and treat complaining as sin, a terrible offense against God—and not as your right to vent your feelings.

What we *think* affects us, but once we verbalize something, it becomes part of us in a much deeper way. People can say things so often that they end up believing them.

Robbie, a second-grader, got to school and started the day by saying, "I wish I could have a birthday party." By morning recess he was saying, "I'm having a birthday party," and by noon he had invited a whole group of classmates to the nonexistent party. When a group of Robbie's classmates showed up at his house after school, his mother was furious.

We think we are a lot smarter than that second-grade boy—but we aren't. The grown-up Israelites in the wilderness talked so much about the "good old days" in Egypt that they forgot how cruel slavery in Egypt had been. Soon they were mad at Moses for bringing them into the terrible wilderness. It took snakebites to bring them to their senses.

Another time some Israelites started complaining that they didn't have meat to eat, and they kept saying that eating manna every day was the pits. Soon they all believed they were deprived, forsaken, and protein-starved. (They forgot that the Creator might also be a nutrition expert.) God then sent them so many quails that the greedy people got sick from eating too much.

If you keep saying something, pretty soon you'll believe it and act upon it. That means you'd better be careful what you say. Because saying and believing the wrong thing is so serious, God must sometimes take drastic measures to keep you on track. Next time you're about to say, "All the people at that church are hypocrites," or "My parents don't care what I do," let visions of snakes or quails keep you from disobeying God!

May the words of my mouth and the meditation of my heart be pleasing in your sight, O Lord, my Rock and my Redeemer. Psalm 19:14

Let your conversation be always full of grace, seasoned with salt, so that you may know how to answer everyone. Colossians 4:6

Day 83

Did You Know That Your Mind Is on Parade?

You know the type. They have names for their teachers, such as "Skinny Neck," "Gestapo George," and "Crazy Carlson." They make nasty comments about the guy with the weird haircut and the girl with the bad complexion. They constantly brag about themselves and put other people down. Their conversations are sprinkled with "I don't care what anyone says," and "Nobody is going to tell me what to do."

Such people get into arguments or fights if anyone says anything even mildly offensive to them. Listening is an activity they avoid because it would deprive them of the opportunity to loudly proclaim what they think. When a person in authority tries to correct them, give advice, or ask them to follow rules laid down for everyone, they interrupt with smart remarks.

The Bible calls people like these "fools" and "mockers"—and says some harsh things about them. By their words they show that they are unwilling to change or accept correction.

Whoever corrects a mocker invites insult; whoever rebukes a wicked man incurs abuse. Do not rebuke a mocker or he will hate you; rebuke a wise man and he will love you. Instruct a wise man and he will be wiser still; teach a righteous man and he will add to his learning. The fear of the Lord is the beginning of wisdom, and knowledge of the Holy One is understanding.
Proverbs 9:7–10

How much of that description of the mocker fits you? Someone once said, "Every time you open your mouth, your mind goes on parade." Start improving the parade by letting God deal with attitudes toward your peers, your authorities, and yourself.

Oh, What a Beautiful Tongue You Have!

People often comment on beautiful eyes, flawless complexion, and lovely smiles, but no one ever says, "Oh, what a beautiful tongue you have!" Yet that would be the nicest compliment you could ever receive—what you say can do so much good. Words of encouragement can help someone through an especially hard day. Telling your mother you love her could brighten her whole month, and saying thank-you to a teacher might make him realize it's been worth the effort.

Your tongue can say something cheerful when everyone else is complaining, and it can say something nice about the person everyone else is putting down. The cruel things people say make living in this world extremely difficult. Your tongue can make a big difference in the atmosphere and make life easier for a lot of people.

Your tongue can also introduce people to Jesus and tell others that God loves them. Your tongue, more than any other part of your body, can make you a person worth knowing—one who brings comfort and cheerfulness wherever you go. Stop concentrating solely on getting the world's best tan and getting your hair to go just right; start praying that God will teach you to say the right things. That's the first step toward having a beautiful tongue.

The tongue of the wise commends knowledge, but the mouth of the fool gushes folly. Proverbs 15:2

A man finds joy in giving an apt reply—and how good is a timely word! Proverbs 15:23

The Sovereign Lord has given me an instructed tongue, to know the word that sustains the weary. He wakens me morning by morning, wakens my ear to listen like one being taught. Isaiah 50:4

Day 85

To Tell the Truth

Talon lived in the inner city, where life was dangerous and survival was top priority. "Keep your nose clean, mind your own business, and remember that you never saw anything," was the advice his father gave. As a sophomore, Talon met Sam, who introduced him to Jesus. A whole new set of challenges kicked in. Kids on the street, even little ones, made fun of him when he walked to church carrying his Bible. The guy across the alley who was a member of a gang seemed to make Talon a special target.

One Saturday afternoon, Talon watched from his apartment window as a gang member jumped out from behind a car to grab a woman's purse. When she resisted, he shot her in the chest and ran. Blaring rock music drowned out the noise and nobody ran to investigate. Talon wanted to help, but his father's warning rang in his head: "Remember—you never saw anything." Finally the sirens came, indicating that someone had called 9-1-1.

That evening the police knocked at the door. It was a routine check. When they asked Talon if he knew anything about the crime, he said no. Telling the truth was just too dangerous. What would you have done?

A truthful witness saves lives, but a false witness is deceitful. Proverbs 14:25

Like a club or a sword or a sharp arrow is the man who gives false testimony against his neighbor. Proverbs 25:18

The devil loves to destroy. The idea that you should never tell on a friend—or a bully—is one of Satan's lies that will erode law and order. You might think that keeping your mouth shut when you see someone steal the test answers, or putting a tack on the teacher's chair, or threatening another student, is harmless. It isn't. It's a contribution to another person's misery.

The days are gone when being a truthful witness was easy. Now it requires great courage and sacrifice. But don't forget that you serve a great God who loves to bless those who take great risks for Him. Tell the truth, even when it's unpopular or dangerous to do so. Trust God to protect you.

Day 86

Evan and Marissa went to a Christian concert in the city and Marissa's curfew was 1:00 a.m. Talking, ordering pizza, and running out of gas made Marissa and Eric two hours late. Marissa was grounded for two weeks.

Marissa boiled over. "You just don't understand me!" she screamed. "If I could leave home, I would—*right now!*" Ignoring the tears in her mother's eyes, she stormed up to her room and slammed the door.

Early the next morning, Marissa's parents found out that her grandmother in Phoenix was ill. Her mother packed to leave on the next plane, then woke Marissa to say good-bye. Marissa was still irritated by her mother, so she shrugged her mom off and rolled over in her bed.

Later, Marissa switched on the TV just as a newscaster was saying, "Flight 682 has crashed near the Phoenix airport. All passengers are feared dead."

"No!" Marissa screamed. "What if I never get to apologize to Mom?"

Her habit of always having to have the final word had backfired. Why couldn't her last words to her mother have been, "Mom, I'm sorry, and I love you"? If only she could have those moments back!

Although holding everything in can be harmful, there's a difference between "exploding in anger" and expressing your views in a way that won't hurt others.

He who guards his lips guards his life, but he who speaks rashly will come to ruin. Proverbs 13:3

Do not let any unwholesome talk come out of your mouths, but only what is helpful for building others up according to their needs, that it may benefit those who listen. Ephesians 4:29

It takes little effort to say something that will cause days or years or even a lifetime of pain. And you can never truly erase what you say. The road to most sins has several exits. But with the tongue, you can ruin someone's reputation, mar another's self-image, or spread deadly gossip in mere seconds. Give your tongue to Jesus and make it abide by all His rules.

Day 87

Some Wisecracks, a Handsome Hunk, and Aunt Nellie

Denika was by nature funny and sarcastic. She made fun of teachers, mimicked politicians, and impersonated other students. She always quipped, "If you don't have brains or beauty, you have to be a comedian."

When it was time for the Christmas banquet at their church, Denika's friend Kaitlyn arranged a double date. Denika was very impressed with Kaitlyn's friend Marc. He was a football player, yet he was gentle and full of fun. Denika cracked her most popular jokes and kept everyone entertained.

After the evening's program, they decided they were hungry for a second dessert. At the pie shop, Denika continued the show. She got started on her "Neighbor Nellie Routine": "Nellie dresses like the 1940s," Denika mocked, "and now her clothes are coming back in style again! She loses something three or four times a day and always comes over to tell my mother about it. One day she said she'd lost her piano—can you believe that?—because she forgot the painters had moved it!"

Kaitlyn and Dan were laughing, but Marc was not. "Is your neighbor's name Nellie Nelson?" Marc asked.

"Why, yes," Denika answered uncertainly. "How did you know?"

"She's my father's aunt," Marc replied. "She had a brain aneurysm twenty years ago, and she's had problems ever since."

Dead silence fell. Denika would have done anything to disappear, but she was face-to-face with the tragedy her tongue had created.

Making fun of people does not help build a better world.

With his mouth the godless destroys his neighbor, but through knowledge the righteous escape. Proverbs 11:9

A man who lacks judgment derides his neighbor, but a man of understanding holds his tongue. Proverbs 11:12

The Bible has some pretty stern things to say about those who use unkind words to hurt another. Before you open your mouth, ask yourself if what you're about to say would make for good conversation if Jesus were sitting next to you. If not, forget it.

Winona met DeShawn at a friend's party. They were mutually attracted and started hanging out a lot, but Winona noticed that De-Shawn's temper erupted with alarming frequency. One day they were driving down the interstate, when a guy in an old clunker accidentally cut off DeShawn. Furious, DeShawn laid on the horn and cut in, almost forcing the other guy into a guardrail.

When DeShawn invited Winona to have dinner with his family, he blew up when he discovered his mom planned to serve soup and sandwiches for dinner. "That's not a company dinner!" he said angrily. "I was planning on steak."

Winona was shocked but said nothing.

One night she asked DeShawn to drive her to a mall so she could buy an anniversary present for her parents. Winona couldn't find exactly what she wanted, but DeShawn had had enough. "I'll give you five minutes to decide," he snapped. "Then we're leaving."

Winona felt fire inside. "What makes you think you can tell the whole world what to do?"

Catching a glimpse of the gathering crowd, DeShawn grabbed her and attempted to clap his hand over her mouth. When store security rushed to the scene, witnesses insisted that DeShawn had been verbally abusive and said they thought he was trying to harm Winona. In the end, two policemen took him to the station in a squad car.

An uncontrolled temper leads to hasty and foolish action, not to mention all the cutting remarks and spiteful words that can never be erased.

A hot-tempered man must pay the penalty; if you rescue him, you will have to do it again. Proverbs 19:19

Do not make friends with a hot-tempered man, do not associate with one easily angered, or you may learn his ways and get yourself ensnared. Proverbs 22:24–25

The root cause of most anger is an I-will-defend-my-rights-at-all-times attitude or a nobody's-gonna-push-me-around mindset. Unless you give *all* your rights to Jesus, you'll never conquer anger. Believe that God runs the universe and *always* does a better job than you could. Remember that God has the right to plan your weekend. He has the authority to tell you to turn the other cheek and the power to enable you to obey.

Mario's family moved in November of his senior year to a place where they were the only Mexican family. Mario couldn't seem to break into a group of friends, until he met Shinji, a Japanese-American guy who was on the basketball team with Mario. Pretty soon they became friends, and being treated as an outsider didn't seem so bad. Both loved basketball, so they played often on the weekends.

At the first varsity game, the other team led by ten points by half time. Then the coach put Mario and Shinji into the game. Nobody expected Mario's outside jump shots, and he quickly sank two baskets! Shinji intercepted the ball and passed it to their star center—for two more big ones. Back in the game, the team battled hard and won.

Still, the other team members treated the two like dirt. They told mean jokes about people with accents and slanted eyes. After a practice, one of the starting players walked up to Shinji and sneered, "You have no right to be in my country, or in my school, or on my basketball team."

Shinji remained calm. He closed his eyes for a minute, and Mario knew he was praying. Then the player cornered Mario. "You dirty wetback! You're not even a U.S. citizen. Go back where you belong."

That did it! Mario downed the guy with one punch to the jaw. It was then Mario realized that he needed to learn Shinji's secret.

A fool gives full vent to his anger, but a wise man keeps himself under control.
Proverbs 29:11

Better a patient man than a warrior, a man who controls his temper than one who takes a city. Proverbs 16:32

When someone insults you, send up a quick prayer. If *you* choose not to fuel a quarrel, it's pretty hard for the other person to keep it going. Replacing a *negative* emotion with a *positive* one brings the desired results. But it's impossible to put this good advice into practice without patience, self-control, and gentleness. Fortunately, the Holy Spirit has all the self-control, gentleness, and patience you need. As you receive more and more from Him, your habits and goals will change.

Day 90

Some Down-to-Earth Advice From Outer Space

Once upon a time on the planet Alpha Sirdraamen IV, lived three extraterrestrials—Ferangin, Kilgonrin, and Ormulin. Emotions on Alpha Sirdraamen IV were actual substances you could feel and touch and the extraterrestrials had apparatuses for gathering these substances. Large storage tanks in their hearts enabled them to accumulate huge quantities of emotions. Huge machines cleaned out heart storage tanks. The black button removed hate, the green button envy, and so forth. It was also possible to fill up with love, peace, and kindness.

Ferangin never cleaned out his heart tank. Whenever someone rubbed his fur the wrong way, black smoke poured out of his mouth. He never had anything kind to say. But Ferangin was very lonely.

Kilgonrin wasn't lonely at all. Whenever hatred, envy, or resentment filled his heart tank, he made sure that none escaped. He always had kind things to say. As a result, he had a great many friends. But he kept stuffing more and more bitterness into his heart tank. One day his heart tank exploded.

Ormulin decided to clean his heart tank each day. Sure, it took time and discipline to connect himself to the heart-purifier but by doing so, he removed the bitterness and hate. He also filled up with love, peace, and kindess.

At first it sounds like a hopeless case—either you lie to cover your resentment, like Kilgonrin, or you reveal your true feelings and become a fool like Ferangin. You can't successfully deal with hatred, envy, and resentment by letting it all hang out, but you can't bottle it all up inside either. Proverbs 10:18 expresses the dilemma: "He who conceals his hatred has lying lips, and whoever spreads slander is a fool."

Don't try to deny feelings of envy, resentment, or dislike for others. Recognize these emotions in order to let God deal with them. Ask God daily to clean out your heart and fill it with His love, joy, and patience.

But now you must rid yourselves of all such things as these: anger, rage, malice, slander, and filthy language from your lips. Do not lie to each other, since you have taken off your old self with its practices. Colossians 3:8–9

Day 91
If The Devil "Made" You Do It, You Blew It!

Jay suddenly started running with the fast-lane crowd. He stopped going to church, his grades went down, and he had frequent fights with his parents. Drinking, drugs, and danger seemed like a lot of fun.

But the party at Devonne's house one evening was not the excitement Jay had expected. Devonne had pulled out two pistols and suggested they do something really crazy—like rob the McDonald's on the corner. He said he'd seen the perfect plot on a TV show, and they organized for action. Though Jay had experienced a twinge of conscience, he agreed to go along with the gang and drive the getaway car. The only problem was that a police cruiser was only half a block away. When it wheeled into the lot, everybody ran. And everybody got away—except Jay.

Hours later, at 4:00 a.m., his parents arrived at the station. His mom was crying and his dad looked pale and nervous. "Son, why did you participate in a holdup?" his father agonized. "How could you do such a thing?"

Jay paused for a moment, then muttered, "The devil made me do it." And he was serious.

But the truth is that Satan can't force anyone to act. The Bible teaches that God has given human beings the ability to choose between right and wrong, and He holds us responsible for our actions.

Choose for yourselves this day whom you will serve. . . . But as for me and my household, we will serve the Lord. Joshua 24:15

We are not puppets or robots. Because God created us with free wills, He will not compel us to obey Him, nor is the devil able to control us. But the devil *is* the world's cleverest con man, and he constantly tries to trick us into thinking that our only choice is to sin. But that is never true. Even in a situation where you'd have to steal food to feed your starving child, the person who believes in a God who answers prayer and performs miracles has an alternative to breaking God's commandments.

"Resist the devil, and he will flee from you" (James 4:7) is still true! So if you say, "The devil made me do it"—*you* blew it.

Day 92

Don't Let the Devil's Masquerade Fool You

Alexis couldn't understand it. She had memorized 2 Corinthians 5:17: "Therefore, if anyone is in Christ, he is a new creation; the old has gone, the new has come!" If the old life was really gone, why did she think so often of going back to her old group of friends? Why did looking through her closet make her wish she could go shoplifting with her girl friend just once more?

Your brain is really a chunk of meat that houses a fantastic computer. It forms thought patterns based on past experiences and on things you've read, heard, and seen. The devil uses these "computer printouts" not only to put thoughts into your mind, but also to impersonate you. He'll speak into your mind, "I really need a hit." Or he'll feed you this line: "I know just what I need to wear to get guys to notice me." Once he convinces you that *you* thought all that, he can go on to the next step—his ultimate weapon. "The Bible must not be true," he whispers. "It says the old has gone, but I can see that real life is different."

Romans 7:20–22 tells us how this all works out in the life of a defeated Christian:

> Now if I do what I do not want to do, it is no longer I who do it, but it is sin living in me that does it. So I find this law at work: When I want to do good, evil is right there with me. For in my inner being I delight in God's law.

The *new* you loves to obey God. That's why you now feel guilty for things that never used to bother you. However, the devil's masquerade is so clever that instead of unmasking him, you just assume that the *real* you wants drugs or stolen clothes or constant attention from the opposite sex.

The truth is that God has made you over again into a transformed person. Accept that as fact and begin acting as the new person you really are. When the devil comes disguised as you, reject each thought he gives you. And remember that you have no guilt—unless you buy the devil's idea and run with it.

Don't let the devil's masquerade fool you. Next time he attacks, just say, "Devil, I'm not listening to your suggestion. Beat it, in the name of Jesus!"

Rafe and Jason were best friends. Jason was a straight-A student, and Rafe got Bs and Cs, but Rafe was a top player on the football team, while Jason warmed the bench. They were such good friends, however, that neither felt jealous.

But when Rafe was voted captain of the football team, he became a local celebrity. His picture was in the paper, he appeared on the *Sports Tonight* show, and he enjoyed instant popularity at school.

One day Jason reminded him of plans they had made to go duck hunting. Rafe blew him off. "Tonight I have a date with Cherry, and tomorrow I have a TV interview. Ducks just aren't on my agenda anymore."

As Jason walked away, Rafe noticed the terribly hurt look on his face. Suddenly he realized that popularity had gone to his head. He knew Cherry wasn't a Christian so he shouldn't even be dating her, plus he felt guilty that he drank to fit in with the "in" crowd.

Jason was the most faithful friend and the best Christian Rafe had ever known! Rafe had always prided himself on not being a fake. How could he have fallen into this trap?

Can you identify with Rafe? Have you ever thought, *That will never happen to me*—only to find yourself doing the very thing you hate? What should be your course of action? First you must recognize that you're not above swallowing the devil's lies.

The heart is deceitful above all things and beyond cure. Who can understand it? Jeremiah 17:9

Next you should realize that temptation is part of life, and you can learn to work it to your advantage. Like fire, temptation can destroy you or serve as your assistant. When you get caught off guard and fall for a temptation you thought you were immune to, decide that you'll learn something from the teacher called temptation. Be thankful that you've discovered the slow leak that could someday cause even greater problems. Confess your sin and ask God to root out the pride, bitterness, unforgiveness, or whatever caused you to fall. Readjust your life and walk on with Jesus just a little wiser from the lesson temptation taught you.

Day 94

Making Points for God's Team

While Eben was grabbing a couple of doughnuts and a cup of instant hot chocolate for breakfast, his brother appeared in the doorway, wearing Eben's new shirt. Eben exploded. "You're such a lazy leech! Don't you dare touch any of my things without asking me!"

An ugly argument ensued, and Eben felt guilty for not having more patience with his younger brother. When he was late for school, the principal's secretary yelled at him for not filling out his tardy pass correctly. Now Eben was in a bad mood. He made a sarcastic remark to his girlfriend, and it hurt her feelings. Then during the pop quiz in geography, his eye caught Lander's paper. Lander always had right answers.

Eben could hear the devil sneer at him. "A fine Christian you are! Your big mouth always gets you in trouble, and you cheat! Why do you even try to do what is right? You'd be a lot happier if you stopped this religious routine and just went along with the tide."

The devil treats all Christians the same way. But getting some facts straight will help you tremendously. First, you need to know that the devil is already defeated. God threw him out of heaven, and Jesus wiped him out completely by dying on the cross and rising again. But he acts like the resentful kid who knows that the dirt bike will never be his, so he tries to wreck it to keep anyone else from ever riding it. Satan tried to be God and failed. So now he uses sin to try to destroy God's children.

Resist him, standing firm in the faith, because you know that your brothers throughout the world are undergoing the same kind of sufferings. 1 Peter 5:9

You are extremely important to God. The devil knows this, so he'll try to sneak spoonfuls of sin into your life. Satan loves sin and the misery it causes, so he tries to torture Christ's followers and spoil God's creation. But you can *hate* sin!

Stand against sin in the power of Jesus. Christians all over the world are fighting along with you, and Jesus is your captain. Every victory you win, by the power of the Holy Spirit, is a point for God's team!

It was Saturday noon, and Talitha sat down with her mom to eat a tuna fish sandwich and a bowl of soup. Talitha's mom flipped on the noon news just in time to hear this report: "A van full of cheerleaders from Westfield High was hit by a train traveling at full speed at Carver's Crossing on Highway 69 at ten-thirty this morning. Eight girls were killed instantly. One is in critical condition."

Talitha's sister, Bonney, was on that bus. Talitha instantly pictured her sister's bloody body and began sobbing. Thoughts flooded in: *I'll never see Bonney again. We'll never share our secrets. God, how could you let such a thing happen?*

After the most horrible ten minutes of her life, it occurred to Talitha to call her father's office. She got his voice mail. Between sobs, Talitha managed to say, "Come home. We think Bonney's dead!"

A half hour later her father called. Hearing his voice, Talitha broke down again. "Talitha!" he soothed. "It's all a mistake. The girls in the accident were from *Washington* High. Bonney's just fine. I was able to get through to her and I talked to her myself."

Talitha was so relieved that she cried again.

As Talitha found out, wrong information can cause real pain. Deception is a powerful weapon, and Satan uses it well. He loves to manipulate our thoughts and emotions. If the devil can convince you that you're hooked on drugs, alcohol, illicit sex, hot fudge sundaes, or spreading juicy gossip, you won't even try to get free. If he can persuade you that God doesn't love you or that everybody despises you or that you're inferior, he's on his way to destroying you.

Misery loves company, so the devil spends twenty-four hours a day wrecking people's lives by trying to make everybody think the Bible's not true, that Jesus won't save, and that it's easier to live for worldly pleasures. But lies evaporate when you know the truth and follow it. Jesus said it all:

Then you will know the truth, and the truth will set you free. John 8:32

Truth, not Houdini, has the patent on the world's greatest disappearing act. When you put the truth about your freedom in Christ to work, Satan has *got* to disappear!

Day 96

When God Says Forget It

Cristi thought once she became a Christian, all her problems would disappear. Her new Christian friends seemed to have it all together, but *she* still got Ds in geometry. She hated cleaning the house as much as ever, and getting up in the morning was no easier than before.

One Saturday, Cristi was halfheartedly vacuuming the living room. "I thought you were one of those saintly born-againers," her mother sneered. "Christians should work hard. You're the laziest thing I've ever seen!"

Cristi lost it with her mom and yelled just what she was thinking. She even used the name of Jesus as a swear word! Her mother responded with a ten-minute lecture that could have been titled "Twenty-Nine Reasons Why Cristi Is Good-for-Nothing." Cristi stormed up to her room.

That she was a hopeless case seemed like a foregone conclusion to Cristi. She'd been through this syndrome before, but now she faced a new phenomenon. Other thoughts invaded her mind: "You've failed as a Christian. Don't ever expect God to forgive you. This sin is just too much for Him. Real Christians are made of stronger stuff."

At that moment, Megan, her Bible study leader, dropped by to say that the study would meet on Thursday this week. But when she saw how discouraged Cristi looked, she gently asked what the problem was.

Breaking into tears, Cristi poured out her heart. Megan listened sympathetically. Finally she said, "I think we've been trying so hard to teach you how to live a victorious Christian life that we've forgotten something very basic. God forgives sin. Your first step is to apologize to your mother. Then confess your sin to God and receive His forgiveness."

While Megan stayed in Cristi's room, Cristi went to make amends with her mother. When she returned, they prayed together and Cristi asked God to forgive her sin. Afterward, she felt new and clean inside.

Opening her Bible, Megan read Isaiah 43:25: "I, even I, am he who blots out your transgressions, for my own sake, and remembers your sins no more."

Cristi smiled. It was nice to hear God say to forget it.

Nervously Lars walked into the youth pastor's office. When Pastor Dale asked him to write down his three biggest problems, number one on his list was "an inferiority complex."

Lars explained that his parents divorced when he was seven. His father had remarried and moved to another state. His mother had a very demanding job and was hardly ever home. They rarely talked or did anything together. He had started to date Julie, but when Darren asked her to the Christmas banquet, Lars was left in the dust. He summed it all up, saying, "I guess I'm not good enough for anybody to really like a lot."

Lars had swallowed one of the devil's biggest lies—that your life is based on what people say rather than on the truth of God's Word.

As the Father has loved me, so have I loved you. Now remain in my love. John 15:9

For God so loved the world that he gave his one and only Son, that whoever believes in him shall not perish but have eternal life. John 3:16

If you want to cash in on everything that God gave you, you *must* be rightly connected to God—the source of your power. If the devil can convince you that you're inferior, you'll be attacked by the temptation to show off, the desire to build yourself up by tearing others down, the craving to take drugs or alcohol—any number of temptations.

Satan knows that if he can get you to believe you're no good (which is ridiculous because Jesus thought you were so valuable that He died for you), all kinds of sins can spring up. But the *Jesus-loves-me-so-I'm-okay* kid won't feel so sorry for himself that he'll eat five bags of potato chips during one TV show. The person who has learned to enjoy God's love doesn't frantically seek attention in socially unacceptable ways.

Build a solid wall against temptation by accepting the fact that God loves you completely and unconditionally. God loves you and that means you are lovable. Period! Stop living in the shack that inferiority built and move into the *God-loves-me-and-thinks-I'm-terrific* penthouse!

Day 98

The Devil's Bestselling Fiction Isn't Fit to Read!

Tyler handed the report card to his mother. He anticipated the reaction that three Cs and three Ds would evoke. And he was not disappointed.

That night, Tyler attended a youth ministry planning meeting. Frankie asked Tyler for the list of members who had paid the fifty-dollar reservation fee for a ski trip. At first Tyler lied and said he had left the list at home. Under further questioning, he confessed that he couldn't remember who had paid him and that he had neglected to keep the money separate from his own—so he didn't really know the exact amount.

Tyler felt like a total failure. Furthermore, he became convinced that God was probably sick and tired of him. He was pretty sure that he had tried God's patience to the limit and that God didn't want him anymore. He decided he really wasn't "Christian material" and that he might as well just give up.

Have you ever felt like that? The devil tries hard to make you (and every other Christian) believe that God doesn't love you anymore. Satan knows that the person who feels that he or she has been abandoned by God will easily fall for any number of temptations. If the devil can make you live by *feelings* instead of by the *fact* of God's Word, he's got you in his trap.

My sheep listen to my voice; I know them, and they follow me. I give them eternal life, and they shall never perish; no one can snatch them out of my hand. John 10:27–28

God doesn't "robotize" His sheep and keep them in cages so they can't escape. Instead, He gives us free wills—and so much security and love that we will want to follow our Good Shepherd. But the devil tries to obscure this *fact* with his *fiction*—that God doesn't love people who make mistakes or act irresponsibly or have bad breath.

Listen to the facts! God offers you total security. He always loves you. He never gives up on you. He will never leave you or forsake you. He is ready to forgive you and create in you a clean heart. The devil's bestselling fiction—that God has just given up on you—isn't fit to read!

Bridget spent a lot of time daydreaming about "Mr. Wonderful." She looked forward to the day she would get married and live happily ever after. Her greatest fear was becoming an "old maid." How she envied the girls who had steady boyfriends. To her, the word *boyfriend* spelled significance, security, success, and the admiration of other girls.

When Allen asked her out, she never even thought to say no. Being the center of his attention was the ego trip she had dreamed of.

Soon they were dating regularly. But Allen was very persuasive. Because her whole self-image was tied up in him, she always gave in. First it was drinking—just a little, to keep him company. Then it was ignoring his bad language. Finally it was having sex.

Even though she felt guilty about dating a non-Christian, Bridget couldn't give him up. In spite of her fear of getting pregnant, she thought that saying no would mean losing Allen. It was easier to stay home from church than to go and feel convicted of her sin.

Are you a Bridget, caught in a similar sin syndrome? Have you bought into a lie from Satan? Do you equate significance with being a great athlete, dating someone who is great looking, getting good grades, or driving a sports car? Do you think security comes from having a steady boyfriend or girlfriend, being popular at school, or singing solos in the choir?

The only way to build a fortress that Satan can't penetrate is to get *all* your security and significance from God. Then you won't fall apart when you receive that "Dear John" letter. If Jesus is *everything* to you, you won't be tempted to compromise your Christian principles for anything or anybody, because nothing will be *that* important to you.

Get off the roller coaster and start traveling on the King's highway!

It is because of him [God] that you are in Christ Jesus, who has become for us wisdom from God—that is, our righteousness, holiness and redemption.
1 Corinthians 1:30

Day 100
Who's a Hypocrite?

When Nathan started dating Kara, the only thing he could see was a vivacious, pretty girl who was considerate and caring. As he got to know her, though, he noticed some negative qualities. Kara was lazy. Whenever she faced a disagreeable task, she simply said, "I can't because I don't have time," or "I'm too tired." If someone irritated her, she made no effort to hide her displeasure.

One day Nathan met Kara forty-five minutes late because of a traffic jam. Kara gave him the silent treatment. This was too much for Nathan. He exploded. "You're one of the biggest hypocrites I've ever seen!"

Kara shouted back, "What do you mean? I don't just pretend I feel loving if I'm ticked off. I might not be perfect, but at least I'm *genuine*."

The dictionary—and the Bible—defines *hypocrite* as a person who pretends to be what he or she is not. The devil's definition of a hypocrite is one who acts differently from what he or she feels. If a married man said, "I don't feel married, so I'll ask my secretary for a date," no one would applaud him for being "honest." He's totally deceived.

As a Christian you're a new creature. Accept what God says is true, not what you feel. If the Bible says, "I can do everything through him who gives me strength" (Philippians 4:13), then you'd better think twice before you say "I can't."

Because Jesus lives inside you, you've got the power to do the things you dislike doing. So saying "I *can't* because I don't *feel* like it" is being a hypocrite. Jesus *can* love through you—to the extent that you are willing to love your enemies. You are a new creature in Christ, with the capacity to love everyone. That's the fact. Living according to your emotions and deciding to hate, punish, or ignore a person who doesn't suit you is hypocritical, because you're just not living like the new you.

My purpose is that they may be encouraged in heart and united in love, so that they may have the full riches of complete understanding, in order that they may know the mystery of God, namely, Christ, in whom are hidden all the treasures of wisdom and knowledge. Colossians 2:2–3

Day 101

Aliyah was so excited she could hardly take it all in. Her family had planned this vacation for so long!

A big metal bird lifted them from the snow and sleet of Chicago and set them down in the balmy paradise of Acapulco. Aliyah's father decided that the first thing on the agenda was a trip to watch the famous cliff divers he had seen on TV. When they stepped out of the taxi, Aliyah could hardly believe that anyone would jump from such a height into water so dotted with craggy rocks. But it was happening right before her eyes! Sensational divers plunged 136 feet off a cliff into the crashing Pacific Ocean.

Concentration was the name of the game. Each action was slow and deliberate. These cliff divers didn't allow their minds to wander or give into their emotions. They acted on fact: there was a way to jump safely and they knew how to do it flawlessly. Inner fears, thoughts of landing on jagged rocks, and wrong information had to be totally discarded.

That night in her hotel room, before going to sleep, Aliyah started reading Romans 6. Verse 11 caught her eye:

In the same way, count yourselves dead to sin but alive to God in Christ Jesus.

It seemed to Aliyah that considering herself "dead to sin" was a lot like those cliff divers who believed they could succeed—even though common sense and normal feelings suggested otherwise. She had never really *felt* "dead to sin." In fact, temptations sometimes seemed overpowering. She was living like a cliff diver who told himself "I can't do it" before each attempted jump. She kept thinking: "I can't resist chocolate sundaes," "I just happen to be a critical person," "I was born moody."

But that didn't change the facts: The Bible said she was dead to sin. Now she realized that if she practiced keeping her mind on God's Word as much as those cliff divers trained their concentration on the ebb and flow of the tide, then God's truth could change her.

That night—for the first time—Aliyah actually believed she could overcome temptation. She really could say, with the apostle Paul, "We died to sin; how can we live in it any longer?" (Romans 6:2).

Day 102

Shopping, Swimming, and Romans 6

Although she usually slept in, Aliyah found herself wide awake at 6:00 a.m. She jumped out of bed and peered through the drapes. Darkness covered the beautiful bay. Since this was a hotel room in Acapulco, she couldn't just head downstairs to get breakfast.

Not wanting to wake her sister, Aliyah took her Bible into the bathroom, and looked up the verse she'd read the night before: "In the same way, count yourselves dead to sin but alive to God in Christ Jesus" (Romans 6:11). She recalled watching the cliff divers who considered themselves dead to feelings of fear and danger, and focused on one simple truth: It was possible to jump safely. She had resolved to believe that victory over sin was possible, because the Bible said she was "dead to sin."

Aliyah memorized Romans 6:11, and she determined to rely on that truth the moment she was tempted by something. Later in the morning, out in the street market, Aliyah found a gorgeous purple dress and just *had* to buy it—even though it meant parting with half of her spending money. Returning to the hotel with her purchase, she met an American who asked her how much she'd paid for the dress. When Aliyah told her, the woman smirked. "You really got ripped off," she gloated. "Mine's exactly the same, and I paid one-third the price."

To top it off, when Aliyah got back to her room, she noticed a big spot on the skirt. Immediately she became crabby. But then she remembered her morning's resolution. Quieting herself, she began to personalize Romans 6:11, paraphrasing it: "In the same way, *Aliyah* will count herself dead to *depression* and *moodiness* but alive to God in Christ Jesus." She repeated it aloud several times and let it sink into her spirit.

Then she realized that it was just like the devil to try to convince her that a spot on a dress and losing some money was the end of the world. But because she took a "Bible break," she conquered her depression.

It was amazing how Romans 6 related to shopping and swimming.

We died to sin; how can we live in it any longer? Romans 6:2

Day 103
Stop Playing Tackle Football With Your Tongue

Cory's mom worked as a warden in a state correctional institution for women—and she was just as strict and unyielding at home as she was on the job. Cory's dad was a construction worker who drank, and they fought a lot. The one thing Cory learned from both of them was that it's a tough world out there, and you've got to learn to defend yourself.

In his sophomore year, Cory met Wes. Wes was different from any friend he'd ever had. Although Wes talked about knowing Jesus, he was no sissy. In fact, he was the best player on the football team. He was self-assured, cool, and he really cared about Cory.

When Cory exploded because the officials declared the ball to be one inch short of a first down, Wes was the first to calm him down. When Cory was sent to the office for mouthing off to his English teacher, Wes took time to listen to his side and talk things through. Wes asked him home for dinner, and everyone made him feel like part of the family. Eventually Wes helped Cory put his faith in Jesus.

Although his character changed in many ways, Cory still battled with his seemingly uncontrollable tongue. At times, Cory felt bad about his "Irish temper," but mostly he blamed others for not understanding him.

May the Lord cut off all flattering lips and every boastful tongue that says, "We will triumph with our tongues; we own our lips—who is our master?" Psalm 12:3-4

At home Cory had learned the motto, "Knock the other guy down before you get knocked down yourself." That's fine in football, but in real life a lot of innocent people get hurt. Now that you know Jesus, you have to fall in step with His principles for right living. The truth is this: It is not up to you to defend yourself. The myth that you must be your own lawyer can lead you into all kinds of sins—criticism, anger, exaggeration, and false accusations, just to name a few. Learn to say with David:

You are my refuge and my shield; I have put my hope in your Word. Psalm 119:114

So stop playing tackle football with your tongue, and rest in the fact that God loves you and cares about you. *He* will protect you.

Day 104

Smart-Alecks Don't Pray, "Lead Us Not Into Temptation"

Colin and Brad decided to go to a party with their old crowd so that they could be a Christian presence in an otherwise corrupt group. But when Brad called to say that his parents were making him do something else, Colin didn't give it a second thought. He pictured himself as the brave and fearless ambassador for Christ, who was immune to all the temptations of his former lifestyle. He went to the party.

Inside, the smell of marijuana awakened in him an old craving. Then Jeannie—the girl he'd always wanted to date—rushed up to him. "It's time you came back to your senses! That Jesus-freak stuff is for sissies. Come with me. I've got some really good coke."

All of a sudden Colin felt completely alone—abandoned by God and open to every temptation. The thought of sharing Jesus never occurred to him. In fact, the desire to get high was more than he could resist—especially since it also included special attention from Jeannie.

When he arrived home at 2:00 a.m., he felt tremendously guilty. Slumping down on the bed, he tried to pray. The words that came out were the Lord's Prayer. When he came to, "and lead us not into temptation, but deliver us from evil," he stopped short.

Suddenly a revelation occurred to him: By relying on his own strength, he had walked right into Satan's trap and got caught. He should have *expected* this outcome, because no human is a match for the devil. He recognized that if he sincerely prayed "lead us not into temptation," it gave God permission to eradicate his pride and change his attitude.

Colin admitted that he was weak and unable to resist temptation. He had to resolve that every time the devil knocked, he would tell Jesus, "*You* go to the door." When Jesus faces Satan's temptation, He is victorious.

Jesus in you can resist sin—but don't undermine yourself by placing yourself in tempting circumstances. If you have a cocky confidence in your own righteousness, then the prayer of your life is, "Lead me *into* temptation. Show me the way!"

Can you honestly pray, "Lead me not into temptation"?

And lead us not into temptation, but deliver us from the evil one. Matthew 6:13

When Jolene gave her heart to Jesus, her life changed radically. She stopped hanging around with her old friends, gave up drugs, and broke up with Grayson. Making new friends wasn't easy, but she did it.

One Saturday night, it seemed as if Satan came to pay her a visit in person. Everyone else in her family had gone out for the night, and her Christian friends had let her down. Then came a knock at the door.

It was Grayson. Smiling and good-natured as always, he began, "I miss you so much, I just can't stay away." To Jolene he looked more attractive than ever, and he was the one person who'd thought of her on a lonely Saturday night. When he suggested they go out for a bite to eat, she couldn't refuse.

As they talked quietly that evening, she soaked in all of Grayson's compliments. The desire to have Grayson take her in his arms became overwhelming. It was like God's ideas about right and wrong ceased to exist.

Getting into the car again, Grayson drove to the bluff that overlooked the Mississippi. There, she enjoyed his physical closeness—and then she surrendered herself to him as she had done so many times before. Of course when she got home, she felt terrible. Forgetting all she had learned about His forgiveness, she was sure that God didn't love her anymore.

The Bible says "Flee from sexual immorality" (1 Corinthians 6:18), and "Flee the evil desires of youth" (2 Timothy 2:22). God's Word never says to face evil like a strong Christian. In fact, our problem with temptation is that we rely on something within ourselves—which just isn't there.

Keep out of the danger zone. Don't stop at your favorite ice-cream parlor, thinking you'll only order a diet soda. Stay miles away from a situation that will bring sexual temptation. Leave the house to avoid throwing a fit that will manipulate your mother into giving you your way.

God can seem far away when your mouth craves that chocolate sundae, your body longs for sexual experience, or your emotions insist on staging a tantrum. At that moment, look for the nearest exit and start running! You'd do well to become a Christian track star.

Therefore do not let sin reign in your mortal body so that you obey its evil desires. Romans 6:12

Day 106

The Decline and Fall of Practically Everybody

Gavin was into being "Mr. Success." When he pitched a good game, he'd loved hearing his dad say, "That's my boy!" If he got straight A's, his mother would comment, "You're my dream for a son come true." To Gavin, acceptance only came from achievement. He knew how to play the game and he played it well.

But during his senior year, a broken leg on a ski trip wiped out his baseball season *and* his dream of leading the team to the state championship. His father's cancer surgery worried him so much that he couldn't concentrate, and his grades started to slip. His girlfriend, Nicole, started dating someone else. Now that Gavin couldn't perform the way he used to, he felt rejected by everyone.

Gavin had done all the right things, but he'd done them in his own strength. Now he had to depend on Jesus to keep some flaky freshman from knocking his crutches out from under him and sending him sailing down the steps. He had to trust Jesus to take care of his father so he could concentrate on chapter 18 in physics. And he had to literally think about Jesus just to keep from falling apart when he passed Nicole and Jeff in the hall on the way to English class.

And whatever you do, whether in word or deed, do it all in the name of the Lord Jesus, giving thanks to God the Father through him. Colossians 3:17

God's criteria is that we act in the name of Jesus through the power of the Holy Spirit for the glory of God. In other words, the Lord grades on motives, not performance.

One of the devil's most subtle temptations is getting you to do the right things with the wrong motive. If you don't want to be part of this "decline and fall of practically everybody" scenario, ask God to show you where you are depending only on your own strength. Consciously ask Jesus to live through you as you do homework and eat pizza and watch television. Those who listen to God's still, small voice don't have to be hit over the head with a ton of bricks.

Ashley's parents were really strict. One of their rules was that she couldn't date until she was sixteen. Chad had recently moved to Indianapolis, and he sat next to her in the trumpet section. He was friendly, studious, and athletic—plus he was a senior and he drove a sports car!

When Chad invited her out for dinner, she said she'd love to go. A little voice in her head said to tell Chad the truth, but she ignored it.

She planned her strategy: She would stay overnight with Kim, so her parents wouldn't find out about the date. Then she realized that Kim's folks might guess what she was up to, so she'd really have to ask Chad to pick her up at *Kathy's* house. Something whispered, *You're not going to get out of this without telling a few lies.* But she reasoned that if her parents weren't so old-fashioned, she wouldn't be forced to go to such extremes.

There were a lot of details to be arranged, but Ashley figured it all out. Chad knocked at the door of Kathy's house, and they were off to Jim's Steak House, where the two-for-one T-bone offer had people lined up out to the sidewalk. After an hour of pleasant conversation and joking, they were seated at a nice candlelit table—right next to Ashley's parents!

Maybe you don't like stories with your-sins-will-find-you-out endings. But these words are from the Bible, and in real life the narrative *always* ends like that. If you want to avoid producing your own autobiography with similar episodes, you must learn the truth of 1 Corinthians 10:13:

> *No temptation has seized you except what is common to man. And God is faithful; he will not let you be tempted beyond what you can bear. But when you are tempted, he will also provide a way out so that you can stand up under it.*

The easiest time to say no to temptation is *before* you've had time to rationalize your way into wrongdoing. Temptation is like a vacuum-cleaner salesman—the sooner you say no, the better. It's a lot easier to meet temptation at the door and say no than to kick it out once it's gotten inside.

Day 108

Levi listened solemnly as his father passed sentence: "Give me the car keys and I'll keep them for a whole month. That will teach you never to lie to me about where you are going."

Levi saw flashing red lights against the orange and yellow swirls on the wallpaper. The swirls turned into words: *Honor your father and your mother*. But Levi decided that those orders were for little kids—and so he spouted off to his dad.

"I'm old enough to look out for myself. I'm the only guy I know who has to face the Family Bureau of Investigation every time I leave the house. I may just run away from home!"

In an instant, he was transferred to the locker room at school. He remembered a dirty joke that was really very funny. This time he saw the neon lights silhouetted against the row of gray lockers. "Nor should there be obscenity, foolish talk or coarse joking" (Ephesians 5:4). But he really didn't want the guys to think he was from Nerdsville, so he told the joke and enjoyed being the center of attention for two whole minutes.

Suddenly he was in a social studies class. "How many of you really believe that God wrote the Bible?" sneered the teacher. Now the neon lights lit up the blackboard with these words: "If we disown him, he will also disown us" (2 Timothy 2:12). But no one else raised a hand, so Levi kept silent.

At that moment, Levi woke up. It was just a nightmare. He puzzled over his strange dream and half-expected to see neon lights in the bathroom mirror.

Falling into sin is a result of deciding to do your own thing instead of obeying the principles found in the Bible. Neon lights might be nice, but having God's Word hidden in your heart will work even better. You really don't need neon lights, fireworks, or voices of angels to stop you from sinning. God's Word alone will do the job—if you decide to obey it.

Blessed are they who keep his statutes and seek him with all their heart. They do nothing wrong; they walk in his ways. Psalm 119:2–3

Day 109

Do You Hide Explosives in the Closet of Your Heart?

Casey had to admit that his sixth-hour social studies class had been interesting. After a heated formal debate about gay rights, the teacher launched into a passionate lecture.

"Some people," he declared, "are *born* homosexuals. Because they're a minority, they've been denied the right to express themselves fully. Americans accept people with black skin, with slanted eyes, and with disabilities, but they still discriminate against homosexuals! It is no sin to be what you *are*. A person cannot change something he was born with."

As Casey listened, an inner horror had gripped him. He feared that he himself was one of those unfortunate guys who had been "born gay." Because he was an extremely talented artist and didn't care for sports, he had always been rejected by the jocks. Deep down inside he felt more attracted to some guys than he did to girls. A voice seemed to be telling him, *Casey, you might as well stop being a Christian. You're already condemned. You'll never be fulfilled unless you follow a gay lifestyle.*

For months his mind was in turmoil. He thought his head was going to burst open. Finally he confided in a Christian friend who promised his prayers and told him to concentrate on the truth in God's Word in order to break free. Even though he still had tempting thoughts, now he knew that another believer was praying for him.

The devil tells this lie to a lot of guys. Although a homosexual *act* is sin, the *temptation* is not. People are tempted to do all kinds of other unnatural things, like destroy their bodies with drugs, abuse children, engage in daredevil exploits in order to show off, or commit suicide. I might be tempted to jump from the Empire State Building, but I don't have to do it—and I don't have to consider myself *suicidal* just because the devil placed that thought in my head. You don't have to call yourself homosexual because of the temptation either!

Ask God to give you someone godly whom you can confide in. It's better not to hide any explosives in the closet of your heart.

A wise man listens to advice. Proverbs 12:15

(If you have a problem similar to Casey's, check out *www.exodus-international.org* or *www.desertstream.org.*)

Day 110

The Temptation That Didn't Make It to First Base

Isabella hurriedly wiped off the tables in the restaurant where she worked. She said good-night to Hank, the owner, then ran to her car and zipped over to the bank to deposit $150 into her savings account.

It was two minutes to nine. She had made it just before closing time.

The transaction completed, she was about to drive off when she noticed something shiny on the ground. She got out of the car and picked up a small sequined purse. Opening it, she gasped with surprise as she counted the roll of bills. In her hand was thirty-five-hundred dollars!

Isabella's first thought was to bring the purse back to the bank the next day. The devil came up with a lot of other ideas—but to Isabella, anything other than strict honesty was unthinkable. When she brought the money into the bank at 9:30 a.m., an older woman was there to greet her. She thrust a crisp hundred-dollar bill into her hands and exclaimed, "It's so nice to know that there are still honest people left in the world!"

The reason that Isabella's temptation didn't even make it to first base was that she really had no desire for money that wasn't rightfully hers.

Jesus never once fell for *any* temptation, because His *only* desire was to obey God in every area of life. Jesus had no discontentment in His life. He harbored no bitterness. He had no inclination to trade righteousness for attention or apparent security, so Satan just couldn't get in anywhere.

James 1:14 explains the way the devil operates:

Each one is tempted when, by his own evil desire, he is dragged away and enticed.

When opportunities arise to steal or shoplift, you must decide if having things is more important than honesty. If you resent your brilliant older brother, temptations to make fun of him or to get back at him will find fertile ground. If you want to get married more than you want to follow Jesus, you lay yourself wide open to falling into a lot of traps.

Check over your desires and line them up with God's Word—regardless of your screaming emotions and mental excuses. When wayward wishes are brought under control, passing a temptation test is easy.

Reina pulled the covers up over her head. Because she'd had to work overtime *and* study for three exams, it had been a long week. She was totally exhausted, and even if it was Friday night, all she wanted was to go to bed and stay there until about noon on Saturday. But at 7:00 a.m. on Saturday morning, Reina heard her mother calling from the bottom of the stairway, "Reina, it's time to get up! Remember, you promised you'd help me clean the kitchen."

Reina's body and emotions rebelled. She groaned and sighed. After such a tough week, she deserved a rest. Couldn't her mother show any consideration? The kitchen would still be dirty at noon, after all. It just wasn't fair. Besides, when her mother cleaned the kitchen, it took all day. When she said clean, she really meant clean.

Reina was badly tempted to scream, "No, I won't! Let me sleep. You're not being reasonable. I promised to clean the kitchen, just not necessarily today." But she remembered her pastor's words: "If the devil can entice you to live according to your feelings instead of by the part of God's Word that applies to your situation, he'll win and you'll lose."

Reina knew what part of God's Word applied to her situation at that moment. She had just memorized Ephesians 6:1:

Children, obey your parents in the Lord, for this is right.

She knew she couldn't pamper her tired body instead of obeying Jesus.

When her mother's second call came—complete with turned-up volume and angry words—Reina answered like a champion who had just won, even though the competition was fierce: "I'm getting dressed, Mom, and I'll be right down."

Sensing Jesus' presence, Reina put her heart into washing walls, scrubbing cupboards, and scouring the stove. It took all day. When they finished, she was as proud of the kitchen as her mother was.

The law of his God is in his heart; his feet do not slip. Psalm 37:31

Day 112

The Failure That Made Victory Possible

Gary felt even smaller and skinnier than he looked in the mirror—more insignificant and rejected too.

Because his father was being transferred to Texas, this was Gary's last day at Eastwood High. Nobody had organized a good-bye party for him. He stuffed the few things he kept in his locker into a sports bag.

For some reason, Gary decided to take a final tour of the building after school. Worried thoughts kept tormenting him: *If I haven't made any close friends here in all this time, what's it gonna be like in Texas?* Then he saw a letter jacket on the bleachers. He noticed that it was his size and that all the medals were in track and skiing.

Suddenly an ingenious idea occurred to him. No one would notice if he stuffed the jacket into his bag. If he took off all the track pins, he could wear the jacket to his new school, posing as a Minnesota ski hero!

When Gary registered at Washington High School, he sported a letter jacket with ski medals. On his first day, he attracted quite a bit of attention. But Pam, who sat next to him in English class, attended his church, and his lies followed him there. One day Pam's comments to Gary's mother blew his cover. He was totally embarrassed and ashamed. Could he ever recover from this failure?

But who are you, O man, to talk back to God? "Shall what is formed say to him who formed it, 'Why did you make me like this?'" Romans 9:20

All of us fail. But there is a way to turn failure into victory. Start by repenting of your resentment against God for not making you some other way. Admit that what you did is wrong. Tell God, "I'm guilty of trying to be somebody I'm not. I hate these terrible sins against you and I'm going to change." Then accept God's forgiveness and forgive yourself.

Receive God's love, be thankful for everything, and find your acceptance from God rather than from those around you. You will find that as you relax and accept yourself just the way God made you, a whole lot of things begin to change.

Frantically, Rachel attempted to do something with droopy hair that defied extra-body shampoo and had responded very poorly to a perm. Besides her complex about having "mouse hair," she thought she was too tall, too thin, and that her feet were much too large.

Surveying her clothes failed to cheer her up. She couldn't find anything sharp to wear to the outreach picnic her youth group had planned. This was the day they were going to put into practice what they had learned about personal evangelism, and she thought looking good might help overcome her nervousness. Everyone labeled her a brain, and she battled a shyness that made her feel socially awkward. She wished she could be pretty, vivacious, and "Miss Personality Plus." Then others would certainly be willing to listen when she shared Jesus with them.

But we have this treasure in jars of clay to show that this all-surpassing power is from God and not from us. 2 Corinthians 4:7

We're the jars of clay and Jesus is the treasure. The glory belongs to Jesus, not to us. Just remember that you're exactly the right container to display the wonderful treasure Jesus really is.

Although it's right to "look your best for Jesus" and be conscious of making a good impression on non-Christians, it's wrong to forget that you're a clay jar. If you try to be "Superman Christian" or "Wonder Woman Witness," you'll fall into temptation. Either you'll become discouraged because you didn't live up to *your* goal, or you'll begin faking it—pretending to be someone you're not.

Remember that the containers God chose to demonstrate His power had weaknesses. Gideon had an inferiority complex. Moses most likely stuttered. Jeremiah was sometimes depressed. Peter made rash decisions. Thomas doubted. The list goes on. God's plan hasn't changed. He still puts the priceless treasure of himself into people who talk too much, who have trouble with math, and who bite their fingernails. Accept the fact that you too are human; you're just a clay jar with an incredible treasure inside—Jesus should be the only thing that people notice about you.

Day 114

Are You Suffocating in Your Isolation Booth?

Torin wished he were back in California. Adjusting to living in a small Midwestern town was more than he bargained for. The kids at school treated him like some kind of transplant from Mars, and they thought he dressed a little weird. If he didn't bowl or play mini golf, there was *nothing* to do. But the hardest part was that the church here was nothing like the one he'd left behind. Only five kids showed up at the youth Bible study, and it was obvious that they knew nothing about the deeper Christian life. Torin decided that he'd get more out of doing his own Bible studies at home.

Soon he discovered a great TV show on Saturday nights and found out that sleeping in on Sunday morning felt good. His plan for attacking the book of Ezekiel got as far as chapter three. But when Torin was in a horrible car accident and had to be hospitalized, he found that the kids from the church he'd written off knew a lot more about caring and helping than he did. He needed them and they needed him.

Be aware that it's Satan's strategy to isolate Christians. If he can get you to think you're too good for the Christians around you, he can use your pride to try to make you think you've got a deeper knowledge of the Bible than anyone else. It's easier for the devil to deceive a loner than a whole group of Christians. You can end up suffocating in your isolation booth. God means for believers to be part of one body, to support and encourage and teach each other as they worship together.

> *Let us not give up meeting together, as some are in the habit of doing, but let us encourage one another—and all the more as you see the Day approaching.* Hebrews 10:25

Each Christian group and each church has strengths and weaknesses. Maybe you think your youth group is not as good at studying the Bible as you are, but they have a generous spirit that reaches out to people in need. Maybe you think your prayer life is deeper than any of your friends', but some of them are bolder in talking to friends about Jesus. You might be able to teach or set an example in some areas, but be ready to learn from the strengths of others.

God is always associated with light. The devil is associated with darkness. Boogeymen, monsters, headless horsemen, and goblins flourish at night but never seem to make appearances in daylight. That's because in darkness nonexistent things can appear to be real. The fear that plagued you at midnight will usually vanish as sunlight streams through your window the next morning. Most crimes are committed by night because people would be afraid or ashamed to do such things in broad daylight.

The devil wants to blind you to the truth and make you live in darkness. Keep in mind that the devil has been defeated by Jesus on the cross and his doom is certain. The devil has already lost the war but wants to win some battles. He works as an undercover agent. His greatest weapons are deception and surprise. A historic event illustrates this point.

During the Revolutionary War, the British recruits at Trenton, who had celebrated Christmas by drinking heavily, were totally surprised when Washington's ragtag army crossed the icy waters of the Delaware River in 1776 and took them all prisoner. By the deception of keeping all the campfires burning, Washington's forces snuck off by night to catch their reinforcements off guard at nearby Princeton and trounce them.

Of course, Washington had to retreat afterward because he didn't have enough soldiers to sustain combat, but the combination of British carelessness plus Washington's deception and surprise rendered the biggest and best army helpless for a while. Like the well-fed and well-trained British army that outnumbered the colonists, you—even though God has provided you with all you need to be victorious—can lose some battles.

Because the devil also uses deception and surprise attacks, you must constantly stay alert and be able to answer Satan's lies with God's truth. The enemy wants you to believe that the Bible isn't trustworthy, that God will never forgive you again, that your problem is too big for God, or that you can't hold out because non-Christians outnumber Christians. You need to avoid the sin and laziness that can trap you while constantly depending on God to rescue you from seemingly impossible situations. This begins by unmasking the devil and his undercover agents.

Undercover Agent

This is the verdict: Light has come into the world, but men loved darkness instead of light because their deeds were evil. Everyone who does evil hates the light, and will not come into the light for fear that his deeds will be exposed. But whoever lives by the truth comes into the light, so that it may be seen plainly that what he has done has been done through God. John 3:19–21

You probably agree that "overcoming evil with good" is logical and scriptural. However, you may still wonder how you can live a holy life without entering a monastery or camping on an uninhabited South Pacific island where there are no drug pushers, porn magazines, or temptations to quarrel with your sister. Well, there is a way. You can cooperate with God so that He can give you His holiness.

The holiness God wants to give you is like a foundation for your Christian life. The foundation of a traditional house is not made from wood but from cement. However, the enduring, strong cement must be poured into wooden forms. Now, you can't make yourself holy, but you can provide the forms for God's holiness. Your turning away from sin and your determination to follow Jesus regardless of the cost are the forms into which God will pour His holiness.

The molds for God's holiness are practical things. Suppose your sister borrows your new sweater without asking and spills spaghetti sauce on it. Your determination to love and forgive her is a form for God's holiness.

God will show you what He is like and how to be like Him as you spend time in prayer and Bible study each day. As you supply more molds—turning down the invitation to attend a wild party, fouling out of an important game graciously, praising God in spite of that D on the physics test, and obeying your father even if your friends laugh at you—God's holiness will fill your molds.

Since we have these promises, dear friends, let us purify ourselves from everything that contaminates body and spirit, perfecting holiness out of reverence for God. 2 Corinthians 7:1

Those who belong to Christ Jesus have crucified the sinful nature with its passions and desires. Since we live by the Spirit, let us keep in step with the Spirit. Let us not become conceited, provoking and envying each other. Galatians 5:24–26

Day 117

Your Personal Body, Soul, and Spirit Guard

Jesus wants to be your personal body, soul, and spirit guard, but you must stay close enough to Him so He can guard you. The Psalm writer says:

"Because he loves me," says the Lord, "I will rescue him; I will protect him, for he acknowledges my name." Psalm 91:14

The devil is always trying to get you out from under God's protection. He distorts Scripture so you won't wholeheartedly obey Jesus. Like Eve, we all find it easy to listen to such distortions and reason ourselves into a lot of trouble. For instance, the Bible commands us to love everybody, even our enemies. Satan will help you rationalize that it's all right to dislike the girl who stole your boyfriend, the guy who constantly puts you down, and people who boss you around for no reason.

However, "love is not resentful" is God's truth. If you don't root resentment out of your life, the devil will see that weak spot and send in his "special agent demons" named Hate, Get Even, and Self-Pity. Unless you reject these, you'll soon be saying and doing things you didn't think you were capable of.

The devil's version of Ephesians 4:29 is "Let no evil talk come out of your mouths—sometimes." Statements such as "This isn't very nice, but it's the truth," "I shouldn't say this, but I know you won't tell anybody," and "I probably shouldn't repeat it, but," all come from the book called *Christian Living Made Easy* by Lucifer and Company. The devil's lie that your situation is an exception to God's Word opens the floodgates of criticism, false rumors, and gossip.

Let those who love the Lord hate evil for he guards the lives of his faithful ones and delivers them from the hand of the wicked. Psalm 97:10

The Lord watches over all who love him, but all the wicked he will destroy. Psalm 145:20

Stay close to Jesus. Obey His every word, love Him better than anyone else, and give Him complete control of your life. Jesus wants to guard you and keep you from evil. He will if you're not out doing your own thing.

A little boy who lived near a lake was instructed by his father never to go swimming without supervision. But one day his father caught him swimming. Soon the innocent-sounding little guy was saying, "But Daddy, I didn't mean to go swimming. It just happened."

"Then why," questioned his father, "did you take your swimsuit with you when you came to play near the lake?"

The little boy answered, "I took it along just in case I got tempted."

Are you like that little boy? Do you devise plans that make it harder for you to obey Jesus' commands, even though you say you love Him? Instead of providing yourself with the possibility for sinning, give yourself every opportunity to do right. If the little boy had left his swimsuit at home, the day would have ended differently.

Take Jesus with you through the day and think, *How would He plan in these circumstances?* Jesus wouldn't even think about lying his way out of an uncomfortable situation. Realizing this, honestly face the problem at hand. You know that Jesus would have you plan a date carefully to avoid situations in which temptation could become strong.

If you give yourself to Jesus, He'll show you how to organize your life so that obeying God's commandments will be easier.

Rather, clothe yourselves with the Lord Jesus Christ, and do not think about how to gratify the desires of the sinful nature. Romans 13:14

And after a while his master's wife took notice of Joseph and said, "Come to bed with me!" But he refused. "With me in charge," he told her, "my master does not concern himself with anything in the house; everything he owns he has entrusted to my care. No one is greater in this house than I am. My master has withheld nothing from me except you, because you are his wife. How then could I do such a wicked thing and sin against God?" And though she spoke to Joseph day after day, he refused to go to bed with her or even be with her. One day he went into the house to attend to his duties, and none of the household servants was inside. She caught him by his cloak and said, "Come to bed with me!" But he left his cloak in her hand and ran out of the house. Genesis 39:7–12

Day 119

When It's Legal to Hate

Do you *hate* sin? God does. You might hear someone say, "Why does God let little children starve and suffer?" But it's not God; the real culprit is sin. It was greed that started the war, alcoholism that misspent the money, and uncontrolled anger that caused the beating. A heresy of our day teaches that finally even the devil will go to heaven! The devil is the author of sin, and he delights in seeing starving children, broken homes, and misunderstood teenagers. You should hate the devil and hate sin.

Sin hurts God and makes people unhappy. If you are to talk to God at all, the first thing you must bring to Him is your sin. You had to confess your sin and bring it to Jesus in order to become a Christian. As a child of God, confession of sin is one of your greatest privileges. God's holiness actually eradicates sin. His holiness is like fire that consumes evil, or like a spot remover that erases every stain.

Our first tendency is to cover sin or try to lessen its impact. Have you noticed that the kid who cheated on the test goes out of his way to be nice to the teacher? If you stay out past the time you promised you'd be in, isn't it easier to clean up the kitchen for your mother than tell her the truth? But sin is so terrible that you can't cover it, patch it up, or rework it. It's like rotting garbage. The only thing to do with it is throw it away. You can never get rid of your sin unless you are completely honest with God and with the people you have wronged.

He who conceals his sins does not prosper, but whoever confesses and renounces them finds mercy. Proverbs 28:13

When I kept silent, my bones wasted away through my groaning all day long. For day and night your hand was heavy upon me; my strength was sapped as in the heat of summer. Then I acknowledged my sin to you and did not cover up my iniquity. I said, "I will confess my transgressions to the Lord"—and you forgave the guilt of my sin. Psalm 32:3–5

Day 120

Does This Shake You Up a Little?

Do you know what God thinks about little white lies? Little white lies are dangerous sins that can break your communication with God and damage your relations with other people. The Bible tells the story of Ananias and Sapphira, a nice Jerusalem couple, who sold their land and gave the money to the church. Now *that's* a very generous thing to do. There was just one problem—they pretended to give all of the money, when they really gave only part of it. When Ananias told this little white lie, Peter answered, "You have not lied to men but to God" (Acts 5:4). When Ananias heard these words, he dropped dead.

Maybe you'd better look at your own life. Do you lie to give false impressions? Do you exaggerate to make people listen to your stories? Do you hint that you are a better athlete than you really are? Would your comments lead others to think that you had more dates than a palm tree? Confess these lies to God. Remember that He loves you exactly the way you are, and it isn't necessary to give a false impression to Him or anyone else. Also ask Him to help you overcome any bragging habits you have established. Never justify your little white lies. Confess them as sin and determine to tell the truth.

> But if you fail to do this, you will be sinning against the Lord; and you may be sure that your sin will find you out. Numbers 32:23

> About three hours later his wife came in, not knowing what had happened. Peter asked her, "Tell me, is this the price you and Ananias got for the land?" "Yes," she said, "that is the price." Peter said to her, "How could you agree to test the Spirit of the Lord? Look! The feet of the men who buried your husband are at the door, and they will carry you out also." At that moment she fell down at his feet and died. Then the young men came in and, finding her dead, carried her out and buried her beside her husband. Great fear seized the whole church and all who heard about these events. Acts 5:7–11

Day 121

Even If They Stone You

The Scarlet Letter, not a popular book nowadays, is an early American novel set in Puritan Massachusetts. In the story, a young minister fathers a child out of wedlock. No one suspects he is the father, and the mother will not disclose his identity. The young minister says from the pulpit that he is the worst of sinners; he constantly condemns himself. At the same time, he refuses to do the one necessary thing—make a direct confession of his specific sin before God and the people, with the intention of facing the consequences. Because he refuses to do this, he is most miserable. Finally, his approaching death makes him confess publicly, but he had no time to enjoy his clear conscience.

It's better to tell God that you have nothing to confess than to confess just for the sake of confessing. Ask the Holy Spirit to point out specific sin in your life. Confess that sin to God—and to another person if you have wronged him or her.

Whenever you feel guilty, ask the Holy Spirit to show you if you've done something specifically wrong. Ask with an attitude of willingness to face God honestly. If God doesn't show you anything, then dismiss the guilty feeling. That "yucky" worthless feeling, which is vague and uncertain, comes from the devil. Ignore it and forget it. However, the conviction of specific sin is from the Holy Spirit, and you have to deal with it immediately.

Against you, you only, have I sinned and done what is evil in your sight, so that you are proved right when you speak and justified when you judge. Psalm 51:4

Achan replied, "It is true! I have sinned against the Lord, the God of Israel. This is what I have done: When I saw in the plunder a beautiful robe from Babylonia, two hundred shekels of silver and a wedge of gold weighing fifty shekels, I coveted them and took them. They are hidden in the ground inside my tent, with the silver underneath." . . . Joshua said, "Why have you brought this trouble on us? The Lord will bring trouble on you today." Then all Israel stoned him. Joshua 7:20–21, 25

Are you able to talk yourself into and out of almost anything? Can you think of a hundred good reasons for not doing your history homework? Are you able to defend yourself for ten minutes straight when your mother mentions that a bulldozer may be needed to get your room cleaned out? Can you rationalize that running with a rowdy group of friends won't hurt you?

If you decide to prove that everything you do is okay, you will hurt yourself immeasurably. People who are really good at rationalizing won't take advice—but it's amazing what you can learn from other people *if you listen.*

Jesus demanded no ifs, ands, or buts from His disciples. If you keep making excuses, you won't obey your parents, your teachers, or God. Probably the worst thing about an excuse-maker is that he or she can't really ask God for forgiveness. If you can't admit that you're dead wrong and you need forgiveness, God won't forgive you. Your confession can't be, "God, if you had to live with my sister, you'd blow your stack too—and besides, she started it. By the way, I'd like forgiveness for getting angry." God wants you to deal directly and honestly with your sin. No excuses are allowed.

For in his own eyes he flatters himself too much to detect or hate his sin.
Psalm 36:2

A certain man was preparing a great banquet and invited many guests. At the time of the banquet he sent his servant to tell those who had been invited, "Come, for everything is now ready." But they all alike began to make excuses. The first said, "I have just bought a field, and I must go and see it. Please excuse me." Another said, "I have just bought five yoke of oxen, and I'm on my way to try them out. Please excuse me." Still another said, "I just got married, so I can't come." Luke 14:16–20

Day 123

Eve Made Me Do It

Nora walked into the principal's office just in time to hear a good-looking guy's "But he started it!" cut off by the principal's booming voice: "I don't care what the other guy did. I want to know what *you* did." Just as the student had to face the principal because of *his own* actions, each of us must face God, knowing that we are responsible for our own deeds; we can't blame anybody else.

My father tells about the first lie he ever heard my sister tell. "Chickie did it. Don't spank me." She was barely two. No one has to teach us to cover up for our mistakes and sins. That comes naturally. If we don't stop blaming other people, we will never build an honest and healthy relationship with God. It doesn't matter if it is 95 percent the fault of the other person. God expects us to confess our part to Him and apologize to the other person—and not in such a way as to force an apology in return.

We are not responsible for making other people confess their sins. We are only responsible for ourselves. One of the devil's best tricks to keep us from having pure hearts is getting us to concentrate on the faults and sins of others. If God had a loudspeaker in the sky to give us constant audible advice, I think we'd often hear, "MIND YOUR OWN BUSINESS." Confess your sin without blaming anyone but yourself.

When Peter saw him, he asked, "Lord, what about him?" Jesus answered, "If I want him to remain alive until I return, what is that to you? You must follow me." John 21:21–22

Who are you to judge someone else's servant? To his own master he stands or falls. And he will stand, for the Lord is able to make him stand. Romans 14:4

The soul who sins is the one who will die. The son will not share the guilt of the father, nor will the father share the guilt of the son. The righteousness of the righteous man will be credited to him, and the wickedness of the wicked will be charged against him. Ezekiel 18:20

Day 124

Do You Enjoy Being Kidnapped?

The newspapers carried the story of a wealthy Italian girl who was kidnapped. Her parents came up with the ransom money, only to find that she liked living with her kidnapper! She refused to be freed.

Do you enjoy your sin? Do you find self-pity comforting? Do you appreciate the way your temper helps you get your own way? Do you find that dwelling on unclean thoughts is an enjoyable pastime? If you answered yes, you'd have to admit that confession of these sins wouldn't be completely sincere. Real confession implies willingness to stop sinning—willingness to hate the sin you're confessing. You still might fall sometimes. However, there is a great difference between trying to go through every red light without getting caught and determining never to go through a red light again, even if you unconsciously do it.

Treat even the thought of sin like a traffic light that has turned red—stop before you get into it. If you have decided always to stop at red lights, your conscious decision soon becomes subconscious, and obeying traffic lights becomes easier and easier. Set your mind completely against sin. Be willing to take any action necessary to follow God. Don't just confess sin. Determine to stop doing it.

Put on the new self, created to be like God in true righteousness and holiness.
Ephesians 4:24

When you spread out your hands in prayer, I will hide my eyes from you; even if you offer many prayers, I will not listen. Your hands are full of blood; wash and make yourselves clean. Take your evil deeds out of my sight! Stop doing wrong, learn to do right! Seek justice, encourage the oppressed. Defend the cause of the fatherless, plead the case of the widow. "Come now, let us reason together," says the Lord. "Though your sins are like scarlet, they shall be as white as snow; though they are red as crimson, they shall be like wool."
Isaiah 1:15–18

Day 125

Repent? You've Got to Be Kidding!

I'll never forget it. At a senior high Bible camp, as we silently sat around the campfire, God's power became very real, and His Holy Spirit began convicting people of sin. A seventeen-year-old boy who had been a troublemaker started sobbing and saying, "I'm a terrible sinner, I'm a terrible sinner." That night kids not only confessed sin, they also genuinely repented.

Repentance means turning around and going in the opposite direction. Those kids were serious about giving their lives to God. Campers cancelled dates so they could go back to their cabins to pray and apologize for wrong things they had said or done. The next day camp seemed a little bit like heaven. The whole atmosphere had changed.

Repentance always includes these things: (1) A deep sense of sinfulness and a realization that a holy God can't look upon our sin. A flippant "All have sinned so I'm a sinner too—big deal" won't make it. We must recognize the seriousness of sin. (2) A desire to get rid of our sin badly enough to obey God in whatever He says must be done. (3) A determination to live our lives for Jesus and not for ourselves. There must be a *complete change of direction*.

You may not hear the word *repent* very often, but if you don't experience the ingredients of repentance, you'll never have a solid relationship with God.

I tell you, no! But unless you repent, you too will all perish. Luke 13:3

Many of those who believed now came and openly confessed their evil deeds. A number who had practiced sorcery brought their scrolls together and burned them publicly. When they calculated the value of the scrolls, the total came to fifty thousand drachmas. In this way the word of the Lord spread widely and grew in power. Acts 19:18–20

Day 126

Sin and Separation

Do you remember doing things such as avoiding Mr. Farnsworth for years because you hit a baseball through his window? Or trying to keep your mother from discovering that you had broken her most beautiful vase? Or hoping you wouldn't meet the kid whose lunch you stole one day when you were extra hungry? If you've ever done anything like that—and most of us have—you know how uncomfortable the person you have wronged can make you feel—even if that person knows nothing about what you have done.

Sin also makes us feel very uncomfortable around God, and there is no way we can hide what we have done from Him. You can never grow as a Christian with unconfessed sin your life. It doesn't matter if it is something you did yesterday or five years ago. To feel close to God again, you must clear up your sin.

If you think back on your life, you may also be able to recall some confessions you did make, and how it completely restored a relationship with another person. When I was a child, my mother left an open can of red paint on the kitchen floor while she went out into the yard. While she was gone, my sister and I were running through the kitchen and dumped the whole thing over. We ran out to tell my mother what had happened. She not only forgave us but said, "When you do something wrong, always tell me right away. Because you told me immediately, I can clean up the floor without permanent damage. If you had tried to hide it, the kitchen floor would have been red for years."

When you do something wrong, remember the can of red paint. If you don't confess it immediately, it will do more harm and will be much harder to confess later. If you have something from your past that must be made right, clear it up immediately before it gets worse.

If we confess our sins, he is faithful and just and will forgive us our sins and purify us from all unrighteousness. 1 John 1:9

Day 127

Hiding in the Garden Is Not Advised

The story of Adam and Eve is so familiar that we forget we can learn something from it. We could title their experience, "All the Wrong Ways to Handle Any Situation." Adam and Eve did all the dumbest things. The sad part is that their actions have been repeated literally billions of times.

Eve listened to the devil as he questioned God. If we do this, it is very dangerous, because we are then assuming that we know more than God and have the right to revise His commandments. Eve hadn't listened to God carefully enough to be sure about what He had actually said, and she inaccurately repeated His instructions.

Next, Eve believed the devil's lies. What he said seemed logical so she bought it. Remember that your logic is never better than God's.

Eve then desired the forbidden fruit. I've heard a mother say to her child, "You can't have it, but it's okay to want it." That is not true when it comes to temptation. If the devil can make you dwell on your desire to have something that's wrong, he has won half his battle.

Misery and sin like company. Eve not only sinned but convinced Adam to join in her sin. Then instead of confessing, they made silly fig-leaf outfits and played the first game of hide-and-seek! To say the least, God was not impressed.

Trying to hide your sin is ridiculous. You don't have to repeat the garden of Eden experiment. The results are always the same.

When the woman saw that the fruit of the tree was good for food and pleasing to the eye, and also desirable for gaining wisdom, she took some and ate it. She also gave some to her husband, who was with her, and he ate it. Then the eyes of both of them were opened, and they realized they were naked; so they sewed fig leaves together and made coverings for themselves. Then the man and his wife heard the sound of the Lord God as he was walking in the garden in the cool of the day, and they hid from the Lord God among the trees of the garden. Genesis 3:6–8

Then, after desire has conceived, it gives birth to sin; and sin, when it is full-grown, gives birth to death. James 1:15

Day 128

If your kidneys failed to function, the only way that you could hope to again live a normal, healthy life would be by receiving a kidney transplant. If I volunteered to donate my kidney to you, you would really owe me your life. If you honestly asked me what you could do to repay me and I told you to give me your antique ring, you'd be obligated to do exactly as I said. To me, that ring would be the most valuable thing you could give me.

Have you ever wondered how the blood of Jesus can take away our sins? Has the Old Testament idea of sacrificing animals to cover sin until Jesus died been a terribly difficult concept for you to understand? Blood is valuable to God because He says it is. God created the world and He made the rules. We couldn't live without blood running through our veins; to give His blood for us, Jesus had to die, showing how terrible sin is and how much it cost God to forgive us.

Yet there is no completely logical way to figure out why blood is valuable to God, so we must accept it by faith. Human logic would say that we should try to do enough good deeds to outweigh the bad ones. But God says no. Our idea is to show penitence and remorse to try and make God feel sorry for us. But that isn't necessary. Jesus already shed His blood for our sins. You can't do a thing to make yourself acceptable in God's sight. Only Jesus' blood can remove your sin. That is what is valuable to God.

This is my blood of the covenant, which is poured out for many for the forgiveness of sins. Matthew 26:28

How much more, then, will the blood of Christ, who through the eternal Spirit offered himself unblemished to God, cleanse our consciences from acts that lead to death, so that we may serve the living God! Hebrews 9:14

In fact, the law requires that nearly everything be cleansed with blood, and without the shedding of blood there is no forgiveness. Hebrews 9:22

Day 129
So Satan Is Accusing You Again!

Do you hear the devil discouraging you? He'll whisper things like, "You're a failure and you might as well stop trying to be a Christian," or "Don't bother trying to confess that sin. God won't even want to talk to you after this."

Obviously, if we have done something wrong and refuse to be honest and confess it, we should feel guilty—because we are. But I'm talking about that vague feeling of failure and discouragement, or the constant rehashing of old sins you've confessed before. The devil loves to accuse Christians, and he spends twenty-four hours a day doing it. The reason we have so much trouble is that we fall for his tricks.

The devil might say, "You're a rotten Christian. You didn't help your crabby neighbor carry in her groceries yesterday—and Christians are supposed to love to help everybody." Our usual reply is something like, "Well, I did mow the lawn without my mother saying a word—so there." Other times we answer, "You're right. I'm a terrible, awful, lousy Christian."

In both cases, we are trying to find righteousness and goodness within ourselves. The right answer for you to give is, "Big deal, Satan. I've already confessed, and Jesus' blood takes away my sin and clears my conscience. Jesus has forgiven me, so I never need to think of that sin again. Besides, you were defeated by Jesus on the cross and will be completely destroyed at the end of the world."

The devil . . . was a murderer from the beginning, not holding to the truth, for there is no truth in him. When he lies, he speaks his native language, for he is a liar and the father of lies. John 8:44

The great dragon was hurled down—that ancient serpent called the devil, or Satan, who leads the whole world astray. He was hurled to the earth, and his angels with him. Then I heard a loud voice in heaven say: "Now have come the salvation and the power and the kingdom of our God, and the authority of his Christ. For the accuser of our brothers, who accuses them before our God day and night, has been hurled down. They overcame him by the blood of the Lamb and by the word of their testimony; they did not love their lives so much as to shrink from death." Revelation 12:9–11

When you have a hassle or a problem, it's nice to have someone stick up for you. The devil is always trying to condemn you. The comments of non-Christians are part of his ammunition: "After all, what can you expect from a religious fanatic?" "I thought you were a Christian," or "But then, everyone from your church is weird."

When you deliberately do wrong, you open the door for the devil because he then has a definite reason to accuse you. Of course, he won't stop with the true accusation. He'll throw in some false ones too, to completely wipe you out. As soon as you confess your sin to God and claim Jesus' blood, you can effectively resist the devil's accusations. Pray honestly, and if God doesn't reveal any specific sin, ignore Satan's whispers. Then remember that *God is on your side*. He loves you, He forgives you, and He sent Jesus to die for you.

You are working for God, not the devil. You would think it strange if the manager of Burger King came over to McDonald's to tell one of the employees that he was making the French fries wrong. He would have no right to criticize the employee of another company. God is the only One who has the right to criticize you. If you are doing God's will, Satan's whispers should not disturb you, and you should ignore the comments of other people unless they're based on Scripture. God is your boss. Serve Him faithfully and listen carefully to His correction, always keeping in mind that *He is on your side*.

The Lord is with me; I will not be afraid. What can man do to me? Psalm 118:6

What, then, shall we say in response to this? If God is for us, who can be against us? He who did not spare his own Son, but gave him up for us all— how will he not also, along with him, graciously give us all things? Who will bring any charge against those whom God has chosen? It is God who justifies. Who is he that condemns? Christ Jesus, who died—more than that, who was raised to life—is at the right hand of God and is also interceding for us. Romans 8:31–34

Day 131

How Did I Become a Sinner?

It isn't true that our every action is preprogrammed so we're free of moral responsibility. But no one can live up to God's standards without supernatural help. None of us likes anger, jealousy, hatred, lying, or selfishness, and we are quite willing to admit that they are bad. Nevertheless, we tend to think of ourselves as good people who get angry only when we have a right to, who hate only people everybody else would hate, and who lie only when we get into especially tough circumstances. Yet if you go on an "I'm-going-to-be-good" campaign, you'll find that something inside you just wants to be bad. Benjamin Franklin tried to eliminate some bad traits by spending a week overcoming each. He was surprised that his experiment failed.

You were born with some things you couldn't help—freckles, curly hair, a long nose—but not sin. You inherited imperfect judgment and independent emotions, which don't help the situation, but you *chose* to sin—just like every other person on this planet. The good news is that Jesus forgives sin and offers supernatural power to overcome it.

"We all, like sheep, have gone astray, each of us has turned to his own way" (Isaiah 53:6). That is why, in yourself, you can't obey God. You're like a train that is headed down the wrong track; the only possibility for you to go the right way is for someone to pick you up and set you on the right track.

If you'll give Jesus control of your life, He can put you "on track" to live in victory.

As for you, you were dead in your transgressions and sins, in which you used to live when you followed the ways of this world and of the ruler of the kingdom of the air, the spirit who is now at work in those who are disobedient. All of us also lived among them at one time, gratifying the cravings of our sinful nature and following its desires and thoughts. Like the rest, we were by nature objects of wrath. But because of his great love for us, God, who is rich in mercy, made us alive with Christ even when we were dead in transgressions—it is by grace you have been saved. Ephesians 2:1–5

Day 132

Whose Slave Are You?

Watching a movie depicting the pre–Civil War South or studying United States history can make you hate slavery. In fact, maybe you can't imagine anything worse than being a slave. But did you know that millions of people are slaves today? *Their master is sin, and sin is a terrible master.* It binds people until they are unable to make choices or see truth.

I remember an object lesson I saw as a child. A visiting pastor picked out one boy from the audience and tied the boy's arms together with a strand of thread. It was easy for the boy to break the thread. Winding the thread around three times made it a little harder to break. Finally, so many threads bound the boy's arms together that he could do nothing. "Sin," the pastor explained to us, "is like that thread. It looks so harmless at first, but it takes away your freedom and makes you a prisoner."

If you know someone who can't stay away from negative influences like bad friends or alcohol, you have seen this principle at work. The only way to break away from sin is to get a new master—Jesus Christ. If you obey Jesus, He gives you power to overcome sin. But you can't be your own master and stay in the "middle of the road." You must either be a slave of sin or a slave of Christ. Whose slave are you?

No one can serve two masters. Either he will hate the one and love the other, or he will be devoted to the one and despise the other. You cannot serve both God and Money. Matthew 6:24

Therefore do not let sin reign in your mortal body so that you obey its evil desires. Do not offer the parts of your body to sin, as instruments of wickedness, but rather offer yourselves to God, as those who have been brought from death to life; and offer the parts of your body to him as instruments of righteousness. For sin shall not be your master, because you are not under law, but under grace. What then? Shall we sin because we are not under law but under grace? By no means! Don't you know that when you offer yourselves to someone to obey him as slaves, you are slaves to the one whom you obey— whether you are slaves to sin, which leads to death, or to obedience, which leads to righteousness? Romans 6:12–16

Day 133
Sin Removal

Do you live as if you are *completely* forgiven? Or do you let the devil whisper things to you like, "You can't expect to live a holy life because a person with a past like yours will never be able to reform," or "What you've done is so terrible that God will never be able to forgive you," or "You're ruined for life. God can't do anything with a mess like you"?

Don't ever listen to those lies. God says He forgives your confessed sin and won't even remember it again. He doesn't just put all the smutty contents of your sin in an envelope so you look good on the outside. He *removes* your sin and actually makes you pure and righteous.

Moses didn't run around saying, "But I killed a man in Egypt, so there's no way that God can use me." Moses knew how to accept God's forgiveness, live close to God, and let God do miraculous things through him.

Peter didn't keep reminding himself that he had denied Jesus at the time when Jesus needed him most. Peter lived like a forgiven man, and that made all the difference. With forgiveness comes God's love, joy, and power to defeat sin. Of course, the earthly consequences of sin will still be around—the murdered man will still be dead, the murderer will still be in jail, the child who never knew his father will keep asking questions, and the person you've hurt deeply may not forgive you. But God in His wisdom and mercy can work His miracles in all of this—if you let Him. A former murderer who lives like a forgiven man, displaying real joy and peace, even in jail, may be one of God's best advertisements. Give God a chance with your life.

For I will forgive their wickedness and will remember their sins no more.
Hebrews 8:12

As far as the east is from the west, so far has he removed our transgressions from us. Psalm 103:12

You will again have compassion on us; you will tread our sins underfoot and hurl all our iniquities into the depths of the sea. Micah 7:19

If I were sending a five-year-old girl out to play in a yard still filled with puddles from last night's rain, I'd give her clear instructions: "Now, don't play in the mud and don't get your teddy bear dirty." If she were an ordinary five-year-old, she'd probably come back into the house covered with mud, and crying, "I'm really sorry. I didn't mean to do it. Please don't spank me."

I could reply, "That's okay, dear. I forgive you and accept you just the way you are." But forgiving her wouldn't be enough. She would still be a mess. Because she was already so dirty, she'd have no reason to stop playing in the mud. And there are lots of things that a clean girl can do that a muddy girl cannot do—a clean girl would be allowed to go many places where a dirty girl would not be accepted. Actually, my scrubbing that little girl and giving her clean clothes would make a *change* in her. She would act differently once she was clean.

God not only forgives our sin, but He also "cleanses us from all unrighteousness." He cleans us up completely. This is not something we can do for ourselves, but we do have a part. The five-year-old cannot do an adequate job of washing herself and providing herself with clean clothes. However, she must cooperate with the person who is bathing her and giving her a fresh change of clothes. Let God cleanse you from the inside out and make you a new and a clean person. The more you long for a clean, pure life, the deeper His cleansing will be.

Have mercy on me, O God, according to your unfailing love; according to your great compassion blot out my transgressions. Wash away all my iniquity and cleanse me from my sin. Psalm 51:1–2

In a large house there are articles not only of gold and silver, but also of wood and clay; some are for noble purposes and some for ignoble. If a man cleanses himself from the latter, he will be an instrument for noble purposes, made holy, useful to the Master and prepared to do any good work. Flee the evil desires of youth, and pursue righteousness, faith, love and peace, along with those who call on the Lord out of a pure heart. 2 Timothy 2:20–22

Day 135

How Many Times Must I Forgive?

"I don't think I can ever forgive him." Have you ever said or thought that? If you have, you are on dangerous ground. The verses that come just after the Lord's Prayer in the Sermon on the Mount are not recited by church congregations or used often as sermon texts, but they are just as much a part of the Bible.

For if you forgive men when they sin against you, your heavenly Father will also forgive you. But if you do not forgive men their sins, your Father will not forgive your sins. Matthew 6:14–15

If you are a Christian, *you must forgive.* Since Jesus, the perfect Son of God, forgave you for everything you've ever done, how can you not forgive another person—no matter what he has done? Your emotions may not be completely under your control, but if, by an act of your will, you choose to forgive, your feelings will sooner or later come into line.

God cannot forgive you if you refuse to forgive others. The Christian with an unforgiving attitude walks straight into trouble—God won't let His children get by with unforgiving attitudes. Peter thought he was being generous if he forgave a person for the same offense seven times. How many times has God forgiven you?

Then Peter came to Jesus and asked, "Lord, how many times shall I forgive my brother when he sins against me? Up to seven times?" Jesus answered, "I tell you, not seven times, but seventy-seven times." . . . *Then the master called the servant in. "You wicked servant," he said, "I canceled all that debt of yours because you begged me to. Shouldn't you have had mercy on your fellow servant just as I had on you?" In anger his master turned him over to the jailers to be tortured, until he should pay back all he owed. This is how my heavenly Father will treat each of you unless you forgive your brother from your heart.* Matthew 18:21–22, 32–35

Day 136
Are You Forgiving Yourself?

Sofia's cousin came one day to play with her, and in her excitement, Sofia told him about the bedroom slippers with tigers on them that she got him for Christmas. Suddenly remembering that this was a secret, she said, "Forget that I ever told you."

The next time her cousin came to visit, he assured Sofia, "I forgot all about the slippers with tigers on them that you're going to give me for Christmas." We can be thankful that God, unlike Sofia's cousin, keeps His promise to forget about confessed sin and never bring it up again.

Is your attitude toward God's forgiveness of your confessed sin influenced by similar experiences you've had with people? Do you really believe that God means it when He says that He will forgive *all* your sin? He does mean it. Confess your sin with complete trust that God will destroy it in the fire of His holiness.

Some people say, "Well, I know that God forgives me, but I can't forgive myself." Since when have you been in the business of forgiving your own sins? Only the extreme pride of putting yourself above God could make you think you're responsible for forgiving your own sins. God says He'll not only forgive your sin, but He'll forget it. Not taking God at His word is unbelief. Accept His forgiveness.

"No longer will a man teach his neighbor, or a man his brother, saying, 'Know the Lord,' because they will all know me, from the least of them to the greatest," declares the Lord. "For I will forgive their wickedness and will remember their sins no more." Jeremiah 31:34

I thank Christ Jesus our Lord, who has given me strength, that he considered me faithful, appointing me to his service. Even though I was once a blasphemer and a persecutor and a violent man, I was shown mercy because I acted in ignorance and unbelief. The grace of our Lord was poured out on me abundantly, along with the faith and love that are in Christ Jesus. Here is a trustworthy saying that deserves full acceptance: Christ Jesus came into the world to save sinners—of whom I am the worst. 1 Timothy 1:12–15

Day 137

Forgiven Sinners, Inc.

I wish I could have seen Jesus heal a blind man or raise Lazarus from the dead. Yet the miracle of Jesus' forgiving and changing the repentant sinner outranks all others. David committed both adultery and murder, but because of his full and sincere confession, he received forgiveness, and God was able to use him to rule His people and write part of the Bible.

As a boy, St. Augustine had taken part in a theft, and as a young man he had lived with his girlfriend, an arrangement acceptable to most of Roman society. After he became a Christian, Augustine lived a holy life that others admired, and he became a brilliant writer and church leader. When he was dying, he asked that Psalm 32 be printed in large letters and hung above his bed so he could read the words and meditate on them. The psalm begins:

Blessed is he whose transgressions are forgiven, whose sins are covered.
Psalm 32:1

It's easy to forget Jesus taught that visible sins are a result of wrong thinking, and that we are responsible for our *thoughts* as well as our *actions*. Therefore, we tend to think that only ex-cons have experienced great forgiveness. But if a film were made of your thoughts, would it be an X-rated movie? All of us need mountains of God's forgiveness. Forgiven sinners are amazing miracles. If you're not a member of Forgiven Sinners, Inc., join 'em!

Then he turned toward the woman and said to Simon, "Do you see this woman? I came into your house. You did not give me any water for my feet, but she wet my feet with her tears and wiped them with her hair. You did not give me a kiss, but this woman, from the time I entered, has not stopped kissing my feet. You did not put oil on my head, but she has poured perfume on my feet. Therefore, I tell you, her many sins have been forgiven—for she loved much. But he who has been forgiven little loves little. Luke 7:44–47

I have seen bumper stickers that say, "Please be patient, God isn't finished with me yet." It's wonderful to know that God doesn't just forgive us and then leave us alone. And He won't suddenly abandon us to work on more promising Christians. The work that God began in you the day you accepted Christ as your Savior, He continues every day of your life and will one day complete in heaven.

God wants to care for everything in your life—earthly or spiritual—because it will affect you for eternity. He will silently continue working in you every moment. All this will happen on one condition—that you trust Him. Absolute trust in God has been the key factor in the lives of people God has mightily used. They weren't the most talented people. Often they didn't possess great charm and wit. They even made mistakes that some other Christians would not have made. But through it all they trusted God to work in them, and God fulfilled His purposes in their lives.

The devil wants to prevent the work of God in your life, and he has some very sneaky ways of doing it. He tries to convince you that it's humble to say or think, "I'm such a poor Christian, I could never work for God," or "Other people can pray or witness or lead a Bible study so much better, so I'll let them do it," or "I've had such a bad background so the devil especially picks on me. I don't have much chance to grow as a Christian." These are not humble confessions. They are *insults* to God, who can do the impossible. He is waiting for you to trust Him enough to take your hands off and let Him work in your life.

> The Lord will fulfill his purpose for me; your love, O Lord, endures forever—do not abandon the works of your hands. Psalm 138:8

> "For I know the plans I have for you," declares the Lord, "plans to prosper you and not to harm you, plans to give you hope and a future." Jeremiah 29:11

> Being confident of this, that he who began a good work in you will carry it on to completion until the day of Christ Jesus. Philippians 1:6

Day 139

God Even Used Peter's Big Mouth

A lot of teenagers can identify with the apostle Peter. He was a leap-before-you-look loudmouth who couldn't be depended on. He wanted to be an authority on topics about which he knew very little. Peter was born with some great natural abilities and characteristics, but his wrong motives made them completely useless to Jesus.

People must have wondered what Jesus saw in him, but He loved Peter and forgave him. Peter accepted this forgiveness and gave his life to Jesus. When Jesus put the right motives within Peter, his willingness to jump into anything became courage, his love for talking was transformed into ability to *preach*—and God made him dependable. Everyone else would have laughed if Jesus had predicted the great things Peter would do.

Jesus never gave up on Peter; also He saw his potential. Jesus sees what you can be, and He won't give up on you—trust Him. If you fail, it's not because you are ugly or have an offensive personality or have a learning disability or have horrible parents. It's because you didn't let Jesus give you His motives and you didn't expect miracles in your life. In order to receive Jesus' motives, you must confess your sin and yield to His correction. Then accept His forgiveness and wait in faith to see what God can do with your big mouth or poor study habits.

Simon, Simon, Satan has asked to sift you as wheat. But I have prayed for you, Simon, that your faith may not fail. And when you have turned back, strengthen your brothers. Luke 22:31–32

Then Peter stood up with the Eleven, raised his voice and addressed the crowd: "Fellow Jews and all of you who live in Jerusalem, let me explain this to you; listen carefully to what I say. . . . Therefore let all Israel be assured of this: God has made this Jesus, whom you crucified, both Lord and Christ." When the people heard this, they were cut to the heart and said to Peter and the other apostles, "Brothers, what shall we do?" Peter replied, "Repent and be baptized, every one of you, in the name of Jesus Christ for the forgiveness of your sins. And you will receive the gift of the Holy Spirit." Acts 2:14, 36–38

If for some strange reason I wanted to rid America of Coca-Cola, it would be pointless for me to do so by defacing every Coca-Cola sign I could find. Even smashing Coke bottles and burying Coke cans wouldn't be effective. I'd have to demolish every factory and destroy every recipe to effectively do the job.

When it comes to fighting sin, we try to overcome sin by bits and pieces—smashing Coke cans—without dealing with the source. The blood of Jesus takes away sins, but the cross has also dealt with the sinful self, the source of sin. In your own strength, you can't die to sin and live to righteousness. You must give yourself completely to God so that His power *within* you can make you strong against temptation. God has promised that He'll never let you face a temptation too strong for you, and He will always provide a way of escape.

Have this attitude: My eyes belong to Jesus; therefore it's impossible for them to look at an NC–17 movie; my mouth belongs to Jesus, who wouldn't think of spreading this gossip; my hands belong to Jesus, so they'll be glad to take out the garbage. This isn't just the power of positive thinking—it's daily yielding the parts of your body to God. Only He can divert your eyes, your tongue, your hands, your feet, and your ears to constantly obey Him. Memorize one of the Scripture verses for today and keep asking God to show you what it means for your life.

He himself bore our sins in his body on the tree, so that we might die to sins and live for righteousness; by his wounds you have been healed. 1 Peter 2:24

You were taught, with regard to your former way of life, to put off your old self, which is being corrupted by its deceitful desires; to be made new in the attitude of your minds; and to put on the new self, created to be like God in true righteousness and holiness. Ephesians 4:22–24

Day 141

Right and Wrong

When God gives us commands, He gives us the power to obey. He wants us to have victory over sin. A lot of our frustration comes because we are confused about what sin really is, and how we can overcome it. God *doesn't* command us to look sharp at all times, appear successful, never be clumsy, and always please everyone. God *does* command us to "Honor your father and mother," "Be still and know that I am God," "Trust in the Lord with all your heart," and "If it is possible, as far as it depends on you, live at peace with everyone."

Victory involves moment-by-moment decisions to apologize to your mother, to concentrate on God's power rather than on the unfair decision, to determine to trust God for the money you need to attend camp, and to be a good worker for the crabby boss. Maintaining an image of a person who never makes mistakes has nothing to do with victory over sin.

Also understand that there is a big difference between willfully disobeying God and unconsciously sinning. In fact, many people define sin as "willful disobedience to God." Every person who has taken care of young children knows the difference between a child purposely disobeying a specific command such as "You must not play in the sandbox with your good clothes on" and a child in his excitement forgetting that the cement is wet and cannot be walked on. Our humanness may prevent us from doing all God wishes; but if we set our wills toward obeying Him, He will always give us the power to obey His specific commands. That ability to obey comes from God who has all power.

[Jesus] replied, "I saw Satan fall like lightning from heaven. I have given you authority to . . . overcome all the power of the enemy." Luke 10:18–19

Therefore, as God's chosen people, holy and dearly loved, clothe yourselves with compassion, kindness, humility, gentleness and patience. Bear with each other and forgive whatever grievances you may have against one another. Forgive as the Lord forgave you. And over all these virtues put on love, which binds them all together in perfect unity. Colossians 3:12–14

Day 142

That Selfishness Inside Me

The basic problem is, how do I get rid of the selfish me that wants its own way and gets into arguments with God? God has provided a way. Paul writes:

> *May I never boast except in the cross of our Lord Jesus Christ, through which the world has been crucified to me, and I to the world.* Galatians 6:14

Crucifixion means death. Since we have proven ourselves to be sinners, there is no way for that sinful self to be eradicated unless it dies. The miracle of the cross is that not only did Jesus shed His blood to take away our sins, but that sinful self within us was crucified when Jesus died. When Paul says, "I have been crucified with Christ," he means exactly that.

Just as Jesus' blood doesn't cleanse your sin unless you have faith in that fact and ask for forgiveness, so too the death of your old sinful self becomes real in you only if you allow it. A cruel slave master wouldn't be able to make a dead slave do anything—no matter how viciously he tortured him. Sin, like that cruel master, is always trying to enslave you. But by giving up your right to have your own way and surrendering totally to Jesus, you can by faith make the miracle of the cross—"by which the world has been crucified to me, and I to the world"—real in your life.

If I give up my right to have everyone think my piano solo was the highlight of the evening, and have faith that God can work in my life through every situation, I don't have to be angry because my number is omitted from the program. The selfish me is dead, and circumstances don't have to cause me to sin.

Know that Jesus took your old self with Him to the cross. Give your will to God. Believe that God can do in you what you can't do yourself.

> *I tell you the truth, unless a kernel of wheat falls to the ground and dies, it remains only a single seed. But if it dies, it produces many seeds. The man who loves his life will lose it, while the man who hates his life in this world will keep it for eternal life. Whoever serves me must follow me; and where I am, my servant also will be. My Father will honor the one who serves me.* John 12:24–26

Day 143

Caterpillars Can Change

Do you ever feel like you're caught in quicksand, a slimy bog, a bottomless pit—a situation you don't think you'll ever be able to get out of? The Bible calls this kind of vicious circle the law of sin and death. There are basically two laws—the law of the Spirit of life in Christ, and the law of sin and death. There is our selfish nature with its inability to obey and love God, and there is God's nature, which loves freely and sets us free from the power of our old nature.

How can one get free from the law of sin and death? Caterpillars have a pretty rough time getting through mud without getting soiled by it. Let's say that the mud is sin. Mud is everywhere and it seems impossible to avoid. The caterpillar can't rise above the mud either—unless it can get rid of its caterpillar self. This, of course, can happen if the caterpillar's old self is discarded and the creature becomes a beautiful butterfly.

Now, if the caterpillar had a choice in this matter and could say, "I want to remain a caterpillar because I like the mud and it's just caterpillar nature to like mud," there would be no victory and no flying above mud. You are faced with the same choice: you can choose to live by God's law and become a butterfly, or you can live by the law of sin and death and crawl like a caterpillar.

Because through Christ Jesus the law of the Spirit of life set me free from the law of sin and death. Romans 8:2

Those who live according to the sinful nature have their minds set on what that nature desires; but those who live in accordance with the Spirit have their minds set on what the Spirit desires. The mind of sinful man is death, but the mind controlled by the Spirit is life and peace; the sinful mind is hostile to God. It does not submit to God's law, nor can it do so. Those controlled by the sinful nature cannot please God. You, however, are controlled not by the sinful nature but by the Spirit, if the Spirit of God lives in you. And if anyone does not have the Spirit of Christ, he does not belong to Christ. Romans 8:5–9

One idea of faith is that it is the acceptance of God's fact. The devil is always trying to get you to doubt truth. But your disbelief of a fact doesn't make it false; it simply becomes inoperative in your life. It is just as possible to walk across a plank that connects the roofs of two five-story buildings as it is to cross one laid on the ground. However, lack of faith, and fear based on lack of faith, will keep one from doing so.

One important Bible fact is:

No one who is born of God will continue to sin, because God's seed remains in him; he cannot go on sinning, because he has been born of God. 1 John 3:9

Watchman Nee, a Chinese Christian writer, explains, "John is not telling us that sin is now no longer in our history and that we shall not again commit sin. He is saying that to sin is not in the nature of that which is born of God." In nature wood floats, but it is possible for wood to sink if it is enclosed in metal or if it is nailed to a dock that is under water.

Now I have a choice. Will I live by God's fact or by what my experience seems to show? If I were blind, I couldn't see a sunset, and if I were deaf, I couldn't enjoy a concert. Yet the elegance of the colors and the beauty of the music would still exist. The wood encased in metal may stay at the bottom of a lake until it rots, not knowing its nature is to float. Even so, the devil may deceive you into thinking there is no deliverance from the power of sin. If you don't believe "no one who is born of God will continue to sin," you live as though that page of your Bible didn't exist. Put your faith in God's facts, not in your experience or feelings.

This is how we know that we love the children of God: by loving God and carrying out his commands. This is love for God: to obey his commands. And his commands are not burdensome, for everyone born of God overcomes the world. This is the victory that has overcome the world, even our faith. Who is it that overcomes the world? Only he who believes that Jesus is the Son of God. 1 John 5:2–5

Day 145

But You Could Fly

The Bible talks about two kinds of life—the life of the spirit and the life of the flesh, natural life. We're living in a world where the things around us are running according to natural life—the life of the flesh. It's a world in which people are expected to stomp on others to get to the top, tell lies when a lot is at stake, and boast about how great they are.

When you start reading the Bible, you learn about selflessness, truth, and humility. The person who uses the resources available in natural life to try to love his enemies will give up in frustration. But God has given His children Spirit-life, and Spirit-life can do what natural life can never accomplish. For example, the law of gravity governs our earth. Whether I throw an algebra book out the window on the eighty-seventh floor (wouldn't you like to sometimes?) or merely drop a pencil, gravity will take over. However, there are other physical laws. Looking up in the sky, you'll have to admit that neither birds nor airplanes seem to worry about the law of gravity. They fly according to a higher law.

Obviously, the person who has never accepted Christ doesn't have the life of the Spirit to give power. However, there are Christians who never use the supernatural Spirit-power they possess. If we try to follow God's rules in our own strength, we are doomed to failure. The devil knows this and is always trying to make us depend on our own strength. If you rely on the supernatural life of Jesus' Spirit, you'll be flying above temptations to sin, but if you trust only yourself, you're bound to crash.

But if Christ is in you, your body is dead because of sin, yet your spirit is alive because of righteousness. And if the Spirit of him who raised Jesus from the dead is living in you, he who raised Christ from the dead will also give life to your mortal bodies through his Spirit, who lives in you. Therefore, brothers, we have an obligation—but it is not to the sinful nature, to live according to it. For if you live according to the sinful nature, you will die; but if by the Spirit you put to death the misdeeds of the body, you will live, because those who are led by the Spirit of God are sons of God. Romans 8:10–14

Day 146

Worth Celebrating

Suppose someone asks you, "Why do you celebrate the pagan festival of Christmas? Don't you know that December 25 was once a Roman holiday?" How will you answer?

It is true that several pagan festivals took place on December 25, which by the old calendar was winter solstice, the shortest day of the year. Nevertheless, there are some good reasons for having a special occasion to remember the birth of Jesus.

First, the Old Testament pattern was to celebrate God's great acts in history. Second, the Bible says, "Do not be overcome by evil, but overcome evil with good" (Romans 12:21). An evil festival can be changed into a good one.

During December, the Romans celebrated Saturnalia, a feast in honor of Saturn, the god of agriculture. People of Europe set bonfires on December 25 to remind the sun to return; by the fourth century, followers of Mithraism were celebrating December 25 as the birthday of the Unconquered Sun. With all the world celebrating, Christians felt that this would be a good time to remember the birth of Christ, who came to save us from sin and give us eternal life.

One of the tactics of the devil is to convince people that anything fun is wrong, and we can make ourselves righteous by giving up all kinds of things. But God, who programmed birds to give concerts and monkeys to put on free comedy shows, certainly wants us to enjoy life. Shouldn't the birth of Jesus be the most enjoyable celebration of all?

Then Nehemiah the governor . . . said to them all, "This day is sacred to the Lord your God. Do not mourn or weep." For all the people had been weeping as they listened to the words of the Law. Nehemiah said, "Go and enjoy choice food and sweet drinks, and send some to those who have nothing prepared. This day is sacred to our Lord. Do not grieve, for the joy of the Lord is your strength." The Levites calmed all the people, saying, "Be still, for this is a sacred day. Do not grieve." Then all the people went away to eat and drink, to send portions of food and to celebrate with great joy, because they now understood the words that had been made known to them. Nehemiah 8:9–12

Day 147

The Greatest Christmas Gift

The celebration of Christmas focuses on the biblical truth that Jesus was both human and divine. The account of the birth of Jesus shows clearly the two natures of Christ. It contradicts false beliefs that are still around today in many forms. Gnosticism said that Jesus was never truly human and that He did not have a real body. Arianism taught that Jesus was neither God nor man but a specially created being with more power than man and less power than God.

The Bible vividly shows the humanity of Jesus—a little helpless baby, born of a human mother, bundled up in a musty feed trough. The animals in His nursery were not on the wallpaper! John summed it up by writing, "The Word became flesh and made his dwelling among us" (John 1:14).

Yet in no way was Jesus less than God. Mary was promised:

He will be great and will be called the Son of the Most High. The Lord God will give him the throne of his father David, and he will reign over the house of Jacob forever; his kingdom will never end. Luke 1:32–33

This prediction could not be describing a mere human being. Isaiah's prophecy was fulfilled:

For to us a child is born, to us a son is given, and the government will be on his shoulders. And he will be called Wonderful Counselor, Mighty God, Everlasting Father, Prince of Peace. Isaiah 9:6

Most people who despise Christmas refuse to believe that Jesus was fully human and fully divine. Understandable, because the fact that Jesus was "made in human likeness" (Philippians 2:7) *is* incredible. Why would God, who created all things, place himself in the position of being fed and cared for by a human mother? Jesus showed us, by becoming human and dying for us, that His love has no equal, even in the imagination of man. Jesus was born in Bethlehem so that He can be born in the heart of every person who accepts the first and greatest Christmas gift.

But when the time had fully come, God sent his Son, born of a woman, born under law, to redeem those under law, that we might receive the full rights of sons. Galatians 4:4–5

When you read in your history book that Christ was born in 4 BC (some books say 5 BC), you might be interested in learning some facts about chronology. People often date things in relation to major events—a big flood, the beginning of a king's reign, or in the case of the Jewish calendar, the exodus of the Hebrews from Egypt. Actually, a Scythian monk named Dionysius Exiguus, who lived from AD 496 until 540, began the practice of numbering our years according to the birth of Christ. It all began while he was preparing a chart to show the correct method of calculating the date of Easter. Because he didn't want to reckon time according to the reign of a pagan ruler, he numbered years according to the birth of Christ. The rest of the world eventually accepted it as well. Every copy of the modern calendar points to the birth of Christ as the great turning point of history.

Actually, Dionysius made a mistake in his calculations. When others corrected those calculations, instead of changing all the other dates, they placed the birth of Jesus in or shortly before the year 4 BC, when Herod died.

After Christ came, nothing could ever be the same again. He brought victory over death. The resurrection meant that people could face death with confidence and serenity. Christ's coming also means that each person has to accept Christ or reject Him, to be for Him or against Him. More than the manger scene on your piano would be missing if Christ had not come. Imagine a world without churches, New Testaments, and Christian music. Hope would be gone.

But Jesus did come. He offers a forever in heaven for those who give their lives to Jesus, a heaven with no death or mourning or pain. But there's also hope for *today*. Jesus came to give you love that no one else has for you. He has hope for you, even if your parents are getting a divorce, even if you feel like the most unpopular kid at school, and even if you're tempted to go back to drugs. Don't live as if Christ had not come. He came—to stay with you forever.

And surely I am with you always, to the very end of the age. Matthew 28:20

For where two or three come together in my name, there am I with them. Matthew 18:20

Was Jesus really born of a virgin? Maybe Joseph and Mary covered up their premarital sex by inventing a story. Does it actually matter whether or not Jesus was born of a virgin? Isn't it just His good life that counts anyway? You'll hear these questions and ideas at some point.

Yes, it does matter. If Jesus was not born of a virgin, many statements He made would be lies: "You are from below; I am from above" (John 8:23); "I came from God and now am here" (John 8:42). If Jesus wasn't born of a virgin, He couldn't have died for our sins; He would have to die for His own.

People in Jesus' time knew very well where babies come from. They certainly didn't expect a supernatural event like this. The people of Nazareth knew Mary and Joseph personally, and they watched Jesus grow up. They knew He was human. Yet Jesus' miracles and resurrection confirmed that He was no ordinary mortal.

God used the incredible purity, self-control, and sacrificial love displayed by Mary and Joseph to make the incarnation possible. Joseph was planning to break up with Mary quietly in order to cause a minimum of pain. But God wanted him to take Mary as his bride. Joseph obeyed—even though it cost him his reputation and a normal honeymoon.

The devil tells you it's okay to have sex with someone you love. But God promises the unlimited power of the Holy Spirit to all His *obedient* children. Mary and Joseph's love story, full of faith and sacrifice, made possible the greatest love story of all: "For God so loved the world that he gave his one and only Son" (John 3:16).

> *His mother Mary was pledged to be married to Joseph, but before they came together, she was found to be with child through the Holy Spirit. Joseph . . . had in mind to divorce her quietly. But after he had considered this, an angel of the Lord appeared to him in a dream and said, "Joseph son of David, do not be afraid to take Mary home as your wife, because what is conceived in her is from the Holy Spirit." . . . When Joseph woke up, he did what the angel of the Lord had commanded him and took Mary home as his wife. But he had no union with her until she gave birth to a son.* Matthew 1:18–20, 24–25

Day 150

Wise Men's Gifts—From a Department Store!

After four hours of frantic Christmas shopping, you discover that not one store has the pink sweater your sister wants. You're ready to believe that gift-giving is a sin inherited from the pagan feast of Saturnalia.

The giving of Christmas gifts *can* be wrong. It is not right for you to purchase presents in a frantic tizzy, in mortal fear that your family and friends won't like what you purchased. Spending extravagantly just to be well thought of reflects impure motives.

Receiving gifts can be just as wrong. If you're more concerned about the gifts you get than the love behind them, something isn't right. The ancient cassette from Aunt Tillie and the old-fashioned mittens from Grandpa shouldn't fill you with disappointment. Remember, it was Jesus himself who said, "It is more blessed to give than to receive" (Acts 20:35).

Whether Christmas gift-giving is pagan or truly Christian depends on *heart attitudes.* Pray for each person on your shopping list and ask God to help you love that person.

The wise men gave Jesus gold, frankincense, and myrrh. Maybe you'd like to give Jesus a birthday present too. There's an old story about a town that instituted a special holiday to honor the birthday of its most distinguished citizen. However, the man spent the day alone as everyone exchanged gifts among themselves. No one seemed to remember that it was *his* birthday. That might sound like Christmas at your house. Well, Jesus said, "Whatever you did for one of the least of these brothers of mine, you did for me" (Matthew 25:40). Christmas is a wonderful time to show love to the lonely neighbor lady, the man in the rest home, or the kid at school who has no friends. Wise men's gifts have no selfish motives.

He who is kind to the poor lends to the Lord, and he will reward him for what he has done. Proverbs 19:17

Each man should give what he has decided in his heart to give, not reluctantly or under compulsion, for God loves a cheerful giver. 2 Corinthians 9:7

Day 151
Did You Miss Christmas?

December 25 is on the calendar every year. But tree-decorating, eating turkey dinner, caroling, attending church, or even giving to the Salvation Army won't guarantee that anything at all will happen inside you. Are you ready for something to happen?

Mary and Joseph were willing to begin their married life in an unconventional way, to be misunderstood, and to flee to Egypt. The shepherds thought that the Messiah was so important that they left their whole flock to visit the baby in the manger. Simeon was "righteous and devout," looking forward to the coming of the Messiah. His seeing Jesus was the crowning point of a lifetime of putting God first. Anna "never left the temple but worshiped night and day" (Luke 2:37). Her number one concern was God and His plan for the world.

The wise men must have had to put up with the displeasure and ridicule of friends and family members whose adjectives for them never included the word "wise." Such a long journey must have cost a lot of money. It certainly meant leaving business and family responsibilities. It must have been terribly tiring. Imagine their disappointment when they found no baby king at Jerusalem! All of these who experienced the first Christmas paid a price, but it was well worth it.

It is no different today. The birth of Jesus takes place again in the lives of those who seek Him with all their hearts. If you seek the beauty and blessing of the Christ-child, you will find Him. But if you're all wrapped up in decorating, cooking, eating, buying presents, and partying, you're certain to miss Christmas.

Now there was a man in Jerusalem called Simeon, who was righteous and devout. He was waiting for the consolation of Israel, and the Holy Spirit was upon him. It had been revealed to him by the Holy Spirit that he would not die before he had seen the Lord's Christ. Moved by the Spirit, he went into the temple courts. When the parents brought in the child Jesus to do for him what the custom of the Law required, Simeon took him in his arms and praised God, saying: "Sovereign Lord, as you have promised, you now dismiss your servant in peace. For my eyes have seen your salvation." Luke 2:25–30

Day 152

Jesus Is Not a "Once Upon a Time" Person

How would you react to a newspaper article that said John F. Kennedy had never been assassinated, that he is hiding out on a Caribbean island, and that he healed many people while he was president? Certainly there would be a lot of questions and investigations into the matter. It's just not possible to make a person into a legend simply by writing a few things about him or her.

Some people have theorized that the New Testament account of Jesus is mostly legend. But the time lapse between the crucifixion of Jesus and the writing of the New Testament was not long enough to allow a legend to develop. New Testament scholars agree that the New Testament books were written within decades of Jesus' death, not the hundreds of years it takes to make a legend.

New Testament readers were in a good position to check up on the facts. The "little town of Bethlehem" really is little. So is Nazareth. In small towns news travels fast. It wouldn't have been hard to find out if the things written about Jesus were true. Because they were persecuted for their convictions, first-century Christians had a lot at stake. They had to make sure the Jesus they believed in was for real.

But you too have reasons for making certain what kind of a person Jesus is. Intellectually, you may have always believed that Jesus is real. But do you treat Him like a real person? Do you spend time talking to Him, reading His Word, and enjoying His presence? Or do you act as if He were just a picture on the wall, a once-upon-a-time person?

We did not follow cleverly invented stories when we told you about the power and coming of our Lord Jesus Christ, but we were eyewitnesses of his majesty. For he received honor and glory from God the Father when the voice came to him from the Majestic Glory, saying, "This is my Son, whom I love; with him I am well pleased." We ourselves heard this voice that came from heaven when we were with him on the sacred mountain. And we have the word of the prophets made more certain, and you will do well to pay attention to it, as to a light shining in a dark place, until the day dawns and the morning star rises in your hearts. 2 Peter 1:16–19

Day 153

Do you feel that no one understands you and that everyone has it together except for you? Just remember that Jesus went through tougher things, so He knows how you feel. Isaiah 53:3 prophesied:

He was despised and rejected by men, a man of sorrows, and familiar with suffering. Like one from whom men hide their faces he was despised, and we esteemed him not.

But Jesus did not become depressed. He knew God's will for His life and realized that nothing else mattered. And He died not only to forgive our sins, but to break the power of sin in the world—to give love to the unloved, to free people from bad habits, and to heal the hurts.

The Spirit of the Sovereign Lord is on me, because the Lord has anointed me to preach good news to the poor. He has sent me to bind up the broken-hearted, to proclaim freedom for the captives and release from darkness for the prisoners. Isaiah 61:1

Jesus stood up in the synagogue at Nazareth and read this passage. Then He said, "Today this scripture is fulfilled in your hearing" (Luke 4:21).

Jesus wants to wipe away our tears and comfort us. But we let self-pity and fear and hatred prevent God's healing from flowing into our lives. The people who really trust God for their lives display a "walking on the water attitude" in spite of handicaps, shattered families, and tragedy.

If you give your life to Jesus, He'll make something wonderful out of it. And don't get discouraged when the molding process hurts. Jesus is there to help you.

So I went down to the potter's house, and I saw him working at the wheel. But the pot he was shaping from the clay was marred in his hands; so the potter formed it into another pot, shaping it as seemed best to him. Then the word of the Lord came to me: "O house of Israel, can I not do with you as this potter does?" declares the Lord. "Like clay in the hand of the potter, so are you in my hand, O house of Israel." Jeremiah 18:3–6

Day 154

Palm Sunday Christians Are Good Friday Traitors

Jesus told His disciples where to find the donkey and the exact words to say to its owner. After they brought the donkey to Jesus, they made a saddle out of their coats and Jesus rode into Jerusalem. People spread garments and palm branches on the way and cheered. "Hosanna! Blessed is he who comes in the name of the Lord!" (Mark 11:9).

This event fulfilled Zechariah 9:9:

Rejoice greatly, O Daughter of Zion! Shout, Daughter of Jerusalem! See, your king comes to you, righteous and having salvation, gentle and riding on a donkey, on a colt, the foal of a donkey.

This was Jesus' declaration of himself as the Messiah. He claimed He came in peace and humility to conquer sin, not the Roman Empire.

Jesus knew His mission and His reason for living. The people did not. The people wanted to follow a Messiah who would require nothing difficult of them. On Palm Sunday, when the sun was shining and Jesus was popular, they shouted their hosannas. But later that week, not one person was willing to defend Him.

If you have not made a full surrender to Jesus, you will always be a Palm Sunday Christian. But Christ doesn't guarantee a life without problems. You can't follow Jesus unless you give up your right to have your own way. When the Good Fridays come along, you've got to be more than a Palm Sunday Christian.

Remember those earlier days after you had received the light, when you stood your ground in a great contest in the face of suffering. Sometimes you were publicly exposed to insult and persecution; at other times you stood side by side with those who were so treated. You sympathized with those in prison and joyfully accepted the confiscation of your property, because you knew that you yourselves had better and lasting possessions. So do not throw away your confidence; it will be richly rewarded. You need to persevere so that when you have done the will of God, you will receive what he has promised. Hebrews 10:32–36

Imagine your history teacher saying, "Napoleon was a tall blond football player who took vacations on an island in the Mediterranean." History is the study of *factual* information about the past, not a field day for imagination. History is based on the assumption that people tell the truth about others, unless they have a reason to lie or are mentally incompetent.

For a long time people searched for a purely human Jesus. But a purely human Jesus never existed. Even ancient historical sources present a *supernatural* Jesus. For example, the Roman historian Tacitus (AD 55–120) tells us of Jesus' crucifixion; the Jewish Talmud explains that He died "in the evening of Passover"; and Josephus, a Jewish historian of the first century, wrote, "Jesus, a wise man, if it be lawful to call him a man, was a doer of wonderful works—a teacher of such men as receive the truth with pleasure. . . . He was [the] Christ; and when Pilate, at the suggestion of the principal men amongst us, had condemned him to the cross, those who loved him at the first did not forsake him, for he appeared to them alive again the third day. . . .' "

Tertullian, a church leader who lived from about AD 155–200, wrote in his defense of Christianity, "Tiberius [emperor under whom Jesus was crucified] . . . having himself received intelligence from Palestine of events which had clearly shown the truth of Christ's divinity, brought the matter before the senate, with his own decision in favor of Christ." Tertullian would never have mentioned this without having reliable information; the Romans kept good records, and the enemies of Christianity were bound to consult them.

Do you sometimes take out a kit and construct your own non-supernatural Jesus? One who can't help you trust people again? Or who can't show you His will for next year? Do you live as though a Jesus who has all power doesn't exist?

Jesus Christ is the same yesterday and today and forever. Hebrews 13:8

And this water . . . saves you also—not the removal of dirt from the body but the pledge of a good conscience toward God. It saves you by the resurrection of Jesus Christ, who has gone into heaven and is at God's right hand—with angels, authorities and powers in submission to him. 1 Peter 3:21–22

All quotations from Richard Wolff, *The Son of Man: Is Jesus Christ Unique?* (Lincoln, NE: Good News Broadcasting Association, 1960).

Day 156

Was Jesus Merely Out of His Mind?

The evening news reports on a man who attracted great crowds. He gave a speech in which he had said such things as "Before Abraham was, I am"; "Because I tell the truth, you do not believe me. Which of you convicts me of sin!" and "If God were your Father, you would love me, for I proceeded and came forth from God; I came not of my own accord, but he sent me. You are of your father the devil."

Your first thought might be that this guy belongs in a psych ward. And if you found out that in his next speech he stated, "He who loves his father or mother more than me is not worthy of me; and he who loves his son or daughter more than me is not worthy of me," you would be more convinced that the man was nuts.

Yet Jesus really said *all* those things. And He was misunderstood. His family, for instance, was worried about His spending too much time with the crowds and not getting His rest. But Jesus displayed none of the indecision and desire to escape reality we usually see in the mentally ill. The poise Jesus showed under the pressure of trial and crucifixion is remarkable. He was never frustrated, never in a hurry, and never too concerned about His own problems to help others. His sleeping through a dreadful storm proves that He was not subject to insomnia. His teachings show balance, profound insight, and beauty that are unmatched.

If Jesus is God—and all evidence proves that He is—He has a right to demand all your love and allegiance. Follow Him where He takes you.

"Come, follow me," Jesus said, "and I will make you fishers of men." At once they left their nets and followed him. When he had gone a little farther, he saw James son of Zebedee and his brother John in a boat, preparing their nets. Without delay he called them, and they left their father Zebedee in the boat with the hired men and followed him. Mark 1:17–20

When they had finished eating, Jesus said to Simon Peter, "Simon son of John, do you truly love me more than these?" "Yes, Lord," he said, "you know that I love you." Jesus said, "Feed my lambs." John 21:15

Day 157

Miracles or Hocus-Pocus?

The Gospel writers devoted a lot of space to the miracles of Jesus. They were willing to give their lives for the messages they preached about Jesus, and part of that message was the miracles. They include details such as names of people and places. Testimonies outside the Scriptures verify Jesus' miracles. Even Celsus, an anti-Christian philosopher who lived in the second century, mentions them. Writing a biography of Jesus without mentioning miracles is like composing a life of Napoleon without referring to a single battle.

But Jesus' life was even more significant than His miracles. The Bible teaches us that the devil can also perform miracles. The Pharisees knew this and accused Jesus of using Satan's power. But Jesus said:

Don't you believe that I am in the Father, and that the Father is in me? The words I say to you are not just my own. Rather, it is the Father, living in me, who is doing his work. John 14:10

Above all, the miracles of Jesus taught spiritual truths. When he fed the five thousand with real bread and real fish, Jesus was saying, "I am the bread of life," the one who can satisfy the hunger in each human heart. When He healed the blind man, He was showing himself as the "Light of the World" who could also open the eyes of the spiritually blind.

Jesus has not changed. He still works miracles with a spiritual purpose in mind. Jesus' *life* was more important than His miracles. And the quality of the life that you lead is more important than the miracles you pray for.

If I have the gift of prophecy and can fathom all mysteries and all knowledge, and if I have a faith that can move mountains, but have not love, I am nothing. 1 Corinthians 13:2

I tell you the truth, anyone who has faith in me will do what I have been doing. He will do even greater things than these, because I am going to the Father. John 14:12

Day 158
Three Days and Three Nights Is Not a Six-Man Rock Band

As a child, not understanding the victory of the cross, I thought Good Friday should be called Bad Friday. As a teenager without much knowledge of Hebrew culture, I wondered how Jesus could have been crucified on Friday, raised on Sunday, and still have spent three days in the tomb.

When asking Pilate for a guard for the tomb, the Pharisees said:

We remember that while he was still alive that deceiver said, "After three days I will rise again." Matthew 27:63

There are two explanations. The first points out that Hebrews of Jesus' time counted parts of days as full days. Because most scholars accept this interpretation of the facts, we still celebrate on Good Friday.

Another explanation suggests that Jesus ate the Last Supper on the Hebrews' Wednesday because their days started at sundown, and that this meal may have been the Passover supper. John 19:14 tells us that Jesus was crucified on the day of Preparation of the Passover, about the sixth hour (noon). He died about 3:00 p.m. (the ninth hour), just as the Passover lambs were being killed, and He was buried before sundown on the Day of Preparation, before the Passover was eaten (John 19:42; Matthew 27:59–60). This could be Wednesday evening of our week, which would mean He spent Thursday, Friday, and Saturday in the tomb. Jesus could have risen from the dead any time after the sun went down on Saturday night because the "first day of the week" began at sundown on our Saturday. Matthew 28:6 only tells us that Sunday morning the angel rolled the stone away and said, "He is not here; for he has risen."

Although it is good to know logical explanations for the apparent contradiction of Good Friday, it is more important to have a time to remember the Savior who made history by His willingness to die for us.

Going a little farther, he fell with his face to the ground and prayed, "My Father, if it is possible, may this cup be taken from me. Yet not as I will, but as you will." Matthew 26:39

Day 159

The Cross and the Crown

King Edward VIII of England fell in love with a woman who was not of royal blood and was unfit to be the Queen of England. He voluntarily gave up his wealth and the throne to marry the woman he loved. Once in exile, he was no less intelligent, no less of royal blood, and no less capable of ruling a country than before. But he had voluntarily limited himself.

In order to save us, Jesus did far more. In John 17, Jesus talks to God about "the glory you have given me because you loved me before the creation of the world" (John 17:24). Jesus gave up everything to be born into this world.

> *Who, being in very nature God, did not consider equality with God something to be grasped, but made himself nothing, taking the very nature of a servant, being made in human likeness. And being found in appearance as a man, he humbled himself and became obedient to death—even death on a cross!* Philippians 2:6–8

He who created everything took the likeness of a creature. He who gave the law became subject to its demands. He who could have called armies of angels endured insults from the Pharisees and misunderstanding from His friends. And then, He, the Author of Life, allowed himself to be painfully executed as a criminal. Jesus sacrificed everything.

During His time on earth, Jesus could truthfully say, "The Father is greater than I"—in position, not in essence. But God raised Him from the dead and exalted Him:

> *Therefore God exalted him to the highest place and gave him the name that is above every name, that at the name of Jesus every knee should bow, in heaven and on earth and under the earth, and every tongue confess that Jesus Christ is Lord, to the glory of God the Father.* Philippians 2:9–11

Jesus gave up all His rights in order to do God's will. He willingly exchanged His crown for a cross so that we could be with God in heaven; then God gave the crown back to Him. All the world will bow to Jesus.

Can you imagine a job more boring than spending a night guarding a corpse in a cemetery? Well, it didn't turn out that way for some men of the first century. The temple leaders who engineered Jesus' crucifixion remembered that He had predicted His own resurrection. They asked Pilate for guards to ensure that the disciples would not steal the body and proclaim to the world that Jesus had risen from the dead.

Even so, by Sunday morning the tomb was empty. Matthew tells us why "graveyard shift" guard duty was so exciting:

> There was a violent earthquake, for an angel of the Lord came down from heaven and, going to the tomb, rolled back the stone and sat on it. His appearance was like lightning, and his clothes were white as snow. The guards were so afraid of him that they shook and became like dead men. Matthew 28:2–4

The first invented explanation for the empty tomb proves that the enemies of Jesus were hard up for excuses.

> When the chief priests had met with the elders and devised a plan, they gave the soldiers a large sum of money, telling them, "You are to say, 'His disciples came during the night and stole him away while we were asleep.' If this report gets to the governor, we will satisfy him and keep you out of trouble." Matthew 28:12–14

However, it's rather strange that they could verify what happened while they were sleeping!

The empty tomb was bound to change history, regardless of those who disbelieved. It offers a message of hope to the world. Jesus said it in a nutshell: "Because I live, you also will live" (John 14:19).

> For my Father's will is that everyone who looks to the Son and believes in him shall have eternal life, and I will raise him up at the last day. John 6:40

> Whoever believes in the Son has eternal life, but whoever rejects the Son will not see life, for God's wrath remains on him. John 3:36

When reading the accounts of the resurrection in the Gospels, it's easy to get the idea that the tomb was a bit like Grand Central Station. Mourning women coming and going, frightened guards, angels, Peter and John, and who knows who else made their appearances. Wouldn't *you* run to see the tomb of a good friend who had reportedly risen from the dead?

Jesus appeared first to Mary Magdalene. John tells us that as Mary sat by the door of the tomb weeping, two angels asked her why she was crying. When Jesus asked her the same question, she thought He was a caretaker. She answered that someone had taken Jesus' body. When He called her by name, she recognized His voice and went to tell the other disciples that she had seen Him.

The authors of the Gospels carefully explain that the women came to anoint the body of Jesus, so it was the women who first learned of the resurrection. They even give the names of these women with no hint that they were anything but reliable, sound-minded, and honest. Only the men of *later* centuries have tried to discredit these women.

There are those who say that the weeping, distraught women went to the *wrong* tomb, but consider some of the facts. First of all, the women knew where the tomb was because Mark says, "Mary Magdalene and Mary the mother of Joses saw where he was laid" (Mark 15:47).

Secondly, the wrong-tomb theorists claim Peter and John *also* went to the wrong tomb, and that Joseph of Arimathea, owner of the tomb, never bothered to straighten things out.

God entrusted two of His most important messages to women. It was a woman who first received word that Jesus was to be born, and it was women who first heard the glorious news of the resurrection. The Bible elevates the position of women.

> *You are all sons of God through faith in Christ Jesus, for all of you who were baptized into Christ have clothed yourselves with Christ. There is neither Jew nor Greek, slave nor free, male nor female, for you are all one in Christ Jesus.*
> Galatians 3:26–28

Day 162
Do You Recognize Jesus?

Neither Mary Magdalene nor the disciples on the road to Emmaus recognized Jesus immediately. But is this reason to doubt that Jesus rose from the dead? One theory states that another man was asked to say that he was the risen Jesus. Others say that the disciples wanted Jesus alive so badly that they imagined another man was Jesus.

Mary Magdalene, whose eyes were blinded by tears, could easily not have recognized Jesus at first. And Luke says about the Emmaus incident, "Jesus himself came up and walked along with them; but they were kept from recognizing him" (Luke 24:15–16).

In other resurrection appearances people had no trouble recognizing Jesus. For instance, when Jesus appeared to the disciples, while they were hiding behind closed doors, He showed them His hands and feet, and they immediately knew who He was. Even Thomas recognized Jesus.

Are there times when you also fail to recognize Jesus? Do you miss Him because you're too busy to listen to the still, small voice that is saying, "Why are you doing all the things you're doing? Stop everything until you get your priorities straight and put *me* first"? Or are you too wrapped up in your youth group activities to show kindness to a sick neighbor or that unpopular girl in your English class? Instead you rush on, not seeing the hurt look in Jesus' eyes. Or do you ignore an opportunity to give to the poor because you "need" those new jeans and you don't hear Jesus saying, "It is more blessed to give than to receive"? Jesus is there. You just don't recognize Him.

Then he will say to those on his left, "Depart from me, you who are cursed, into the eternal fire prepared for the devil and his angels. For I was hungry and you gave me nothing to eat, I was thirsty and you gave me nothing to drink, I was a stranger and you did not invite me in, I needed clothes and you did not clothe me, I was sick and in prison and you did not look after me." They also will answer, "Lord, when did we see you hungry or thirsty or a stranger or needing clothes or sick or in prison, and did not help you?" He will reply, "I tell you the truth, whatever you did not do for one of the least of these, you did not do for me." Matthew 25:41–45

Day 163

Pink Elephants and a Picnic Breakfast

Jesus' disciples saw Him alive many times after His resurrection. The people who don't want to believe it have a story that goes like this: "Sure, they saw Him. People have also seen pink elephants and have had visions of Egyptian pharaohs."

The disciples, however, were not having hallucinations. Neither were the burly fishermen nor doubting Thomas. They were startled and frightened when they saw Jesus standing among them (Luke 24:36–37).

Paul says in 1 Corinthians 15:5–7:

> *He appeared to Peter, and then to the Twelve. After that, he appeared to more than five hundred of the brothers at the same time, most of whom are still living, though some have fallen asleep. Then he appeared to James, then to all the apostles.*

The breakfast by the Sea of Galilee was the worst possible environment for a hallucination. After tugging away at a net so full of fish that the seven of them were unable to pull it in, Peter jumped into the water to swim ashore. The men all ate breakfast with Jesus that morning, and then Jesus talked with Peter about his future.

How real is Jesus to you? Is He just someone you imagine at times in a daydream? Or do you talk over every detail of your life with Him, let Him help you with your homework, invite Him to go on dates with you, and let Him tell you what to do with your life?

> *The third time he said to him, "Simon son of John, do you love me?" Peter was hurt because Jesus asked him the third time, "Do you love me?" He said, "Lord, you know all things; you know that I love you." Jesus said, "Feed my sheep. I tell you the truth, when you were younger you dressed yourself and went where you wanted; but when you are old you will stretch out your hands, and someone else will dress you and lead you where you do not want to go." Jesus said this to indicate the kind of death by which Peter would glorify God. Then he said to him, "Follow me!" John 21:17–19*

Can you imagine eating tuna sandwiches for Christmas dinner or having our Congress adopt a flag that's orange and purple? Would you object to having school begin at 6:00 a.m. or having the boys' basketball team wear kilts? People just don't change familiar ways unless they have a good reason for doing so.

Now, the Jewish people had a very strong tradition supported by one of the Ten Commandments: "Remember the Sabbath day by keeping it holy" (Exodus 20:8). They observed a special day of rest and worship each Saturday because when God created the world, He rested on the seventh day.

Only something drastic would cause Jewish people to change their day of worship. But the most important event of history, the Resurrection, occurred on the first day of the week. Jesus' death and resurrection is so important that everything changes. The person who accepts Jesus is transformed from the inside out. The Jews observed the Sabbath because the law required it. But Christians made Sunday their Sabbath because they wanted to celebrate their resurrection life.

In 1 Corinthians 16:2 and Acts 20:7, we find Christians meeting on the first day of the week. In Colossians 2:16–17, Paul writes that no one should pass judgment on another regarding "a Sabbath." Ignatius, the Bishop of Antioch, wrote in AD 110 that Christians no longer observed the Sabbath but the "Lord's Day" [Sunday], remembering that "our life also arose through Him."

The fact that Christians worship on Sunday is one of the great historical proofs that Jesus rose from the dead. The twelve apostles—all Jewish—wouldn't have started having services on Sunday just for the fun of it. And we won't begin Thursday schools or Tuesday morning worship services, because nothing as great as the resurrection of Jesus will ever again take place in history.

Our Sunday worship should be more than a remembrance of the resurrection. It should remind us that the Jesus who walked on the water, healed the blind, and conquered death is capable of repeat performances.

Day 165

No Zits in Heaven

Before Jesus died, He committed His spirit to God, then took His last breath. Ecclesiasters 12:7 teaches that death is a separation of the body from the spirit: "And the dust returns to the ground it came from, and the spirit returns to God who gave it."

Romans 8:11 teaches us that God raised Jesus in *physical* form *through* the Holy Spirit:

> And if the Spirit of him who raised Jesus from the dead is living in you, he who raised Christ from the dead will also give life to your mortal bodies through his Spirit, who lives in you.

That the risen Jesus had a physical body is clearly demonstrated. When Jesus appeared to the disciples, they "clasped his feet" (Matthew 28:9). Jesus told Thomas to put his hand into His side (John 20:27).

The Bible teaches that because Jesus rose from the dead, our mortal bodies will also be resurrected. Jesus promised:

> Do not be amazed at this, for a time is coming when all who are in their graves will hear his voice and come out—those who have done good will rise to live, and those who have done evil will rise to be condemned. John 5:28–29

If you have given your life completely to Jesus, you'll be very interested in this resurrection life. Paul writes,

> But our citizenship is in heaven. And we eagerly await a Savior from there, the Lord Jesus Christ, who, by the power that enables him to bring everything under his control, will transform our lowly bodies so that they will be like his glorious body. Philippians 3:20–21

Some day you'll have a glorious body just like Jesus. There won't be any zits in heaven!

Day 166

Now Offering Eternal Life Membership!

Numb and tearless, Kay took one last look at the open grave and the casket that contained the body of her mother. It was as if a hidden movie projector that had no Off button insisted on replaying the tragic events of the past four days: the note from the school office for her to leave class immediately; the tears in her aunt's eyes as she told Kay that her mother had been in a serious car accident; the hours in the intensive care waiting room; the endless parade of people offering their sympathy. No longer could she get her mother's opinion on what clothes to buy, and never again would she eat the homemade cinnamon rolls her mother made on Saturday mornings. She felt engulfed in loneliness

Even if you haven't been separated from anyone by death, you may sometimes identify with Kay. Maybe you're the "foreigner in the family." Perhaps you experience that "fifth-wheel" feeling wherever you go. Do you ever wonder where you can feel accepted?

The union of your parents put your life within your mother and put life from your parents in you. Because your brothers and sisters were formed the same way, you have a special unity with them—you're all part of a family. It's the same way spiritually. Jesus lives in your heart, but in an equally unexplainable way, you are in Jesus, Jesus is in the Father, and those who have experienced the miracle of this new birth are united in Christ. Jesus explained to His disciples:

> Before long, the world will not see me anymore, but you will see me. Because I live, you also will live. On that day you will realize that I am in my Father, and you are in me, and I am in you. John 14:19–20

Because Christians don't all look alike or think alike or have the same last name or get together all at once for a family reunion, we sometimes forget about our brothers and sisters in Christ. When misunderstandings and differences of opinion seem to divide us, we must remember that God has offered us eternal life membership in His family—and you can't just switch families whenever you wish. You belong to God. That's where you fit; that's where you are accepted. And nothing can separate you from Him.

Day 167

About That F on the Faith Exam

ABRAHAM

Have you ever wished the teacher would give you one big exam, and after you'd passed that one, you'd never have to take another test again? Good learning requires constant review to prevent forgetting, and tests motivate you to review. You'd never know if you'd mastered the new material unless you've been tested. If you want to follow God, you might as well get used to the idea of tests, because God uses them frequently.

The life of Abraham shows how—and how not—to take God's tests. Abraham's test, in this case, was a famine. A food shortage is a pretty serious problem, but Abraham's experience should have kept him from panic. Abraham had enjoyed God's protection and guidance. The famine was only a review test for Abraham. But he failed.

Abram went down to Egypt to live there for a while because the famine was severe. As he was about to enter Egypt, he said to his wife Sarai, "I know what a beautiful woman you are. When the Egyptians see you, they will say, 'This is his wife.' Then they will kill me but will let you live. Say you are my sister, so that I will be treated well for your sake and my life will be spared because of you." Genesis 12:10–13

Abraham failed because he tried to solve the problem with his own plan—he moved to Egypt. What a bad trip! First he gave up the opportunity to learn to trust God more. Then he sinned to protect himself by indicating that Sarah was his sister and not his wife. Sarah was very beautiful; the king could murder anybody he wished. Thus, by making a beautiful woman a widow, he could take her into his harem. Abraham fell not only into fear and insecurity, but also into selfishness, since he cared more about his own safety than his wife's welfare.

Failing a test, however, is not nearly as important as your attitude about failing. Abraham failed, but he learned from his mistakes. He admitted he was wrong, faced humiliation, and returned to face the famine and trust God. Are you willing to be humble, admit you are wrong, and go back and find out how to do the math problems (or the faith problems) correctly? Will you let God teach you from your failures?

Day 168

Go-for-It Faith

ABRAHAM

You've just passed your driver's test and can't wait to prove your skill as a licensed driver. Your grandmother congratulates you.

"I'm very proud of you. I know you'll be a safe and careful driver. I do have an appointment with the doctor this afternoon, but—uh—I couldn't ask you to do that. It'll be during the worst rush-hour traffic of the day. I'll call a cab." Crushed, you realize your grandmother has no faith in your driving ability—in spite of her encouraging comments. Only put-your-money-where-your-mouth-is faith can be considered genuine.

Faith requires initiative, but it doesn't independently venture out without hearing from God. That is presumption. Because of this danger, the "go-for-it" element of faith is often overlooked.

The Lord said to Abram after Lot had parted from him, "Lift up your eyes from where you are and look north and south, east and west. All the land that you see I will give to you and your offspring forever. . . . Go, walk through the length and breadth of the land, for I am giving it to you." Genesis 13:14–15, 17

Abraham had to "go for it." God gave him the promise of the land, but He asked him to walk through the land, to claim it by a specific act of obedience. You can't please God by doing things your own way. Give up your own plans and seek God's. Keep Scripture in your mind to help you remember God's promises. Then you're ready to act.

You and your mother have fought a hundred times about how often you are to stay home and take care of your younger brother and sister. The matter sits like a bomb ready to explode. Admit to God that you're helpless, and in faith ask Him for the solution. Then face God's Word— "Children, obey your parents" (Ephesians 6:1)—and realize disobeying your mother is never God's will. Give up your own desires and be willing to baby-sit if that's God's plan. Find a Bible verse, a promise to claim (for example, "Blessed are the peacemakers, for they will be called sons of God"). Then go to your mother and discuss the baby-sitting situation. That's "go-for-it" faith. You have no need to fear; God rewards those who obey Him.

Day 169

The Faith-Obedience Plan

ABRAHAM

Some people forget that their relationship with God and their motives for obeying Him are as important as the obedience itself. They obey God only because they are afraid of what will happen if they don't obey. Obviously, these people don't consider God their intimate friend. Obedience that comes from love and faith is the only kind that satisfies. Obedience doesn't have to be a drag. It wasn't for Abraham.

> So Abram said to Lot, "Let's not have any quarreling between you and me, or between your herdsmen and mine, for we are brothers. Is not the whole land before you? Let's part company. If you go to the left, I'll go to the right; if you go to the right, I'll go to the left." . . . The king of Sodom said to Abram, "Give me the people and keep the goods for yourself." But Abram said to the king of Sodom, "I have raised my hand to the Lord, God Most High, Creator of heaven and earth, and have taken an oath that I will accept nothing belonging to you, not even a thread or the thong of a sandal, so that you will never be able to say, 'I made Abram rich.'" Genesis 13:8–9; 14:21–23

Abraham's generosity came from obeying God in faith. He knew that God would take good care of him, even if Lot received first choice of the land. And he knew better than to place his confidence in the generosity of people like the king of Sodom who wanted to give him gifts. Abraham knew that accepting presents from that powerful king would obligate him to the king. Abraham wanted to be obligated only to God.

Abraham's view of material possessions clearly shows an obedience based on faith. First, Abraham left a big, beautiful house in Ur. Second, he lived in a tent. A tent won't hold much, so a person can't store up anything for the future. Abraham believed that the God who owned the whole world had plenty of riches to supply his needs.

Put God first and trust Him for your worn-out wardrobe, your empty wallet, or your school tuition. He will take care of you.

Day 170

Is Your God As Good As His Word?

ABRAHAM

Someone once said, "Hope says, 'God will do it,' but faith says, 'God has already done it.'" You probably have friends you trust implicitly, but do you include God in that category? What God has said is as good as done. Although you realize the logic of trusting an all-powerful, all-wise, all-loving God to carry out His promises, you probably succumb to the human tendency to figure things out for God and give Him some help. Even Abraham, a great man of faith, was guilty of this.

Abraham and his wife were old when God promised them a son. Only a miracle could make this happen. As years passed and the promise remained unfulfilled, Abraham and Sarah began to wonder. They didn't have enough faith to believe in the promise from God. When Abraham was eighty-six and Sarah seventy-six, Sarah finally advised Abraham to have a son by her maid, Hagar. This was the logical, culturally acceptable way to solve the problem.

> Now Sarai, Abram's wife, had borne him no children. But she had an Egyptian maidservant named Hagar; so she said to Abram, "The Lord has kept me from having children. Go, sleep with my maidservant; perhaps I can build a family through her." Abram agreed to what Sarai said. . . . So Hagar bore Abram a son, and Abram gave the name Ishmael to the son she had borne.
> Genesis 16:1–2, 15

What a disaster! Isaac and Ishmael became enemies, and to this day, the sons of Ishmael (Arabs) are still fighting the sons of Isaac (Jews). But God didn't give up on Abraham and Sarah. He forgave them, built up their faith, and sent them a son when Abraham was one hundred and Sarah was ninety—an even greater miracle than it would have been before.

Now compare yourself with Abraham and Sarah. Do you believe God can help you pass final exams? Do you trust Him to make you healthy? Of course you must cooperate with God, but to "help" Him with schemes of your own is to distrust Him. Whatever He has promised isn't "as good as done"; it's *already done*. Your God is as good as His word.

Day 171

An Arranged Marriage—God's Way

ISAAC

You probably have imagined it all: Someday you'll meet him or her—attractive, polite, charming, intelligent. You'll look into this person's eyes and feel special. You'll fall in love, and you'll know *this* is the one for you! But maybe you've forgotten the most important ingredient in your idea of a "marriage made in heaven"—God's will and plan for your life.

Isaac trusted God to choose a wife for him. According to the custom of that time, parents arranged a marriage, usually without the consent of the children they'd matched up. Abraham wanted to make sure his son didn't marry a local idol-worshiper, so he sent his servant to Abraham's relatives to find the woman God had chosen for Isaac. God arranged it beautifully, and everyone recognized God's guidance.

> *Laban and Bethuel answered, "This is from the Lord; we can say nothing to you one way or the other. Here is Rebekah; take her and go, and let her become the wife of your master's son, as the Lord has directed." . . . So they called Rebekah and asked her, "Will you go with this man?" "I will go," she said. . . . Isaac brought her into the tent of his mother Sarah, and he married Rebekah. So she became his wife, and he loved her; and Isaac was comforted after his mother's death.* Genesis 24:50–51, 58, 67

God's choice was the best. God chose the right woman for Isaac. Isaac was quiet and easygoing, but Rebekah had spunk—any girl who offered to water ten camels must have been hardworking and decisive! No one can arrange a marriage better than God can.

Ask the Holy Spirit to show you how the principle of this story applies to dating and marriage in your life. Ask God whom to date. Ask God to sort out your emotions and to give you the dates that would be best for you.

Don't make a list of qualifications and start hunting. Seek God's will, remembering He is all-powerful. Isaac was forty years old and living in a country without one suitable marriage partner! But that posed no problem for God. Even if you, like Isaac, live in a Christianless wilderness, God can find for you the right friends and the right person to date—if you're willing to wait in faith and cooperate with Him.

A famine is no fun. When lack of rainfall caused a crop failure and a shortage of grass for his animals, Isaac had to make a decision. Egypt had plenty of grain, so he considered going there. God, however, had promised Isaac's father, Abraham, that Canaan was the land for him and his descendants. If Isaac moved to Egypt, he would leave this Promised Land. While Isaac was trying to decide what to do, God appeared and told him to avoid Egypt, even though it meant giving up the security of knowing where his food would come from.

Now there was a famine in the land—besides the earlier famine of Abraham's time—and Isaac went to Abimelech king of the Philistines in Gerar. The Lord appeared to Isaac and said, "Do not go down to Egypt; live in the land where I tell you to live. Stay in this land for a while, and I will be with you and will bless you. For to you and your descendants I will give all these lands and will confirm the oath I swore to your father Abraham." Genesis 26:1–3

You may wish life could be that simple for you—if only you could see an angel or hear a thundering voice from heaven or read flashing neon signs in the sky, you'd obey God perfectly.

One command God has made clear is not to "go to Egypt"—in other words, not to pursue the first idea that pops into your head. Find out what God wants you to do.

Look to the Lord and his strength; seek his face always. 1 Chronicles 16:11

You don't need an angel or a thundering voice or neon lights to tell you not to go to Egypt. You already have God's clear command. You can know what to do and how to live because you have the Holy Spirit to lead you into the truth of God's Word. And that is enough.

I hold fast to your statutes, O Lord; do not let me be put to shame. I run in the path of your commands, for you have set my heart free. Teach me, O Lord, to follow your decrees; then I will keep them to the end. Psalm 119:31–33

Day 173

New Software for Old Habits

ISAAC

Isaac's easygoing nature made it easy for him not to rebel against his parents or God. But such a temperament was also a pitfall. When obeying God required pioneering a new path and standing against pressure, Isaac didn't have the "right stuff"; in the land of the Philistines, he followed his father's example, right into trouble.

> *So Isaac stayed in Gerar. When the men of that place asked him about his wife, he said, "She is my sister," because he was afraid to say, "She is my wife." He thought, "The men of this place might kill me on account of Rebekah, because she is beautiful." When Isaac had been there a long time, Abimelech king of the Philistines looked down from a window and saw Isaac caressing his wife Rebekah. So Abimelech summoned Isaac and said, "She is really your wife! Why did you say, 'She is my sister'?" Isaac answered him, "Because I thought I might lose my life on account of her." Then Abimelech said, "What is this you have done to us? One of the men might well have slept with your wife, and you would have brought guilt upon us." Genesis 26:6–10*

Isaac knew it was wrong to say his wife was his sister, but he jumped at the only solution he knew.

You don't have to repeat your parents' mistakes. To begin solving problems Jesus-style, retrain yourself to think as the new creation in Christ that the Bible says you are (2 Corinthians 5:17). Reprogram your mind as you would a computer. Instead of reacting according to the computer memory from previous experiences, learn to pray, "Jesus, how would you solve this problem?"

God's Word is the secret of the reprogramming process. It renews your mind and gives general guidelines for problem-solving: "Overcome evil with good," "serve one another in love," "share with God's people who are in need," and so on. As you meditate on God's Word, it will fill your "software" with God's guidelines for action, and God's methods will become your natural reactions.

Learn from Isaac. Decide not to repeat his mistake. Let God free you from the tendency to automatically react according to familiar patterns. Give God a chance to reprogram your mind.

Do teachers' pets make you feel inferior? Maybe your parents give your little brother more attention. Favoritism also occurs at work and even at church, when superiors make special allowances for the people they like best.

Playing favorites is one of the easiest traps to fall into. Do you go through the yearbook and decide who's personality plus, personality minus, and too weird to categorize?

The boys grew up, and Esau became a skillful hunter, a man of the open country, while Jacob was a quiet man, staying among the tents. Isaac, who had a taste for wild game, loved Esau, but Rebekah loved Jacob. Genesis 25:27–28

Isaac was guilty of the sin of favoritism; he loved Esau more than Jacob. He was proud of this brave, athletic hunter, and he enjoyed the wild game Esau prepared for him to eat. Isaac made his choice only on personal preference. Jacob, however, was quiet, and he enjoyed staying around the tents—nothing wrong with that. But Isaac admired an expert hunter, so he loved the son who fulfilled *his* expectations.

Isaac failed to deal with his sin, and thus caused great trouble in his family. Jacob followed the example of his father, and out of his twelve sons, Jacob favored Joseph. This caused Joseph's brothers to hate him and sell him into slavery.

If you don't deal with your tendency to choose one person over another, and thus withhold your friendship from people you don't appreciate, you, like Isaac, will cause friction and heartache. Examine yourself before God. Have you been trying hard to impress someone while ignoring other people? God doesn't put people into categories. God is in the business of changing people, and He wants to use your love and acceptance to help someone become likable and friendly.

If you really keep the royal law found in Scripture, "Love your neighbor as yourself," you are doing right. But if you show favoritism, you sin and are convicted by the law as lawbreakers. James 2:8–9

Day 175

The Minus That Makes a Real Plus

JOSEPH

How do you feel when the teacher picks on you, your boss gives you the worst jobs, and your little brother gets away with everything?

After surviving his father's favoritism, his brothers' hatred, and finally slavery, Joseph was unjustly imprisoned. He certainly had reason to be bitter. But he wasn't.

When his master heard the story his wife told him, saying, "This is how your slave treated me," he burned with anger. Joseph's master took him and put him in prison, the place where the king's prisoners were confined. But while Joseph was there in the prison, the Lord was with him; he showed him kindness and granted him favor in the eyes of the prison warden. So the warden put Joseph in charge of all those held in the prison, and he was made responsible for all that was done there. The warden paid no attention to anything under Joseph's care, because the Lord was with Joseph and gave him success in whatever he did. Genesis 39:19–23

Later, when Joseph—as prime minister—had authority even to kill his brothers, he never tried to repay their evil deeds. Although he tested them to see if their characters had changed, he was never bitter. Instead, he told them, "You intended to harm me, but God intended it for good to accomplish what is now being done, the saving of many lives" (Genesis 50:20).

With such an outlook, you also can overcome bitterness. React with love when the teacher unfairly accuses you. Humility and helpfulness will touch the heart of your boss, who gives you the hard jobs because you don't complain. And maybe your little brother needs a role model.

Joseph trusted God to give him an attitude of forgiveness. He decided not to brood over the wrongs done to him and attacked the job at hand. He had no time left to be bitter.

Someone has said hardships either make you bitter or better. Let Joseph be your example for the "better." Don't let injustice, tragedy, or indifference sour you. A life minus bitterness is a real plus.

See to it that no one misses the grace of God and that no bitter root grows up to cause trouble and defile many. Hebrews 12:15

How Far Is It From Under the Pile to on Top of the World?

JOSEPH

Do you feel like a permanent resident of "under the pile"? Just when you wish you could take things a bit at a time, everything comes at once. Sixth-hour biology gets more boring by the day. Your ex-boyfriend's new fling just moved into the locker on your left. Your father fears he'll be losing his job. When life overwhelms you, you're under the pile.

How can you handle overwhelming problems that seem as if they'll never go away? Take a good look at Joseph.

So the chief cupbearer told Joseph his dream. . . . "This is what it means," Joseph said to him. . . . "Within three days Pharaoh will lift up your head and restore you to your position. . . . But when all goes well with you, remember me and show me kindness; mention me to Pharaoh and get me out of this prison." . . . The chief cupbearer, however, did not remember Joseph; he forgot him. Genesis 40:9, 12–14, 23

For Joseph, both slavery and imprisonment appeared hopelessly permanent. First came the loss of freedom and never-ending work. Then chains and dungeon gloom darkened the picture.

Faith made Joseph successful, even in prison, enabling him to bring cheer to others. You need faith that believes God will never allow you to experience trials greater than He will give strength to handle. Never let the devil convince you that God doesn't care.

Displaying faithfulness in all you do not only is your responsibility to God and others, but it's good for you. Because Joseph faithfully performed his tasks in prison, he unknowingly prepared for a glorious future.

Concentrating on doing your best for God in each task will give you little time to nurse your broken heart. And it will give God a chance to reveal your future "on top of the world." You can get there, regardless of your circumstances, if you follow the formula of faith plus faithfulness.

Dear friends, do not be surprised at the painful trial you are suffering, as though something strange were happening to you. But rejoice that you participate in the sufferings of Christ, so that you may be overjoyed when his glory is revealed. 1 Peter 4:12–13

Day 177

Are You a Product of God's Remodeling Factory?

JOSEPH

Do you feel as if you can't do anything right when under pressure? You expect God to help you stop sinning, but you've probably thought He won't do anything to change your personality defects. Not true.

Joseph grew up among shepherds, then endured slavery and imprisonment. Imagine coming from such a background—then being instantly promoted to the palace! Talk about a pressure situation. But Joseph didn't cave in under the pressure. Instead, the pagan king was amazed, and he recognized that Joseph's poise and inner strength had come from God. He was even impressed by the discreetness of Joseph—who had once blurted out all his dreams to anyone within earshot.

So Pharaoh asked them, "Can we find anyone like this man, one in whom is the spirit of God?" Then Pharaoh said to Joseph, "Since God has made all this known to you, there is no one so discerning and wise as you." Genesis 41:38-39

Joseph willingly went through God's remodeling factory. He had sustained pain and suffering, and he trusted God to do His work. Joseph learned the lesson of patient waiting. Slaves and prisoners, of course, have no choice but to wait, so Joseph was in an ideal situation for remodeling—personality remakes take time. And he learned to wait for God's instructions on how to handle his brothers, even though Joseph, as prime minister, had complete authority over people.

Do you often jump from the mold that would reshape your character and improve your personality? Do you forget that people's emotions are delicate and must be handled with God's wisdom, and impatiently fumble each chance God gives you for learning tact and poise? Would you choose to improve your study habits by rubbing Aladdin's lamp rather than by working hard? Would you prefer to receive an injection that will instantly heal your broken heart rather than slowly learn God's lessons?

If you find yourself guilty of these attitudes, it's time for you to start acting like a product, rather than a boss, in God's remodeling factory.

And we know that in all things God works for the good of those who love him, who have been called according to his purpose. Romans 8:28

Then Joseph said to his brothers, "Come close to me." When they had done so, he said, "I am your brother Joseph, the one you sold into Egypt! And now, do not be distressed and do not be angry with yourselves for selling me here, because it was to save lives that God sent me ahead of you. For two years now there has been famine in the land, and for the next five years there will not be plowing and reaping. But God sent me ahead of you to preserve for you a remnant on earth and to save your lives by a great deliverance. So then, it was not you who sent me here, but God." Genesis 45:4–8

When your friend is voted captain of the football team or gets the lead part in the school play, does your friend still have time for you? Or are you lucky to get an appointment with the new star—as long as you plan six months in advance? The temptations that accompany sudden power, prestige, or popularity can ruin a nice person.

Joseph was propelled instantly to the peak of authority and influence, the ultimate rags-to-riches story. Now he had the power to even the score with his brothers. But the same truth that sustained Joseph through slavery and imprisonment kept him from caving in under the temptation to misuse his authority. He knew God had promoted him in order to fulfill His purpose. Joseph realized God had sent him to Egypt and granted his high position to save God's chosen people. So Joseph identified himself with his relatives and invited them to live in Egypt. Christ would come from these people, and His coming would be history's most important event. All of this hinged on Joseph's willingness to let God use his life.

If God gives you popularity and influence, remember that a star's purpose is to *give light*. God makes you popular because He wants to use you for His kingdom, not because you're more intelligent or more talented than others. Determine to use each honor, each position, each talent for God and His kingdom. Don't become a falling star.

No one from the east or the west or from the desert can exalt a man. But it is God who judges: He brings one down, he exalts another. Psalm 75:6–7

Day 179

Are You Listening to a "From-the-Pit" Recording?

MOSES

Moses had to make a drastic choice. Becoming the Pharaoh would require him to identify himself with the pagan Egyptian religion, and it would mean abandoning his people in their slavery. He had to either give up his right to the Egyptian throne with its vast power and wealth or compromise with God.

> By faith Moses, when he had grown up, refused to be known as the son of Pharaoh's daughter. He chose to be mistreated along with the people of God rather than to enjoy the pleasures of sin for a short time. He regarded disgrace for the sake of Christ as of greater value than the treasures of Egypt, because he was looking ahead to his reward. By faith he left Egypt, not fearing the king's anger; he persevered because he saw him who is invisible. Hebrews 11:24–27

Moses chose God's way, changing history forever.

You, like Moses, must make important decisions that affect a lot of people's lives, so you need to establish a standard by which every decision can be made, and you must make every decision in the light of *eternity*. Will you study the Bible more or watch more TV? Will you cheerfully obey your parents or argue and complain? Will you pray for and share Jesus with your non-Christian friends, or follow their ways? Will you give more money to God's work, or spend it on yourself?

As you think about college, are you considering how to better yourself for serving God, or how to get a plush job? As you consider a marriage partner, will you leave the decision to God, or will you look for the person who satisfies your twenty-five-point checklist? A nasty recording inside your head may be telling you it doesn't matter what you choose. But it does. So don't listen to that "From-the-Pit" recording. You are extremely important to God. You're part of the greatest enterprise in the world: spreading God's good news to all people. The world can be different because of your choices. Make decisions that will count for eternity.

> "I tell you the truth," Jesus said to them, "no one who has left home or wife or brothers or parents or children for the sake of the kingdom of God will fail to receive many times as much in this age and, in the age to come, eternal life." Luke 18:29–30

Day 180
It's What's Inside That Counts
MOSES

Moses made the "right" decision—he renounced the Egyptian throne in order to identify with his people. He knew God promised that Abraham's descendants would be freed after four hundred years of slavery, so he meant to assist God in His plan for their deliverance. Yet though his choice was admirable, his attitude was not.

One day, after Moses had grown up, he went out to where his own people were and watched them at their hard labor. He saw an Egyptian beating a Hebrew, one of his own people. Glancing this way and that and seeing no one, he killed the Egyptian and hid him in the sand. The next day he went out and saw two Hebrews fighting. He asked the one in the wrong, "Why are you hitting your fellow Hebrew?" The man said, "Who made you ruler and judge over us? Are you thinking of killing me as you killed the Egyptian?" Then Moses was afraid and thought, "What I did must have become known." When Pharaoh heard of this, he tried to kill Moses, but Moses fled from Pharaoh and went to live in Midian, where he sat down by a well. Exodus 2:11–15*

Moses intended to deliver God's people in his way and in his strength. So when he spotted an Egyptian beating up an Israelite, he simply killed the Egyptian. Consequently, he messed up everything.

The road to a dead end is the attitude that says, "I'll do great things for God. After all, I'm attractive and popular, I get great grades, and I'm a natural leader." If this is your attitude, get off your cloud, because Moses had more going for him than you do, and he had a zero success rate.

Stop depending on your abilities. Wait for God's time rather than rushing into things as Moses did. Receive the guidance of the Holy Spirit.

If you think you've surrendered the outward parts of your life to Christ, you'd better check things out inside. Don't be like the rebellious little boy who, after being told to sit, declared to his mother, "I'm sitting down on the outside, but on the inside I'm still standing up." Learn to obey from the depths of your heart. It's the inside that counts.

Day 181

All You Need Is a Blank Check

MOSES

But the king of Egypt said, "Moses and Aaron, why are you taking the people away from their labor? Get back to your work!" . . . That same day Pharaoh gave this order to the slave drivers and foremen in charge of the people: "You are no longer to supply the people with straw for making bricks; let them go and gather their own straw. But require them to make the same number of bricks as before; don't reduce the quota. They are lazy; that is why they are crying out, 'Let us go and sacrifice to our God.' . . . The Israelite foremen realized they were in trouble when they were told, "You are not to reduce the number of bricks required of you for each day." When they left Pharaoh, they found Moses and Aaron waiting to meet them, and they said, "May the Lord look upon you and judge you! You have made us a stench to Pharaoh and his officials and have put a sword in their hand to kill us." Exodus 5:4, 6–8, 19–21

You're puzzled. You broke up with your non-Christian boyfriend and you haven't had a date in a year. You studied hard for the English test, resisted a perfect chance to cheat, and got a D-. You resolved to always obey your parents because it is God's will, and now your mother gives you all the housework to avoid conflict with your brother. Shouldn't God instantly reward you for following Him?

Moses felt the same way. He had chosen to obey God—risking his life by facing Pharoah, leader of the world's strongest army, and risking his sanity and health by attempting to lead an entire nation across a desolate desert. He had tremendous faith to willingly accept such danger and responsibility. But the whole project appeared to blow up immediately.

Facing rejection from the very people he was trying to help, Moses had to make his most important decision. Would he stick with God when everything was going against him? Or would he give up?

Unlike forty years earlier, Moses didn't run from the crisis. Although there was no human support system, he knew God had sent him. Putting God's will above his own, he decided to trust solely in the Lord.

In revealing himself to Moses as I AM, God was telling him, "I will be to you whatever you need" [not everything you desire at the moment]—like a blank check that can be filled out by faith. God was saying, "I AM your strength. I AM your security. I AM your wisdom. I AM the one who loves you." So Moses staked his life on I AM. And I AM proved to be all Moses needed. God's miracles convinced the Egyptians to give the Israelites their gold—just to get rid of them!

Like Moses, you'll obey God only to discover that everything seemingly is falling apart. Will you trust God or will you turn away? Your God is almighty—He hasn't changed since He spoke to Moses. His name is still I AM: I AM _____ (whatever you need). It's a blank check you can fill in by faith.

Day 182

Why Not Choose the Best?

MOSES

The choices you make show where your priorities lie. Will you fork over a few dollars for your church's missionary in Nigeria, or spend the money on pizza? Will you spend your afternoon visiting a friend in the hospital or playing tennis? Moses has a chariot-load of lessons to teach about priorities.

The next day Moses said to the people, "You have committed a great sin. But now I will go up to the Lord; perhaps I can make atonement for your sin." So Moses went back to the Lord and said, "Oh, what a great sin these people have committed! They have made themselves gods of gold. But now, please forgive their sin—but if not, then blot me out of the book you have written." The Lord replied to Moses, "Whoever has sinned against me I will blot out of my book." Exodus 32:30–33

After God gave the Israelites the Ten Commandments, Moses went to the top of Mount Sinai to talk with God. There he spent the most amazing forty days any man had ever experienced—only to return to the most horrifying sight he could imagine: his people dancing around and worshiping a gold calf. They were rebelling against the God who had performed mind-blowing miracles to bring them out of Egypt!

Moses first must have thought, *Get rid of the whole bunch. I won't put up with such a thankless lot!*

But remembering God's promises, Moses prayed for the people. He knew God had predicted that a great nation would come from Abraham, and from that nation would come the Messiah. So he pleaded with God to let them live.

Spend time with God. Get to know Him and love Him so much that choosing His work, His honor, and His will above your own interests becomes automatic. If you know God like that, you, like Moses, will experience God's glory.

But in your hearts set apart Christ as Lord. Always be prepared to give an answer to everyone who asks you to give the reason for the hope that you have. But do this with gentleness and respect. 1 Peter 3:15

After the death of Moses the servant of the Lord, the Lord said to Joshua son of Nun, Moses' aide: . . . "No one will be able to stand up against you all the days of your life. As I was with Moses, so I will be with you; I will never leave you nor forsake you. Be strong and courageous, because you will lead these people to inherit the land I swore to their forefathers to give them. Be strong and very courageous. Be careful to obey all the law my servant Moses gave you; do not turn from it to the right or to the left, that you may be successful wherever you go. Do not let this Book of the Law depart from your mouth; meditate on it day and night, so that you may be careful to do everything written in it. Then you will be prosperous and successful. Joshua 1:1, 5–8*

Do you feel imprisoned by your circumstances—by tension at home, temperamental friends, hard subjects in school, and a puppy who refuses to be housebroken? Joshua could have felt hemmed in too. He had a high-pressure job trying to fill the shoes of Moses, one of the greatest leaders in history. He had to lead a whole nation of stubborn complainers. Caught between the scorching desert behind him and the heavily fortified cities before him, he had no way out without God. But Joshua took God up on His promise to be there and give success if he followed the Scriptures and the Lord's guidance.

God has promises for you too. But Satan doesn't want you to know about them. You can find God's This Way Out sign for each tough situation by standing on an appropriate Scripture. (If you don't know your Bible very well, ask someone to help you choose the right verse to internalize.)

For example, maybe you're the only committed Christian in your school. Walking down the halls, you try to avoid looking at locker-door graffiti and block out nasty air pollution. You feel desperately lonely and out of place. The things you're taught clash with your biblical values and any idea you offer is met with scorn. It seems that you're the only one who studies instead of joining the organized cheating. You desperately need some help.

Day 183 (CONTINUED)

Under the Circumstances, Over a Barrel, or in Jesus?

JOSHUA

Let's say you pick 2 Chronicles 16:9 as your lifesaver verse: "For the eyes of the Lord range throughout the earth to strengthen those whose hearts are fully committed to him." Write the verse on a card so you can carry it with you and read through it a couple of times at the end of each class. Read it out loud and visualize God constantly watching you, ready to empower you. Meditate on the verse until it's a part of you. Treat is as a fact of life, praying, "God, I receive your strength not to laugh at the dirty joke," "Lord, I'm depending on you to help me befriend the new kid so I can share Jesus' love with him," "God, give me the courage to tell the truth if the principal asks me who stole the teacher's glasses."

As you permit God to strengthen you, it won't just be a matter of survival, but you'll be able to let your light shine in the darkness of your school. History is different because Joshua took God at His Word and lived in the supernatural. God's promises will change your biography too. If you're really in Jesus and His Word is in you, you won't be living under the circumstances, and nothing will put you over a barrel.

Day 184

Crossing River Impossible

JOSHUA

Joshua told the people, "Consecrate yourselves, for tomorrow the Lord will do amazing things among you. . . . As soon as the priests who carry the ark of the Lord—the Lord of all the earth—set foot in the Jordan, its waters flowing downstream will be cut off and stand up in a heap." . . . So the people crossed over opposite Jericho. The priests who carried the ark of the covenant of the Lord stood firm on dry ground in the middle of the Jordan, while all Israel passed by until the whole nation had completed the crossing on dry ground. Joshua 3:5, 13, 16–17

God told the Israelites to cross the Jordan River at flood stage without as much as a rowboat—a seemingly impossible order for a bunch of non-swimmers who had spent their lives in the desert! In addition, they were told to do things that most people would consider crazy. But God cleared the way, and the people crossed the river on dry ground.

Joshua acted on God's promise before there was any evidence that God would come through. He did what God told him to do. Do you believe God can even help you understand physics? Instead of saying, "I'll flunk the final for sure," say in faith, "With God's help I'll pass it." Then you can study in faith instead of frustration.

But what about a person who hurt you? How can you possibly love him? In faith. God commands you to love: "Love each other as I have loved you" (John 15:12), not "Love unless the person has hurt you." So in faith obey this command. Defy your emotions and put your feet into the Jordan by deliberately doing something to show love for that person. Pray for him every day. Be friendly. Then ask God what you can do for that person that would help him. Take conscious steps of faith to forget that hurt.

Next time something seems impossible, remember how the Israelites crossed the Jordan at flood stage. In good weather your River Impossible can seem bad enough, but when thunderstorms of problems soak you and the river starts to overflow, panic comes easily. Don't give in. Instead, as the Israelites looked to the Ark—the symbol of God's presence—keep your eyes on Jesus and act in faith on God's promise to you.

Day 185

Losing the Game But Winning the Championship

JOSHUA

Has something like this ever happened to you? You rededicated your life to Jesus, and the next week you had a great time sharing Him with some friends at school. Then disaster struck. Your mother yelled at you for not cleaning your room, and you lost your cool and lashed back at her. Afterward you felt completely defeated.

The same thing happened to the Israelites. After watching the walls of the strongest city in the country fall down flat, they were defeated by the defenders of the little hick town of Ai. Israel had decided Ai was so weak that only two or three thousand soldiers could easily take it. They forgot that God doesn't use the same strategy for each problem. He did not plan the same kind of defeat for Ai as He used for Jericho. And the Israelites never bothered to ask God about His method for capturing Ai.

Joshua was devastated. God used the occasion to point out that Israel had sinned, and Joshua went tribe to tribe until he found the offender, Achan.

Then the Lord said to Joshua, "Do not be afraid; do not be discouraged. Take the whole army with you, and go up and attack Ai. For I have delivered into your hands the king of Ai, his people, his city and his land." Joshua 8:1

Even if you blow it completely, you can recover lost ground, just as Israel defeated Ai and again lived in victory. But that return to victory was not easy; Israel had to eradicate the sin and selfishness that caused defeat. Confess your pride and independence, then ask God what to do next. Although God forgives immediately, a minute of disobedience may require hours, days, or months of obedience before the wrong is wiped clean from the mind of the person you offended.

Don't let pride create an Ai for you. But if you do suffer a defeat, remember there is a road back to victory. You may have lost a game, but Christ in you can still win the championship.

Through love and faithfulness sin is atoned for; through the fear of the Lord a man avoids evil. Proverbs 16:6

Life With an Anti-Boredom Guarantee

JOSHUA

You're late to the concert where you're supposed to sing a solo. Your friend forgets to pick you up for the away game, so you spend Friday night alone. You misplace your paycheck. Do you exhibit faith in everyday life?

The Israelites found themselves in a situation where the little things would determine their entire future. They had conquered all the major kings. The only remaining fighting would consist of mopping-up operations. The leaders had assigned each tribe a portion of land, and each tribe was to drive out the enemies in its territory. Some tribes were raring to go. Others were not.

The people of Joseph said to Joshua, "Why have you given us only one allotment and one portion for an inheritance? We are a numerous people and the Lord has blessed us abundantly." "If you are so numerous," Joshua answered, "and if the hill country of Ephraim is too small for you, go up into the forest and clear land for yourselves there in the land of the Perizzites and Rephaites." The people of Joseph replied, "The hill country is not enough for us, and all the Canaanites who live in the plain have iron chariots, both those in Beth Shan and its settlements and those in the Valley of Jezreel." Joshua 17:14–16

The people of Joseph cowered in fear and missed the blessing.

One reason for not cashing in on God's promises is laziness. Rather than fighting any more battles, some Israelites let the Canaanites stay in their territory. The descendants of Joseph doubted an all-powerful God could do anything about iron chariots. Maybe sometimes you also prefer to compensate for your weaknesses instead of letting God get rid of them.

You could live to be a hundred and still not exhaust God's power to change you. His plans for your life come with an anti-boredom guarantee—if you claim it by faith.

Ask and it will be given to you; seek and you will find; knock and the door will be opened to you. For everyone who asks receives; he who seeks finds; and to him who knocks, the door will be opened. Matthew 7:7–8

Day 187

When Hope Is Gone

RUTH

Ruth grew up in the pagan country of Moab. Happily, she learned about the true God and a better way to live when she married a man from Israel. And she grew to love his mother, Naomi, a very kind person. But when Ruth's father-in-law, her husband, and her brother-in-law all died, life suddenly seemed hopeless.

When Naomi started traveling back to Bethlehem in Israel, her two daughters-in-law walked with her. But Naomi, aware of the hard life a widow in a strange country could face, urged Orpah and Ruth to return to their homes. At this, Orpah kissed her mother-in-law good-bye and left for home, but Ruth would not go back.

"Look," said Naomi, "your sister-in-law is going back to her people and her gods. Go back with her." But Ruth replied, "Don't urge me to leave you or to turn back from you. Where you go I will go, and where you stay I will stay. Your people will be my people and your God my God. Where you die I will die, and there I will be buried. May the Lord deal with me, be it ever so severely, if anything but death separates you and me." Ruth 1:15–17

Ruth decided to follow the God of Naomi—no matter the cost—and the cost was great. In choosing to follow the Lord, Ruth gave up the right to make her own decisions. Because she was going to her mother-in-law's country and would be living with her, Ruth would be at Naomi's mercy. But worse, if something happened to Naomi, Ruth would be alone in a foreign land.

When Ruth said to Naomi, "Your God will be my God," she gave up everything. But look again. Once Ruth gave God her life, God gave back to her more than she ever could have dreamed. The same can be true for you. God can make something beautiful out of your mixed-up life if you let Him.

Make this promise yours:

Surely God is my salvation; I will trust and not be afraid. The Lord, the Lord, is my strength and my song; he has become my salvation. Isaiah 12:2

Day 188

Jesus Says, "Take Two Giant Steps"

RUTH

If you face some tough choices, take some pointers from Ruth.

Notice the steps Ruth took to get out of her tragic situation. First she decided to follow God, no matter what the cost. Then she took the advice of a godly person who cared about her—Naomi. And because Ruth took advice from the right person, she made wise decisions.

Ask God to show you a wise, committed, strong Christian from whom you can get good advice. This might be your pastor or a Christian friend. Even if you can't think of such a person right now, keep praying until God shows you one, because you need sound, spiritual advice.

Her mother-in-law asked her, "Where did you glean today? Where did you work? Blessed be the man who took notice of you!" Then Ruth told her mother-in-law about the one at whose place she had been working. "The name of the man I worked with today is Boaz," she said. . . . Naomi said to Ruth her daughter-in-law, "It will be good for you, my daughter, to go with his girls, because in someone else's field you might be harmed." So Ruth stayed close to the servant girls of Boaz to glean until the barley and wheat harvests were finished. And she lived with her mother-in-law. Ruth 2:19, 22–23*

You make two kinds of decisions. One kind of decision is a matter of wisdom, such as deciding what to do with the money you've saved. Wise, godly advice can help you make the right decision. The other kind of decision is a matter of submission—whether or not to obey authority. Because Naomi was Ruth's mother-in-law, Ruth had a responsibility to obey Naomi. And because Ruth obeyed Naomi, even when she could have raised some logical objections, she was delivered from her miserable state. If you obey authority, God will also give you deliverance.

Obeying authority can be difficult. The devil tries so hard to break down respect for authority, because taking godly advice and obeying authority are two giant steps toward a new and better life.

Plans fail for lack of counsel, but with many advisers they succeed. Proverbs 15:22

Day 189

Rejects Recycled

RUTH

Are you afraid of saying the wrong thing and giving others a bad impression of you? Are you afraid that your attempt at friendliness might be rejected? Fear of rejection can be paralyzing.

One day Naomi her mother-in-law said to her, "My daughter, should I not try to find a home for you, where you will be well provided for? Is not Boaz, with whose servant girls you have been, a kinsman of ours? Tonight he will be winnowing barley on the threshing floor. Wash and perfume yourself, and put on your best clothes. Then go down to the threshing floor, but don't let him know you are there until he has finished eating and drinking. When he lies down, note the place where he is lying. Then go and uncover his feet and lie down. He will tell you what to do." "I will do whatever you say," Ruth answered. Ruth 3:1–5 (Ruth and Boaz were not alone. As usual, all who participated in the harvest came to sleep under the stars near the threshing floor after the celebration meal.)

Because Israelite custom obliged Ruth to find a husband—and she was required to make the first move!—Ruth could have let fear of rejection ruin her life. Although Boaz, as a relative of her deceased husband, was obliged to marry Ruth, another law forbade intermarriage with foreigners. This was a complicated situation, to say the least.

Naomi's plan must have seemed bizarre to Ruth at first, yet she obeyed her mother-in-law and the laws of Israel. And because she was doing God's will, she knew she was accepted by God, even if she were rejected by Boaz. This love story has a happy ending, but Ruth didn't know that. When she lay down at the feet of Boaz, she risked rejection.

God wants to work in your life so others will be drawn to Him because of the good things He is doing through you. He wants to eliminate your fear of rejection so others will be favorably impressed by you, not so you can win a personality award, but so you can win other people into His kingdom.

If the Lord delights in a man's way, he makes his steps firm; though he stumble, he will not fall, for the Lord upholds him with his hand. Psalm 37:23–24

The temptation to give up hits often. When geometry gets difficult, you drop the course rather than face hard work. When the job gets boring, you quit. When your friend lets you down, you dump him. When hardly anyone shows up for Bible study, you quit too.

Overcoming the effects of tragedy and the scars of life requires hard-to-develop qualities like perseverance and loyalty—a willingness to stick with it no matter what. Ruth developed loyalty. She gave up everything to follow God, and even when she was lonely in a new country and exhausted from overwork, she didn't slip back into idol worship. When going to the field to pick up grain day after day became tiring and boring, she didn't quit. And when Ruth married Boaz, she could easily have forgotten all about Naomi. But she didn't. In fact, her love for Naomi was so obvious that everyone in Bethlehem talked about it.

So Boaz took Ruth and she became his wife. Then he went to her, and the Lord enabled her to conceive, and she gave birth to a son. The women said to Naomi: "Praise be to the Lord, who this day has not left you without a kinsman-redeemer. May he become famous throughout Israel! He will renew your life and sustain you in your old age. For your daughter-in-law, who loves you and who is better to you than seven sons, has given him birth." Ruth 4:13–15

The principles that worked for Ruth will work for you. First, *discover what is good and start doing it.* You find out what the right thing to do is by studying the Bible. Then *stick with it.* Honoring your mom is easy—until a really difficult situation arises. Working with enthusiasm comes naturally during the first two months of school—but maintaining that attitude through two semesters is tough. Helping people isn't difficult—until they take advantage of you or display some of their unlovable characteristics. But hanging in there and obeying by faith, when no results are showing, will make the difference.

You must continually do what is right—stick with it—because the side streets on the narrow road leading to eternal life all have names like Trouble Trail, Discouragement Drive, and Loser's Lane.

Day 191

Change the S to P and Add aul

SAUL

Saul in the Old Testament—His Beginning:

There was a Benjamite, a man of standing, whose name was Kish. . . . He had a son named Saul, an impressive young man without equal among the Israelites—a head taller than any of the others. 1 Samuel 9:1–2

He ends with: "Surely I have acted like a fool and have erred greatly" (1 Samuel 26:21).

Saul in the New Testament—His Beginning:

Meanwhile, Saul was still breathing out murderous threats against the Lord's disciples. He went to the high priest and asked him for letters to the synagogues in Damascus, so that if he found any there who belonged to the Way, whether men or women, he might take them as prisoners to Jerusalem. Acts 9:1–2

He ends with: "I have fought the good fight, I have finished the race, I have kept the faith" (2 Timothy 4:7).

King Saul of the Old Testament was an outstanding young man apparently headed for great success, but he killed himself. The Saul of the New Testament, because of Hebrew custom, changed his name to Paul following the greatest experience of his life. This Saul began his life breathing threats against the disciples of the Lord, determined to annihilate Christianity. He ended up becoming a great apostle.

Saul's and Paul's lives show that the outcome of your life will depend on the choices you make along the way, and at each fork in the road—each chance to decide for or against God. Once he became a Christian, Paul chose God every time, and his life ended in triumph. In contrast, Saul repeatedly scorned God's ways, and his life ended in tragedy.

Decide not to ride the fence, dividing your interests between God and the things of the world. Decide that God will own your heart. Trust Him, and be willing to admit when you're wrong.

Such a life will be demanding—you'll never be able to sit back and take it easy. Doing what is foolish and making your life a mess is easy, but following God and making your life count for Him requires combat. The apostle Paul called it a fight of faith. But someday you will, as Paul did, look back and evaluate your life. Will you have been a Saul or a Paul?

Day 192

Forgetting to Forgive and Flights of Fantasy

SAUL

When Saul became king, he was tenderhearted, ready to forgive people who slighted him and refused to honor him as king. When men questioned his ability to lead, he kept silent (1 Samuel 10:26–27). After his first military victory, instead of killing those who had not wanted him to be king, Saul gave God the credit for his victory: "No one shall be put to death today, for this day the Lord has rescued Israel" (1 Samuel 11:13).

The people of Israel responded enthusiastically, appreciating the sense of security such a king gave them. Saul began his reign with kindness, willing to overlook the sins of others.

The experiences of Saul and the teachings of Jesus show that a spirit of forgiveness isn't just a nice ornament, an optional extra for your personality. It's an absolute necessity. Ephesians 4:32 is a command: "Be kind and compassionate to one another, forgiving each other, just as in Christ God forgave you."

Somewhere along the line, Saul got tired of forgiving people—a temptation that strikes almost everyone. His life as king of the people of Israel, of course, was not easy. Once Saul's subjects began complaining, they didn't stop. Saul finally became fed up. He decided to stop tolerating the griping, and he stopped forgiving.

Soon Saul was not only refusing to forgive people who had offended him, but he was imagining that everyone was against him. Eventually, plagued by fantasies, Saul could no longer think rationally. He even turned against David, who had always shown him loyalty—he went after David with an army of three thousand men.

What happened to Saul could happen to you. You're not made of different stuff. If you refuse to forgive, little things will grow into mountains, and you'll soon imagine no one is treating you justly. You'll make unreasonable demands of others and exaggerate your own sense of importance. You'll soon be against everyone, and everyone will be against you.

So do a little self-examination. If you've fallen into "Saulish" thinking, forgiving others is the cure.

Bear with each other and forgive whatever grievances you may have against one another. Forgive as the Lord forgave you. Colossians 3:13

Day 193

Five-Page Assignments, Paper Airplanes, and Three Simple Words

SAUL

The class is out of control so the exasperated teacher finally yells, "If one more person throws a paper airplane, the whole class will get a five-page homework assignment!" You know the scenario.

If you've helped with the Girl Scouts or baby-sat for the neighbor kids or coached Little League, you know that once you're in a position of authority, the temptation to make rash statements and give impetuous orders increases greatly. And once you've said something in front of the whole group, it takes a lot of courage to admit that you're wrong and back down.

When King Saul was chasing Philistines, he didn't even want his men to stop to eat. Anyone who did would be killed! But his own son, Jonathan, did not hear the order and ate some honey he found.

Saul said, "May God deal with me, be it ever so severely, if you do not die, Jonathan." But the men said to Saul, "Should Jonathan die—he who has brought about this great deliverance in Israel? Never! As surely as the Lord lives, not a hair of his head will fall to the ground, for he did this today with God's help." So the men rescued Jonathan, and he was not put to death.
1 Samuel 14:44–45

Stubbornness that never says, "I'm sorry, I was mistaken," or "I was wrong and I want to apologize," causes tremendous problems. A big factor in Saul's first step to failure was stubbornness. He refused to choke back his pride and admit that his ban on eating during the battle was an unwise decision. He began to lose the respect of his subjects. And more tragic, he began to lose the blessing of God.

Don't be a Saul. When you hastily say foolish things, correct your statements. Revise every false remark. Three simple words, "I was wrong," can do wonders for your spiritual life. Do you have the attitudes that make these three words possible?

Blessed are the meek, for they will inherit the earth. . . . Blessed are the peacemakers, for they will be called sons of God. Matthew 5:5, 9

Day 194

Having a Heart Checkup

SAUL

Saul had a terrific start, depending on God's advice as he ruled Israel. Saul's heart, however, grew cold as he neglected to study God's law and make it part of his life. He didn't trust God. He disregarded one of God's commandments—that only a priest could offer a special sacrifice—and he only partially obeyed God's instructions.

When Samuel reached him, Saul said, "The Lord bless you! I have carried out the Lord's instructions." . . . Samuel said, "Although you were once small in your own eyes, did you not become the head of the tribes of Israel? The Lord anointed you king over Israel. And he sent you on a mission, saying, 'Go and completely destroy those wicked people, the Amalekites; make war on them until you have wiped them out.' Why did you not obey the Lord? Why did you pounce on the plunder and do evil in the eyes of the Lord?" "But I did obey the Lord," Saul said. "I went on the mission the Lord assigned me. I completely destroyed the Amalekites and brought back Agag their king. The soldiers took sheep and cattle from the plunder, the best of what was devoted to God, in order to sacrifice them to the Lord your God at Gilgal." But Samuel replied: "Does the Lord delight in burnt offerings and sacrifices as much as in obeying the voice of the Lord? To obey is better than sacrifice, and to heed is better than the fat of rams. For rebellion is like the sin of divination, and arrogance like the evil of idolatry. Because you have rejected the word of the Lord, he has rejected you as king." 1 Samuel 15:13, 17–23

God told Saul to attack the Amalekites, and then destroy them and their possessions. But Saul *purposely* disobeyed God's order, then made pious excuses to cover up his disobedience.

Sin always harms others, and the result of Saul's sin almost wiped out God's people a few hundred years later.

What would be the worst thing that could happen to you? Losing your entire family? Failing all your classes? Being rejected by all your friends? No. The worst thing that could happen is hardening your heart against God—becoming so calloused that your conscience no longer registers guilt. That will ruin your life—and your eternity.

Day 195

God's Honor Society

DAVID

You probably were just a little tyke when you first heard the exciting story of David, the shepherd boy, killing big, bad Goliath, the giant. As a child, however, you probably missed the point of the incident. David was not trying to play hero by showing off his bravery; rather, he was applying a spiritual principle: God defends His honor.

> *Then he took his staff in his hand, chose five smooth stones from the stream, put them in the pouch of his shepherd's bag and, with his sling in his hand, approached the Philistine. Meanwhile, the Philistine, with his shield bearer in front of him, kept coming closer to David. He looked David over. . . . David said to the Philistine, "You come against me with sword and spear and jave-lin, but I come against you in the name of the Lord Almighty, the God of the armies of Israel, whom you have defied. This day the Lord will hand you over to me . . . and the whole world will know that there is a God in Israel. All those gathered here will know that it is not by sword or spear that the Lord saves; for the battle is the Lord's, and he will give all of you into our hands." . . . So David triumphed over the Philistine with a sling and a stone; without a sword in his hand he struck down the Philistine and killed him.*
> 1 Samuel 17:40–42, 45–47, 50

Goliath had no respect for the God of Israel, but David believed God could do anything. David boldly told the giant he would kill him so "the whole world will know that there is a God in Israel" (1 Samuel 17:46).

Because God's honor was so important to him, David had no time to think about himself. He had no time to get scared of Goliath, who was much larger than he was. He had no time to bask in the glory of being a national hero. He had no time to nurse a grudge against Saul, who would not reward him.

God honors those who honor Him. He promises, "Humility and the fear of the Lord bring wealth and honor and life" (Proverbs 22:4). It's worth the effort to become a member of God's Honor Society.

David answered Ahimelech the priest, "The king charged me with a certain matter and said to me, 'No one is to know anything about your mission and your instructions. . . . Give me five loaves of bread, or whatever you can find.' . . . So the priest gave him the consecrated bread. . . . David asked Ahimelech, "Don't you have a spear or a sword here? I haven't brought my sword or any other weapon, because the king's business was urgent." The priest replied, "The sword of Goliath the Philistine . . . is here . . . take it." . . . Then the king sent for the priest Ahimelech. . . . Saul said to him, "Why have you conspired against me, you and the son of Jesse, giving him bread and a sword and inquiring of God for him, so that he has rebelled against me and lies in wait for me, as he does today?" . . . The king said, "You will surely die, Ahimelech, you and your father's whole family. 1 Samuel 21:2–3, 6, 8–9; 22:11, 13, 16*

It escapes from your lips too quickly—that lie or exaggeration just to make a better impression.

Lying implies God can't be trusted to guard your reputation or get you out of a tight spot. So you try to lie your way out. David fell into the lying trap. True, he was running for his life and the pressure was on, but when the same thing had happened before, David had gone to the prophet Samuel for help. If David had again sought safety with Samuel, the lying could have been avoided.

Because David didn't ask God what to do, he found himself fleeing from an army, with no food and no weapon. He stopped to ask a priest for food, but the priest was suspicious because David was traveling alone. He gave David another chance to tell the truth, but David blew it. His lie caused the deaths of an innocent priest and his family.

Lies dishonor God, hurt other people, and destroy you. Break the habit by replacing each lie with the truth—follow God's Word. God's truth, like a B–52 bomber, will demolish the fib factory in your life.

Therefore each of you must put off falsehood and speak truthfully to his neighbor, for we are all members of one body. Ephesians 4:25

Day 197

The Price of a Promise

DAVID

[David] asked, "Is there no one still left of the house of Saul to whom I can show God's kindness?" Ziba answered the king, "There is still a son of Jonathan; he is crippled in both feet." . . . When Mephibosheth son of Jonathan, the son of Saul, came to David, he bowed down to pay him honor. David said, "Mephibosheth!" "Your servant," he replied. "Don't be afraid," David said to him, "for I will surely show you kindness for the sake of your father Jonathan. I will restore to you all the land that belonged to your grandfather Saul, and you will always eat at my table." 2 Samuel 9:3, 6–7

You make promises every day. "I'll be there at eight-o'clock sharp." "I'll send you a picture later." "I'll pay you back at the end of the month." "I'll do all the assignments tonight and hand them in tomorrow."

How much are your promises worth? Maybe you never realized that sticking by your word is an important part of honoring God.

David went to great lengths to fulfill a promise he had made years before to Jonathan, son of King Saul. David was hiding from Saul when he learned that his good friend Jonathan had been killed in battle. Seven years later he became king over all of Israel. He then had to defeat the enemies of his nation, capture Jerusalem, and set up his capital city there. But David did not forget his promise. As soon as he had a little rest, he went all-out to find any living relatives of Jonathan. When he found Mephibosheth, the son of Jonathan, he gave him all the land that had belonged to his grandfather Saul, and invited him to live at the palace and eat at his table.

God always keeps His promises. If you don't keep your promises as a child of God, you make a mockery of your Father who based His entire revelation to man on His promises. If you are sloppy about keeping your word, you'll have difficulty putting your faith in the promises of God and living by them. You'll tend to value God's promises as you value your own. Here are words to live by:

It is better not to vow than to make a vow and not fulfill it. Ecclesiastes 5:5

Day 198

A Secret Sin That Everyone Knows About

DAVID

One evening David got up from his bed and walked around on the roof of the palace. From the roof he saw a woman bathing. The woman was very beautiful, and David sent someone to find out about her. The man said, "Isn't this Bathsheba, the daughter of Eliam and the wife of Uriah the Hittite?" Then David sent messengers to get her. She came to him, and he slept with her. (She had purified herself from her uncleanness.) Then she went back home. The woman conceived and sent word to David, saying, "I am pregnant." 2 Samuel 11:2-5

David fell into sin because of spiritual laxness. Although he couldn't help the first look, the second look was sin. Rather than taking another peek, he should have walked away.

You'll inevitably see tempting billboards or fashions—but you don't have to look twice. God expects you to guard your eyes. Temptation is often unavoidable, but sin is never accidental.

David misused his power in order to cover up his sin—he had Bathsheba's soldier husband positioned in the battle so he would be killed. Then David could legally marry the widow carrying his child.

Do you take advantage of being older and smarter than your little brother, or are you always fair to him? Do you exploit your seniority at work by joining the plot to make the new employee do all the dirty work? Consider carefully how you use the power entrusted to you.

When David finally came to his senses, he repented fully and God forgave him. But his secret sin became world news—people are still reading about it in their Bibles. And David, whose heart's desire was to honor God, realized what a terrible example he had been.

Learn from David's mistakes. The story of David and Bathsheba doesn't need any modern reruns.

In everything set them an example by doing what is good. In your teaching show integrity, seriousness and soundness of speech that cannot be condemned, so that those who oppose you may be ashamed because they have nothing bad to say about us. Titus 2:7-8

Day 199

Facing the Big Bad World Alone

ELIJAH

What reaction would you get if you told your lunchroom gang that you always come in by curfew and never try to sneak out without permission? Would you lose all your friends if you reminded your geometry classmates you all deserved the punishment homework and that you planned to complete it? Do you feel like you are the only one in the whole school who really wants to know God and obey Him? Does it seem that being good is old-fashioned and out-of-style?

Well, the Bible tells us about a guy who faced your problem: Elijah.

Now Elijah the Tishbite, from Tishbe in Gilead, said to Ahab, "As the Lord, the God of Israel, lives, whom I serve, there will be neither dew nor rain in the next few years except at my word." 1 Kings 17:1

Because Jezebel, wife of King Ahab, had made idol worship the state religion of Israel, very few people were following the true God. As Elijah looked around him, he felt very much alone. Following the Lord had meant risking his life to deliver a message from God to the king.

Elijah knew God as He really is—alive, all-powerful, never bummed-out, always ready with an answer to every problem. This he hadn't learned from his grandmother, but from daily depending on the almighty God. And that's the way you too can learn to receive strength from God.

God is never overwhelmed when evil surrounds you. He knows light shows up best in a very dark place, so He intends to give you the power to be that light. You may be facing a big, bad world, but you don't have to face it alone.

Be strong and courageous. Do not be afraid or terrified because of them, for the Lord your God goes with you; he will never leave you nor forsake you. Deuteronomy 31:6

Popularity, Self-Confidence, a Bulletproof Vest, & Money in the Bank

ELIJAH

Then the word of the Lord came to Elijah: "Leave here, turn eastward and hide in the Keanth Ravine, east of the Jordan. You will drink from the brook, and I have ordered the ravens to feed you there." So he did what the Lord had told him. . . . Some time later the brook dried up because there had been no rain in the land. Then the word of the Lord came to him: "Go at once to Zarephath of Sidon and stay there. I have commanded a widow in that place to supply you with food." . . . After a long time, in the third year, the word of the Lord came to Elijah: "Go and present yourself to Ahab, and I will send rain on the land." So Elijah went to present himself to Ahab. 1 Kings 17:2–5, 7–9; 18:1–2

There's an epidemic of insecurity going around. Most cases are the common chronic variety, but some are acute—for instance, the dread that rises within you when you read about a stabbing in the school across town, or when you remember the guy who tried to break into your house last month. Fear can cripple you.

Gutsy Elijah had told wicked King Ahab there would be no rain for three years. Elijah's popularity plummeted as the land dried up, and he found himself ripe for a case of acute insecurity: Ahab's henchmen were ready to kill him on sight, supplies of food and water were withering, and no one seemed willing to trust and obey God.

But Elijah had a secret for coping with immense problems: unquestioning obedience to God's instructions. And those instructions sounded a bit strange. First he was to camp by a brook and be fed by ravens; then he was to get food and lodging from a poor widow in a foreign country; finally he was to again—horrors!—confront Ahab. Strange orders, yes, but Elijah did not argue.

God honored Elijah's trust. The ravens daily delivered meat and bread. God miraculously supplied the widow with flour and shortening to make bread. And Ahab ended up obeying Elijah.

If God calls you to be an Elijah, don't run away. Stick around and watch for miracles. The security He provides is a lot better than popularity, self-confidence, a bulletproof vest, or money in the bank.

Find rest, O my soul, in God alone; my hope comes from him. Psalm 62:5

Day 201

Fire From Heaven

ELIJAH

Do you ever imagine yourself giving the perfect speech in English class that will convert the teacher and the entire class? Or being the hero of the football game and telling the news reporters God deserves the credit?

Hold it. Get back on the Reality Train.

At the time of sacrifice, the prophet Elijah stepped forward and prayed: "O Lord, God of Abraham, Isaac and Israel, let it be known today that you are God in Israel and that I am your servant and have done all these things at your command." . . . Then the fire of the Lord fell and burned up the sacrifice, the wood, the stones and the soil, and also licked up the water in the trench. When all the people saw this, they fell prostrate and cried, "The Lord—he is God! The Lord—he is God!" 1 Kings 18:36, 38–39

Elijah didn't prepare the big show on Mount Carmel. If he had, there would have been no fire—and no rain afterward. Mount Carmel was simply the culmination of walking with God and obeying Him in the little things. When he heard God's voice, he knew exactly what He wanted. Elijah had the calm courage of one who was a friend of God.

Daydreaming aside, the Mount Carmel fireworks are a wonderful reminder that a lone servant of God can conquer 450—or a million for that matter—prophets of Baal, or any other false belief system. Elijah's power and courage came from God, and you can have it too. "One with God is a majority" is more than a nice-sounding platitude. It's the truth.

Let the God of Elijah be your God. Let Him make you the person who is unafraid of what other people think or say. But like Elijah, get specific instructions from the Lord. Follow Him step by step. Don't try to be Incredi-Christian. Don't attempt Wonder Woman witnessing. Don't write your own Fire From Heaven manual. Your plans will fail; God's will not.

Yet the Lord longs to be gracious to you; he rises to show you compassion. For the Lord is a God of justice. Blessed are all who wait for him! Isaiah 30:18

Day 202

Panic and a Picnic

ELIJAH

The Lord said, "Go out and stand on the mountain in the presence of the Lord, for the Lord is about to pass by." Then a great and powerful wind tore the mountains apart and shattered the rocks before the Lord, but the Lord was not in the wind. After the wind there was an earthquake, but the Lord was not in the earthquake. After the earthquake came a fire, but the Lord was not in the fire. And after the fire came a gentle whisper. When Elijah heard it, he pulled his cloak over his face and went out and stood at the mouth of the cave. 1 Kings 19:11–13*

After the fire from heaven had proven who was the true God, and rain had fallen for the first time in three and a half years, Elijah had expected the nation—even the king and queen—to turn to God. Instead, Jezebel was determined to kill him by the next morning.

After a panicked run into the desert, Elijah fell beneath a scrubby bush. He had no food or water. He begged God to let him die.

Although Elijah deserved it, God did not yell at him or give him a long lecture or write him off His list. Rather, He sent an angel to bake a cake for Elijah and give him water—a picnic in the desert! And then He spoke to Elijah with a still, small voice. He understood how Elijah was feeling.

God also understands when the pressure on you is too great. He wants to meet your physical, emotional, and spiritual needs. When you're tempted to mope, ask God what you should do next. It usually will be something ordinary like cleaning your room, apologizing to your father, or getting to bed at a decent time. God assigned Elijah several tasks. As he completed them, his depression vaporized. Ask God for your next assignment.

God sent Elijah right back into Jezebel's territory. Don't panic or make rash decisions. Be willing to stay exactly where you are until God tells you what to do.

Elijah could have eaten his picnic in much more pleasant surroundings if only he hadn't yielded to his fears. God has some picnics planned for you too. If you trust Him, you'll enjoy them much more than Elijah enjoyed his.

Let us not become weary in doing good, for at the proper time we will reap a harvest if we do not give up. Galatians 6:9

Day 203

God Always Means What He Says

JONAH

The word of the Lord came to Jonah son of Amittai: "Go to the great city of Nineveh and preach against it, because its wickedness has come up before me." But Jonah ran away from the Lord and headed for Tarshish. He went down to Joppa, where he found a ship bound for that port. After paying the fare, he went aboard and sailed for Tarshish to flee from the Lord. Jonah 1:1–3

"I'm praying about whether or not to steal the money."

"God wouldn't let me fall in love with Erich if it weren't His will for me to date him."

"I got the last ticket available for the heavy metal concert, so I know it's God's will that I attend."

Wait a minute!

Jonah may have used the same kind of reasoning to duck out of God's command to go to Nineveh and warn the people. Jonah had good reasons for not wanting to go there. The Assyrians were the cruelest people in the Middle East, and Nineveh was their capital. He had some very good excuses.

But quality of excuses wasn't the point. God had told Jonah to go. Period. Jonah wasn't supposed to say, "How unpatriotic to help Israel's enemies. And God should punish the Ninevites for being so cruel. Oh, wow! I just heard there are no tickets for Nineveh until next month, but I can get a ticket for Tarshish now."

If your mom asks you to buy a carton of milk at the store, you don't spend two hours trying to decide what your mother's will is. You buy a carton of milk. Just as your mother clearly states her instructions, God clearly spells out His will in His Word; no amount of rationalizing will alter God's words. And God means what He says—every time.

Once you get used to obeying God, you'll develop an instinctive "feel" for God's will. It's a natural result of listening. By regularly studying God's Word and asking the Holy Spirit to show you verses you need and how to apply them to your life, you'll soon know God very well. So well, in fact, that sometimes you'll sense in your spirit what He wants without even looking for a verse, because you'll be hearing His voice.

But Jonah ran away from the Lord and headed for Tarshish. He went down to Joppa, where he found a ship bound for that port. After paying the fare, he went aboard and sailed for Tarshish to flee from the Lord. . . . Then they took Jonah and threw him overboard, and the raging sea grew calm . . . But the Lord provided a great fish to swallow Jonah, and Jonah was inside the fish three days and three nights. Jonah 1:3, 15, 17

If Jonah had relied on circumstances and opinion polls to show him God's will, all of them would have indicated he should not go to Nineveh. (1) It was a long, hard trip. (2) The Assyrians of Nineveh were enemies of Israel. (3) The Assyrians were so cruel that everyone else in the world thought the destruction of Nineveh was a good idea. (4) None of Jonah's friends would have encouraged him to go. But God doesn't pay attention to such statistics.

Some issues of God's will are very clear because God has provided specific Scripture on the topic. For example, you don't have to sit around wondering if you should love your enemies; the Scriptures say you must, so you obey—regardless of the circumstances. Other issues, though, are not as clear, so you need guidance from the Scriptures and from the Holy Spirit. These issues include decisions such as what subjects to take, whether or not to buy a motorcycle, which college to attend, what career to pursue, and where to live. And there are some choices that God may leave completely to your discretion, such as what color shirt to buy, what to eat for lunch, or which football team to cheer for. In every decision, however, you must be sensitive to the Holy Spirit.

Jonah knew God's will, but he didn't want to obey Him. He rushed into action based solely on his view of the circumstances. He did not listen to God's clear guidance, so Jonah's stubbornness and resulting ignorance led to his experience of whaling and wailing! Willingness to obey, waiting for the voice of the Holy Spirit, and expecting God to show you His way will save you from a Jonah and the whale experience.

I will instruct you and teach you in the way you should go; I will counsel you and watch over you. Psalm 32:8

Day 205

The God of the Second Chance

JONAH

No matter how bad you feel, Jonah felt even worse. After all, he was a prophet, so he should have known better than to run away from God. Now he was sliding down the throat of a great fish. He saw no possibility of making amends. But in this tough situation, he repented and promised to go to Nineveh. He said, "What I have vowed I will make good" (Jonah 2:9). And God performed a complete miracle to give Jonah a second chance. Then He used him in a great way.

> Then the word of the Lord came to Jonah a second time: "Go to the great city of Nineveh and proclaim to it the message I give you." Jonah obeyed the word of the Lord and went to Nineveh. Now Nineveh was a very important city—a visit required three days. On the first day, Jonah started into the city. He proclaimed: "Forty more days and Nineveh will be overturned." Jonah 3:1-4

No matter what you've done, you can repent and get back into God's will. When you repent you turn around. You have to retrace your steps. So where did you get off the track in the first place? What were you unwilling to do? God won't make any deals. He expects obedience on the very issue that kept you from God's will in the first place. Jonah had to go to Nineveh. You must go to your Nineveh. There is no other way to get right with God.

Don't wait as long as Jonah did to return to God. Don't ignore that uneasy feeling of guilt. Don't decide you'll keep sinning just a little longer. Don't buy a ticket to Tarshish. Don't become so insensitive that only a big shock will bring you around—three days in a fish's stomach is not a pleasant experience. If you are out of God's will, take the second chance that God offers. And take it now.

> Seek the Lord while he may be found; call on him while he is near. Let the wicked forsake his way and the evil man his thoughts. Let him turn to the Lord, and he will have mercy on him, and to our God, for he will freely pardon. Isaiah 55:6-7

The Supply Is Unlimited—Just Help Yourself

JONAH

Do you wonder how a missionary can live with a jungle tribe in unsanitary conditions, struggle through language barriers, and eat toasted beetle grubs, just to teach about Jesus? Do you fear that God's will is too hard for you to do?

Jonah certainly could have used that argument. Nineveh was over five hundred miles away straight across the desert, but much farther by common trade routes. The trip would be long and lonely. The people of Nineveh were famous for cruelty. Certainly some foreigner prophesying the destruction of their city would be a prime candidate for torture and death.

The Ninevites believed God. They declared a fast, and all of them, from the greatest to the least, put on sackcloth. When the news reached the king of Nineveh, he rose from his throne, took off his royal robes, covered himself with sackcloth and sat down in the dust. . . . When God saw what they did and how they turned from their evil ways, he had compassion and did not bring upon them the destruction he had threatened. Jonah 3:5-6, 10

Interestingly, once Jonah decided to obey, he was able preach in Nineveh—and the people listened and repented!

True obedience comes from a heart of faith and love—not merely from a sense of obligation. You can obey either from fear or from faith! If you obey God from fear, you aren't in a position to receive the grace and power God has to give. But if you obey in faith, doing God's will is a joy. The task that appeared hard will become an adventure with God; you will expect miracles and a new depth of relationship with Him.

When you go out on a limb to obey God, you'll be in very good company. By faith, Abraham left Ur, Moses crossed the Red Sea, Joshua conquered Jericho, and David faced Goliath. Take the risk to join them.

Direct me in the path of your commands, for there I find delight. Turn my heart toward your statutes and not toward selfish gain. Turn my eyes away from worthless things; preserve my life according to your word. Psalm 119:35-37

Day 207

But That's Not the Future I've Planned

JEREMIAH

You have dreams for your future—a happy marriage, a prestigious job, skiing vacations, and Caribbean cruises. Will they come true?

Jeremiah also had dreams, but he didn't get to live out the future he had planned. His fellow Israelites' hypocrisy, rebellion, and idol worship were about to bring God's judgment. And God wanted to use Jeremiah as His messenger. His life would not be at all what he had expected.

When Jeremiah learned God had chosen him to be a prophet, he was surprised. He was very shy and tenderhearted; Jeremiah's personality didn't seem to fit the job description. But God promised to put His words in Jeremiah's mouth and put courage and strength in his heart.

> The word of the Lord came to me, saying, "Before I formed you in the womb I knew you, before you were born I set you apart; I appointed you as a prophet to the nations." "Ah, Sovereign Lord," I said, "I do not know how to speak; I am only a child." But the Lord said to me, "Do not say, 'I am only a child.' You must go to everyone I send you to and say whatever I command you. Do not be afraid of them, for I am with you and will rescue you," declares the Lord. Jeremiah 1:4–8

Maybe you also feel you don't have what it takes. Be assured God will give you what you need to accomplish His purpose. God gives assignments that seem too hard so you will depend on Him to complete them.

Do you really want the boring, predictable future you've planned? There's something wonderful about living on the cutting edge, experiencing the agony and ecstasy of being on the front lines. Maybe the future won't turn out the way you planned, but you can live an action-packed life.

> Then the Lord reached out his hand and touched my mouth and said to me, "Now, I have put my words in your mouth. . . . Get yourself ready! Stand up and say to them whatever I command you. Do not be terrified by them." Jeremiah 1:9, 17

You can see it on the screen—cities enveloped in flames, a world staggering with radioactivity, slow death, and suffering; life reduced to a daily struggle against a hostile environment. You can hear it in church—a stirring sermon proving you are living in the last days. You can read it in the newspaper—street violence, guerilla warfare, and terrorism. Everything seems to say: "The end of all things is near" (1 Peter 4:7).

Jeremiah experienced the end of the world as he knew it. The Babylonians' knocking down the gates of Jerusalem frightened him as much as thoughts of a glowing mushroom cloud terrify you. Life as a captive in a foreign land, which appeared to be his future, made him feel hopeless.

> "Have you not brought this on yourselves by forsaking the Lord your God when he led you in the way? Now why go to Egypt to drink water from the Shihor? And why go to Assyria to drink water from the River? Your wickedness will punish you; your backsliding will rebuke you. Consider then and realize how evil and bitter it is for you when you forsake the Lord your God and have no awe of me," declares the Lord, the Lord Almighty. Jeremiah 2:17-19

Today, as in Jeremiah's time, God gives prophecies to His people so they can know how to prepare for what's coming. God not only used Jeremiah to prophesy impending doom—the fall of Jerusalem and the need to repent—but also to explain His total plan. God would use the destruction of Jerusalem and the captivity in Babylon to cure the survivors of idol worship, so they would return to their land. Then He would send them a Savior and bring them to a time when,

> I [God] will put my law in their minds and write it on their hearts. I will be their God, and they will be my people . . . they will all know me, from the least of them to the greatest. Jeremiah 31:33-34

In the midst of despair, God was giving them hope!

We are living in difficult times. But God has everything planned. He has a pattern and purpose, even in this falling-apart world. But if you've given your life to Jesus, your future couldn't be brighter.

Day 209

"Stop the World, I Want to Get Off"

JEREMIAH

The Lord said, "It is because they have forsaken my law, which I set before them; they have not obeyed me or followed my law." . . . This is what the Lord says: "Let not the wise man boast of his wisdom or the strong man boast of his strength or the rich man boast of his riches, but let him who boasts boast about this: that he understands and knows me, that I am the Lord, who exercises kindness, justice and righteousness on earth, for in these I delight," declares the Lord. Jeremiah 9:13, 23–24

Life seems overwhelming. School is a parade of locker-room jokes, swearing "seminars," anti-Bible opinions, wholesale cheating, and harassment of honest people. Home is a hotbed of bickering and selfishness. If life were a bus, you'd probably ask the driver to let you off.

Jeremiah would know what you're talking about. Often Baruch, his secretary, was the only one who stood with him. Wickedness was increasing rapidly, false religion was flourishing, and the international situation was dreadful. Does this sound just like today? It was.

Jeremiah realized that knowing the God of kindness, justice, and righteousness was more important than doing anything else, and he lived that way, in complete dependence on God. He couldn't count on his family or the people he preached to for comfort, so he got it directly from God. God's presence and words were the joy of his life.

What was his secret? A deep love relationship with God that went far beyond simple knowledge. Jesus said the real test of love is obedience, and Jeremiah's obedience proved he loved God more than anyone or anything.

Don't let your love for Jesus grow cold. Be willing even to suffer for Him in a sick, sad, and sinful world, and be ready to receive from Him all you need to live above the mess.

I have loved you with an everlasting love; I have drawn you with loving-kindness. Jeremiah 31:3

Where Does Courage Come From?

JEREMIAH

"I will make you a wall to this people, a fortified wall of bronze; they will fight against you but will not overcome you, for I am with you to rescue and save you," declares the Lord. "I will save you from the hands of the wicked and redeem you from the grasp of the cruel." Jeremiah 15:20–21

As you read in the papers about brainwashing, genetic engineering, "holy" war, and the possible death of our solar system, you may shudder with fear—thinking that if the world doesn't end soon, it may not be fit to live in. But fear can hit much closer to home, when you walk a few blocks alone at night or when a girl was murdered three blocks from your house. At those times you may wonder, *Where does courage come from?*

Jeremiah was in constant danger. People wanted to kill him. Even his family turned against him. The government and religious leaders wanted him executed for treason. He endured verbal attack, house arrest, and even imprisonment in the mucky bottom of a cistern. Yet through all this, Jeremiah displayed remarkable courage. What was his secret?

Jeremiah's secret was *faith*. God had promised to protect him, and Jeremiah believed Him. He realized that confidence in God's promises was better than any sword or bodyguard or karate lesson. When the powerful, influential men of Judah wanted to kill him, he told them bluntly that God had sent him to give a message, so if they killed him they would be responsible to God.

God gave Jeremiah a super-hazardous job *and* perfect protection, so if He asks you to take a big risk, be assured He will take care of you. He may ask you to take a dangerous assignment, but you can have courage by placing complete confidence in God and His promises of protection—and there's a bunch. Study those promises. Memorize them. Make them part of you. Allow the God of promises to be your God, your friend, and your protector.

The Lord is my strength and my shield; my heart trusts in him, and I am helped. My heart leaps for joy and I will give thanks to him in song. Psalm 28:7

Day 211

God's Magic Master Plan

ESTHER

Stories of kings and queens are fascinating. How romantic to have riches, power, and prestige! Well, life in ye old palace isn't always so great, as Queen Esther discovered. Although she was queen of the huge Persian Empire, she was married to a king much older than she. He was not known as an even-tempered man, and it had been more than a month since he had asked to see her.

To make matters worse, the king's prime minister was plotting to kill all the Jews in the empire; and Esther knew she was the only person who could ask the king to save her people. Yet the law stated that if anyone approached the king without invitation, that person would quickly be killed—unless the king decided otherwise. And since the king had not called her for thirty days, what was she to do?

When Esther's words were reported to Mordecai, he sent back this answer: "Do not think that because you are in the king's house you alone of all the Jews will escape. For if you remain silent at this time, relief and deliverance for the Jews will arise from another place, but you and your father's family will perish. And who knows but that you have come to royal position for such a time as this?" Esther 4:12–14

God had a master plan for Esther's situation—she was used by God to save her people. God can work out His will from the midst of the worst of problems. He uses former drug addicts to spread the news about Jesus to people who might listen to no one else. He takes kids from broken, mixed-up families and gives those kids emotional stability and winsome personalities—so they can be great advertisements of His power. So whatever your situation, there is hope for you. And God may choose to use you in a most extraordinary way.

"O house of Israel, can I not do with you as this potter does?" declares the Lord. "Like clay in the hand of the potter, so are you in my hand, O house of Israel. If at any time I announce that a nation or kingdom is to be uprooted, torn down and destroyed, and if that nation I warned repents of its evil, then I will relent and not inflict on it the disaster I had planned. Jeremiah 18:6–8

Then Esther sent this reply to Mordecai: "Go, gather together all the Jews who are in Susa, and fast for me. Do not eat or drink for three days, night or day. I and my maids will fast as you do. When this is done, I will go to the king, even though it is against the law. And if I perish, I perish." Esther 4:15–16

When Queen Esther chose to risk her life to plead for her people, she was afraid. But she knew courage came from God, so she spent some time fasting, which was a way of separating oneself from the routine of daily life in order to seek God. Esther didn't think about the dinner menu because she wasn't going to eat dinner. She didn't think about what to do in the evening because she wouldn't be going anywhere. The time was completely given over to God. Fasting gave unhurried time for prayer. The events in the story of Esther prove she prayed much during her three days of fasting.

Through fasting, Esther became a different person. When the king saw her come before him, he was pleased with her. Had she been frantic, frazzled, and frustrated—and fearful (as she had been three days earlier), the king might have turned away from her in disgust. But that day Esther entered his court with dignity and poise. Discreetly she withheld her request, rather than blurting it out. She had received God's wisdom for the problem and was willing to wait for His perfect timing.

Esther's God is your God. He can replace your fear with courage. Instead of worrying about losing the football game or flubbing your solo, set aside a chunk of time to be alone with God. Think about the great ways in which God delivered frightened people in the past: the Israelites at the Red Sea, David facing Goliath, Daniel in the lions' den, Paul on a sinking ship, and Peter in prison waiting to be executed. Then think of the ways God has helped you and your friends. Thank Him for being a God who helps His children.

You don't have to be frantic, frazzled, and frustrated. After all, God is not like that, and He lives inside you. He wants you to pick up His attitudes. Spend enough time with Him and you will.

Day 213

A Banquet for a Big Shot

ESTHER

If I have found favor with you, O king, and if it pleases your majesty, grant me my life—this is my petition. And spare my people—this is my request. For I and my people have been sold for destruction and slaughter and annihilation. If we had merely been sold as male and female slaves, I would have kept quiet, because no such distress would justify disturbing the king. . . . Now write another decree in the king's name in behalf of the Jews as seems best to you, and seal it with the king's signet ring—for no document written in the king's name and sealed with his ring can be revoked. Esther 7:3–4; 8:8

When Esther felt the king was about to do something wrong, she appealed to him and gave him all the facts so he could make a better decision. She did it with a humble, submissive attitude. She first spent time with God to discover the best way to present her petition. Then she invited the king to a banquet where he relaxed. She wisely made the king coax her request out of her instead of laying it on the line. Because she hadn't forced her request on him, the king never doubted her respect for authority. And he granted her request. Esther's method can work for you.

If your teacher gives an unfair test, don't rush up and complain. Find a way to tactfully and respectfully suggest a solution to the problem. If your boss makes you work every Saturday night so his nephew can have time off, let God show you a way to appeal to him and reasonably work out the problem.

But if your appeal to authority fails, you must obey, trusting God to deliver you—even as Esther was willing to die if her banquet didn't succeed. After all, God is all-powerful and able to show you how to handle the consequences. He can help you live through a D- on a test. He has a wonderful way of protecting people who really want to obey Him.

Having God's view of authority cancels out fear because it prevents reacting wrongly to the person in charge. When you respect and obey authority, you're obeying the God you love, the God who always has your best interest at heart.

Everyone must submit himself to the governing authorities, for there is no authority except that which God has established. The authorities that exist have been established by God. Romans 13:1

Day 214

Faith Remembers What Fear Forgets

ESTHER

It's probably happened to you. You trusted God completely for last year's biology final and He worked a miracle, giving you supernatural calm and peace as you studied for and took the test. This year, however, you're a nervous wreck before the first chemistry exam.

You trusted God to run your social life last year, and you thoroughly enjoyed yourself. But now you're desperate because all your friends seem to be happily dating. You feel left out.

God hasn't changed! So what is the problem?

Yesterday's faith doesn't automatically cover today's fears. You have to continually stick close to Jesus, constantly renew your mind by letting the Bible speak to you, and daily receive the power of the Holy Spirit. One way to keep your focus on God is to remember with joy and thanks what He has done in the past.

> *This happened on the thirteenth day of the month of Adar, and on the fourteenth they rested and made it a day of feasting and joy. . . . And these days of Purim should never cease to be celebrated by the Jews, nor should the memory of them die out among their descendants.* Esther 9:17, 28

Purim commemorates God's deliverance for the Jews in the Persian Empire. Recalling God's great deeds of the past focuses your mind on God's power. When fear threatens to smother your faith, recall how God has helped you in the past; then remind yourself how He will help you now. Learn to effectively use the memories of victories God has won for you.

When fear invades, try this prescription: On a sheet of paper, write in big letters across the top, "Jesus Christ is the same yesterday and today and forever" (Hebrews 13:8). Beneath that verse, list all the times Jesus has given you victory. After each point add, ". . . and God can do it again." You'll find it impossible to think about the greatness of God and be afraid at the same time. Faith remembers what fear forgets.

> *I will remember the deeds of the Lord; yes, I will remember your miracles of long ago. I will meditate on all your works and consider all your mighty deeds.* Psalm 77:11–12

Day 215

The Time of Your Life

NEHEMIAH

Should you sign up for Spanish II because your best friend did? Should you apply for the first job you see in the want ads? Should you attend the college that's closest to home? Aren't you tired of making spur-of-the-moment decisions that get you into trouble?

When Nehemiah heard the wall of Jerusalem was in shambles, he had to decide whether or not to go and supervise its rebuilding—a job that would take much time and effort. How did he make such a big decision?

They said to me, "Those who survived the exile and are back in the province are in great trouble and disgrace. The wall of Jerusalem is broken down, and its gates have been burned with fire." When I heard these things, I sat down and wept. For some days I mourned and fasted and prayed before the God of heaven. Nehemiah 1:3-4

First, he was willing to do God's will, no matter what the cost. He was willing to leave his prestigious palace job, with all its fringe benefits. He was willing to risk infuriating a king by requesting a leave of absence. God's will was worth any sacrifice.

Second, Nehemiah prayed—extensively. He recognized he could give up everything to serve God and still be completely out of God's will, so Nehemiah spent four months praying about it before he took action.

One man who, as a young person, was confused about choosing the right occupation, was told by a friend, "Spend five minutes each day praying about this decision." He took the advice and got his answer.

Why don't you try it? Instead of complaining to everyone, pray about it every day. Nehemiah was willing to make the necessary sacrifices, and then he spent enough time praying to discover God's plan for his life. God, in turn, took care of the king's attitude and marvelously opened the way for Nehemiah to go and rebuild the wall. If you will dedicate your time to God and ask Him what walls He wants rebuilt, you, like Nehemiah, will receive His guidance and see His miracles. But don't try to build the wrong wall. If you'll spend the time of your life for God, you'll have the time of your life.

Day 216

Orders From the General Himself

NEHEMIAH

The devil loves using the opinions of others to mix up your priorities and keep you from accomplishing the jobs God assigns you. When the devil tried this tactic on Nehemiah, however, it failed. Nehemiah simply ignored the insults and continued building.

> When Sanballat heard that we were rebuilding the wall, he became angry and was greatly incensed. He ridiculed the Jews, and in the presence of his associates and the army of Samaria, he said, "What are those feeble Jews doing? Will they restore their wall? Will they offer sacrifices? Will they finish in a day? Can they bring the stones back to life from those heaps of rubble—burned as they are?" Tobiah the Ammonite, who was at his side, said, "What they are building—if even a fox climbed up on it, he would break down their wall of stones!" Hear us, O our God, for we are despised. Turn their insults back on their own heads. Give them over as plunder in a land of captivity. . . . So we rebuilt the wall till all of it reached half its height, for the people worked with all their heart. Nehemiah 4:1–4, 6

The devil tries to use "public opinion," such as ridicule from unbelievers or discouraging comments from Christian friends, to make you ineffective. If you drop basketball so you can lead a Bible study, people will think you're crazy. If you decide to get by on last year's wardrobe so you can give more money to missions, you're more apt to get an eye roll than an eye flutter.

God wants you to ignore them, relax, and keep His priorities: obedience to authority and working to the best of your ability. When a member of the Ego Demolition Squad quips, "Did you get your haircut at the poodle boutique?" don't let Satan convince you to hide for a month. When some self-crowned princess remarks that your skirt must have come from your grandmother's attic, don't decide that all the kids hate you because your wardrobe isn't up-to-date. Learn to ignore the abuse and keep building the wall that God has given you to build.

How should you handle discouraging comments? Again, ignore them. Although God often will use the council of other Christians to confirm what He has already told you, be careful to always get your orders from God first. In the army, the commander-in-chief's orders cancel all other suggestions and orders. A fellow private's advice can never outweigh the words of the General himself.

Day 217

Easy Street Is Boring

NEHEMIAH

Overcoming constant opposition gives life a certain excitement, a cutting edge. Nehemiah and his people, for instance, weren't basket cases because an enemy was harassing them. They decided that they could guard against danger and continue to build the wall. The opposition inspired cooperation, a renewed dedication to the job, and a greater trust in the Lord. God allowed their priorities to be tested so they could strengthen their faith.

> When our enemies heard that we were aware of their plot and that God had frustrated it, we all returned to the wall, each to his own work. From that day on, half of my men did the work, while the other half were equipped with spears, shields, bows and armor. The officers posted themselves behind all the people of Judah who were building the wall. Those who carried materials did their work with one hand and held a weapon in the other, and each of the builders wore his sword at his side as he worked. But the man who sounded the trumpet stayed with me. Nehemiah 4:15–18

Life without a challenge is boring. Playing football against third graders would be easy—but not fun. Canoeing the kiddie canal at the amusement park or skiing the bunny hill would be effortless—but dull. That's why God allows constant challenges in your Christian life—so you'll grow, both physically and mentally.

The sooner you quit seeking a safe, boring, easy Christian life, the better. You must always be on guard against Satan's attacks; today's victory will not help you tomorrow. You will have to stay close to Jesus and let Him protect you, because wandering out on your own will get you into deep trouble.

In a way, the Christian life is like a science-fiction cartoon, with you as the main character. God has given you secret power against the devil. Whenever you venture off on your own, any attack of Satan crash-lands you on a hostile, lonely planet. But if you stay close to Jesus, He'll always win the battle for you—and everybody likes to be on the winning side.

> Be on your guard; stand firm in the faith; be men of courage; be strong.
> 1 Corinthians 16:13

So on the first day of the seventh month Ezra the priest brought the Law before the assembly, which was made up of men and women and all who were able to understand. . . . On the second day of the month, the heads of all the families, along with the priests and the Levites, gathered around Ezra the scribe to give attention to the words of the Law. Nehemiah 8:2, 13

All sorts of jobs had been postponed so the wall could be built. But instead of caring for any of these pressing needs, Nehemiah and his people took two days off to hear the Word of God. Impractical? In addition, they set aside other days that month to observe the celebration God had prescribed in the Law of Moses. Returning to God and obeying His Word was more important to them than work that "just has to get done."

Maybe you're already aware that life can grind on like a relentless machine—classes, homework, part-time jobs, choir rehearsals, sports games, and then you start another carbon-copy week. Maybe you've noticed that making time payments, keeping up with the Joneses—or the kid at school—and trying to accomplish too many things at once can imprison you. It can seem like a not-so-merry-go-round that never stops!

A man once remarked, "Your greatest danger is letting the urgent things crowd out the important." You may be groaning in response, "If only I could discover what things are important. Straightening out priorities isn't possible."

Start discovering God's priorities by reading and studying His Word. If you are obeying God's general biblical teachings about money, work habits, or heart attitudes, you can expect specific guidance about what is your next important step. So take time to study the Bible every day.

You will also discover God's priorities by praying. Rather than bolting out of bed at the last moment and dashing off to school, get up earlier and spend time talking to God about your activities.

Be willing to obey God, and stick so close to Him that you won't wander down a wrong path. Let Him decide what will be first on your agenda. Your life will be much better if you spend it doing only the things He has planned for you.

Day 219

Do You Need a Degree From Whale Seminary?

"So a fish swallows Jonah, Jesus walks on the water, and the Red Sea opens just in time, making a spectacular splash for the Miracles on Water show. Does God do as well on land?" Faithless Freddy may have even more to say, but at least he has one issue straight—your concept of God determines your attitude toward miracles. If you really believe in an all-powerful Creator God, you believe that God could "minnowize" that big fish so Jonah could swallow the whale!

It is interesting that nonbiblical sources mention the miracles of Jesus, and His enemies do not deny them. Josephus, a Jewish historian of the first century, calls Him a wonderworker. Later Jewish religious writings say He did His miracles by black magic. This is also the explanation given by Celsus, a philosopher who criticized Christianity in the second century.

All of our historical sources agree that Jesus did miracles. Jesus did miracles in public where everyone could see them. He even performed miracles in the presence of people who didn't believe in Him. He didn't have just one trick up His sleeve; He did a variety of miracles over a period of time. People who were cured spread the word.

Bible miracles have a purpose. God gets concerned if His people disobey Him. Take Jonah, for instance. His degree from Whale Seminary made him obedient and showed the world forever that it's a big deal when a person boards a ship for Tarshish if God has told him to go to Nineveh.

From inside the fish Jonah prayed to the Lord his God. He said: "In my distress I called to the Lord, and he answered me. From the depths of the grave I called for help, and you listened to my cry. . . . The engulfing waters threatened me, the deep surrounded me; seaweed was wrapped around my head. . . . Those who cling to worthless idols forfeit the grace that could be theirs. But I, with a song of thanksgiving, will sacrifice to you. What I have vowed I will make good. Salvation comes from the Lord." And the Lord commanded the fish, and it vomited Jonah onto dry land. Jonah 2:1–2, 5, 8–10

Does your biology book claim that life just happened—with no help from a Creator? Some biology texts, though they do not give *God* the credit for making the world, are honest enough not to make up their own creation story. For example, one such book says, "The question of how life originated remains open to investigation." But if your science teacher explains in detail how energy over zillions of years formed toadstools, horned owls, and Mrs. Jones, don't decide to resign from the human race or throw out the Bible. Just do some thinking.

Where did the universe come from? There are only two possibilities: (1) It came from something non-living and impersonal, or (2) It began with a Personal Being.

If everything began with something impersonal, such as mass, energy, or motion, why do people have individual personalities, consciences, and curiosities? Did simple energy form into individual beings with intelligence, emotions, and a hunger to know God? The formula for this theory seems to be: *the impersonal + chance + time*. Yet most people would not consider throwing the parts of a watch into a clothes dryer and expecting the energy to produce a watch—even if the machine could run for a billion years. It seems even less likely that energy could generate the *parts* of a watch no matter how many billion years were involved. And we haven't even discussed how *living* things originated.

However, if a Personal Being created everything, there is an explanation for humanity's questioning mind, creative genius, and capacity for caring about others. Also, if a personal God created *you,* there is a reason for your existence. You weren't a chance occurrence. When you feel blah and worthless, turn to your Creator and thank Him for creating you to be unique. Then ask Him what important thing He wants you to do each day.

By the word of the Lord were the heavens made, their starry host by the breath of his mouth. Psalm 33:6

Day 221
What Does God Look Like?

When you think of God, what picture comes to your mind? Do you think of a kind-looking old gentleman in a rocking chair on some cloud? A "no you can't" computer? An enlarged replica of your father when he's angry? The Bible says God is none of these. Jesus taught:

God is spirit, and his worshipers must worship in spirit and in truth.
John 4:24

Jesus came to the earth not only to die for our sins, but to tangibly demonstrate to us what God is like. Jesus claimed that if someone "looks at me, he sees the one who sent me" (John 12:45). In other words, getting to know Jesus was discovering God in human form.

Although God the Father does not have a physical body, Christ took on a physical body. The Jesus who was born in Bethlehem had a physical body, but He let people worship Him as God. After He rose from the dead, He continued to have a body. Zechariah predicts that when Jesus comes back again, His *feet* will touch the Mount of Olives and people will "look on the one they have pierced" (John 19:37).

Perhaps you feel like you got the raw end of the deal because the disciples got to see Jesus personally but you can't. Just remember what Jesus said to Thomas: "Because you have seen me, you have believed; blessed are those who have not seen and yet have believed" (John 20:29).

Philip said, "Lord, show us the Father and that will be enough for us." Jesus answered: "Don't you know me, Philip, even after I have been among you such a long time? Anyone who has seen me has seen the Father. How can you say, 'Show us the Father'? Don't you believe that I am in the Father, and that the Father is in me? The words I say to you are not just my own. Rather, it is the Father, living in me, who is doing his work." John 14:8–10

Have you ever tried to get advice from your dog? That wagging tail could mean "get a different job," "drop algebra," or "break up with Sally." But you know it only means, "I like it when you pet me."

Ability to communicate verbally—using a spoken language—is one huge difference between people and animals. Every normal baby in the world can learn to talk. Where did this ability come from?

It would take a lot of faith to believe that mass or energy could invent language and enable people to speak it. It seems that only a personal God who wanted to communicate with the people He made—and wanted them to talk with each other—could and would create language.

Without language there is little communication. If God can't speak to us, we can't really know Him; we would all be agnostics. But you may be asking, "If God can talk, why doesn't He say something to *me*?" It could be that you are expecting the wrong thing, or maybe you are making it impossible for God to speak to you.

Although God has on occasion spoken out loud to people, He usually reveals His will through the *thoughts* He puts into our minds. These are accompanied by a deep inner assurance in our spirits. He also speaks to us through His words in the *Bible,* but even these do not necessarily make sense unless the Holy Spirit explains them to us.

God can't speak to you if you won't quiet down and listen. Do you ever get away from the TV or turn off the computer in order to find a quiet place to open your Bible and *let* God speak to you? God won't come running after you with a megaphone! Once you hear His voice, you won't need an intellectual argument to convince you that God can use language.

The grass withers and the flowers fall, but the word of our God stands forever.
Isaiah 40:8

Your word, O Lord, is eternal; it stands firm in the heavens. Psalm 119:89

Day 223

Are You Trying to Play God?

Every person wants to understand him or herself and answer the question, "Who am I?" The Bible teaches that you best understand yourself by getting to know the God who made you and believing what He has to say about human nature.

Socrates was into a "know thyself" trip. Shakespeare took up the theme with his "to thine own self be true" bit. Some swami has stated, "The inner self of everyone is supreme. It is not sinful."

If you're going to believe that truth is to be found inside *you,* by self-realization, you must believe that you have no sin and that you, not God, are the source of truth. Yet there are many visible proofs of human sin—the child who suffers because of an alcoholic father, the misfit who is treated cruelly by others, and the people who trample on everyone just to make more money. Unless you believe that the real world is an illusion, you can't possibly consider yourself the ultimate source of truth.

Here's the way Rabi Maharaj, who was a Hindu yogi before he gave his life to Jesus, describes it: "I believed as a Hindu that I was divine . . . that everything was divine. I knew it was impossible for man to become God. So that was my first and major dilemma, not knowing the real God but knowing He was there and not being able to find Him in Hinduism. Then . . . as Hindus believed that I was perfect and divine and whereas I tried to believe it with my head, I knew my own imperfections, my own limitations. I did what every good Hindu does to find the truth: I looked into myself. . . . When I looked into myself, I didn't see God. I saw sin."*

Ask the God who made you to run your life and give you understanding about yourself from the Bible. It's as sensible as reading the manufacturer's directions instead of asking your alarm clock, "What makes you tick?" You don't have to be another stage failure trying to play God.

Through him all things were made; without him nothing was made that has been made. John 1:3

He did not need man's testimony about man, for he knew what was in a man. John 2:25

*(Rabi Maharaj, "Rebirth of a Yogi—Rabi Maharaj's Story" (Berkeley: Spiritual Counterfeits Project, no date) 6.

Some people insist that everything in the universe is part of God and that evil doesn't really exist, it is only wrong thinking.

The Bible teaches exactly the opposite.

The Mighty One, God, the Lord, speaks and summons the earth from the rising of the sun to the place where it sets. From Zion, perfect in beauty, God shines forth. . . . He summons the heavens above, and the earth, that he may judge his people. Psalm 50:1–2, 4

God is perfect, He is apart from the things He has created, and He has the right to judge them. The Bible also tells us that there is a devil and a horde of demons who are very dangerous. Ephesians 6:11 tells us how to resist him: "Put on the full armor of God so that you can take your stand against the devil's schemes."

Yet Christianity is not a belief in dualism with a good god and a bad god. The devil is a once-good angel who was created by God but fell into pride and rebellion. In order to do evil, the devil—or any person—must have intelligence and free will (good things created by God). Even though God made all things and rules over them, evil is real and so is the devil. The Bible also teaches that God is much more powerful than the devil, so the person who sticks with God has nothing to fear.

However, if everything is part of God and God is everything in the world, there is no such thing as evil, because everything is one and that one is God. If this were the case, it would mean that murdering an innocent baby and giving your hungry friend your last dollar would be equally "God's work." It would mean that you could experiment with anything you wish because nothing is dangerous. If God is in everything and all is God, there is no danger of being deceived by demons and evil spirits.

Christians know better. Meditate on God's Word and don't let your mind remain inactive. Keep the bad guys out!

Good and upright is the Lord; therefore he instructs sinners in his ways. He guides the humble in what is right and teaches them his way. Psalm 25:8–9

Day 225

Why Isn't God Giving Cash Prizes?

Many people think God should give prizes for good behavior. Others think that since God is love, people should be able to demand from Him whatever they wish. They think God should eliminate hard tests, household chores, arguments, and suffering—not to mention war and the rising price of chocolate. However, love is not God's only characteristic, and it is held in balance with His perfect wisdom, knowledge, justice, and holiness, as well as His decision to give humans free will.

God did not create you to be a programmed robot. You have the ability to talk back to your parents and to put down the kids in your class that nobody likes. However, God did not create a world without consequences for sin. You can't rebel against your parents without becoming a bitter and unhappy person. You can't ignore God's commandments without pain and heartbreak.

It just isn't fair to blame God for the greed that causes war or the selfishness that prevents the rich from sharing with the poor. The stubborn refuse to admit that individuals' sinful acts are responsible for the world's problems. God's love doesn't cancel out human ability to make wrong decisions.

When the Bible states that God is love, we must remember that its definition of love differs from our sentimental notions.

But God demonstrates his own love for us in this: While we were still sinners, Christ died for us. Romans 5:8

If you love me, you will obey what I command. John 14:15

God showed His love for us by sending Jesus to die for our sins, not by raining Hershey's Kisses from heaven.

We have to change our definition of love. When we learn God's justice perfectly balances His love, we'll be glad He doesn't give cash prizes.

Righteousness and justice are the foundation of your throne; love and faithfulness go before you. Blessed are those who have learned to acclaim you, who walk in the light of your presence, O Lord. They rejoice in your name all day long; they exult in your righteousness. Psalm 89:14–16

Jesus believed that the Old Testament was God's Word. In fact, He gave it supreme importance in His life. Jesus quoted from at least twenty-four different Old Testament books.

When Jesus was tempted by the devil, He used Bible verses to defeat Satan. "Man does not live on bread alone, but on every word that comes from the mouth of God" (Matthew 4:4). He used the Old Testament to confirm His logic, saying, "Scripture cannot be broken" (John 10:35). He assured His listeners,

> *Do not think that I have come to abolish the Law or the Prophets; I have not come to abolish them but to fulfill them. I tell you the truth, until heaven and earth disappear, not the smallest letter, not the least stroke of a pen, will by any means disappear from the Law until everything is accomplished.* Matthew 5:17–18

Jesus believed the controversial stories of Noah and Jonah. He said, "For as Jonah was three days and three nights in the belly of a huge fish, so the Son of Man will be three days and three nights in the heart of the earth" (Matthew 12:40), and "Just as it was in the days of Noah, so also will it be in the days of the Son of Man. People were eating, drinking, marrying and being given in marriage up to the day Noah entered the ark. Then the flood came and destroyed them all" (Luke 17:26–27).

Maybe the Amalekites, the Amorites, and the Assyrians mix you up a little, and you wonder why the Hebrews were so interested in who a person's great-great-grandfather was, but if you're willing to study and dig a little, you'll find great treasures in the Old Testament. After all, it's the only book Jesus put on His recommended-reading list.

> *He said to them, "This is what I told you while I was still with you: Everything must be fulfilled that is written about me in the Law of Moses, the Prophets and the Psalms." Then he opened their minds so they could understand the Scriptures.* Luke 24:44–45

Day 227

The Sun Stood Still—Oops!

If the chemistry teacher asks you if you saw the beautiful sunset last night, you wouldn't reply, "Don't you even know that the *earth* revolves around the *sun?* The sun never sets!" We also use "sunset" as an expression to describe what *appears* to happen. We even have figures of speech such as "the four corners of the globe" or "the wind sang its haunting melody," and we all know what they mean.

Yet when the Bible uses expressions, people say it's unscientific. When Isaiah says that the mountains will sing and the trees will clap their hands (55:12), it doesn't mean that there were mountain choirs and trees with hands. Always look for the intention of the author and the context of the statement.

On the other hand, it is ridiculous to say such things as "The Bible says that Jesus walked on the water, but He just knew where the sand bar was"—in one of the world's deepest lakes! It doesn't make sense to say that the account of Adam and Eve is just a nice story to illustrate a truth. Time after time the Bible traces the ancestry of people back to Adam, and the New Testament keeps mentioning him.

Study the Bible with a great deal of prayer, keeping in mind the intention of the writer. If a solar spectacular of the type described in Joshua's day were to be written up today, some author might still write,

> So the sun stood still, and the moon stopped, till the nation avenged itself on its enemies, as it is written in the Book of Jashar. The sun stopped in the middle of the sky and delayed going down about a full day. Joshua 10:13

The Bible often uses poetic language to express the attributes of God to give us comfort and hope.

> He who dwells in the shelter of the Most High will rest in the shadow of the Almighty. I will say of the Lord, "He is my refuge and my fortress, my God, in whom I trust." Surely he will save you from the fowler's snare and from the deadly pestilence. He will cover you with his feathers, and under his wings you will find refuge; his faithfulness will be your shield and rampart. Psalm 91:1–4

God didn't write the Bible on scrolls and throw them down from heaven. He didn't even dictate it to His mortal secretaries. He used men to write His words, working through their personalities so that each could use his individual style of writing. Because of this, we say the Bible was "God-breathed" (2 Timothy 3:16). One scholar explains, "By inspiration we mean that holy men of God—under the influence of the Holy Spirit—wrote what God wanted written." And that is quite different from saying that Shakespeare was "inspired" to write great plays.

Obviously, the Bible must quote what people really said, so if a person said something that is not true, it is quoted as such. If a person is accurately quoted as saying something false, or if a figure of speech is used, this is not an error. But a lot of people will tell you that the Bible contains both truth and error. Evidently, they think that each person is to determine for himself what is truth and what is error.

No! Teachers would have a fit if you did that with your textbooks and decided that everything you didn't understand was an error! Doing this with the Bible is preposterous. It makes each person a little god with his or her own system of truth.

You may agree with every word on this page and still try to hedge when the Bible says, "Children, obey your parents," and "Do everything without complaining or arguing." But if all the words in the Bible were put there by God, you'd better obey them.

All Scripture is God-breathed and is useful for teaching, rebuking, correcting and training in righteousness. 2 Timothy 3:16

How does Esther's risking her life for her people relate to your attitude toward dirty jokes? What does Moses' parting the Red Sea have to do with your geometry test on Tuesday? A lot—if you'll just listen.

The Bible is *relevant*. If God could help David kill Goliath, He can give you the strength to tell your friend about Jesus. If God could give Daniel power to pray in front of His enemies and then deliver him from the lions' den, He surely can help you stand up for what's right when your classmates choose drugs, deceit, and defiance.

If you were deciding whether or not to take some new cold pills, which evidence would be most convincing: (1) laboratory experiments that proved the tablets killed germs; (2) testimony from a person who got relief from symptoms; or (3) someone's beautiful poem about pills? Since rat poison may also kill cold germs, and poetic words don't create reality, you'd be smartest to accept the testimony of the person who really took the pills.

God goes to great lengths to show us that His Word is talking about real people who lived in real places and did real things.

> *In the fifteenth year of the reign of Tiberius Caesar—when Pontius Pilate was governor of Judea, Herod tetrarch of Galilee, his brother Philip tetrarch of Iturea and Traconitis, and Lysanias tetrarch of Abilene . . .* Luke 3:1

This verse gives the distinct impression that Luke is about to relate something that really happened! And for a long time many people said that Luke made an error because the only Lysanias known in history was the one whom Antony executed to fulfill Cleopatra's wish thirty-six years before Jesus was born. But a Greek inscription has been found that mentions Lysanias the tetrarch and fits Luke's dating accurately.

The Bible is not a Cinderella story with the moral that pretty girls get the goodies in the end. It's a book about a real God for real people.

> *Many have undertaken to draw up an account of the things that have been fulfilled among us, just as they were handed down to us by those who from*

the first were eyewitnesses and servants of the word. Therefore, since I myself have carefully investigated everything from the beginning, it seemed good also to me to write an orderly account for you, most excellent Theophilus, so that you may know the certainty of the things you have been taught.
Luke 1:1–2

Day 230

Quoting Hezekiah 6:8 and Other Crazy Things

When Patti Persecutor goes around school telling everybody that the Bible says, "There is no God," just ask for chapter and verse. Then study the Bible for yourself. The words "There is no God" are found in the Bible, but the *whole* verse reads, "The fool says in his heart, 'There is no God'" (Psalm 53:1).

Some people are good at taking biblical statements out of context. The writer of the book of Ecclesiastes, for example, tells of the intellectual struggles of his life. At one point in his life he believed that death was nothingness, and that the most important thing in life was enjoyment. But at the end of his life he sees the importance of God, and he changes his viewpoint.

> *Then man goes to his eternal home and mourners go about the streets . . . and the dust returns to the ground it came from, and the spirit returns to God who gave it. . . . Now all has been heard; here is the conclusion of the matter: Fear God and keep his commandments, for this is the whole duty of man.* Ecclesiastes 12:5, 7, 13

The entire book must be studied to understand any one of its verses.

When Irwin the Irresponsible says, "*I* heard that *he* said, when *he* quoted the world's greatest authority, that the *Bible* says . . . ," ask him to show you *where* the Bible says it.

By the way, laziness is a sin, and we are commanded to *study* God's Word. Many young people have landed in strange cults because they were too lazy to investigate and study what the Bible really says. You should know that Hezekiah is not a book of the Bible and that "Do your own thing" is not a Bible verse.

> *Now the Bereans were of more noble character than the Thessalonians, for they received the message with great eagerness and examined the Scriptures every day to see if what Paul said was true.* Acts 17:11

Have you ever sneaked into the football game by saying that your buddy inside has your money and you'll be right out to pay? Or given a false excuse for not handing in your book report on time? If you have, you have collided directly with commandments of the Bible, such as: "Do not lie" (Leviticus 19:11).

The Bible's claim to absolute truth for all people, for all time, is not very popular in our if-it-feels-good-do-it society. But then neither is anything or anyone who keeps people from doing exactly what they wish to do at any particular moment. Popularity, however, does not determine truth.

Even common sense tells you that people can't be happy if they are continually trying to steal from each other and lie to each other. Leaving the decision to each individual to "do the best thing in the given situation" is a frightening prospect. Consider how easy it is to rationalize selfishness in order to save face.

The Bible not only tells us the rules by which to live; it explains how we each can be transformed by the power of the Holy Spirit so that God can fulfill these laws in us.

The book *Valley of the Kwai* by Ernest Gorden beautifully shows how this worked in a tough situation. Gorden had been imprisoned by the Japanese during World War II. The starving prisoners, who were stealing from each other and living like animals, decided to read the New Testament together. These skeptics came to trust in Christ, who gave them power to obey the commandments of the New Testament and have genuine love for each other. The prison camp was transformed.

Can you honestly thank God for all His rules, even the ones that are hard to obey? When you're tempted to say, "I did my book report, but my little sister used it for her finger-painting," thank God for His commandment and say, "I didn't finish my book report because I put it off until the last minute. It's my fault." That kind of obedience will bring you freedom and joy, which will convince you of the wisdom of God's commandments.

I delight in your decrees; I will not neglect your word. Psalm 119:16

Day 232
But Jesus Didn't Say He Was God

Queen Elizabeth doesn't need to say, "I am the Queen of England." She just goes around acting like the Queen of England. She opens Parliament, she represents her country on state visits, and at times she wears a crown.

You won't find any record of Jesus saying, "I am God." But He did *act* like God. And He claimed the right to do things that only God can do, such as the ability to forgive sins.

When Jesus was speaking in a private home to an overflow crowd, friends of a paralyzed man removed tiles from the roof and lowered their friend on a cot just in front of where Jesus was standing. Jesus said, "Son, your sins are forgiven." Onlookers wondered why He would say such a thing. After all, no one can forgive sins except God.

"Which is easier: to say to the paralytic, 'Your sins are forgiven,' or to say, 'Get up, take your mat and walk'? But that you may know that the Son of Man has authority on earth to forgive sins . . ." He said to the paralytic, "I tell you, get up, take your mat and go home." He got up, took his mat and walked out in full view of them all. This amazed everyone and they praised God, saying, "We have never seen anything like this!" Mark 2:9–12

One person telling another that he is forgiven of *all* his sins makes no sense. One can only forgive sins committed against *himself.* But since all sins are committed against God, He can forgive a person of all his or her sins. This is exactly what Jesus claimed to do, and He healed the paralytic in order to prove that His claim was not mere words.

The people in these biblical accounts accepted the forgiveness of Jesus. Will you? Of course you have a guilt complex. You're guilty, aren't you? But if you admit your wrongdoing and wrong thinking, and accept Jesus' pardon, He will set you free. Jesus is God, and He wants to prove it to you.

My dear children, I write this to you so that you will not sin. But if anybody does sin, we have one who speaks to the Father in our defense—Jesus Christ, the Righteous One. He is the atoning sacrifice for our sins, and not only for ours but also for the sins of the whole world. 1 John 2:1–2

I once heard a story about a Texas family who saved and scrimped, going without many things in order to pay off the mortgage on their farm. All the while, these people were ignorant of one fact: *There was oil under their land.* Lack of knowledge condemned them to poverty.

Of course, even after discovering oil, those people could have chosen to ignore this resource and remain poor. Many people treat the promises in God's Word the same way. Although they know the promises, they refuse to act upon them, and their lives remain unchanged. They want to have their lives changed, but they doubt whether God would really do such good things for them.

Unlike people, God doesn't promise anything He is unwilling to give or do. He doesn't resent being reminded of His promises. In fact, when you claim one of His promises, He *loves* it!

We often get into trouble when we pray because, being ignorant of God's promises, we ask for things God has never promised to give. For example, if a kind rich man promised to send a poor boy to an expensive private school, would the boy be justified in complaining that the rich man hadn't bought him a ten-speed bike or given him a free trip to Disney World? Obviously the man would be held responsible only for what he had *promised* to give the boy. We need to remember that God didn't promise sunshine for all our picnics, but He did promise to give us peace "which transcends all understanding" (Philippians 4:7).

Claim a promise from God's Word. Stick with that promise and keep asking God to make it real in your life.

God is not a man, that he should lie, nor a son of man, that he should change his mind. Does he speak and then not act? Does he promise and not fulfill? Numbers 23:19

Through these he has given us his very great and precious promises, so that through them you may participate in the divine nature and escape the corruption in the world caused by evil desires. 2 Peter 1:4

I'll always remember one particular Saturday morning. I got up early to attend a Bible study. I'd gone to church all my life and thought I knew my Bible pretty well. But as we studied the first chapter of Ephesians, I learned for the first time that the power of the Holy Spirit within me is the same power that raised Jesus from the dead. Wow! That's a lot of power! I could never again say that I was powerless to do what God asked of me. I had within me the power that raised Jesus from the dead. That Bible truth has made a big difference in my life.

The Bible is full of spiritual principles the Holy Spirit wants to apply to our lives. How many people have to look back on their lives and sadly say, "If I had only known and applied what the Bible teaches, this would not have happened to me"?

An increasing knowledge of God's Word and a deeper obedience to God's commands will assure you of an abundant and joyful life. The Bible is like a huge gold mine—you'll always keep finding more treasure if you're willing to search for it. But what you don't know about the Bible can hurt you.

My people are destroyed from lack of knowledge. Because you have rejected knowledge, I also reject you as my priests; because you have ignored the law of your God, I also will ignore your children. Hosea 4:6

While they were bringing out the money that had been taken into the temple of the Lord, Hilkiah the priest found the Book of the Law of the Lord that had been given through Moses. . . . Then Shaphan the secretary informed the king, "Hilkiah the priest has given me a book." And Shaphan read from it in the presence of the king. When the king heard the words of the Law, he tore his robes. He gave these orders to Hilkiah, Ahikam son of Shaphan, Abdon son of Micah, Shaphan the secretary and Asaiah the king's attendant: "Go and inquire of the Lord for me and for the remnant in Israel and Judah about what is written in this book that has been found. Great is the Lord's anger that is poured out on us because our fathers have not kept the word of the Lord; they have not acted in accordance with all that is written in this book." 2 Chronicles 34:14, 18–21

Suppose Jesus came in person and spoke to your church, youth group, or Bible study. Would you daydream through His talk, fall asleep, whisper to your friends, or try to get the attention of your buddy across the room? I didn't think so. But have you ever realized that since God is the author of the Bible, each of us has a tremendous responsibility each time we hear it read and explained? How you *hear* the Word of God can determine whether you go to heaven or hell, whether you will follow Jesus or not.

Inattentiveness to God's Word can ruin your life. The devil knows this and will try to make you think that goofing around or daydreaming during a Bible study or keeping someone else from listening to a Scripture lesson is innocent fun. It isn't.

Really listening isn't easy; neither is concentrating when you read the Bible for yourself. You will need God's help. Confess any wrong attitudes you may have in this area and ask God to show you how to change. Don't ever come to a meeting thinking, "This is easy. All I have to do is sit and listen." Pray for God's help each time you are to listen to His Word. Make up your mind to listen attentively every time you hear a Scripture reading, a sermon, or a Bible talk. Take notes—even if no one else does—because it helps you concentrate. When you study the Bible for yourself, decide to get everything possible out of it. Really hearing God's Word will be, like so many hard things, completely worthwhile.

And though the Lord has sent all his servants the prophets to you again and again, you have not listened or paid any attention. They said, "Turn now, each of you, from your evil ways and your evil practices, and you can stay in the land the Lord gave to you and your fathers for ever and ever." . . . "But you did not listen to me," declares the Lord, "and you have provoked me with what your hands have made, and you have brought harm to yourselves." Therefore the Lord Almighty says this: "Because you have not listened to my words . . . this whole country will become a desolate wasteland, and these nations will serve the king of Babylon seventy years." Jeremiah 25:4–5, 7–8, 11

Day 236

But I Thought You Said "Hit It"

The Word of God contains truths that will give you an abundant and joyful life—if you hear them, understand them, and apply them. Doing this is a little bit like eating a meal. You aren't ready for more food until you've at least partially digested what you last put into your mouth. If you listen carefully and obey God's Word, it will become part of you, and you will be ready to receive more.

> The Lord said to Moses, "Take the staff, and you and your brother Aaron gather the assembly together. Speak to that rock before their eyes and it will pour out its water. You will bring water out of the rock for the community so they and their livestock can drink." . . . Then Moses raised his arm and struck the rock twice with his staff. Water gushed out, and the community and their livestock drank. But the Lord said to Moses and Aaron, "Because you did not trust in me enough to honor me as holy in the sight of the Israelites, you will not bring this community into the land I give them." Numbers 20:7–8, 11–12

God expects us to listen to Him and obey. Moses hit the rock instead of speaking to it as God had commanded. As punishment, he was not allowed to enter the land God promised His people, the land that was the goal of Moses and his people for forty years. Whether Moses thought that giving the rock a couple whacks with his rod would help God get water from the rock, whether he was letting out his frustration because the people were getting on his nerves, or whether he never listened carefully in the first place, we are not told. However, the story shows that God expects us to listen to His Word so attentively that we can obey it exactly. Listening is an art. Ask God to help you listen better to His Word, and listen more carefully to your parents, teachers, and friends.

> Therefore consider carefully how you listen. Whoever has will be given more; whoever does not have, even what he thinks he has will be taken from him. Luke 8:18

Your spiritual growth depends, in large measure, on how you "eat" the Word of God. It is spiritual food, and a malnourished Christian, one who neglects that food, will certainly be weak. It's not the quantity of food on the *table,* but the quantity that gets *inside* you that is important.

If the Bible is to really become a part of you, it is necessary to remember that your *heart* is more important than your *mind* when you are studying the Bible. With your mind you understand and comprehend, but with your heart you desire, love, and hold fast to Jesus. *Your mind must be the servant of your heart.* You have given your *heart* to Jesus because He is the Son of God, He is truth, and He knows everything. The little bucket of your mind will not be able to contain the ocean of God's truth.

Spiritual truth is different from *intellectual* truth. It's not IQ but dedication to God that makes spiritual truth clear. Even in our human relationships, our hearts' sense of love and compassion is more important than intellectual understanding of every action and statement. Use your mind, but remember that Bible study is not an intellectual exercise—it's fellowship with the living God. Let Him speak to you very personally and intimately through His living Word. If your heart is always hungry for more of God's truth, Bible study will be a real feast.

> However, as it is written: "No eye has seen, no ear has heard, no mind has conceived what God has prepared for those who love him"—but God has revealed it to us by his Spirit. The Spirit searches all things, even the deep things of God. For who among men knows the thoughts of a man except the man's spirit within him? In the same way no one knows the thoughts of God except the Spirit of God. We have not received the spirit of the world but the Spirit who is from God, that we may understand what God has freely given us. This is what we speak, not in words taught us by human wisdom but in words taught by the Spirit, expressing spiritual truths in spiritual words.
> 1 Corinthians 2:9–13

Day 238

Seeds Need Time to Grow

Have you ever opened your Bible, read a few verses, and closed it again without feeling or learning anything? Then the devil whispers, "You might as well quit reading the Bible. You don't get anything out of it anyway."

When this happens to you (and it will), don't get discouraged. When you start your Bible study, do you *pray in faith,* asking the Holy Spirit to teach you from His Word? God honors faith. It is said that if you expect nothing, you'll get it every time.

Studying the Bible is *hard work.* You sometimes need to do quite a bit of prospecting before you find gold. You may read a whole chapter or more before you come to the verse that the Holy Spirit wants to apply to your life for that day.

The most important thing to keep in mind is that seeds need time to grow. Suppose your neighbor said, "I planted my garden last night and it looks exactly the same this morning. It doesn't do any good to plant seeds." You would quickly tell him that he should wait longer.

In Luke 8:11 we read, "The seed is the word of God." We all know that seed has to be planted in good soil. Reading and memorizing God's Word is like planting seed. If you sincerely desire to see God work in your life, the time you spend in Bible study is never wasted. It's like planting a seed. It may take time, but it will grow. Your *attitude* determines the kind of soil the seed of God's Word has to grow in. Don't just read the Bible, meditate on it. Obey it and live by it. Keep it with you all through the day, and it will work in you.

As the rain and the snow come down from heaven, and do not return to it without watering the earth and making it bud and flourish, so that it yields seed for the sower and bread for the eater, so is my word that goes out from my mouth: It will not return to me empty, but will accomplish what I desire and achieve the purpose for which I sent it. Isaiah 55:10–11

When you fall in love, you cherish the words of the person you love. Those words change you, and you are comforted to know that he or she loves you and will stick with you no matter what.

After a parent has died, children still remember his or her words of advice and often allow that advice to direct their lives.

The problem is that there are limits on the power of human words. The person who has stated, "I'll love you forever" may forget that promise within a month, and the once-comforting words become painful memories. Parents can give wrong advice, and the changes this advice makes in the lives of their children may be devastating.

God's Word is different. It is *always* true, *always* reliable, and *always* the best advice. Do you have the kind of love relationship with God that makes His words all-important to you? Do you ponder the verses you read, keep them in your heart, and think about them all day long? If hearing God's words is only an intellectual exercise, your life won't change. But if God's words reach your heart so that you cherish them and determine to obey them, God will use His words to transform your life.

May your unfailing love come to me, O Lord, your salvation according to your promise; then I will answer the one who taunts me, for I trust in your word. Do not snatch the word of truth from my mouth, for I have put my hope in your laws. I will always obey your law, for ever and ever. I will walk about in freedom, for I have sought out your precepts. I will speak of your statutes before kings and will not be put to shame, for I delight in your commands because I love them. I lift up my hands to your commands, which I love, and I meditate on your decrees. Psalm 119:41–48

Day 240
Powerful Stuff

Bible study is not necessarily pleasant. The old expression "the truth hurts" has validity. Honestly facing ourselves and being willing to change is not easy, but earnest Bible study requires us to do just that.

Often God's words don't "get through" to us because we rationalize. We take God's Word and try to soften its impact with our own reasoning. The Bible may say, "Be still and know that I am God," but our reasoning says, *That's okay for Old Testament shepherds, but things are so bad for me I have to do something—run away from home, drop out of school, get married—anything to get out of this mess.*

When we use our own reasoning, the Bible becomes nothing more than a book to study, and its power to change our lives is useless. Others, like the Pharisees of Jesus' day, have added things from their own culture or their own personalities, distorting its true meaning. Because of this, it is very important to ask the Holy Spirit to help you interpret the Bible. Only the Holy Spirit can help you apply the truths of the Bible to everyday life.

All of us approach the Bible with a lot of preconceived ideas and misinformation. We hear the axiom, "You've got to work for what you get," so often that we easily get caught up in earning our way to heaven or winning God's approval. No doubt you've also heard, "God helps those who help themselves" so often you think it's a Bible verse. It isn't. From this statement we get the false idea that asking God's help should be a last resort—after everything else has been tried. But we must approach God's Word as little children who know nothing and who expect it to change our attitudes and actions. When we let the Bible speak to us and remake us, God's Word is powerful stuff.

For the word of God is living and active. Sharper than any double-edged sword, it penetrates even to dividing soul and spirit, joints and marrow; it judges the thoughts and attitudes of the heart. Nothing in all creation is hidden from God's sight. Everything is uncovered and laid bare before the eyes of him to whom we must give account. Hebrews 4:12–13

LeRoy spends hours in the lotus position trying to meditate to achieve "oneness with the universe." Ken goes door-to-door every day, whether he feels like it or not, to try to convert people to his religion. Keesha has piled up enough good works to fill a grain elevator, yet continues to volunteer for every charitable organization that will accept her services.

The sad part is that none of these people feels certain that he or she has done enough to please God.

The major thing that differentiates true Christianity from the other religions is *salvation by faith based on grace*—God's willingness to show His mercy and kindness in order to save us, even though we don't deserve it.

Titus 3:5 tells us:

> *He saved us, not because of righteous things we had done, but because of his mercy. He saved us through the washing of rebirth and renewal by the Holy Spirit.*

Jesus died for our sins. When we give ourselves totally to God and invite the Spirit of Jesus to live inside us, we become new people in Christ Jesus.

If you have accepted Jesus into your life, don't ever forget that you're saved by grace, made righteous by faith, and kept safe in Jesus by the mighty hand of God. The devil will come up with things like, "Hey, you lied. So now you've lost your salvation forever." If Satan tries these tricks, just tell him the truth: "Of course I'm not good enough for God, but He wants me anyway." Or say, "Look here, Mr. Devil, 1 John 1:9 says, 'If we confess our sins, he is faithful and just and will forgive us our sins and purify us from all unrighteousness.' Lying was wrong. But I can confess my sin and receive forgiveness."

If you don't want to be another casualty, find out God's truth in His Word, and tell the truth to the devil. Never let Satan try to talk you out of receiving God's grace.

> *For it is by grace you have been saved, through faith—and this is not from yourselves, it is the gift of God—not by works, so that no one can boast.*
> Ephesians 2:8–9

Day 242

The Dream That Came True

It was only a dream, but it was fun while it lasted.

Doug had a fear of meeting new people. In his dream, he had to enter a room full of strangers and witness about his faith in Christ to someone in the room. Doug was terrified, and he felt that it should be a job reserved for self-assured jocks. Just then a beautiful white dove landed on his shoulder and kindly began to speak: "Don't worry, I'll help you. Just go and ask the first person his name and tell him yours."

Doug did it, even though he stuttered a lot.

"That's fine. You did your best," cooed the dove. Then it explained, "Ask this guy how things are going, and his reply will give you an opportunity to tell him about Jesus."

Doug obeyed. Although he hesitated several times and forgot the Bible verse he wanted to use, the man listened. The dove smiled. "That's wonderful. You're learning to be a witness for Jesus."

The good news is that God's grace—His favor, kindness, and mercy—is with you just like that dove that sat on Doug's shoulder. It's there if you listen to the Holy Spirit, the Comforter, and don't chase Him away by accepting one of the devil's lies.

The psalmist continues, "No *good* thing does he withhold from those whose walk is blameless" (Psalm 84:11). If you are following Jesus with all your heart, God's kindness, favor, grace, and mercy are yours twenty-four hours a day. God's grace can be yours not only for sharing your faith, but also when you get a traffic ticket, when the teacher gives a pop quiz, and when you get blamed for what your little brother did. It's possible to sense so much of God's care and acceptance that these things don't throw you. By receiving God's grace and the power of the Holy Spirit, Doug's dream can come true for you. You can escape from the prison formed by your fear. You can reign in life because there will always be enough of God's grace for you to be on top of things.

How much more will those who receive God's abundant provision of grace and of the gift of righteousness reign in life through the one man, Jesus Christ.
Romans 5:17

Day 243

Is God Wearing His Happy Face Today?

Perhaps you've read the book *Call of the Wild*. Beaten constantly by his master and nearly starved to death, a dog named Buck was rescued by a man named John Thornton. In return for the genuine love and care he received, Buck willingly risked his life for his master.

God has done so much more for you than John Thornton did for Buck. He sent His only Son to die for you so you could be saved from hell. He constantly sends His love and grace and mercy and blessing your way. He has a wonderful plan for your life, plus forever in heaven with Him. Who wouldn't want to obey a God like that?

When you realize the depth of God's grace and kindness and mercy, you'll want to obey Him. In fact, you'll count it a joy to give up something for Jesus. Receive the grace of God. Every day expect to see more of God's kindness, favor, and mercy in your life. Constantly thank God for His grace, and things will change.

> *All over the world this gospel is bearing fruit and growing, just as it has been doing among you since the day you heard it and understood God's grace in all its truth.* Colossians 1:6

The more you experience of the riches of God's grace, the more natural your Christian obedience and outreach will become.

The devil tries to feed us lies and get us to act on them so we can no longer enjoy God's grace. When you swallow the devil's lies that you're no good, that it's impossible to please God, that He's a big meanie anyway so you might as well go and sin some more—God in His compassion must show His stern face. After all, a kind person doesn't smile and cheer as he watches someone edging closer to a dangerous cliff.

Whether you're seeing God's happy face or God's frowning face depends totally on whether you're letting His grace transform your life. From your point of view, is God wearing His happy face today?

> *Consider therefore the kindness and sternness of God: sternness to those who fell, but kindness to you, provided that you continue in his kindness.* Romans 11:22

Day 244

When Thinking Could Be Hazardous to Your Health

What kind of thoughts do you have about yourself? Positive Pete stands in front of the mirror for hours proclaiming, "I'm super-intelligent and I'm the handsomest guy in my class." But he still gets Ds in English and hasn't succeeded in broadening his shoulders. Only in his dreams do hordes of girls run in his direction.

On the other hand, Humble Henrietta sprinkles her conversation with "I know *I* can never learn to drive a car" and "I need to wear a lot a makeup—it helps hide my face." Somehow people fail to see her as a billboard advertisement for true humility.

The problem is that the devil has a special strategy for getting people to think of themselves in the wrong way. He'll dish out superiority or inferiority, whichever lie you'll swallow. Paul, who says the grace of God made him a new person, explains something he learned. He says,

> *For by the grace given me I say to every one of you: Do not think of yourself more highly than you ought, but rather think of yourself with sober judgment, in accordance with the measure of faith God has given you.* Romans 12:3

Faith to think of yourself in the right way comes from God and His Word. The idea is that you must get your opinion of yourself from God. Remember that the Bible says:

> *I always thank God for you because of his grace given you in Christ Jesus. For in Him you have been enriched in every way—in all your speaking and in all your knowledge.* 1 Corinthians 1:4–5

Reject the devil's lies. And when some ray of thought from outer space suddenly descends with, *I'm the handsomest guy in our church—any girl who gets my attention should count her blessings,* don't let your mind wallow in such daydreams. Recall that God says: "Man looks at the outward appearance, but the Lord looks at the heart" (1 Samuel 16:7).

You'll never be emotionally and spiritually healthy if you don't let God define who you are. Return Satan's thoughts without opening the package.

The newspaper headline caught Jane's eye: "Volunteer Serves Prison Sentence for Gang Leader." When a tough gang leader robbed a bank, his lawyer dug out a two-century-old law that was still on the books and arranged to serve jail time himself so the boy could go free.

"I'm seventy years old," the lawyer explained, "and I've lived my life. I want Kirby to be able to live his."

It's a heartwarming story—until you find out how it ends. When asked how he felt about having his freedom, Kirby quipped, "It's great. Now I can rob banks and Mr. Warwick can sit in jail."

Something is wrong. It just doesn't make sense that someone should take the rap for Kirby so he can enjoy right standing with the law while he continues to be personally corrupt.

It seems that some people view Jesus' death for our sins exactly the way Kirby perceived the sacrifice Mr. Warwick made for him. Like the lawyer in the story, Jesus took your place. He suffered the penalty of your sin so that God can count you as righteous—*perfect*—in His sight. You, who have sinned like everyone else in the human race, can go to heaven because Jesus died in your place. No matter how many times you hear it, never fail to appreciate the wonder of what Jesus did for you.

"God made him who had no sin to be sin for us, so that in him we might become the righteousness of God" (2 Corinthians 5:21) means more than God viewing us as sinless, because Jesus died to erase all imperfections. It implies a change on the inside so profound that it transforms our attitudes and actions. It isn't only receiving God's forgiveness and righteousness by faith in order to get saved from hell; it's constantly appropriating the righteousness of Jesus by faith. It's saying, "Jesus, I can't love that person, but by faith I'll reach out in kindness, and I'll trust you to supply the love." It's obeying your mother with the faith that God will change her unreasonable attitude and protect you in the meantime. Receiving God's righteousness isn't a whitewash job that only covers up all the muck. It's a total exchange. You give Jesus your sin and He gives you His righteousness. It's the best trade you'll ever make.

Day 246

But You've Got to Build the Dam!

"Evie, you're lazy and undisciplined. Your room is a disgrace. Look at you—forty pounds overweight and eating candy." Most of the time Evie politely stared at her mother as she tuned out the words. But this time she listened and felt terrible. The guy she had a crush on said something that really made her think. " Evie," he had said, "if you'd lose weight, you'd be the prettiest girl around." But what could she do?

> *Do not offer the parts of your body to sin, as instruments of wickedness, but rather offer yourselves to God, as those who have been brought from death to life; and offer the parts of your body to him as instruments of righteousness.* Romans 6:13

In faith, relying on the power of the Holy Spirit, tell your body that it will eat tossed salad and fish instead of cupcakes, potato chips, and chocolate bars, so it will be in better shape to serve God. Instead of getting down on yourself, remember that you're a new creature in Christ and that "the righteous will live by faith" (Romans 1:17). Believe that God can show you organizational skills and make you a good worker.

Your body, mind, emotions, and will are somewhat like the destructive flood waters of spring. They can't go unchecked or they wreck everything in their path. To control them, it's essential to put faith in a capable engineer to build the right kind of dam. Once the rushing waters are under control, they become an asset. You must believe that God can change you and willingly endure whatever pain is necessary to place your body, mind, emotions, and will under the domination of the Holy Spirit to aid you in obeying God. But you must cooperate in getting the dam built no matter what the cost. The Holy Spirit must be the designer of that dam because your blueprints, like those of millions of others who tried out their own ideas, will fail.

> *For if you live according to the sinful nature, you will die; but if by the Spirit you put to death the misdeeds of the body, you will live.* Romans 8:13

As Derrick, a new Christian, began reading the Ten Commandments, he thought being a Christian would be pretty easy. He had never had a problem with idol worship, and he thought quitting lying would not be a problem. Stealing wasn't a temptation for him, and swearing was easy enough to stop. But the command "Honor your father" really blew his mind. The Sermon on the Mount laid it on even thicker—"Love your enemies" (Matthew 5:44). Derrick didn't know if he could even tolerate his stepfather—to say nothing of loving him.

Derrick's stepfather resented Derrick and took everything out on him. Derrick had grown to hate him.

Do you face a similar situation? The answer is wrapped up in these few words: "The righteous will live by faith." Derrick must put faith in God's power to give him love for his stepfather.

For it is God who works in you to will and to act according to his good purpose. Philippians 2:13

Derrick, empowered by the Spirit to live by faith, will be able to change his words and deeds. He can use the next available opportunity to tell a friend, "My stepfather is an intelligent man and a hard worker. He just became vice-president of the company he works for." And Derrick can pray for his stepfather every day.

The neat thing is that as you obey by faith, God works a miracle in you—He changes you into the person who can obey His commands from the heart. By faith you rise out of the temptation to try to lower God's standards so you can live up to them. And by faith you receive His supernatural power to live a supernatural life. "Now to him who is able to do immeasurably more than all we ask or imagine, according to his power that is at work within us" (Ephesians 3:20).

Ability to live right is a gift. Receive it by faith and open the package.

However, to the man who does not work but trusts God who justifies the wicked, his faith is credited as righteousness. Romans 4:5

Day 248

Do You Have Some Extra Faith in the Bank?

When Tyson became a Christian, he stopped doing drugs. He believed that God would help him stay in school and become a better student, and his faith was rewarded. He believed that God could give him love for his family, and he experienced a miracle inside. Whenever he felt the depression that he used to alleviate with drugs, he read his Bible and used praise and thanksgiving as his weapons. And it worked.

But when Tyson added a job to his already busy schedule—and then came down with a bad case of the flu—he became very discouraged. He got into a huge argument with his father, and he felt that old hatred creeping back. Facing a week's makeup work, he wanted to drop out and forget it. The devil was right there to try to steal all his faith.

Satan tries to destroy our faith because he too knows that "we live by faith, not by sight" (2 Corinthians 5:7). In order to make you sin, he must rob your faith. Your first line of defense is not using your willpower to resist temptation; it's guarding your faith and building it up by meditating on God's Word.

Once you were alienated from God and were enemies in your minds because of your evil behavior. But now he has reconciled you by Christ's physical body through death to present you holy in his sight, without blemish and free from accusation—if you continue in your faith, established and firm, not moved from the hope held out in the gospel. Colossians 1:21–23

But you can't wait until you're sick and are bombarded with all kinds of trials and temptations to establish yourself in the faith. Put something in your bank account *now* and save it for a rainy day. In this way you'll build a strong wall against attack. If you have a tendency to quit when things get tough, arm yourself with Scripture passages on perseverance and hard work. If you're often tempted to return to drugs and alcohol when you feel depressed, learn with the psalmist how to praise and thank your way out of those nasty moods. Do you have some extra faith in the bank? You're going to need it.

Build yourself up in your most holy faith. Jude 20

I once asked a student if he'd had a good weekend. "No," he replied. "It was terrible. I ran a red light and hit a police car. Besides that, I was driving without a license!" To that student, the law was a real curse.

The Bible says Christ redeemed us from the curse of the law (Galatians 3:13). Some people think this means that Christians can do whatever they wish. That simply isn't true. God's moral laws still apply.

A red light doesn't need to be a curse. It can be a real blessing! In fact, it's designed for your safety. It's only when you're paying the traffic ticket or staring at that crumpled front fender that you find the law unreasonable.

Jesus died not to take away God's eternal standards but the curse of the law. Jesus paid the price for your sin once and for all—you never need to enact another ceremony to be cleansed of it! If you confess and forsake your sin, He'll forgive you.

Jesus not only died, but He rose again as conqueror over Satan and sin. Forgiveness and the victory over sin can be yours because of Jesus' death.

The death he died, he died to sin once for all; but the life he lives, he lives to God. In the same way, count yourselves dead to sin but alive to God in Christ Jesus. Romans 6:10–11

In addition to taking advantage of His forgiveness when you fail, realize that God has good reasons for all the commandments in the Bible, and He offers you supernatural power to obey them.

God's commandments are great if you trust God's wisdom in giving them, have asked forgiveness for breaking them, and are depending on the Jesus-power inside you for keeping them. Jesus, the curse-remover, wants you to have a new perspective on life. And that's what stopping at red lights has to do with eternal redemption.

We wait for Jesus Christ, who gave himself for us to redeem us from all wickedness and to purify for himself a people that are his very own, eager to do what is good. Titus 2:13–14

Day 250

Faith—the Price Tag of a New Life

Shania looked at her protruding tummy. She wouldn't be able to hide her pregnancy much longer. Her mother was already suspicious.

Why had she ruined her whole life? Why had she believed Nathan when he said sex was the only way they could truly express their love for each other? Why had he left her when she told him she was going to have his baby? Would God ever forgive her? She felt so alone and so scared.

Maybe you, like Shania, feel marked for life by the consequences of sin. Perhaps past wrongdoing continues to haunt you, and you wonder if you'll ever be free from guilt. As you view the shambles of your existence, do you doubt your ability to become a success?

Listen to the story of King Manasseh. He not only worshiped idols, but he sacrificed his sons to them and carried images of them into God's temple. He practiced witchcraft and ignored the Lord when He tried to speak to him. But as a POW in Assyria, he repented. God not only pardoned him but gave him back his throne and used him to destroy all the idols and lead his people back to God. (Read the whole story in 2 Kings 21.)

No matter what you've done, you can return to God and receive His complete forgiveness and power to live a new life. Micah knew this.

Who is a God like you, who pardons sin and forgives the transgression of the remnant of his inheritance? You do not stay angry forever but delight to show mercy. You will again have compassion on us; you will tread our sins underfoot and hurl all our iniquities into the depths of the sea. Micah 7:18÷19

Because of Jesus' death, God can trade you your sin for His righteousness! It's the best deal in the world. The only price is faith. You can have faith when He says He'll forgive you completely and give you an entirely new life. When you face each moment knowing that a loving and all-powerful God is in control, there is no reason to sin. The price tag on that brand-new life you need says "faith."

For in the gospel a righteousness from God is revealed, a righteousness that is by faith from first to last, just as it is written: "The righteous will live by faith." Romans 1:17

Jaeden's mind kept flashing back to the one day he just couldn't forget. It was the last day of school and students had been dismissed at eleven-thirty. Steve had invited the guys over for a couple cases of beer. Celebrating the end of school with abandon, Jaeden drank a lot. "Let's go to McDonald's," someone suggested, and four friends hopped into his car.

Jaeden was driving Indianapolis–500-style when suddenly a four-year-old boy ran in front of the car. The boy was killed instantly.

That limp little body, the hysterical cries of his mother, and the heartless questions of the policeman rushed across his mind as he relived the scene. And then came the unforgettable words that came back to torture him: The mother had screamed, "You killed my boy!" Mentally, Jaeden received his six-hundred-eighty-ninth conviction of murder.

Six months after the accident, Jaeden had accepted Jesus as his Savior. Although he knew his sins were forgiven and he could go to heaven, the cloud of guilt would not leave him. He was redeemed, but he didn't feel redeemed.

Moses was a murderer, David was an adulterer, and Paul a persecutor of Christians. God forgave each of these men and used them mightily. The reason God could re-tool their lives and make them into heroes of the faith is that they received God's pardon and lived like forgiven men.

Let God's Word sink deep into your spirit.

For as high as the heavens are above the earth, so great is his love for those who fear him; as far as the east is from the west, so far has he removed our transgressions from us. As a father has compassion on his children, so the Lord has compassion on those who fear him; for he knows how we are formed, he remembers that we are dust. Psalm 103:11–14

Who are you to argue with God and decide not to feel forgiven? One big crash (or mistake or set of circumstances) can't ruin your life because of redemption—the restoration of ruined lives.

Put your hope in the Lord, for with the Lord is unfailing love and with him is full redemption. Psalm 130:7

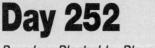

Day 252

Boredom Blasted by Blessings

Kirk sighed as his physics teacher launched into his "When-I-was-in-high-school-students-respected-their-teachers" speech. In Kirk's next class, he had to listen to thirty oral reports on the dangers of nuclear war. And finally in language lab, the most exciting thing that happened was repeating a *new* French phrase over and over again.

Having worked at a fast-food joint for two years, Kirk longed for a more challenging job. Even the church youth group seemed boring—always singing the same songs and endlessly discussing which movies and TV shows were okay for Christians to watch.

One day as he thumbed through his Bible, a couple of verses jumped out at him.

With joy you will draw water from the wells of salvation. Isaiah 12:3

For he has rescued us from the dominion of darkness and brought us into the kingdom of the Son he loves, in whom we have redemption, the forgiveness of sins. Colossians 1:13–14

This really meant that the price had already been paid not only to forgive Kirk's sins, but to bring him into another dimension of living. He really could draw waters from the wells of salvation with the assurance that God wanted to do something about his lackluster life!

Because people tell God how to rescue them and give Him their time-table, they "lose their faith," thinking God did not answer. Your part is to put your faith in Jesus as your Savior and Redeemer from the present problem, and claim the deliverance God has promised. Maybe you, like Kirk, need to hold on in faith until the headlines of your life read: "Boredom Blasted by Blessings!"

For you know that it was not with perishable things such as silver or gold that you were redeemed from the empty way of life handed down to you from your forefathers, but with the precious blood of Christ, a lamb without blemish or defect. 1 Peter 1:18–19

Karina surveyed her disorderly room. Dirty clothes filled one corner. Her dresser was stacked high with textbooks, scattered pages of a term paper, and half the CDs she owned. On her vanity were enough bottles and jars to stock the health and beauty department at Wal-Mart. Dreading what she might find under the bed, Karina tried to mentally change the subject. Why couldn't she be more tidy?

Karina knew that if God said she was redeemed from futile ways, it was true. But she certainly didn't *feel* redeemed. And if she were totally honest, keeping a clean room seemed like an utter impossibility. Why couldn't she be different?

And everything that does not come from faith is sin. Romans 14:23

Suddenly Karina realized the root of her problem—she considered herself hopeless, the thought of cleaning her room an impossibility. The Bible called her lack of faith sin, and she had to confess it as such.

Although Karina knew it would be uphill all the way, she could see that nobody was ever redeemed without faith. People even miss heaven because of lack of faith. And she couldn't take advantage of God's power to restore and renovate areas of her life without stick-to-it faith and action based on firm trust in God. Karina also saw how the devil continually tried to cause her to put her mind on all the past failures in this area to snuff out any faith that might be rising within her. She determined to believe that God could rectify the situation, and she prayed for specific changes.

Karina resolved to ask God to soften her heart and give her the next step, and the next, and the next. She thought, *God really does have a way of vaporizing vicious circles.* Then she lifted up her bedspread and started putting away the things she found under her bed.

You are my hiding place; you will protect me from trouble and surround me with songs of deliverance. Psalm 32:7

Have you met Phydo, my fluffy French poodle? I've decided that he should be a new liberated dog. Instead of his friendly, cuddly self, he'll be a fierce watchdog—this will remove any doubts he may have about his masculinity. And I will give him talking lessons, because no dog can be really free unless he can express his desires in words. He will have neither discipline nor restraints.

Wait a minute! Can you imagine the frustration poor Phydo will experience if someone tries to change his true personality and forces him to attempt the impossible? His lack of success will evoke scolding and rejection from those who should be part of his support group. Is this freedom?

What is freedom for you? Do you know? Honest human beings would have to say no. Those who say they're looking for freedom either exchange one set of chains for another or seem to build for themselves rather formidable prisons. The knowledge that "I did it my way" isn't very comforting when one surveys the mess that has been created.

How do you start on the freedom trail? The Bible tells us:

> *But the man who looks intently into the perfect law that gives freedom, and continues to do this, not forgetting what he has heard, but doing it—he will be blessed in what he does.* James 1:25

God's rules found in the Bible will correctly define freedom for you. God created you, and His plan is to make you totally free to be your true self.

Don't say things like, "If only my parents weren't so strict, if only I didn't have to attend boring classes every day, if only I could get to a bigger city where something exciting is happening, then I'd feel free." Listen to what God says. His formula for freedom starts on the inside, not on the outside. Because it's not dependent on what others do or say or think, the freedom God gives has a lifetime guarantee. Use God's Word to start on the road to freedom—freedom to be the real you that God created.

Adam had been as excited as anyone else about this trip to Paris with his French class. It had been a great adventure. They were leaving for home at six the next morning and this, their last day in Paris, was a free day. When Lucy decreed that everyone should go shopping, no one objected. But because he hated to shop, Adam decided to return to the Louvre, one of the greatest museums in the whole world. When would he get another opportunity to see so many treasures from the past?

Overconfident in his French and his sense of direction, he left his map in the hotel room. He hopped on a bus only to discover, after a while, that he had no idea where he was going. When he asked for directions, no one seemed to understand him. He was totally dependent on other people—their captive. His only hope was to put himself at the mercy of some cab driver. Adam was frightened.

Without a map or a working knowledge of French, Adam surrendered his freedom. Not knowing the right way to go put him in a jail constructed of unfavorable circumstances. Similarly, ignorance of the Bible and of scriptural principles can cause you to end up in a spiritual prison.

If you hold to my teaching, you are really my disciples. Then you will know the truth, and the truth will set you free. John 8:31–32

Don't strike out on your own. Although you should listen respectfully to advice of mature Christians, don't be bound by what people tell you. Your freedom depends on your following what God says in His Word and letting the Holy Spirit apply that word to each situation in your life.

God's Word is like Adam's map. It will tell you where to go. The Holy Spirit in you, in some ways, can be compared to a mastery of French, which enables you to work out the details in your journey and arrive at the desired destination. Knowing God's truth, letting the Holy Spirit apply that truth to your situation, and obeying it conscientiously will keep you out of jail—and lead you into freedom.

I will walk about in freedom, for I have sought out your precepts. Psalm 119:45

Day 256
Slave Escapes From Devil's Den

The date is January 1, 1863. Abraham Lincoln has just announced that all slaves in the Confederate states are free. Yet Emmie, a young slave girl whose overseer is especially cruel, continues her drudgery in the cotton fields from sunup until sundown. Why? A war is still going on. The South has not yet been conquered, so the new law can't be enforced.

On April 9, 1865, the day the South surrenders, Emmie is still slaving away. The knowledge that she is no longer a slave doesn't really free Emmie. Neither do changes in the system. Working for pay on the same plantation, she still believes that she is inferior. She is still a slave in her heart.

Maybe you're an Emmie-type Christian. Even though you've accepted Jesus as your Lord, you don't feel free from Satan and sin and condemnation.

Let's look at what you need to do to live in the liberty that's yours in Jesus. Although Jesus has declared you free because He totally defeated Satan on the cross, the master liar will constantly try to enslave you with chains of deception. You must fight to stay free. Your weapon is the truth found in God's Word. If the devil points out fifteen reasons why this will be a bad day and you feel like a slave to circumstances, you can answer: "But thanks be to God, who always [even on rainy days when I don't understand the math homework] leads us in triumphal procession in Christ" (2 Corinthians 2:14).

The only power the devil has is that sort of deception. But you must take to heart biblical warnings like these: "Watch and pray so that you will not fall into temptation" (Matthew 26:41), be "watchful and thankful" (Colossians 4:2), and "be self-controlled and alert" (1 Peter 5:8). The devil can never get you as long as you use God's Word as ammunition.

You don't have to remain an Emmie, whose factual freedom has never become an inner reality. Ask Jesus to show you deep in your spirit the freedom you have in Him. Meditate on the verses about freedom in Christ and join the ex-slaves that are escaping from the devil's den.

It is for freedom that Christ has set us free. Stand firm, then, and do not let yourselves be burdened again by the yoke of slavery. Galatians 5:1

Henry Smid stole a large amount of money from a German bank when he was a youth. He managed to escape from prison and immigrate to America. Here he formed a prosperous business, retired well-off, and enjoyed a fine reputation in the community. Not even his wife knew of his former life of crime. So the people of Forest Hill were shocked to learn that ninety-year-old Mr. Smid had returned to Germany and given himself up to the authorities.

"I was never free on the inside," he explained. "I just couldn't live with myself any longer." Even after he received a pardon, Henry insisted on serving out his prison sentence.

You can't erase sin any easier than Henry could. You can rationalize your actions, declare yourself forgiven, and get everyone else to say that what you're doing is okay. Still, the nagging sense of guilt remains. Without a pardon from Jesus, you'll never be free. Confess and forsake every sin—no matter how long ago you did it, no matter how embarrassing that confession might be. Then *fully accept* the pardon of Jesus. Don't be like Henry.

Jesus declared to the people in the synagogue at Nazareth: "He has sent me to proclaim freedom for the prisoners" (Luke 4:18). But He didn't run around letting people out of jail. Instead, He freed the Samaritan woman at the well from her ignorance and her sin. He broke the chains of the fear of death for the dying thief on the cross. What is your prison? Jesus can set you free. Your part is to obey and receive. The truth is that you were born again to be free.

Let them give thanks to the Lord for his unfailing love and his wonderful deeds for men, for he breaks down gates of bronze and cuts through bars of iron.
Psalm 107:15–16

Day 258

Freedom at Bargain Prices

The Wuol family is sitting down to dinner when Nina exclaims, "I'm really excited about my new diet! I can eat all I want, I just have to eat the right things."

Her brother, Tyler, interjects, "Yeah, right. You won't stick with it. Don't you remember your New Year's resolution to go running every day? Your jogging outfit is as good as new. Who are you kidding?"

Does Nina's story remind you of similar failures in your life? The ability to "stick with it" seems to be a missing ingredient in modern life. Humans are notably deficient in daily disciplines that form correct habits. It's the very reason that, although Jesus offers liberty to believers, so few Christians are really free. Inner freedom has two aspects: letting the Holy Spirit reign in our lives and relying on His power to put Bible principles into practice.

Now the Lord is the Spirit, and where the Spirit of the Lord is, there is freedom. And we, who with unveiled faces all reflect the Lord's glory, are being transformed into his likeness with ever-increasing glory, which comes from the Lord, who is the Spirit. 2 Corinthians 3:17–18

Now that you know these things, you will be blessed if you do them. John 13:17

After you learn some biblical principles of freedom, you must *continually* put them into practice; you must *constantly* renew your mind by meditating on Scripture, and by *daily* obedience you will maintain your freedom. The devil so successfully uses wrong thought patterns to erase scriptural truth that you must retrain your mind. Whenever you realize that you have violated God's Word, you must confess your sin and turn in the opposite direction.

Following Jesus by confessing and forsaking sin is *much more important* than anything else. Jesus has made you a new creation with power from His Holy Spirit to obey God. When your body complains, don't listen. Be led by the Spirit. Claim the truth of Scripture and act promptly each time Satan tries to put some chains around you.

What picture comes to your mind when you think of a winner?

Do you see a smiling track star brushing a wisp of unruly hair off his forehead as he repeats some humble-sounding words over the microphone, shakes the hand of the coach, and receives his trophy? Or do you visualize hours of hard training, turning down pizza before the track meet, getting up at 5:00 a.m. to go on a long run before school? Do you imagine the trophy and the celebration for South High's undefeated football team? Or do you look back to sweaty boys practicing day after day under the sweltering August sun, the pain of torn muscles, and the discipline of sticking by the training rules?

It might seem strange, but winning and suffering go together. The apostle Paul knew that. Beaten and put into prison unjustly, he acted every bit like a winner. Knowing that he served a God who never lost a tournament, he organized a midnight pep rally. He and Silas sang praises to the Lord, God sent an earthquake, and soon they were free.

As a passenger on a ship during a terrible storm, he trusted God. One night God sent His angel to assure Paul that his life and the lives of those who traveled with him would be saved, even though the ship would be lost. Paul announced this to everyone and proceeded to take charge—certainly one of the few men in history to organize a successful shipwreck! Even in the suffering of being a prisoner, Paul was not a victim. His motto was "For to me, to live is Christ and to die is gain" (Philippians 1:21).

Because you are in Jesus, you play on the winning team. The power of Jesus within you gives you the capacity to triumph in every situation. But you can just sit on the bench and watch other Christians suffer, fight, and win. Or you can be a full participant. Winning and suffering go together, but the winning is wonderful.

Don't ever forget that it's "onward Christian soldiers," not "onward Christian couch potatoes!"

Let us fix our eyes on Jesus, the author and perfecter of our faith, who for the joy set before him endured the cross, scorning its shame, and sat down at the right hand of the throne of God. Hebrews 12:2

Day 260

The Invisible Victory

Perhaps you're saying "Hey, don't give me any of this theoretical stuff about being a winner. I'm defeated and I know it."

Remember one thing: If the devil can get your eyes on something other than Jesus, you will live in defeat.

In late 1944, U.S. military leaders knew that Hitler's defeat was only a matter of time. Hitler, however, wanted another victory and concocted a scheme so unlikely that, for a while, it worked. He chose several English-speaking German soldiers and put them in American uniforms. Road signs were changed, and these Germans guided U.S. troops straight into a trap. Hitler got his victory, known in history as the Battle of the Bulge.

Although one American unit was entirely surrounded by German forces, its commander, Antony McAuliffe, recognized that the situation was temporary and that U.S. troops not only had the capacity to rescue him, but they could win the war. In spite of the worst possible circumstances, his reply to the German demand to surrender was, "Nuts!" His faith in an unseen reality made a successful rescue operation possible.

The devil will see to it that your life is full of Battle of the Bulge situations. Maybe your parents are getting a divorce or your best friend really lets you down—God asks you not to waver but to believe that He has the power to rescue you. God knows that this is not easy to remember.

Therefore put on the full armor of God, so that when the day of evil comes, you may be able to stand your ground, and after you have done everything, to stand. Stand firm then. Ephesians 6:13–14

Because God acts in response to our faith, it is not a matter of living through the day but of expecting the victory even when nothing but defeat seems possible. When General McAuliffe said "nuts" to the surrender demand, nothing in his circumstances had changed. But he had made the decision that would make help possible. By faith, win some invisible victories right now. Then let God bring them into reality.

Do not be afraid. Stand firm and you will see the deliverance the Lord will bring you today. Exodus 14:13

Reading through the Bible, you meet a lot of members of the faith hall of fame: Moses at the Red Sea, Gideon and his three hundred, David facing Goliath, Daniel in the lions' den, and Paul and Silas in prison. Faith is the common ingredient found in all these victories.

Moses could have surrendered to Pharaoh's army; Gideon could have run away; David could have let someone else volunteer to fight the giant; Daniel could have prayed in secret; and Paul could have groaned and complained all night. These men weren't different from you and me—we're all made out of the same stuff. Their secret was finding the faith connection and plugging in.

And without faith it is impossible to please God, because anyone who comes to him must believe that he exists and that he rewards those who earnestly seek him. Hebrews 11:6

Do you really believe that God gives victories to those who want Him more than anything else? Are you sure that God takes charge of the situations we truly turn over to Him? If God rewards those who diligently look for Him, your job interview will turn out differently if you take the time and effort to find the faith connection.

Because we need to break through layers of habit, hypocrisy, and ignorance, we must let God be the judge of our diligence in seeking Him. It's too easy to think that if our first effort isn't good enough, we can give up. We moan, "I really prayed about it, and everything went wrong," forgetting about the perseverance factor.

The Bible says God *rewards* those who *earnestly* seek Him. You must believe that. In fact, you can't be a winner if you don't take that verse literally. God does give special prizes to those who search for Him with all their hearts. Acting on that promise is the key to the faith connection.

For everyone born of God overcomes the world. This is the victory that has overcome the world, even our faith. John 5:4

Day 262

Spark Plugs for Christians

Clark was totally discouraged. He had volunteered to pass out invitations to a city-wide youth outreach event. But it wasn't going well. Most people were throwing away the flyers as soon as they got them—if they were even nice enough to take one from Clark in the first place. One student he approached said, "Leave me alone. I just can't believe that a straight-A student like you could fall for such religious nonsense." Gulping, Clark managed a nervous, "We all have our own opinions."

This final encounter took the wind out of Clark's sails. He didn't talk to anyone else about the city-wide event.

What would you think of a quarterback who grounded the ball the minute it looked as if someone might tackle him? How would you view the firefighter who, when he saw how big the blaze was, turned and left for home? The truth is, getting tackled doesn't kill a guy who's in good condition, and a firefighter with proper training and equipment *can* put out a very big fire. Believing the right thing makes such a difference.

Truth is the spark plug you need to ignite the power of the Holy Spirit in you so you can live victoriously. The devil may say, "You've failed—you can't really share your faith with anybody anyway." But God's truth is:

Though a righteous man falls seven times, he rises again. Proverbs 24:16

Satan may whisper, "No one in your school even cares to hear about God." But truth answers:

Let us not become weary in doing good, for at the proper time we will reap a harvest if we do not give up. Galatians 6:9

So open your Bible. Truth is power, and you could use a few spark plugs.

The law of the Lord is perfect, reviving the soul. The statutes of the Lord are trustworthy, making wise the simple. The precepts of the Lord are right, giving joy to the heart. The commands of the Lord are radiant, giving light to the eyes. Psalm 19:7–8

Jorji stared into the darkness. The digital dial on her snooze alarm blinked 1:20, but sleep was the furthest thing from her mind.

Jorji and four other girls had walked over to Colleen's apartment for Bible study on Friday after school as usual. Supportive and always kind, Colleen talked to them about being open with their problems, sharing their weaknesses, and remembering that God is love. "We're all weak," Colleen had said, "but God loves us anyway, and He understands."

That same evening, Jorji and her friends went to hear a special speaker at Hope's church. He talked about enduring hardship and being a strong Christian. "Don't come up with any excuses. Don't say you're weak. The battle's too tough for sissies. You've got to be strong."

Jorji was sleepless with confusion. "If I don't admit my weaknesses, I'm a liar. But if I'm weak, I'm failing because I'm not a strong soldier."

He [the Lord] said to me, "My grace is sufficient for you, for my power is made perfect in weakness." Therefore I will boast all the more gladly about my weaknesses, so that Christ's power may rest on me. 2 Corinthians 12:9

Paul didn't just admit his weaknesses, he bragged about them. But he didn't make the mistake of misinterpreting them. God wants neither weaklings who refuse His strength nor self-sufficient people who try to spread a little of God's power on top of human ability. It's kind of like the positive force of God's strength attracts our negatively charged weaknesses, and the fusion of the two produces the same kind of stability and potential power that's found in the atom. If we try to neutralize the negatives of our insufficiency or ignore the positive of God's strength, the potential power of combining the two won't ever materialize.

Don't choose to be a self-propelled engine when you could become an atomic power plant. Just admit that you're a minus looking for a plus. Your weakness plus God's strength is dynamite!

Day 264

Are You a Crybaby Christian?

Dora loved Jesus with all her heart. She was faithful in church, obedient to her parents, and kind to others. But Dora had one very big problem: the use of the words "I can't."

Whenever she was asked to do something, she'd reply, "I can't do it very well, but I'll try." She assumed that others were more capable.

Dora could admit her weaknesses, but she had no faith to expect God's power to more than make up for her deficiencies. She operated with an "expect-nothing-and-you'll-get-it-every-time" mentality. She didn't really believe that God was her strength. Apostle Paul said, "When I am weak, then I am strong" (2 Corinthians 12:10).

Have you swallowed any crybaby Christian myths? Have you played the "world-is-getting-so-wicked-that-all-Christians-can-do-is-hibernate" tune on your violin? Have you decided that you can't learn good study habits or stop overeating or give up smoking pot? Are you in a prison of fear or self-consciousness that is so confining you feel you can't escape?

If you are, you're in the perfect place for the next miracle to happen! James tells us to count it all joy when we face trials, because they test our faith and teach us patience. Paul said he delighted in weaknesses, because in Christ he could get all the strength he needed. Gideon had a full-blown inferiority complex, but he was a scaredy-cat who opened his heart to receive God's strength. He and his three hundred men defeated a huge army without firing a gun, shooting an arrow, or even touching an enemy soldier.

It's about time you stopped being a crybaby Christian and really started asking God for strength in every area of weakness. "I can do everything through him who gives me strength" (Philippians 4:13). This is more than a memory verse that nearly everyone can quote: its truth is meant to touch you so deeply that *crybaby* changes to *can-baby*.

Have I not commanded you? Be strong and courageous. Do not be terrified; do not be discouraged, for the Lord your God will be with you wherever you go. Joshua 1:9

As Jack sat down at his desk, he felt the weight of the world on his shoulders. Every day after school he had basketball practice, and every Friday night there was a game. Saturday he worked all day, and as leader of his youth group's planning committee, he not only attended but planned all the Saturday night youth meetings. He had to squeeze in school assignments—and he was taking honors and AP classes. It was already 10:00 p.m. and he was just starting his homework. Jack didn't have time to sleep, let alone have personal devotions.

Worn out and discouraged, Jack put his head down on his desk and began to pray. Straight-A student, basketball star, spiritual giant on the outside, Jack was really weak and close to falling apart on the inside.

In repentance and rest is your salvation, in quietness and trust is your strength. Isaiah 30:15

Strength comes from the Lord, and if you're never still before Him, you'll never hear His voice. Part of repentance is letting God revise your schedule. He will eliminate the things that keep you from spending time with Him. Rest also rebuilds us physically, and you need it.

Sometimes *God* calls you to do things that require extraordinary strength. If you're obeying Him, you can cash in on the abundant supply of spiritual adrenaline available to God's servants. It's a promise: "He gives strength to the weary and increases the power of the weak" (Isaiah 40:29).

But God doesn't give His supernatural strength on a daily basis to over-programmed people. In order to revive your energy, take the time to bind yourself to Jesus. So many forces try to tear you away—busyness, laziness, following *your* dreams instead of God's instructions, and marching in step with the world instead of listening to the heavenly cadence.

Come to me, all you who are weary and burdened, and I will give you rest. Take my yoke upon you and learn from me, for I am gentle and humble in heart, and you will find rest for your souls. For my yoke is easy and my burden is light. Matthew 11:28–30

Day 266

Don't Call the Fire Department

Don was lead guitarist in the band their youth pastor had organized. After a lot of practicing and praying, they went on a week's tour. Monday night the response was tremendous. People loved the music and listened attentively to the testimonies and the preaching.

But after giving the same program four nights in a row, it became routine. Prayer became more of a ceremony than a time to receive desperately needed help from God. On Friday night, the sound system failed to function properly, Debbie forgot the words to her solo, and the whole concert was dry. The Holy Spirit power connection had been unplugged.

Your source of strength is the Holy Spirit—not natural ability, experience, or talent. Like an old-fashioned locomotive that needs fire in its engine to pull the train, you need the power of the Holy Spirit in your spirit. The Bible tells us, "Do not put out the Spirit's fire" (1 Thessalonians 5:19).

Without enough fuel, a fire will die. The Holy Spirit uses Scripture as the catalyst to bring revelation to your heart. If you don't meditate on the Bible, how can that fire keep burning? If you don't claim the strength of the Holy Spirit in prayer, you start running on your own power, and you'll wear yourself out.

Winds of trials and difficulty will attempt to extinguish the blaze. But wind can either snuff out a fire or whip it into a fury. Adopt an attitude that says, "Though war break out against me, even then will I be confident" (Psalm 27:3).

Another thing to remember is that the fire department of public opinion is always ready to fight the fire of the Holy Spirit. Worldly friends and lukewarm Christians will feel uncomfortable around "on-fire fanatics."

Decide to take orders from heavenly headquarters. And whatever you do, don't call the fire department.

For this reason I remind you to fan into flame the gift of God, which is in you through the laying on of of my hands. For God did not give us a spirit of timidity, but a spirit of power, of love and of self-discipline. 2 Timothy 1:6–7

Because God miraculously opened many doors, I was able to teach an elective history course called "Bible and Archeology" in a public high school for several years. Especially when I finished the Old Testament and came to the life of Christ, I was aware of a tremendous spiritual battle. As students from extremely varied backgrounds came face-to-face with the claims of Jesus Christ, the persistent opposition of satanic forces was evident. But after a while I noticed something very interesting.

Whenever there were Christian pupils in my class, it seemed that their very presence dispelled darkness and their influence caused others to accept more truth. I remember one class in which there wasn't a single Christian. It was by far the toughest Bible class I've ever taught. On the other hand, when there were three or four grounded believers taking the course, I found teaching relatively easy. And even a weak, struggling Christian made a noticeable difference. John 1:4–5 explains, "In him was life, and that life was the light of men. The light shines in the darkness, but the darkness has not understood it."

Jesus is the *big* light who ignites a flame in the heart of each believer—and unless you intentionally cover it up, your little light will shine.

Stop to consider it. You *are* the light of the world. Jesus didn't say, "Try to be a little candle burning in the night." He declared, "You are the light of the world." You and all the other Christians have the truth that keeps this planet from complete chaos and disintegration. Let your light shine.

Even a small light can be seen for a great distance in the darkness. During World War II, complete blackouts were ordered for entire cities. Even a burning candle could aid an enemy pilot in finding his target. You'll never know how much the light you display will accomplish.

Obviously, you should do everything possible to make your light as effective as possible. But right now concentrate on this: "I have the light of life. I am a light in this world." While others complain that the younger generation is going to the dogs, that the world is more wicked than ever, and that being good is old-fashioned, you guide your life by this fact: "I am the light of the world. Darkness can never hurt light."

The powers of darkness are afraid of light. And you are the light of the world!

Day 268

Please Pass the Salt

Do you complain about the service in restaurants, the prices in stores, and other drivers on the road? Do you murmur about your boss, your teachers, and your school assignments? Do you use anger to get your own way? Do you constantly defend your rights and spout your opinions—whether or not anyone is interested? If you do, you're losing an opportunity to be a good advertisement for Christianity and ignoring the clear teaching of Scripture: "We who are strong ought to bear with the failings of the weak and not to please ourselves" (Romans 15:1).

Jesus gave a warning that all of us should heed:

You are the salt of the earth. But if the salt loses its saltiness, how can it be made salty again? It is no longer good for anything, except to be thrown out and trampled by men. Matthew 5:13

Salt preserves, cleanses, and brings out flavor. People who obey the Word of God in the power of the Holy Spirit are the salt of the earth. They uphold standards of right and wrong. They spread light and love in an atmosphere of distrust and discouragement. Seeing life from Jesus' point of view, they have a zest for living that is contagious.

As long as salt doesn't mix with other substances, it maintains its full strength. But when you dilute God's truth with the newest psychological theory or public opinion polls, you lose your saltiness. Compromising with the world discredits your testimony. If there is any salt in your life that has lost its flavor, throw it all out and start over with Jesus.

But if you stay salty, you're a terribly important person. Potatoes or planets without salt are worthless. And remember one thing: Salt isn't usually noticed—only its absence is worthy of mention. Live so that when you graduate or change jobs or move to another city, people will in their own way say, "Please pass the salt," "I sure miss her," "She was always so cheerful," "You could never find a more honest and reliable employee," "He's the one who told me about Jesus before I became a Christian."

But thanks be to God, who always leads us in triumphal procession in Christ and through us spreads everywhere the fragrance of the knowledge of him. 2 Corinthians 2:14

Mitch just sat there and said nothing. The biology teacher had asked for volunteers for a debate between creationists and evolutionists. Three people volunteered to debate on the side of evolution, but only Chloe said she wanted to represent the creationist point of view. Mitch was a Christian, and he believed that the Genesis account of how God created the world was totally correct—it's just that he was afraid of what the other kids would think of him.

Have you ever been in Mitch's situation? Thinking seriously about it, you'd have to admit that it's totally illogical for the light of the world to refuse to shine. Jesus said it this way:

No one lights a lamp and puts it in a place where it is hidden. Luke 11:33

Let your light shine before men, that they may see your good deeds and praise your Father in heaven. Matthew 5:16

As you stay close to Jesus, you automatically reflect His light. But you might ask, "How do I do that?" And the answer to your question is, "By the power of the Holy Spirit." The Holy Spirit is the infallible computer on the inside of you that tells you when you're straying away from Jesus, gives you power to stand up for Jesus in a hostile crowd, and tells you what to say and how to say it when opportunities to share your faith arise. Until you give the Holy Spirit free rein to manifest himself to you any way He wishes, your Christian witness will be weak and anemic.

In 1 Thessalonians 5:19 we read, "Do not put out the Spirit's fire." Resisting what the Holy Spirit wants to do through you dims your light. Learn from the Holy Spirit how to stay close to Jesus and let your light shine. Only the Holy Spirit can keep you from hiding your light or using a spotlight that blinds instead of illumines. And if you ever wonder, *How can I—the person who has trouble loving my little brother, who annoys me daily and begs me to drive him and his friends places—ever be a Son reflector who lights up the world?* The answer is this:

"Not by might nor by power but by my Spirit," says the Lord Almighty. Zechariah 4:6

Day 270

Linda sat there stunned. Her father had just announced that he was leaving and moving in with his secretary. Where was God? How could He allow such a thing to happen in her family?

For weeks Linda operated in a fog. Her prayers seemed to bounce back at her, and she couldn't concentrate when she tried to read the Bible. She felt guilty for being a bad testimony, but it seemed as if the light had disappeared from her life. Finally a verse got through to her and slowly things began to change.

When Jesus spoke again to the people, he said, "I am the light of the world. Whoever follows me will never walk in darkness, but will have the light of life." John 8:12

Linda resolved not to allow the visible clouds to obscure the invisible light.

As Christians, we're to mirror the light of Jesus. But sometimes the whole sky appears cloudy, and we feel like we can't find any light to reflect. We forget that behind the clouds, the Son is still shining, God's Word is still true, and God's love is constant no matter how we feel.

Light does come through clouds. It's not pitch black on a cloudy day—you can even get sunburn. Clouds of tragedy, stress, and heartbreak can't eradicate the light of the Son. You need to learn that clouds can't keep you from being a Son reflector. Only the panic that makes you light your own fires instead of trusting God can place you in a position where you receive nothing from the Light of the World.

When things fall apart, remember that you can keep on enjoying the Son light, even on cloudy days.

Light is shed upon the righteous and joy on the upright in heart. Psalm 97:11

Bruce didn't know how to fit Romans 8:29—"For those God foreknew he also predestined to be conformed to the likeness of his Son, that he might be the firstborn among many brothers"—into his theology. He wondered how Christians could be called brothers and sisters of Christ, and he didn't know how to deal with his friend's godlike aspirations.

Although Jesus laid aside His power as God to come to earth, His nature as God did not change. At every point during His earthly life, Jesus deserved the honor due only to God. Wise men worshiped Jesus as a baby. When the blind man who had received his sight found Him, "the man said, 'Lord, I believe,' and he worshiped him" (John 9:38). Jesus accepted the worship He deserved.

But because of His human body and His decision to come to earth, Jesus did not exercise all the rights He had as God. Jesus voluntarily made himself dependent on the Father's life inside Him and declared, "It is the Father, living in me, who is doing his work" (John 14:10).

The most amazing thing is that Jesus came to earth to die and rise again—not only to save us from hell, but to share with us everything He has by adopting us into His family.

The Spirit himself testifies with our spirit that we are God's children. Now if we are children, then we are heirs—heirs of God and co-heirs with Christ.
Romans 8:16–17

It's completely mind-boggling, but it's true. Because you're His adopted kid, Jesus wants to share His power, authority, riches, peace, and joy. And you desperately need to see what great changes you'll experience in your daily life when you start acting like a co-heir of Jesus Christ.

Jesus' offer to give us everything He has is like a king deciding that his doorman will share his palace, his money, his power, and his honor. The doorman can enjoy his newfound position to the fullest, but he must remember that he has no royal blood and is forever indebted to the king. Jesus is willing to give us everything that is His, and He treats us as brothers and sisters. But we must never forget that we are totally God-dependent.

Sure, we get to enjoy using His power and authority, but He owns the property, and the title is still in Jesus' name.

Day 272

All This and Heaven Too!

The year is 1932. Clyde lived on a Kansas farm. Drought and the Great Depression made the struggle for survival fierce. Even during good times, Clyde's family possessed little. Now they had even less. But one day word came that Clyde's great-uncle, who had gone to South Africa to mine diamonds and gold, had named him as his heir. A check came for $500 million with the explanation that this was just his guarantee money until all of his great-uncle's mines were sold and he came into his full inheritance!

You may never have fully realized it, but you're a Clyde with a similar inheritance. Ephesians 1:13–14 tells us:

Having believed, you were marked in him with a seal, the promised Holy Spirit, who is a deposit guaranteeing our inheritance until the redemption of those who are God's possession—to the praise of his glory.

As a born-again Christian, you are a co-heir with Jesus. You'll get to share all the excitement of heaven with Him.

No eye has seen, no ear has heard, no mind has conceived what God has prepared for those who love him. 1 Corinthians 2:9

Jesus told His disciples, "But you will receive power when the Holy Spirit comes on you" (Acts 1:8). The same power that raised Jesus from the dead lives in you (Ephesians 1:17–20). It's the power you've always wanted to live a victorious Christian life and to win your world for Jesus. Besides the complete set of Christlike qualities and dynamite power, the Holy Spirit gives specific spiritual gifts to Christians—your special present from God.

Start taking advantage of all you can receive through "the deposit guaranteeing your inheritance," the precious Holy Spirit. Live like a co-heir of Christ, receiving more and more from the Holy Spirit each day. His blessings are yours to enjoy—all this and heaven too!

". . . Or Are You Going to Spend the Rest of Your Life Surfing the Net?"

Jennica was in charge of the homecoming assembly. For weeks she worked so everything would go perfectly. A lot of students participated, and the performance went like clockwork. When it was all over, only a couple of friends complimented her on the fine job she had done. By Monday morning no one even remembered that there had been a homecoming assembly.

Do you sometimes wonder if you're doing anything worthwhile with your time? Never forget that if you know Jesus, you're part of something wonderful and exciting!

The Spirit himself testifies with our spirit that we are God's children. Now if we are children, then we are heirs—heirs of God and co-heirs with Christ, if indeed we share in his sufferings in order that we may also share in his glory.
Romans 8:16–17

As a Christian and co-heir of Christ, you get to share His work—not as a servant who just follows orders with no idea what's going on, but as a partner whose contribution to the kingdom of God is important. The neighbor kid from a broken home can grow up experiencing Christ's love because you took time to invite him to your weekly Bible stories. The letter you write to the school secretary who just lost her husband can show her that there is hope in Christ. You really can cooperate with Jesus to change your world for the better. You have the privilege of spending your time and energy accomplishing great things for time and eternity.

Are you going to invest your time in spreading the life-changing message that gives hope to the lonely and changes eternal destinies? Or are you going to spend the rest of your life surfing the Net? It's your choice.

The man who plants and the man who waters have one purpose, and each will be rewarded according to his own labor. For we are God's fellow workers.
1 Corinthians 3:8–9

Day 274

Welcome to the World's Greatest Enterprise

Do you ever dream of being the jungle pilot who brings the missionary doctor the right medicine just in time to save the whole village? Of winning an Olympic gold medal and giving the credit to Jesus? Of liberating Muslim women with the gospel? Dreams are great, and reaching the world for Jesus is exciting—it's the world's greatest enterprise.

However, the devil loves dreamers with marvelous plans who do practically nothing. Your vision of making a difference for Jesus will only come true if you start right now. Take a friend out for pizza with the specific purpose of telling him or her about Jesus. When you get to choose any topic in speech class, make yours on "What Jesus Means to Me." Visit a neighbor in the hospital and give him a good Christian book to read. Invite friends to tune in to the teen program on Christian radio. Get permission from your neighbors and start a Bible club for the younger kids in your neighborhood.

Use every opportunity to prepare yourself for greater usefulness in the kingdom of God. Join a Bible study group, take a course on evangelism, or sacrifice to attend the Christian conference. Show up on the Saturday dedicated to beach evangelism.

Don't become a grass-is-always-greener-someplace-else dreamer. Find the place God has for you and stay there—even if it's hard. Serve faithfully even if others are retreating or looking for places where they would have better opportunities for becoming heroes. It's not the realization of *your* dreams or visible results, but the fulfillment of *God's* plan for you that makes you a success in the world's greatest enterprise.

> The first thing Andrew did was to find his brother Simon and tell him, "We have found the Messiah." And he brought him to Jesus. Jesus looked at him and said, "You are Simon son of John. You will be called Cephas" (which, when translated, is Peter). . . . Philip found Nathanael and told him, "We have found the one Moses wrote about in the Law, and about whom the prophets also wrote—Jesus of Nazareth." John 1:41–42, 45

The most important thing you'll ever do is introduce someone else to Jesus.

Day 275

Cristina finally arrived home at 9:30 p.m. She had been rushing non-stop through a day filled with noisy hallways, warning bells, end-of-the-hour buzzers, lunchroom chaos, classroom disorder, and pressure—always more pressure. After school, her boss insisted that she work extra hours in the department store where December shoppers never gave her one minute's rest.

She arrived home frazzled and frustrated, wishing she could spend the rest of her life skiing silently down a mountainside. On the table was a blue envelope with her name on it. Inside was a beautiful blue and gold Christmas card that said, "Peace on Earth. Good will to men. Jesus is our peace." Cristina sighed. She was sure that Jesus had plenty of peace. But how could *she* get some?

Peace is not dependent on circumstances. Because you are a new creature, you have the supernatural life of Jesus within you. As a co-heir with Him, you get to share all that He has, and one of these things is His peace. You receive peace as a gift. Jesus declared:

Peace I leave with you; my peace I give you. I do not give to you as the world gives. Do not let your hearts be troubled and do not be afraid. John 14:27

Receiving the gift of peace involves the conscious decision to ignore the chaotic circumstances and accept the peace Jesus offers. It comes down to a determination to live by faith in God's promises, regardless of how much our emotions protest. The Bible is the truth, and it says, "Do not fear." "Do not let your hearts be troubled." Your emotions will scream, "I can't help being scared, nervous, and upset!" Your will must intervene: *I'll live by the Bible, not by my emotions. I'll let the peace of Jesus rule my heart.*

Peace is the gift Jesus wants to give you. But if you're not willing to drop everything and come with empty hands to receive, it will never be yours.

Do not be anxious about anything, but in everything, by prayer and petition, with thanksgiving, present your requests to God. And the peace of God, which transcends all understanding, will guard your hearts and your minds in Christ Jesus. Philippians. 4:6–7

Day 276

People Are Hard to Figure Out

Do you notice that the football hero who gives a humble speech at the banquet won't even speak to ordinary mortals in the halls? And that the all-smiles-and-sweetness cheerleader tries to destroy the girl who stole her boyfriend? It seems impossible to truly understand people. You probably don't even understand yourself.

To understand people, we need the knowledge given in the Bible. The Bible teaches that people were created good, but through the sin of Adam and Eve, all people became flawed (Romans 5:12). Born without the perfection of Adam and Eve, we're suckers for selfishness—which leads straight to sin.

For all have sinned and fall short of the glory of God. Romans 3:23

A girl may break a promise made to you, but she'll say it's unfair if you break a promise you made to her. No one thinks that a traitor or a double-crosser is doing the right thing. People know there is a standard of behavior they are responsible to live up to, but they lack the power to do it.

This is where Jesus Christ comes in. He died and rose again to forgive us for the moral laws we've broken *and* to give us power to live up to the standard that God expects of us. We just need to accept Him into our lives. People have been ruined by sin, but there is hope for them—in Jesus Christ. People may be hard to figure out, but God wants to take them with all their contradictions and idiosyncrasies and reshape their lives.

For since death came through a man, the resurrection of the dead comes also through a man. For as in Adam all die, so in Christ all will be made alive. 1 Corinthians 15:21–22

Therefore, if anyone is in Christ, he is a new creation; the old has gone, the new has come! 2 Corinthians 5:17

Day 277

Nerds, Weirdos, and Rejects

Many people today consider themselves and others to be zeros. A person is viewed as just a bunch of predetermined chemical responses, a sort of robot-zombie. Life, therefore, has no meaning, and people's actions have no significance. If all this is true, good actions and bad actions alike are meaningless; humans have no guilt, no responsibility for their actions.

I once toured Colorado State Penitentiary. We listened in on a discussion group for inmates. An intelligent man was serving a life sentence because he had entered a shopping center and shot everybody in sight. He said, "It was just something I had to do." He had no guilt. To him, no action had meaning. No country could afford to have people with his philosophy of life.

If each human is a zero, hope, purpose, love, significance, beauty, and relationships mean nothing. We're all lost. Where do people get the idea that a human being is a machine or that a human being is a beast run only by instincts? Of course, if humans evolved from slime, energy, apes, or anything else, that is a logical conclusion. And if humans are part of some life-force—everything is God and God is everything—then an individual has no personal significance either.

However, if humans were created by a personal God in His own image, a human being is very valuable. God gave us personality and freedom of choice. Though we are now flawed because of sin, our inner sense of hope, love, and beauty remind us of what people should be and what we can be in Jesus Christ.

We're not a bunch of nerds, weirdos, and rejects. We're God's special creations. The strawberry malt, horseback riding in the country, the rosy sunset, and the cuddly black puppy have meaning as a part of the life God gave you to enjoy.

So God created man in his own image, in the image of God he created him; male and female he created them. Genesis 1:27

Know that the Lord is God. It is he who made us, and we are his; we are his people, the sheep of his pasture. Psalm 100:3

Day 278
Illogical Logic

Human reason can be corrupted by many things. The salesman who needs money can become blind to all the faults of his product. Many people won't risk embarrassment, loss of prestige, or ridicule, so they lie. Others become so involved in their own ideas that they refuse to listen to anyone else.

Our ability to reason is also warped by things that we have been repeatedly taught. A lot of people believe that humans are basically good, just because that's what they've been told. Yet an afternoon of baby-sitting a two-year-old could cure them of this notion.

You're going to have to decide whether you will believe the Bible or trust what your biology text or some famous psychologist says about truth. In making this decision, you must realize that all human reasoning can be wrong. Proverbs 3:5 says, "Trust in the Lord with all your heart and lean not on your own understanding." Attitudes and opinions of educated and uneducated people alike are affected by many things. PhDs doing research fight with their spouses, carry chips on their shoulders, and hold irrational opinions, just like other people do.

God's Word should be the standard that determines the truth of what you study—and don't forget that it is also the yardstick for your own reasoning. All of us are susceptible to illogical logic. We need to learn from the Creator of the universe.

Then the Lord answered Job out of the storm. He said . . . "Where were you when I laid the earth's foundation? Tell me, if you understand. . . . Have you ever given orders to the morning, or shown the dawn its place. . . . Have you entered the storehouses of the snow or seen the storehouses of the hail. . . . Do you send the lightning bolts on their way? Do they report to you, 'Here we are'? . . . Do you give the horse his strength or clothe his neck with a flowing mane? . . . Does the eagle soar at your command and build his nest on high?" Job 38:1, 4, 12, 22, 35; 39:19, 27

Because people come from different cultures and different climates, religious practices vary. People see God differently. The American Indians conceived the "happy hunting grounds" because in their earthly existence, plenty of game to hunt meant an easy life. Muslims, many of whom come from the hot desert where food spoils quickly, view heaven as a garden where people will eat and drink with good digestion. Founders of some religions had to base their doctrines on very practical considerations. For example, Muhammad included a pilgrimage to Mecca so the merchants of that city would get back their traditional pilgrimage business—and thus accept the Islamic faith.

People tend to fill the "God-shaped vacuum" by inventing their own gods and religious systems. These religions basically have the same themes, such as good works and rituals, along with peculiar teachings, but usually there is just enough truth to make people swallow the errors as well.

People can be very sincere—and very wrong. Taking the wrong medicine by mistake won't cure you even if you believe it will. Sincerely believing the gas pedal is the brake pedal won't prevent an accident.

People may be talented at inventing religions, but they are all like blind people, each describing the small section of the large elephant they feel. (One thinks it's like a tree, another thinks it's like a rope.)

The only cure for this mess is *revelation*—God breaking into human history and *showing* what the right way is. Jesus' life, death, and resurrection demonstrated that we must "let God be true, and every man a liar" (Romans 3:4).

The Spirit clearly says that in later times some will abandon the faith and follow deceiving spirits and things taught by demons. Such teachings come through hypocritical liars, whose consciences have been seared as with a hot iron. They forbid people to marry and order them to abstain from certain foods, which God created to be received with thanksgiving by those who believe and who know the truth. For everything God created is good, and nothing is to be rejected if it is received with thanksgiving. 1 Timothy 4:1–4

Day 280

The Truth About Worry

As the story goes, a Sunday school teacher got this definition of a lie from a little boy: "A lie is a terrible sin but an ever-present help in trouble." It often seems easiest to bail ourselves out by stretching the truth. Probably all of us sometimes try to alter Scripture so we won't feel guilty. But that's dangerous.

If you listen to great orators or read famous books, you'll find that an authority in a specific field is often quoted to prove a point. Jesus, however, was His own authority. The people who heard Him recognized the authority with which He spoke. They were amazed and asked, "How did this man get such learning without having studied?" (John 7:15). When Jesus finished speaking, the crowds were astonished because He taught with such authority (Matthew 7:28–29).

Here's the problem: If what Jesus said is true, you'll have to change the way you live! You can no longer rationalize greed, selfishness, or even worry. If you're going to conquer worry, you first must confess it as *sin,* because Jesus *commands* you not to do it, and worry is a slap in the face to the God who takes such good care of you. The second step is to trust the Holy Spirit for a faith-filled response in each situation. The God who can send a blizzard bad enough to close down your city—and who brings spring every year—certainly can protect you from the teacher who has it in for you, and can show you what to do this summer. The Son of God who has all power and all knowledge told us the truth about worry. He commanded you not to worry.

> Therefore I tell you, do not worry about your life, what you will eat or drink; or about your body, what you will wear. Is not life more important than food, and the body more important than clothes? Look at the birds of the air; they do not sow or reap or store away in barns, and yet your heavenly Father feeds them. Are you not much more valuable than they? Who of you by worrying can add a single hour to his life ? And why do you worry about clothes? See how the lilies of the field grow. They do not labor or spin. Yet I tell you that not even Solomon in all his splendor was dressed like one of these. Matthew 6:25–29

Day 281

Lord, May I Change My Mind?

"I don't particularly feel like being a Christian today." Most people feel that way at some time or another. You may want to sneak out when your parents have grounded you. Goofing around in geometry class may be more fun than doing your assignment. Or maybe you'd like to go to a party because all the popular kids are invited, but you know it won't be a party a Christian should attend.

Sometimes it seems so hard to be a Christian that you'd rather not try than try and fail. When you're afraid that you can't hold out as a Christian, you're forgetting that God is all-powerful, and that it's not *your* ability to hold on to Him that matters, but *His* ability to hold on to you.

If you've given your life to Jesus, the Holy Spirit is at work inside you. Just as a kitten or a pine tree grows large because of the life inside, so you grow as a Christian because of the life of the Holy Spirit inside you. Choosing to sin will squelch that life inside you, but you can choose to obey. As you grow in the soil of God's grace, the formula for going on with Jesus is very old and very simple—"trust and obey."

But grow in the grace and knowledge of our Lord and Savior Jesus Christ. To him be glory both now and forever! 2 Peter 3:18

Let us acknowledge the Lord; let us press on to acknowledge him. As surely as the sun rises, he will appear; he will come to us like the winter rains, like the spring rains that water the earth. Hosea 6:3

And if you ever think, *I don't feel like being a Chritian today,* it's time to change your mind.

Day 282
Assurance

The night you invited Christ into your life, you felt so clean inside and so full of joy. God seemed so near that you were sure you could never doubt Him again. But then you had to go back to "real life." There was Friday's book report, and you hadn't even picked out a book to read. As usual, the kitchen was a disaster the night you had to load the dishwasher and clean up, and you complained the whole time. The boss yelled at you at work, and life seemed no different from before. You heard the devil's sneering whisper, "See—you're no different. You're not really a Christian after all!" You might even have answered, "Well, I surely don't *feel* any different."

Maybe the beautiful bride feels no different after the trip to the altar either. Three days later, with a terrible sore throat and a temperature of 103 degrees, she may not *feel* one bit married. But the fact is, she *is* married. If she keeps acting on that fact, sooner or later she'll feel married.

If you truly accepted Christ, you are God's child, regardless of feeling. Trust that fact. Also remember that even if you're the weakest, newest Christian, you're still a child of the King of Kings. If you stay close to Jesus, you will grow and mature in your Christian life. But if you keep doubting that you are a Christian, you'll never grow.

All that the Father gives me will come to me, and whoever comes to me I will never drive away. For I have come down from heaven not to do my will but to do the will of him who sent me. And this is the will of him who sent me, that I shall lose none of all that he has given me, but raise them up at the last day. John 6:37–39

I write these things to you who believe in the name of the Son of God so that you may know that you have eternal life. 1 John 5:13

Do you want to be happy? You might respond, "That's a dumb question. Everyone wants to be happy!"

God loves you and wants to give you real joy, but like everything He has for us, it must be on *His* terms, not ours. If you're looking for gladness, you won't find it, because you're looking for a feeling, for something within yourself. Look to Jesus, follow Jesus, believe in Jesus, and joy comes. Joy is deeper than pleasant emotions caused by favorable circumstances. Does your happiness come from the fact that Jesus really satisfies you and that you enjoy doing His will? If it does, it won't disappear on a cloudy day.

In the Bible, light and joy usually go together. When gloom descends, it's because of one of these reasons: (1) ignorance of all God can do; (2) doubt that God can work in a tough situation; (3) unwillingness to give up everything to Jesus; or (4) sin.

God can give you joy and light in the middle of absolutely terrible circumstances; there are Christians around who prove it by their lives. I'll never forget Helen. I met her when I was eighteen. Helen was a hunchback lady, caring for her dying mother in a rickety old house on an out-of-the-way farm. She had never been able to realize her dream of attending a Bible school, and now found herself in a very lonely and difficult situation. But Helen's face beamed as she talked constantly of the Lord and His many blessings. She knew that if she had Jesus, it was possible for her to find all her happiness in Him.

Jesus assured us that whoever follows Him "shall not walk in darkness." Deep-down joy doesn't necessarily mean absence of pain and heartache. Only hopelessness causes depression—but the Christian can always have hope and faith in any situation because God is all-powerful.

It is because of him that you are in Christ Jesus, who has become for us wisdom from God—that is, our righteousness, holiness and redemption.
1 Corinthians 1:30

If you obey my commands, you will remain in my love, just as I have obeyed my Father's commands and remain in his love. I have told you this so that my joy may be in you and that your joy may be complete. John 15:10–11

Day 284

"Living It Up" Can Be a Real Downer

It was a gorgeous fall day—but as Kayla walked home from school, she couldn't appreciate the spectacular red oaks along the boulevard or the brilliant oranges and yellows of her mother's chrysanthemums lining the front walk. She was still too embarrassed to think straight. "How could I have said anything so dumb?" she berated herself.

Painfully, Kayla relived what had happened during lunch. Jenna had announced to everyone at the table that she was madly in love with someone named Isaac something. Hearing the name meant nothing to Kayla and she asked innocently, "Does he go to our school?" Uproarious laughter followed. "Do you live under a rock?" asked one girl. "He's a rock star!"

Kayla knew the story would spread throughout the school, and she'd be Nerd of the Year. For the first time in her life, she let herself have doubts about Christianity. After all, she was young and maybe she needed to live it up. She seemed to be missing out on a lot—the comments of other students proved it: "The party was a blast." "You haven't lived until you've gotten high." "Going out parking with Rick makes my weekend."

Kayla was tempted to do whatever it took just to fit in.

Do not envy wicked men, do not desire their company; for their hearts plot violence, and their lips talk about making trouble. Proverbs 24:1–2

The devil has a well-designed strategy to make wrongdoing look attractive. His tactics will include the mirage that sin is fun and being good will hurt you. The devil plays on a teen's tendency to look at things by the day, not by the year or the decade. Right this minute, the guy who uses cocaine and brags about his sexual conquests may seem happier than you are—but don't let this carry you to the illogical conclusion that non-believers have more fun. This is disproven by the famous movie star who committed suicide, by the girl whose abortion plummetted her into depression, and by the guy whose shoplifting expedition made the evening news.

When you're tempted to fit in because you don't see the benefits of being good, remember that God doesn't give a time limit for fulfilling the desire of the righteous.

What do you think when you hear phrases such as "total consecration," "full surrender," or "giving your life completely to Jesus"? Possibly you picture raising your hand at a meeting and going forward or selling all your possessions and giving to the poor. Maybe the whole idea scares you.

One of the devil's chief lies is that God is a big meanie; that as soon as you surrender your life to Him, He will send you straight to the armpit of Africa, that He'll tell you to give up chocolate-chip cookies forever, and force you to learn Hebrew.

Suppose a little boy came running to his father and said, "Daddy, I love you so much I'll do anything you ask me to do." The father wouldn't reply, "That's just what I've been waiting for. I'm locking you in the closet for twenty-four hours. When you get out, you'll have to eat spinach three times a day, and you will never be allowed to play baseball again." Even the worst earthly father wouldn't respond this way, and certainly God wouldn't.

On the other hand, the father of the three-year-old wouldn't cancel all dental appointments because the boy hated the dentist. God *will* give us His best if we surrender our lives totally to Him. But everything will not necessarily seem good or enjoyable at the time.

Giving your life completely to Jesus may seem impossible and impractical. However, it is clear in Scripture that Jesus expects absolute commitment to himself. Maybe you feel that the demand is something you can't attain. Remember that you are not under the law that demands but gives no power to fulfill. You are under grace (God's special favor and strength enabling us to do things we could not accomplish otherwise). The grace of God within gives you the power to surrender yourself totally to Him. If you try to do it in your own strength, your knuckles will turn white from hanging on for dear life.

Give your life to Jesus, because you love Him and you know He loves you.

Anyone who loves his father or mother more than me is not worthy of me;

anyone who loves his son or daughter more than me is not worthy of me; and anyone who does not take his cross and follow me is not worthy of me. Whoever finds his life will lose it, and whoever loses his life for my sake will find it. Matthew 10:37–39

Still another said, "I will follow you, Lord; but first let me go back and say good-bye to my family." Jesus replied, "No one who puts his hand to the plow and looks back is fit for service in the kingdom of God." Luke 9:61–62

As you commit yourself to Jesus, you'll discover the need for ever deeper levels of consecration. You commit to Him everything that you are and have. However, you may not be the least aware of the fact that your sense of humor is offensive to Jesus, but when the Holy Spirit shows you this, you must give it over to Him. Later, He may point out that you manipulate people, even though you don't realize it. Then you must give this over to Jesus and determine to stop it.

Each time you gain a new position or possession, you must ask the Holy Spirit how to give it completely to Jesus. Last year you didn't have to think about how to give being captain of the football team to Jesus. This year you will. You may suddenly find yourself needing to know how to give your dating relationship to Jesus. God requires of us a "living sacrifice"—a daily giving of our lives to Jesus.

Someone has remarked that the trouble with a living sacrifice is that it keeps trying to crawl off the altar. Confess your sin immediately when you sense you're trying to take back the commitment you've made. Give it all to God. Your living sacrifice is made to your living Lord. Your close relationship and personal attachment to Him are the secret of being a living sacrifice and loving it.

Therefore, I urge you, brothers, in view of God's mercy, to offer your bodies as living sacrifices, holy and pleasing to God—this is your spiritual act of worship. Romans 12:1

Day 287

Mountaintops

When you became a Christian you probably thought you'd never have another problem. You may have gone to a retreat or a Bible camp where you felt very close to God. Maybe at one point you surrendered yourself completely to Him and experienced the supernatural power of the Holy Spirit. You saw clearly for the first time how much God loved you, and you realized that you could trust Him for everything.

We have to understand that Jesus died for us before we can personally accept Him. We have to see that God loves us completely before we can yield our lives totally to Him. We have to know that Jesus' Spirit within us can overcome sin before we think we can live a victorious life.

First we know something, then we act on it. Often this action is a crisis or "mountaintop" experience. But after scaling the peak, we must face entering the valley—you must still talk to your father about borrowing the car and face your old boyfriend or girlfriend.

No Christian experience will exempt you from having to decide each day how to stay close to Jesus.

The temptation of sitting back and relaxing is a real one—one the devil uses a lot. The real test is living day by day in the new light, insight, and power you have received. The way to do this is to spend time praying and reading the Bible each day. Build a deep relationship with God. Determine that nothing, not even good things, will take up so much of your time, energy, or emotional involvement that God will ever take second place. When you fail, receive God's forgiveness and keep pressing forward.

Not that I have already obtained all this, or have already been made perfect, but I press on to take hold of that for which Christ Jesus took hold of me. Brothers, I do not consider myself yet to have taken hold of it. But one thing I do: Forgetting what is behind and straining toward what is ahead, I press on toward the goal to win the prize for which God has called me heavenward in Christ Jesus. Philippians 3:12–14

Day 288

Falling Off Cloud Nine and Other High Places

Are you a "superstar Christian" one day but blow it the next? Just when you think you've made a spiritual giant step, do you fail miserably? Has the devil ever whispered to you, "You're such a lousy Christian you might as well give up"? Falling short of *your* goal is not failure in the Christian life. God didn't intend for you to be a permanent resident of cloud nine! Failure is falling short of *God's* requirement.

The fact of failure is not nearly as important as your attitude toward it. There are two extremes to avoid. The first is *discouragement*. No verse in the Bible says that because you failed, God doesn't love you or want you anymore. Don't ever believe that lie. Don't decide that you must not really be a Christian just because you messed up.

The other extreme is flippancy. The attitude, *Well, I bombed again. Big deal,* is not God's will either. Saying, "I might as well learn to accept failure since I'll fail all the time anyway" is very dangerous. It's saying that God is so weak, He cannot keep you from failing.

Parents expect a child who is learning to walk to take a few tumbles. Even so, as you mature spiritually, there will be growing pains and falls. But your Heavenly Father watches your progress with the same joy that earthly parents have when their child learns something new. God is always there with comfort for the child who needs it. The child who stumbles doesn't fail to learn to walk. That could only happen if the child refused to try again.

The reason you fail is because you have not relied on Jesus in complete faith. Jesus never fails, and with Him directing your life, even though you may stumble, you will get up again. His path for you might not lead to success that the world will admire, but it will please God.

The path of the righteous is like the first gleam of dawn, shining ever brighter till the full light of day. Proverbs 4:18

To him who is able to keep you from falling and to present you before his glorious presence without fault and with great joy—to the only God our Savior be glory, majesty, power and authority, through Jesus Christ our Lord, before all ages, now and forevermore! Amen. Jude 24–25

Day 289

How to Run the Rat Race Without Becoming a Rat

Do you ever feel like screaming, "Stop the world! I want to get off!" Does the fast pace, the time squeeze, and the list of things to be done sometimes make you think you're going crazy?

The answer to this dilemma, as well as all others, can be found in the power of the Holy Spirit. Jesus spent unhurried time in prayer and received the guidance of the Holy Spirit. He could therefore handle the crowds and the many demands placed upon Him. He also knew when to "get away from it all" in order to spend time alone with God in prayer.

There were many unhealed lepers in the Holy Land, many who had not heard Jesus preach, and many who had rejected Him. Yet He could say to God, "I have brought you glory on earth by completing the work you gave me to do" (John 17:4).

He received His orders from God instead of deciding on His own what to do. He did only what God told Him to do.

Put faith in the fact that the Holy Spirit lives in you; He will direct you. The person receiving directions must be quiet and concentrate. This is where so many of us in this activity-oriented society fall down. We have difficulty being quiet long enough for the Holy Spirit to speak to us.

Unfortunately, most prayer is a one-way conversation. We dictate to God our shopping list and say "Amen." If we really want the peace of God, we can't come to our devotions with the attitude of a rat making a quick pit stop before rejoining the race. The Bible talks about "waiting on God," and waiting is something most of us are not very good at. But unless we wait until we can clearly hear His instructions, we'll never experience God's direction in our lives.

Whether you choose to run the rat race is up to you, but there is a way out.

Very early in the morning, while it was still dark, Jesus got up, left the house and went off to a solitary place, where he prayed. Mark 1:35

The fruit of righteousness will be peace; the effect of righteousness will be quietness and confidence forever. Isaiah 32:17

A woman who found herself in a difficult situation went to a friend for advice. As she explained the problem, she cried, "But I don't understand!"

Her friend replied, "At a time like this, you don't need to understand. You need to *trust*. Trusting God is not a feeling. It's a *decision*."

Do you ever try to gauge your faith by how you feel? Do you feel that you must not trust God because you're too scared to fly in an airplane? Do you think that the person who doesn't cry at a funeral trusts God more than you do? The truth is, our emotions can be kept under control, even if we aren't exercising faith in God.

Whether or not you trust God depends on your *decision,* not on your emotions. For example, let's say that you have been dating a non-Christian but you know you shouldn't. Besides the fact that you really care about this person, you feel there's no one else around you would ever date. In this case, you are not trusting God with your social life or with the life of the other person. If you decide to break off this relationship and trust God with your social life and the other person's emotions, you may feel worse for a short time—but keep trusting God.

You may have to pray ten times a day, "God, I give my friend to you and know that you can help my friend more than I ever could. I give my dating life and my emotions to you." Your decision to trust God will eventually bring your feelings into line, though this may take time. Your decision to trust God rather than your emotions is the all-important thing.

My soul finds rest in God alone; my salvation comes from him. He alone is my rock and my salvation; he is my fortress, I will never be shaken. . . . Find rest, O my soul, in God alone; my hope comes from him. He alone is my rock and my salvation; he is my fortress, I will not be shaken. My salvation and my honor depend on God; he is my mighty rock, my refuge. Trust in him at all times, O people; pour out your hearts to him, for God is our refuge.
Psalm 62:1–2, 5–8

Day 291

Roller Coaster Rides and Christians

Is your Christian experience a little like riding a big roller coaster? Are the ups and downs just too much, and is getting off the roller coaster the best part of the ride? Are you one day nearly walking on water only to be in the pits of despair the next, wondering if God really exists? That is not God's will for you. The Bible says:

The way of the sluggard is blocked with thorns, but the path of the upright is a highway. Proverbs 15:19

When you look at the road of life before you, it may resemble a stretch of highway in the Austrian Alps. But God wants to fill in the valleys and level the mountains, making the way smooth for you as you trust Him. The valleys are caused by lack of faith in God. Why do you think your parents' last fight depressed you? Why do you think your friend's insults devastated you? It's because you didn't trust God for your parents or for your reputation.

The peaks that are so hard to descend from are also your creations. If you imagine yourself as the guy who will kick the nearly impossible field goal with ten seconds remaining to win the game, it's difficult to face that eleven-yard punt. If you've dreamed and dreamed of becoming homecoming queen, having no date for the game is really hard to take. Do you discuss your dreams and hopes with God so He can change them? He wants to replace your daydreams with reality. Do you read His Word and let Him teach you to trust Him in every problem? Only Jesus can make your path into a level highway.

The path of the righteous is level; O upright One, you make the way of the righteous smooth. Isaiah 26:7

Fear arises in at least three different circumstances: emergency panic situations, long-term problems such as disastrous financial or family difficulties, and an uncertain future. God doesn't want the devil to paralyze you with fear. God can give you peace even when you've missed your last bus home. He can keep you calm if you trust Him with your parents' divorce, your sister's attitude, or your physical handicap.

Satan loves to exploit your fear of the unknown. Your imagination can make you afraid that you'll flunk out of the college you haven't even entered, or that you'll get fired from the job you haven't even applied for, or that you'll get cancer and die before you graduate from high school.

Satan also uses fear of the *spiritual* unknown. He tries to make us afraid of giving God everything. As we imagine ourselves captured by terrorists and beheaded, the devil whispers, "That's what happens to all people who give God everything." Even though the Bible and hundreds of Christian biographies prove otherwise, we're still dumb enough to believe it. Although there are twenty-first-century martyrs who will be richly rewarded in heaven, we forget that God gives supernatural strengths to Christians in especially tough circumstances, and He usually protects us from harm. Our part is to trust Him and expect that power.

God wants to free us from fear. Someone once said, "Fear knocked at the door. Faith answered. No one was there." Fear is a nobody.

David also said to Solomon his son, "Be strong and courageous, and do the work. Do not be afraid or discouraged, for the Lord God, my God, is with you. He will not fail you or forsake you until all the work for the service of the temple of the Lord is finished." 1 Chronicles 28:20

So do not fear, for I am with you; do not be dismayed, for I am your God. I will strengthen you and help you; I will uphold you with my righteous right hand. Isaiah 41:10

Day 293
Eradicate the Panic Button

Do you get a sinking feeling in your stomach when you discover that you've just lost your keys? Do you break out in a cold sweat when you realize there's a big biology test and you haven't even read the chapter? Do your knees knock when you give a report in front of the English class? Are you always pushing the Panic button? When you panic, you are saying, "God, you just can't take care of me. What on earth will I do?"

There are two kinds of fear: a self-preservation instinct and an insecurity when facing difficult or new situations. Fear that keeps you from crossing a busy street with your eyes closed, or keeps you from jumping out of a third-story window, and at least sometimes keeps you from a horrible sunburn, is God's protection. Most fear is not only harmful, it is also wrong. And God would not command us to "fear not" if He could not give us peace to replace fear.

As a Christian facing a tight situation, you have two choices: you can panic or pray in faith. It may take time for your emotions to catch on to the fact that your will has determined to pray and trust God rather than panic, but bring your fears immediately to God and ask Him to calm you.

Reaction to emergency is habitual. Habits are broken slowly, just as they are formed slowly. Decide to bring each panic situation to God. Ask for forgiveness if you go through a crisis without even thinking about God. After a while, you'll start forming the habit of praying rather than panicking; but it all starts with a decision to trust God in every situation.

In God, whose word I praise, in God I trust; I will not be afraid. What can mortal man do to me? Psalm 56:4

Then he got into the boat and his disciples followed him. Without warning, a furious storm came up on the lake, so that the waves swept over the boat. But Jesus was sleeping. The disciples went and woke him, saying, "Lord, save us! We're going to drown!" He replied, "You of little faith, why are you so afraid?" Then he got up and rebuked the winds and the waves, and it was completely calm. The men were amazed and asked, "What kind of man is this? Even the winds and the waves obey him!" Matthew 8:23–27

Probably one of the reasons children enjoy adventure stories is that they know everything will turn out fine in the end. In the "happily ever after" story, the worse the problems get, the better the ending will be.

If you're determined to trust Jesus and live for Him, you're one of the characters in a real-life happily-ever-after story. Not only is there heaven at the end, but your heavenly Father has designed your life to bring glory to Him—the difficulties you face are opportunities for Him to work His miracles. But God won't work miracles unless you trust Him.

Paul demonstrated faith that overcomes the worst of situations. He was aboard a ship during a storm so bad that nobody except Paul expected to survive. But Paul prayed and listened to God's voice. When they finally landed on the island of Malta, they were treated well. Paul's faith was a testimony to everyone on the ship.

However, if he had had a complaining, bitter attitude, Paul would have hated the whole winter he spent there. Have you learned how to trust God and enjoy being shipwrecked?

Before very long, a wind of hurricane force, called the "northeaster," swept down from the island. The ship was caught by the storm and could not head into the wind; so we gave way to it and were driven along. . . . When neither sun nor stars appeared for many days and the storm continued raging, we finally gave up all hope of being saved. After the men had gone a long time without food, Paul stood up before them and said: "Men, you should have taken my advice not to sail from Crete; then you would have spared yourselves this damage and loss. But now I urge you to keep up your courage, because not one of you will be lost; only the ship will be destroyed. Last night an angel of the God whose I am and whom I serve stood beside me and said, 'Do not be afraid, Paul. You must stand trial before Caesar; and God has graciously given you the lives of all who sail with you.' So keep up your courage, men, for I have faith in God that it will happen just as he told me." Acts 27:14–15, 20–25

Day 295

Either the Mountain or the Faith Will Have to Go

When you decide to trust God completely and follow the path He has for you, do you ever feel as if not just one mountain, but the entire Himalayan Range, is stopping you? Moving mountains is a God-sized task. He only requires that you obey and trust Him. Don't get out your little pickax and start hacking away at the mountain yourself. Keep following God and going forward, because the mountains you see up ahead aren't stopping you yet.

The mountains in your life can be removed little by little or in one chunk. They can be removed tomorrow or ten years from now. That is for God to decide. It is your job to trust God in every situation and not depend on your feelings.

Most of us have seen Christians victoriously face terrible situations, such as a death in the family, an alcoholic parent, or a crippling accident. We've also seen Christians go to pieces over minor things like a shopping trip, striking out in the ninth inning, or a sick dog. If you don't have faith in God and His Word, there will be impassable mountains at every turn. But if you have complete confidence in God, the mountains will disappear. Either the mountain or the faith will have to go.

"Have faith in God," Jesus answered. "I tell you the truth, if anyone says to this mountain, 'Go, throw yourself into the sea,' and does not doubt in his heart but believes that what he says will happen, it will be done for him. Therefore I tell you, whatever you ask for in prayer, believe that you have received it, and it will be yours." Mark 11:22–24

Let the morning bring me word of your unfailing love, for I have put my trust in you. Show me the way I should go, for to you I lift up my soul. Psalm 143:8

Someone once said, "God has designed each day so that we can't get through it without faith."

The twenty-four-hour period will pass whether or not we trust God, and we may even still be alive at the end of it! The point is: How do we want to get through each day?

Moses had a pretty tough day ahead of him. In front of him and the thousands of frightened people was the Red Sea, and behind them was Pharaoh's army. They could have either drown or let the army use them for target practice. But instead, Moses put his faith in God. It became the most exciting and wonderful day of their lives. Walking through the Red Sea on dry ground must have been fun!

God put the Red Sea in front of the Israelites so they would have to trust Him, and they got to see His power demonstrated. He also gives *us* obstacles so *our* faith has a chance to grow. The opening night of the school play, the final biology test, and your first job interview are all opportunities for you to trust God.

Approach the Red Sea in your life with faith and confidence. God put it there to strengthen your walk with Him.

Moses answered the people, "Do not be afraid. Stand firm and you will see the deliverance the Lord will bring you today. The Egyptians you see today you will never see again. The Lord will fight for you; you need only to be still." Then the Lord said to Moses, "Why are you crying out to me? Tell the Israelites to move on. Raise your staff and stretch out your hand over the sea to divide the water so that the Israelites can go through the sea on dry ground." . . . Then Moses stretched out his hand over the sea, and all that night the Lord drove the sea back with a strong east wind and turned it into dry land. The waters were divided, and the Israelites went through the sea on dry ground, with a wall of water on their right and on their left. Exodus 14:13–16, 21–22

Day 297

"Pardon Me, Your Attitude Is Showing"

We live in a world where people admire how many A's you get on your report card, how many home runs you hit, or how much money you make in a year. Some people could care less if Sasha cheated her way to straight-A's if the champions bribed the pitcher of the opposing team, or if Nolan got a good job because the boss owed his father money. Everything seems to be measured by output and performance, not by motives and heart attitudes. Working for Jesus is the exact opposite. In God's book, *obedience* is the important thing.

If you're proud because you're the only person your age who goes door-to-door witnessing with your church every Sunday, you're not really obeying God. He hates pride. If you're inviting people to church just to win a prize at the end of the month, your motives are wrong. If you and another Christian quarrel over the best way to share your faith, neither of you is walking very close to Jesus. If you rattle off a spiel to a person just so you can say you witnessed, but you have no love or care for the person, it's wrong. Scripture tells us we are to be "speaking the truth in love."

Your witnessing will have no lasting effect if it is done with the wrong motives. That does *not* mean that you are excused from sharing your faith. Jesus commands us to "go into all the world and preach the good news" (Mark 16:15). James 4:17 also tells us:

Anyone, then, who knows the good he ought to do and doesn't do it, sins.

You became imitators of us and of the Lord; in spite of severe suffering, you welcomed the message with the joy given by the Holy Spirit. And so you became a model to all the believers in Macedonia and Achaia. The Lord's message rang out from you not only in Macedonia and Achaia—your faith in God has become known everywhere. Therefore we do not need to say anything about it, for they themselves report what kind of reception you gave us. They tell how you turned to God from idols to serve the living and true God.
1 Thessalonians 1:6–9

Day 298

Sitting in English class, Paolo didn't hear Mrs. Martinez bawl out the class and threaten to flunk anyone who didn't turn in a term paper on time. Instead, he was thinking of what it would be like to go sailing in the Mediterranean.

He was just passing the French Riviera when Mrs. Martinez walked up to his desk and demanded to see what he had written so far. Paolo blinked out of his daydream and handed over a pack of empty note cards and a couple sheets of paper with an introduction and a few ideas.

"Young man, do you expect this to evolve into a term paper in just two weeks?" demanded Mrs. Martinez. Everybody laughed.

When the grammar lesson began, Paolo drifted off to the Riviera again.

Escaping the reality of daily living is *not* one of your basic needs. Jesus left heaven to become a man needing food, rest, and transportation.

Proverbs is full of advice on dealing with personal relationships, managing money, guarding your tongue, living successfully in this work-a-day world. What's necessary is learning to obey God *here* and *now*—sensing Jesus' presence and strength as you board the school bus, order hamburgers, call your friend, and take driver's training.

True Christianity is about overcoming, not escaping. It's about conquering, not running; miracles, not manufacturing masks to hide behind.

A discerning man keeps wisdom in view, but a fool's eyes wander to the ends of the earth. Proverbs 17:24

Folly delights a man who lacks judgment, but a man of understanding keeps a straight course. Proverbs 15:21

People of God have always been involved in the real world. Paul gave his fellow travelers some commonsense advice; Dorcas made clothes for needy children; the early church took care of widows; and Jesus himself washed the disciples' feet. If you want to count for God, you'll finish your homework and clean up the mess you made.

Day 299

Are You a Slave to "Curiosity"?

Barry invited Ian over to his house after school so they could work on their project for the science fair. When Ian saw all the magazine pictures on Barry's bulletin board and a stack of pinup magazines, he let out a gasp of surprise.

"Ian, are you still an innocent little boy?" Barry mocked. "I can lend you a couple copies."

Not wanting to risk more ridicule, Ian carefully hid two copies in his notebook.

When he got home, he stashed the magazines in his bedroom. After supper, he helped his dad clean out the garage, finished his homework, and then got ready for bed. Setting the alarm clock, he crawled into bed and turned off the light. But as he lay there in the darkness, he was overcome by a wave of curiosity. What was he missing out on, anyway?

Ian switched on the light and dug out a magazine.

He got hooked fast. He borrowed more magazines from Barry and even bought some of his own. His once-innocent thoughts changed drastically, but he convinced himself that he was just a normal, red-blooded teenage boy. He didn't realize that pornography was about to ruin his life.

A basic necessity for your health and happiness is holy living, which includes having clean thoughts. If you have questions about sex, direct them to a mature Christian who can give you correct answers. The devil is out to destroy every young person, and he'll use every lie and deception available to pollute your mind and drive you into sexual sin. Be smart enough to resist.

Stay away from a foolish man, for you will not find knowledge on his lips. The wisdom of the prudent is to give thought to their ways, but the folly of fools is deception. Fools mock at making amends for sin, but goodwill is found among the upright. Proverbs 14:7–9

A fool finds pleasure in evil conduct, but a man of understanding delights in wisdom. Proverbs 10:23

For three days, B.J. had studied for the big biology test. He hardly cared what grade he got anymore; he just wanted it to be over. The class filed in more silently than usual, and he tried to keep from biting his fingernails.

Mr. Boyer stood by his desk. As soon as the bell rang, he made his announcement. "I'm sorry, but I wasn't able to type up the test last night. My little girl became extremely ill and we had to rush her to the hospital. We'll have the exam on Monday instead."

Shane rose to his feet. "That's not fair!" he shouted. "We're all psyched for the test *now*. You just ruined my weekend. You tell us to plan ahead. If *I* gave you some excuse and asked to take the test another day, you wouldn't let me. I'm going to the office to protest."

The following Tuesday, B.J. listened to Shane's Newman-the-Nerd routine as he made fun of his gym teacher.

Just then Justin walked by.

"Teacher's pet!" sneered Shane. "You don't have a brain in your head, but Newman-the-Nerd gives you straight A's because you lift weights."

"That's right, I got an A on the last exam," Justin shot back, "*and* I have perfect attendance. You deserve to flunk! The only muscle you have is in your mouth."

At that, Shane became furious—and his fist missed Justin's face only because Justin ducked. B.J. didn't realize how dangerous it was to have Shane as a friend; he couldn't yet tell how many of Shane's attitudes he was adopting.

Saying anything you want and acting just as you please is *not* something you need. These things characterize a fool. True happiness comes from permitting Jesus to work inside you to remove all the seething lava of hate and bitterness that could erupt into antisocial behavior.

Mockers stir up a city, but wise men turn away anger. Proverbs 29:8

A fool shows his annoyance at once, but a prudent man overlooks an insult. Proverbs 12:16

Day 301

Wise Up

Sure, Michael loved Jesus and wanted to follow Him. He hoped his life would count for something. But he felt he had too many strikes against him. Too much to overcome. He'd been hit by a car while playing in the street as a child, and the injury had left him with a disability. On top of that, his mom was an alcoholic and brought home a string of men. He didn't even have any idea who his father was.

Michael had accepted Jesus as his Savior at a Christian camp for underprivileged children. But even among the poor, he felt like the bottom of the barrel. And though the people at the church he attended showed him love and concern, he felt out of place. They dressed nicer than he did. Other kids did things with their families, but he had nobody.

One day he read a verse in the Bible:

A wise servant will rule over a disgraceful son, and will share the inheritance as one of the brothers. Proverbs 17:2

In that passage Michael saw a very important principle: The key to rising above his background and circumstances was to obtain God's wisdom.

He thought of his favorite Bible character, Joseph. Even when he was sold as a slave, Joseph kept seeking God's wisdom. The day came when he ruled over all of Egypt. He got the job because, as Pharaoh noticed, "there is not one so discerning and wise as you."

Michael saw that there was always more of God's wisdom to learn. God's wisdom gives power and protection, and He takes care of those who follow Him. As you receive God's wisdom, you'll sense His strength and strategy for dismantling the devil's strongholds in your life and in the world around you. The person who's filled with God's wisdom demands respect. When the Queen of Sheba visited Solomon, she was super impressed with his God-given wisdom.

A king delights in a wise servant, but a shameful servant incurs his wrath. Proverbs 14:35

A man is praised according to his wisdom, but men with warped minds are despised. Proverbs 12:8

Although Aaron daydreamed through most of Sunday's sermons, he caught "God promises to bless the person who tithes and is generous to others." Aaron decided to tithe.

Blair and Aaron worked together at a fast-food joint. Blair was a go-getter who did most of the work while Aaron did most of the complaining. One night, Blair went home sick and Aaron was stuck with everything. When the manager asked if he'd cleaned the floor yet, Aaron saw that it looked pretty good. "Sure did," he replied, hoping his lie would go undetected.

Receiving his next paycheck, he triumphantly gave his tithe, plus a tidy contribution to the senior citizens. And he waited for the wealth that would soon pour in.

Blair was promoted to cashier, and Aaron was asked to train a new guy on the grill. For the first hour, he almost kept up with the orders—but finally everybody was yelling at him. Complaints from the customers brought the manager to the scene. When he chewed Aaron out, Aaron blamed the new guy. The next day, Aaron was fired.

Aaron was furious! How dare the devil try to rob him of the blessing! He had tithed and was generous to others. Aaron didn't realize that honesty and faithfulness are also biblical requirements for God's blessing.

Lazy hands make a man poor, but diligent hands bring wealth. Proverbs 10:4

It's a lot easier to grab a verse or two and base an entire doctrine on a few words than it is to thoroughly search the Scriptures. And it's a lot more dangerous.

According to the Bible, the prerequisites for God's prosperity (which is not just material well-being but contentment and peace of mind), include these: righteousness, application of God's wisdom, hard work, responsibility, tithing, and generosity. And that doesn't mean you may not be tested, like Job, or voluntarily give up great wealth to serve God's people as did Moses.

Laziness—both physical and spiritual—is one cause of poverty. God wants you to tithe, but it won't cover up for the basic dishonesty included in laziness. God can't put His blessing on anything that lacks integrity. Obeying God's Word demands knowing your Bible well and putting its principles into practice.

Day 303

The Problem Called Pride

Travis looked at the fluorescent dial on his watch. It was midnight. Because of the burning pain in his right leg, he couldn't get to sleep. When he pushed his button to call a nurse, no one came.

Although it seemed like ages ago, it was only yesterday that he had been voted Outstanding Student of Meadowbrook High. Thunderous applause greeted him when the announcement was made. When the three-o'clock bell rang, his friends mobbed him. Being a celebrity was great!

He had dreamed about being chosen Outstanding Student of the Nation and shaking hands with the president. Whisking a comb through his hair, Travis turned his thoughts to his other triumphs. He was popular with the girls, a better-than-average guitar player, and if he kept learning more stunts on his unicycle, he might just have to turn down a chance to join the circus.

After baseball practice, the unicycle group met to shape up their act for the annual Meadowbrook High carnival. They were still waiting for Cal when Travis began to show off a little. A moment later, his stunt hurled him onto the cement.

Excruciating pain shot through his body right before he blacked out, and the next thing he knew, he was being carried into the emergency room.

There's a difference between feeling good about yourself as you completely depend on God, and being conceited.

> On the appointed day Herod, wearing his royal robes, sat on his throne and delivered a public address to the people. They shouted, "This is the voice of a god, not of a man." Immediately, because Herod did not give praise to God, an angel of the Lord struck him down, and he was eaten by worms and died.
> Acts 12:21-23

Herod's problem wasn't that he had authority and talent recognized by other people. It was that he didn't give God the credit. Humility isn't saying that you're ugly, that you're a klutz, or that you don't have a brain in your head. It's recognizing that God gave you all the talent you possess, and you should be using it for His glory.

Angel was discouraged, angry—and totally unaware of the big "chip" she carried on her shoulder.

As always, nothing seemed to be going right. She thought that her teachers picked on her, that her mother paid more attention to her younger sister, and that her aunt forgot her birthday on purpose. One afternoon, Angel was called into the counselor's office. That was a switch. Usually Angel was the one who made pity-party appointments so that she could complain to someone about her grades or the unfair treatment she was getting from one teacher or another.

"Angel," Mr. Whitener began, "I've been watching you lately, and I've noticed how miserable you are. I want to help you, and I have some advice I hope you'll consider. What I have to say is going to be hard to hear, though. Your pride and self-centeredness are making you unhappy. Every time someone fails to notice you, or when things don't go your way, you explode. You don't consider the feelings of others. You don't give anyone the benefit of the doubt."

This was not what Angel wanted to hear. She couldn't believe that her counselor didn't understand how she was being mistreated—and she remained oblivious to the fact that she was addicted to pride. If you see some of Angel in yourself, take the biblical perspective for your problem.

Do not be overcome by evil, but overcome evil with good. Romans 12:21

Because pride is totally self-centered, the arrogant person constantly has hurt feelings. Instead of solving problems, pride invents them. Pride creates quarrels and dissention. Pride looks down on others and refuses to take advice. The conceited person forgets God and writes off anyone who doesn't fit into his or her scheme of things.

When pride comes, then comes disgrace, but with humility comes wisdom. Proverbs 11:2

The proud and arrogant man—"Mocker" is his name; he behaves with overweening pride. Proverbs 21:24

Day 305

The Bargain

John had dreamed for so long of having a car of his own. Wheels spelled independence and freedom. He'd been carefully saving his money, but as he looked at the prices, he became more and more dismayed. The thousand dollars he'd saved wouldn't buy anything.

A gray-haired man approached him. "I have a beautiful car in my garage, and I'll sell it to you for five hundred dollars. It's worth more, but I remember what it was like to be young."

The shiny red car in the man's garage had impeccable black vinyl seat covers and almost-new tires. Impulsively, John handed him five hundred dollars in cash. The man smiled, gave him the key, and went inside his house.

When John turned the ignition key, the engine choked and sputtered. The old man came to the door and explained, "I haven't driven it for ten years, so it needs to warm up. After a couple hundred miles, it'll run like a rabbit."

John tried again and finally got it going. It jerked and coughed, and at one intersection the engine died. The light changed three times before he got started again.

When John got home, his father took one look at the car and moaned. "They stopped making this car *years* ago. You can't get parts for it. You just threw your money away."

Do you make impulsive decisions before checking on the facts?

Every prudent man acts out of knowledge, but a fool exposes his folly.
Proverbs 13:16

A simple man believes anything, but a prudent man gives thought to his steps.
Proverbs 14:15

If you make rash decisions, you are disregarding God's Word. If you act without gaining the advice and knowledge that will enable you to choose wisely, you're asking for trouble. Even if you feel God has directed you to say or do something special or unusual, it's almost always advisable to ask Him for confirmation from a friend before rushing into action.

Have you ever thought how different your life would be if you lived in Old Testament times before Jesus died on the cross for your sins? Your church would be a slaughterhouse where animals were constantly being killed for wrongs done. Leviticus states that as a penalty for sins committed, the person must bring a lamb or goat to be sacrificed.

Could you imagine having a priest kill a lamb every time you sinned? You would relive the episode of your talking back to your mother as you looked into the innocent brown eyes of Dolly. Aren't you glad that this is no longer needed?

The Bible teaches that after Jesus died on the cross, the priests that descended from Aaron were no longer necessary. Hebrews explains that Jesus is now our permanent high priest. Because the job of the priest was to take the sacrifice and be a "middleman" between God and the people, there is a sense in which every true Christian is a priest. (But let's not confuse this with the role of priest as a pastor or minister.) Since Jesus died, we can go directly and ask forgiveness for our sins without a sacrifice, and therefore perform the function of a priest for ourselves. Martin Luther called this the priesthood of all believers.

But we are priests only in the sense that we need no special person or group of people to arrange for our forgiveness or our instruction. We still need our High Priest, the "one mediator between God and men, the man Christ Jesus" (1 Timothy 2:5). Jesus is there 24/7 to forgive us and help us.

Therefore, since we have a great high priest who has gone through the heavens, Jesus the Son of God, let us hold firmly to the faith we profess. For we do not have a high priest who is unable to sympathize with our weaknesses, but we have one who has been tempted in every way, just as we are—yet was without sin. Let us then approach the throne of grace with confidence, so that we may receive mercy and find grace to help us in our time of need. Hebrews 4:14–16

Day 307

Are You Ready to Get Into the Wheelbarrow?

Usually if you believe something strongly enough, you will act on it. If you're convinced that understanding chemistry will help you get into an Ivy League school, you'll study hard. On the other hand, if you're certain you won't make the cheerleading squad, you won't even try out. But can you have it both ways? If you really believe the ice will hold, you'll go snowmobiling on the frozen lake. Saying, "I believe the ice will hold, but I'd never walk out on it," would reveal your lack of faith.

If you really believe in Jesus, you'll want to trust Him. An old story tells about a man who walked on a tightrope across Niagara Falls. Next, he wheeled an empty wheelbarrow across the rope above Niagara Falls. Then he asked his applauding crowd, "Do you believe that I can put a man in the wheelbarrow and still make it across?" Everyone shouted, "Yes!" Then he asked, "Who will get into the wheelbarrow?" No one volunteered.

Real faith will initiate action. Do you have "getting into the wheelbarrow" faith? This is the kind of faith needed to receive salvation.

Whoever believes in the Son has eternal life, but whoever rejects the Son will not see life, for God's wrath remains on him. John 3:36

If your faith is genuine, it will produce changes in your life. Paul describes what active faith meant in his life. To get the whole story, read chapters nine and twenty-six of Acts.

So then, King Agrippa, I was not disobedient to the vision from heaven. First to those in Damascus, then to those in Jerusalem and in all Judea, and to the Gentiles also, I preached that they should repent and turn to God and prove their repentance by their deeds. Acts 26:19–20

A six-year-old boy was terrified to walk past the house of a big bully. This bully would always beat him up. Then one day the boy's fifteen-year-old brother walked past the house with him. The bully never even appeared.

The six-year-old was safe as long as he was accompanied by his brother. But one day he became overconfident and decided to go past the home of the big bully all by himself. He was again beaten up. At first he was afraid to tell his big brother, but when he did, the big brother taught the bully a lesson. He also instructed his little brother never to walk by that house alone again.

Jesus intends that we have victory over sin—not once in a while, but constantly. If we approach life in our own strength, sin will defeat us just as the bully beat up the child. However, Jesus within us is all-powerful and He has never yet lost a fight with the devil.

Stay close to Jesus and be afraid to venture into anything without His presence and approval. Bring every sin to Him. Never try to deal with it yourself. It is as ridiculous for you to try to deal with sin by yourself as it is for a vulnerable six-year-old to take on a big bully. Jesus will forgive you and give you strength for the next time. Jesus is a Savior from sin. You don't overcome sin with a little help from Jesus, but when Jesus himself lives within you, He can ensure victory over sin.

And you are to give him the name Jesus, because he will save his people from their sins. Matthew 1:21

I can do everything through him who gives me strength. Philippians 4:13

Day 309

Are There Any Goliaths in Your Life?

Admitting that you were wrong, saying no to drugs, starting the homework that's due on Friday, or returning the stolen bike sometimes can seem like beady-eyed nine-foot-high giants. Life is full of Goliaths. Jesus is the One with the power to win the victory over each of them, and He wants to give that power to us.

The story is told of a mother who visited her son's dorm room at college. She was disappointed to see the walls filled with immoral pictures. She said nothing but mailed her son a present—a beautifully framed picture of Christ. He put it on the wall, and as he looked at it, he thought of his religious beliefs and morals. He was forced to take down the other pictures. The power of Jesus is like that—it wins over wrong thoughts and sinful actions.

The power of Jesus is not just for facing emergencies and full-grown Goliaths. Do you realize that Goliath was once a cute, helpless little baby? The most innocent or potentially worthwhile thing can become a monster unless it is under the control and guidance of Jesus. Even a search for love can turn into a horrible experience if Jesus is not in charge of it.

Take all your plans, all your decisions, and all your temptations to Jesus. Let Him fight the Goliaths in your life.

David said to the Philistine, "You come against me with sword and spear and javelin, but I come against you in the name of the Lord Almighty, the God of the armies of Israel, whom you have defied. This day the Lord will hand you over to me, and I'll strike you down and cut off your head. Today I will give the carcasses of the Philistine army to the birds of the air and the beasts of the earth, and the whole world will know that there is a God in Israel. . . ." Reaching into his bag and taking out a stone, he slung it and struck the Philistine on the forehead. The stone sank into his forehead, and he fell face-down on the ground. 1 Samuel 17:45–46, 49

Day 310

The High Cost of Disobedience

Brad's church supported missionaries who ran an orphanage in Mexico. The youth group decided to help out by collecting used children's clothing and school supplies to send to them. Winter was coming, and they wanted to send these poor children sweaters, jackets, and socks.

Because of his gift for leadership, Brad was put in charge of the project. The youth director had to be out of town for two weeks, and his final instructions to the group were to collect the clothes, wash them, and pack them in the boxes provided. "Don't send anything until I return," he emphasized. "There are special shipping instructions we have to follow."

Brad organized a small group to go door-to-door asking for used clothing for kids. When the kids in the youth group realized how much work was involved, most of them dropped out. But Brad just did all the extra work himself. A little sacrifice wouldn't hurt him.

The youth director phoned the church to say that he'd be returning a week late, and Brad thought that he'd better just go ahead and send the clothing. "You can't," Paula declared. "The last thing Wayne told us was not to send anything until he gets back."

"But winter is almost here," Brad protested. "The kids need the clothes."

"Call Wayne before making any decision," Paula warned.

Without checking, Brad took the boxes to the post office. It was more expensive to send them than he'd imagined. He emptied the youth group treasury and added fifty-four dollars of his own money—he'd been saving for new running shoes. When Wayne returned, Brad learned that there was a less expensive way to ship packages to missionaries, and it would have left the youth group treasury almost untouched. His lack of submission to authority had cost him and others a whole lot.

Listen, my son, and be wise, and keep your heart on the right path. Proverbs 23:19

To do what is right and just is more acceptable to the Lord than sacrifice. Proverbs 21:3

Day 311

You're the Kind of Person I Like to Do Business With

Malinda's single mother constantly had problems making ends meet. Malinda longed to be able to give her mom what she most wanted for Christmas, but at fifteen, Malinda didn't have a job.

One day a friend told her about selling jewelry to earn money, so Malinda stopped by the business, signed for samples, and started selling. Malinda worked hard and sold more than she even dreamed possible. Nobody could turn down a charming girl who wanted to buy her widowed mother a refrigerator for Christmas.

But on the first day of school in January, Malinda's friend Mariel had some startling information: "Malinda, I'm sure you didn't know it, but the jewelry you sold wasn't fourteen-carat gold—it was fake. My uncle is a jeweler, and he checked it over. He said it was costume jewelry. He said the price would have been great for gold, but it was three times what the necklace is worth." Malinda was dumbfounded. What should she do? Actually, the Bible gives her the answer. Malinda told her customers the truth. And when she started selling for a reputable company, she heard, "You're the kind of person I like to do business with!"

The Lord abhors dishonest scales, but accurate weights are his delight. Proverbs 11:1

Do not repay anyone evil for evil. Be careful to do what is right in the eyes of everybody. Romans 12:17

The Lord does not close His eyes even to our "little" dishonesties. He sees you peek at John's paper just to check if the answer you had for number five is correct. He notices if you fail to return the extra money the clerk gave you in change. Your exaggeration of the merits of the product you're selling offends God.

On the other hand, God is honored when you give up the perfect chance to cheat and accept an F on the quiz because you didn't study hard enough. Openly acknowledging that it was your fault, or that you are wrong, honors the Lord. You should be the kind of person others would enjoy working with.

Day 312

But I Want My Own Way

Nothing can cause you to *want* to obey your teachers, your principal, your boss, and your parents unless two issues are settled in your life.

First, you must be willing to *obey God regardless of what He asks you to do*. Your parents may have been wrong for grounding you when the reason you were late was because your car broke down and your cell phone died, so you couldn't even call. Yet if you love Jesus so much that honoring your parents is more important to you than being wrongly accused, you'll willingly take the grounding.

Second, you must *have faith in the God who changes people and situations*. If God did not have supernatural power, then obedience to delegated authority would not seem reasonable. But God can use your obedient spirit and your prayers for your boss, teachers, and parents to *change* them. If your English teacher is constantly crabby and your father seems unreasonable, determine to obey them and pray every day that God will transform their lives.

There may come a time when you will have to go against authority in order to obey God. Your English teacher may assign a book that you as a Christian have no business reading. First, talk with the teacher and volunteer to read another book, even if it is a longer one. Involve your parents or your pastor if necessary, but don't demand your rights in an un-Christlike way. If this does not work, respectfully explain your position and be willing to take a lower grade. But as you pray for that teacher, expect God to change his or her attitude. Remember that God runs this universe, and He will take full responsibility for His obedient children.

Then Nebuchadnezzar said, "Praise be to the God of Shadrach, Meshach and Abednego, who has sent his angel and rescued his servants! They trusted in him and defied the king's command and were willing to give up their lives rather than serve or worship any god except their own God." Daniel 3:28

Teach slaves to be subject to their masters in everything, to try to please them, not to talk back to them, and not to steal from them, but to show that they can be fully trusted, so that in every way they will make the teaching about God our Savior attractive. Titus 2:9–10

Day 313

Getting Blamed for Shawn's Mistake and Obeying God

What does obeying God have to do with being polite to your boss when you get scolded for something you didn't do? Does God really care if you do the three-page assignment the whole class got because one student's cell phone rang? Does God expect you to stay after school for talking in health class when the teacher singled you out of a group of chattering students? These are important questions, and you may not like God's answer.

God insists on obedience to authority, and He gave bosses, teachers, police officers, and principals that authority. Disobeying their authority is just like disobeying God.

The Bible says:

The authorities that exist have been established by God. Consequently, he who rebels against the authority is rebelling against what God has instituted.
Romans 13:1–2

This does not mean that the person in authority is always right, but it does mean that your attitude must be one of willingness to obey. You may calmly offer an explanation that proves your innocence, but even if you receive an unjust punishment, you should accept it with a humble spirit. It's not always easy to sort out the truth. Look at such issues from the point of view of the teacher or the boss. The only time you can disobey authority is when you are asked to go against one of God's specific commands. Even then, your attitude must be one of gentleness.

Honestly facing the issue of obedience to authority will convince you that you need God's supernatural power. If you ask Him in faith, He will teach you how to submit to authority.

Slaves, obey your earthly masters in everything; and do it, not only when their eye is on you and to win their favor, but with sincerity of heart and reverence for the Lord. Whatever you do, work at it with all your heart, as working for the Lord, not for men, since you know that you will receive an inheritance from the Lord as a reward. It is the Lord Christ you are serving. Colossians 3:22–24

Are you a straight-pin Christian—"pointed" in one direction and "headed" in the other? Would you like to be a missionary to Japan one day and a professional racecar driver the next? Are you planning a camping trip one minute and staying home to bathe the dog the next? Do you study hard for a month and then consider dropping out of school? Are you enthusiastic about your job the first week but ready to quit after the boss criticizes your work?

Jesus' life was not like that. He didn't flit from one thing to another. He had one goal, and everything He did related to that great goal. That goal was so important that He could say:

> *My food is to do the will of him who sent me and to finish his work.* John 4:34

Jesus' life had peace and order. If you are a follower of Jesus, you are to be like Him. You must first settle the main issue. Is your goal to please God and not yourself? If it is, two practical suggestions will help you.

First, *finish what you start*. If you followed this motto, you'd spend more time praying about what you should start. The Bible has many verses that tell us to wait on God and wait for God, but not one that says, "If you don't like it and it gets hard, quit, leave, or change your mind."

Second, remember that *it is NEVER God's will for you to do nothing* for a long period of time. Although the saying, "An idle mind is the devil's workshop," is very old, it is also true. Get a job, even if it is not the job you'd choose. Stay in school even if it's hard. God did not intend your life to be an extended vacation.

> *In the name of the Lord Jesus Christ, we command you, brothers, to keep away from every brother who is idle and does not live according to the teaching you received from us. For you yourselves know how you ought to follow our example. We were not idle when we were with you, nor did we eat anyone's food without paying for it. On the contrary, we worked night and day, laboring and toiling so that we would not be a burden to any of you.*
> 2 Thessalonians 3:6–8

Day 315

Don't Quit Just Because It's Hard Work

Do you complain about going from school to work every day? Don't gripe at your teachers or your boss. Work is God's idea.

Six days you shall labor and do all your work. Exodus 20:9

That's smack in the middle of the Ten Commandments! And research shows that physical work helps keep people physically and mentally healthy. Work is good for your health!

Laziness and selfishness often keeps us from the hard work necessary to write a good term paper or mow the lawn. Messiness or lack of organization can also make us very ineffective, and the only cure for either one is a willingness to work hard.

God not only has individual work projects that are His will for us, but also group projects such as redecorating the church, raising money to support an orphan in the Philippines, or helping an elderly woman move. Working together can be a way of worshiping God.

The story of Nehemiah is a good example of how God's will can only be accomplished by hard workers who "stick with it." The Babylonians had completely destroyed the city of Jerusalem and taken the Jews as captives to Babylon. Years later the Persians allowed the Jews to return to the ruined city, but it was not safe to live there until a wall was built. Their enemies tried to stop the work by armed attacks and false rumors. Through obedience, faith, and an unbelievable amount of hard work, the wall was completed.

If these people had stopped building the wall because of backaches, vacation plans, and fatigue, history would have been different. A proper attitude toward work is the key to success and victory.

So the wall was completed on the twenty-fifth of Elul, in fifty-two days. When all our enemies heard about this, all the surrounding nations were afraid and lost their self-confidence, because they realized that this work had been done with the help of our God. Nehemiah 6:15–16

Do you realize that your homework, your job performance, and your attitude toward the tasks you do around the house are terribly important to Jesus? Our self-centered society has the idea that a person can quit a job any time he or she wishes, regardless of how it will affect other people. Another popular idea is that no one should have to do anything he or she does not like. When a job becomes difficult or a class requires a lot of work, the first thought is to find an easier way.

This philosophy makes sense if there is no purpose in life except to get as much pleasure out of seventy years as possible. However, that is not God's intention for our lives. We were put on earth to prepare for eternity, to bring honor to God, and to let God work through us to restore peace in our tiny corner of His universe. God, through the Holy Spirit, will give us all the power we need to live like that.

Our honesty, willingness to do the hard jobs, and faithfulness to our work can help bring people to Jesus. When the work is hard and we feel like quitting, we can offer it as our sacrifice to Jesus and receive His strength to do it. When we work for Jesus and feel His approval, the fact that other people criticize or don't even notice won't be that important.

A Middle Ages monk named Brother Lawrence delighted in the presence of God as he daily scrubbed the pots and pans for the monastery. Do you clean your room or take out the garbage or mow the lawn for Jesus? Do you do algebra problems for Jesus or seek to honor Him in the way you make French fries or stock store shelves? Work is God's plan for you; offer your work as worship to Him.

So whether you eat or drink or whatever you do, do it all for the glory of God. 1 Corinthians 10:31

So God created man in his own image, in the image of God he created him; male and female he created them. God blessed them and said to them, "Be fruitful and increase in number; fill the earth and subdue it. Rule over the fish of the sea and the birds of the air and over every living creature that moves on the ground." Genesis 1:27–28

Day 317

Noah—The Man Who Started Before It Rained

Procrastination is "no" on the installment plan. The students at Edison High School weren't particularly happy about the principal's new list of school regulations, one of which was that a student could be suspended for defying a teacher's "reasonable request." So several students formed the "later" club: Rather than saying no to teachers' requests, they'd just say "later." Needless to say, the instructors weren't overjoyed by their delaying tactics.

One of the problems with putting everything off until the last minute is that once you've waited long enough, it's literally impossible to do what you set out to do. If you've stayed in bed until seven-thirty, you can't get to first-hour class on time. If you've waited until the night before the semester project is due, it's impossible to finish the assignment for the next day. The devil likes to fool you into thinking that you're just a last-minute person and the world should make allowances for you.

One of the bad things about procrastinators is that they tend to be dishonest in making excuses for their inaction. But if you didn't ask anyone to be on the program until the day before, you can't say that it had to be cancelled because of lack of cooperation. If you waited until the last minute, you don't have a right to complain about the unreasonable assignment. If you started twenty minutes late in the first place, it's not honest to blame your tardiness on a two-block detour.

Imagine Noah standing in the rain, trying to come up with a good excuse for why the ark wasn't finished yet. If he had procrastinated in building that boat, you and I wouldn't be here today!

God wants to make you into a Noah who plans ahead and works hard so that His work can be accomplished through you.

I went past the field of the sluggard, past the vineyard of the man who lacks judgment; thorns had come up everywhere, the ground was covered with weeds, and the stone wall was in ruins. I applied my heart to what I observed and learned a lesson from what I saw: A little sleep, a little slumber, a little folding of the hands to rest—and poverty will come on you like a bandit and scarcity like an armed man. Proverbs 24:30–34

Are you sick of being the doormat? Do you get the worst schedules at work because you complain the least? Are you tempted to talk back the way everyone else does, but you don't because you know it's not right? Does the boss always make *you* mop the floor at cleanup time?

First you need to ask God to show you how to be happy in your present circumstances. Someone once quipped, "Bloom where you're planted. Then maybe God will move you to a bigger pot." Paul says:

I have learned to be content whatever the circumstances. Philippians 4:11

God will bless your decision to get all your approval from Him. Don't worry that no one will recognize your genius, appreciate all your hard work, or listen to your great ideas. Thank God for your school and your job, just the way it is.

Step two is the frosting on the cake, but you have to bake the cake first. After you have told God you're willing to put up with anything and that you'll trust Him, start praying for changes—not a new location, but improvements in your present situation. Once your bitterness and rebellion are gone, God will answer those prayers and teach you how and when to appeal to unjust authority.

God will show you how to defend your answer to the history teacher in a respectful and acceptable manner. He'll make someone else request to work every Saturday night, or He'll cause the new Christian kid to be transferred into your biology class so there are two of you who believe God created the world. He'll show you how to ask for time off to go to the Christian retreat and how to make the most of mopping the floor. If your school or work situation were perfect, you'd miss out on a lot of exciting answers to prayer.

Now to him who is able to do immeasurably more than all we ask or imagine, according to his power that is at work within us, to him be glory in the church and in Christ Jesus throughout all generations, for ever and ever! Amen. Ephesians 3:20–21

Day 319

Are You a Secret-Service Christian?

Do you squirm when someone talks about those "crazy religious fanatics"? Are you scared to share your faith with your new friend? Would you be willing to tell the captain of the football team that you're a Christian? Are you willing to stick up for Jesus anyplace and anytime?

You must deal with the fear of other people. Either you care about what other people think or you care about what God thinks.

Be willing to follow God in *every* situation. If you fail, confess it, and ask God for a second chance to make a Christian stand. God is the God of the second chance. He will teach you if you're willing to let people think you are different, pathetic, or crazy.

Sometimes the fear of standing up as a Christian comes from unwillingness to live the consistent Christian life expected of a person who shares his or her faith. If your teacher knows you are a Christian, she'll expect you to do your homework. If your teammates know you're a Christian, they'll watch how you react when you fumble twice in one game. Bosses think Christians should be good workers. Are you willing to constantly live your Christianity and risk ridicule?

There is a legitimate fear of making a fool of yourself; fear of doing something that would tarnish God's reputation. You don't have to put Bible verses on your letter jacket, preach hellfire and brimstone sermons in speech class, and carry a ten-ton Bible to prove that you're a Christian. Ask God to free you from fear of what other people think and give you His wisdom and discernment in all you say and do.

I am not ashamed of the gospel, because it is the power of God for the salvation of everyone who believes: first for the Jew, then for the Gentile.
Romans 1:16

Are not two sparrows sold for a penny? Yet not one of them will fall to the ground apart from the will of your Father. And even the very hairs of your head are all numbered. So don't be afraid; you are worth more than many sparrows. Whoever acknowledges me before men, I will also acknowledge him before my Father in heaven. Matthew 10:29–32

Let the Holy Spirit Be Your Coach

You may be wondering, *How can a shy and timid person like me ever tell anybody about Jesus? How can I keep from sounding like a little robot who spouts off the same words to everyone without being sensitive to their needs? How will I know when to keep quiet and when to speak? How will I know what to say?*

Someone once said, "The answer to every 'how' question in the Christian life is the Holy Spirit." The Holy Spirit can make a naturally shy person into a bold witness. The Holy Spirit can tell you the right words to say at the right time and show you when to keep silent.

You experience the power of the Holy Spirit by spending time in prayer, by being willing to obey instantly, and by having faith that the Holy Spirit will act. It has been said, "If you're not spending more time talking to God about people than talking to people about God, something is wrong." Pray for the people you'd like to witness to, and pray for them every day.

When you know you should say something, say it. Get the first word out, and the Holy Spirit will bless your obedience by giving you the right things to say.

There are other things you can do too. Take a class on evangelism techniques so you can learn better how to share your faith. Lend or give away good Christian books. Invite people to church and Christian club meetings. Some letters you write will give you a good opportunity to share Christ. Always remember that your obedience to God, not necessarily the response of the people to whom you talk about Jesus, is the important thing. Ask God to give you opportunities to share the good news, and He will answer that prayer.

I am sending you out like sheep among wolves. Therefore be as shrewd as snakes and as innocent as doves. Be on your guard against men; they will hand you over to the local councils and flog you in their synagogues. On my account you will be brought before governors and kings as witnesses to them and to the Gentiles. But when they arrest you, do not worry about what to say or how to say it. At that time you will be given what to say, for it will not be you speaking, but the Spirit of your Father speaking through you.
Matthew 10:16–20

Day 321

"But I can't teach a Sunday school class or speak in front of a group or go door-to-door to talk about Jesus or . . ."

Well, if you can't, you may just be the right person for the job. God isn't looking for the super-talented, showy worker who will expect the attention and applause of every onlooker. God is after the person who will serve Him in deep humility and be completely dependent on Him at all times.

This doesn't mean God wants choirs made up of monotones or a blind man to drive the church bus. It also doesn't mean that God condones laziness. You should practice your solo or get that science project done on time. It does mean that spiritual work can't be accomplished without complete dependence on God or without a sense that you're working for Him because you love Him.

If you're really dependent on God, whether you succeed or fail will be *God's* concern, not yours. As an employee in a restaurant, it is your responsibility to do your job well. You let the owner worry about whether or not the restaurant is making a profit. In the same way, God's big requirement from you is faithfulness. The Holy Spirit will take the responsibility for success or failure.

The Bible promises that we will reap a harvest if we don't give up (Galatians 6:9). God decides when the proper time for harvest is, not us! As soon as we become wrapped up in the number of people we share our faith with, the number of hours we spend preparing, or the number of compliments the praise band receives, we're not thinking of Jesus.

We like to do the jobs we feel comfortable doing. But Jesus, our Boss, may decide that a position in which we feel very uncomfortable will best build our character. It brings great glory to God when someone demonstrates His power by letting Him accomplish through him or her what would naturally be impossible. Let Jesus decide what you should do.

Now it is required that those who have been given a trust must prove faithful.
1 Corinthians 4:2

But we have this treasure in jars of clay to show that this all-surpassing power is from God and not from us. 2 Corinthians 4:7

Day 322

Walking Around Walls and Other Crazy Behavior

The Bible tells you to obey your parents and show proper respect to everyone. These commandments are just words on a page unless you decide that you will obey God and believe Him for miracles in your life. Decide you will clean your room every time your mother tells you to. Ask God to give you the right attitude, and He will. If you obey your mother and faithfully expect God to change you, He will smooth things between you and your mom and make you a better housekeeper.

When you realize that "Show proper respect to everyone" includes your crabby chemistry teacher, "Mr. Formula," you will decide to always be courteous to him and pray for him. Soon God will change your attitude toward him.

Read the Bible intending to obey it or you'll miss out on all the good stuff—*miracles* in your very own life!

When Joshua received God's directions for defeating the city of Jericho, he didn't say, "My devotions this morning were especially interesting. By the way, would anybody like to go on a picnic?" or "The Lord gave me some directions, but His methods seem too old-fashioned. If we didn't have modern weapons, I could understand just trusting the Lord." Joshua *obeyed* God, and all the Israelites saw the walls of Jericho crumble before their eyes. Joshua believed God's Word was not only to be heard and read but also to be obeyed.

On the seventh day, they got up at daybreak and marched around the city seven times in the same manner, except that on that day they circled the city seven times. The seventh time around, when the priests sounded the trumpet blast, Joshua commanded the people, "Shout! For the Lord has given you the city!" . . . When the trumpets sounded, the people shouted, and at the sound of the trumpet, when the people gave a loud shout, the wall collapsed; so every man charged straight in, and they took the city. Joshua 6:15–16, 20

Day 323

Reaching the Finish Line

The youth planning team needed a fund-raising project for their winter ski retreat. Someone suggested selling microwave popcorn in small bags outside the mall. Jan invited everyone to her house on Saturday morning, and three people promised to bring microwave ovens so they could get the popcorn popped faster.

When Elijah arrived a half hour late, nobody else had shown up yet. Jan already had an impressive quantity of bagged popcorn on the counter. Ten minutes later, Morganne breezed in, explaining that she could stay for only a half hour.

After she left, Elijah said, "Jan, this is ridiculous. Let's just throw this popcorn away and enjoy our Saturday. This is a *group* project, and it's not fair for two people to do all the work."

"Elijah!" Jan exclaimed. "I'm surprised at you! Throwing away all this good popcorn would be wasting the Lord's money. Besides, we're working for God, and *He* sees what we're doing."

"You can do what you want," Elijah replied, "but I've got enough sense to give up a lost cause." With that, he left. But Jan and her little sister sold all the popcorn that morning and even made some to sell in the afternoon. What would you have done?

He who works his land will have abundant food, but the one who chases fantasies will have his fill of poverty. Proverbs 28:19

The way of the sluggard is blocked with thorns, but the path of the upright is a highway. Proverbs 15:19

It is said, "Time is the stuff of which life is made." Letting hours and days slip by without accomplishing anything means wasting part of your life. Seeking God's wisdom for initiating the projects *He* wants you involved in, and then sticking with them until they are completed, is essential if your life is to count for God. If you present your best schoolwork as a living sacrifice to God, you'll receive His blessing.

Treat each undertaking in your life as a venture for God that merits your best work until it's finished.

Day 324

A Job Well Done

Rod challenged the students in his Bible study to memorize the book of Jude. Response was enthusiastic, and then Rod handed out workbooks on Jude that had to be completed in two weeks. "Do half of a chapter each day," Rod said, "and you'll finish three days early."

Trey did his workbook assignment for two nights in a row, but on Wednesday, he really wanted to watch his favorite TV shows. An hour later, it took all the energy he could muster to get back to work.

The next evening he felt totally exhausted. He prayed for strength instead of telling himself it was impossible to work that night.

And on Friday evening before the Saturday Bible study, he turned down an invitation to go out for pizza—all so he could turn in his completed workbook on time.

Next, they were to memorize the entire book of James—all 108 verses! Rod said that by learning two verses a day, they could complete it in less than two months.

They quizzed each other over the phone and met twice a week to encourage each other. Because he'd always been so lazy, Trey didn't even know that he was good at memorization. Actually, he learned the verses faster than the others. And he began to enjoy it.

During spring break, Rod's cousin came and drilled the Bible study group for four hours every morning so they could enter a national contest. Staying home to watch TV or sleeping in occurred to Trey, but by now he was able to resist these temptations. He was learning to carry his weight and take satisfaction in doing his best.

All hard work brings a profit, but mere talk leads only to poverty. Proverbs 14:23

Whatever your hand finds to do, do it with all your might. Ecclesiastes 9:10

It's God's will that you be ambitious and hardworking, that you learn to do things well—and that you bring glory to Him by the way you work. A job well done is a gift you can present to God.

Day 325

Robbing God's Bank to Buy a Blue Sweater

After saving her money for another week, Stephanie would be able to buy that blue sweater at Nordstrom. She hoped she'd have someplace special to wear it. Her mom had been nagging her about tithing, but surely that could wait until after the sweater. Although Stephanie felt convicted and guilty, she just couldn't part with any of her money. That night she dreamed about robbing God's bank to buy a blue sweater.

Will a man rob God? Yet you rob me. But you ask, "How do we rob you?" In tithes and offerings. You are under a curse—the whole nation of you—because you are robbing me. Malachi 3:8–9

Tithing (giving 10 percent to the Lord) is a way of honoring God by putting Him first in every area of your life. Just listen to the rest of what God says:

"Bring the whole tithe into the storehouse, that there may be food in my house. Test me in this," says the Lord Almighty, "and see if I will not throw open the floodgates of heaven and pour out so much blessing that you will not have room enough for it." Malachi 3:10

If you're faithful to God, He'll be faithful to you. He knows you need jeans and hamburgers and tennis rackets. Trusting Him is a great adventure. Keeping everything you get all to yourself gets boring, stale, and unsatisfying after a while. Budgeting by faith means receiving from God and generously giving back to Him and others. That will give you prosperity and the adventure of watching how God will return what you give to Him.

If you give to God first, He'll take good care of you.

Give, and it will be given to you. A good measure, pressed down, shaken together and running over, will be poured into your lap. For with the measure you use, it will be measured to you. Luke 6:38

Honor the Lord with your wealth, with the firstfruits of all your crops; then your barns will be filled to overflowing, and your vats will brim over with new wine. Proverbs 3:9–10

Ryan and Nick were best friends. One day, they stopped by the electronics store together. The new computer Ryan had wanted for so long was on sale. By putting down two hundred dollars and paying the rest in monthly installments, he could take it home that day.

"Nick, do you have any money on you?" Ryan asked.

Nick was saving for a fishing trip to Canada, but he still had three months to save the money, so he gave Ryan what he needed for the computer.

When Ryan got paid, he bought some new software and some extra memory instead of paying Nick. A month went by and Nick mentioned the fact that Ryan hadn't paid anything on the debt. "You said you didn't need the money until July," answered Ryan. "I'll give you some money next payday."

But Ryan owed his mother money and she put up such a fuss that when payday came, he forked over his whole check. This put him behind on his payments with the electronics store, so he had to make two payments the next month plus a small penalty.

Nick realized he would not get the money back in time for his fishing trip—he might never get it back. And now he didn't even want to be around Ryan, because seeing his friend made him so angry about the lost money. And Ryan avoided Nick because he didn't want the constant reminder of his guilt.

Give everyone what you owe him: If you owe taxes, pay taxes; if revenue, then revenue; if respect, then respect; if honor, then honor. Let no debt remain outstanding, except the continuing debt to love one another. Romans 13:7–8

The Bible is very clear that being in debt is a curse, not a blessing, and not paying your debts is sin. Pay what you owe and kick the borrowing habit.

Day 327
The Devastating Detour

Josh didn't like his job at Taco Bell. The manager was always on his back, and Josh didn't think he made enough money. He felt like quitting. When Josh saw a magazine ad with the title, "How You Can Earn Over $20,000 a Year and Work Only Ten Hours a Week," he sent for information. Immediately Josh quit his job and started dreaming about what he'd do with $20,000. All he had to do was get some of his friends to help him sell some CDs. They were willing to give it a try, but they didn't keep good records, so Josh spent extra hours straightening things out before he sent in the orders.

When the CDs arrived, they were of poor quality and the company had made substitutions. Over half the people wanted their money back. Josh hadn't read the fine print that said he was responsible to return money to unsatisfied customers. The next month was a nightmare. Josh had to borrow money from his father, and he got a bill from the company for more CDs instead of a paycheck.

How had this all happened? Didn't God promise prosperity?

Choose my instruction instead of silver, knowledge rather than choice gold, for wisdom is more precious than rubies, and nothing you desire can compare with her. Proverbs 8:10–11

Dishonest money dwindles away, but he who gathers money little by little makes it grow. Proverbs 13:11

God intends that financial prosperity be the result of hard work and good planning. Get-rich-quick schemes are built on some catch—deceptive advertising, overaggressive sales techniques, or inferior products. And they're devastating detours, not highways to real prosperity.

Proverbs warns you against being eager to get rich. Wanting instant wealth implies laziness, willingness to cheat, or lack of trust in God. Jesus taught us to pray, "Give us this day our daily bread," not "Grant me a bank account so large that I never need to mention money to you again."

When Crystal was elected to the National Honor Society, her mom beamed with pride. "Here's my Visa card," she said. "Take it and buy a nice new outfit. I want you to feel confident when you stand in front of the whole school."

At the store, Crystal ran into Alicia. "My mom's giving me a new dress for the National Honor Society installation," Crystal said. "She let me take her Visa card."

"I wish I had parents like that," Alicia complained.

Crystal spied the kind of dress she'd been looking for. The price was within reason. Meanwhile, Alicia found a stunning outfit. They met at the three-way mirror outside the dressing rooms.

"Crystal," Alicia begged, "couldn't you charge this on your mom's card? I'll pay you back by the end of June. I already have a job with Parks and Recreation."

Crystal hesitated—but she felt sorry for Alicia. Being generous was something Crystal enjoyed. "Okay," she heard herself say, "but you have to repay the money as soon as possible. My mom trusted me with this card."

Suddenly Alicia said, "Oh no! I left my purse in the dressing room! Crystal, could you please run and get it before someone steals it?"

Crystal looked everywhere but she didn't see the purse.

When she returned, Alicia was smiling. "I just remembered I put my purse in the bag with the yarn I bought for my mother. But thanks for looking."

She handed Crystal the Visa card, and they walked out with their packages.

At home Crystal paid her mom for Alicia's outfit; she would wait for Alicia to pay her back. A couple of weeks later Crystal heard her mom let out a yell. The bill from the store was nearly five hundred dollars more than the cost of the two outfits. Crystal knew then she'd never get any of the money back from Alicia.

Proverbs 17:18 tells us:

A man lacking in judgment strikes hands in pledge and puts up security for his neighbor.

However, Jesus tells us:

But love your enemies, do good to them, and lend to them without expecting to get anything back. Luke 6:35

It's wiser to give than to lend, and if you do, lend only an amount you can live without—having decided ahead of time to forgive the person if he or she does not pay you back.

You're never doing a favor by helping someone go into debt for a luxury they can't afford. But God hates stinginess, and you should be ready to give or lend (expecting not to be paid back) for worthy causes. If you seek God's wisdom *before* making a decision, you'll never face Crystal's problem—making an enemy to love.

What if you suddenly became a multimillionaire? Would you enjoy deciding what to spend your money on? What if someone asked you to contribute every penny to the poor, and then become his slave?

You'd probably say "Forget it," without thinking twice.

What if the person who asked was Jesus? A rich young man asked Jesus what he needed to do to have eternal life. Jesus told him to sell everything, give it to the poor, and follow Him. The young man turned away in sorrow; what Jesus asked was more than he was willing to give Him. Matthew 19:20–24 commented that it was easier for a camel to go through the eye of a needle than for a rich man to enter heaven. This reminded the disciples of what they had left to follow Jesus. Peter, Andrew, James, and John had left their fishing nets. Matthew had quit his job as a tax collector.

Peter observed, "We have left everything to follow you!" (Matthew 19:27). Jesus gave him an answer that no one but God could have given:

Jesus said to them, "I tell you the truth, at the renewal of all things, when the Son of Man sits on his glorious throne, you who have followed me will also sit on twelve thrones, judging the twelve tribes of Israel. And everyone who has left houses or brothers or sisters or father or mother or children or fields for my sake will receive a hundred times as much and will inherit eternal life." Matthew 19:28–29

If Jesus is not the real owner of your possessions, something is wrong. You may not have any houses or land to leave for Jesus, but He may be asking you to share your clothes with your sister, lend your skis to your little brother, or give more money to missions. And you may need God's special grace, even to get this little camel through the eye of the needle.

Do not store up for yourselves treasures on earth, where moth and rust destroy, and where thieves break in and steal. But store up for yourselves treasures in heaven, where moth and rust do not destroy, and where thieves do not break in and steal. For where your treasure is, there your heart will be also. Matthew 6:19–21

Day 330

Humble Harry Strikes Again

Jesus is the example of true humility. His formula was *truth plus complete self-sacrifice*. Jesus was never a showoff. He never performed a stunt miracle. He always put the welfare of others before His own. He left the glories of heaven and took on human form. He talked to the Samaritan woman at the well even though He was exhausted and may have preferred solitude. He took time to bless the children, and He washed the disciples' feet. He willingly died for the world and cared for the thief dying next to Him. His best friends left Him in the lurch, and even Peter pretended he didn't know Him. No one has ever made a greater sacrifice for others than Jesus did.

True humility isn't being Milquetoast Matilda or Humble Harry. We should never say something false in order to appear humble. For example, a talented football player would be lying if he said, "I don't pass very well." Humility would comment, "I thank God for giving me a good throwing arm." Paul, in Ephesians 4:15, defines humility in speech as, "speaking the truth in love."

Humility sometimes means keeping your mouth shut even though you know all the right answers. It means washing the car with a smile or offering to work on homecoming night so your friend can go to the game. It means being willing to get a lower grade on the chemistry test by using your study time to visit a sick neighbor. It means graciously admitting that you are wrong. It means telling the truth and putting your rights last.

Jesus knew that the Father had put all things under his power, and that he had come from God and was returning to God; so he got up from the meal, took off his outer clothing, and wrapped a towel around his waist. After that, he poured water into a basin and began to wash his disciples' feet, drying them with the towel that was wrapped around him. . . . When he had finished washing their feet, he put on his clothes and returned to his place. "Do you understand what I have done for you?" he asked them. "You call me 'Teacher' and 'Lord,' and rightly so, for that is what I am. Now that I, your Lord and Teacher, have washed your feet, you also should wash one another's feet."
John 13:3–5, 12–14

Children outgrow letters to Santa Claus, and grown-ups realize that the president can't do anything about the weather, pneumonia, or making someone fall in love. Actually, it's ridiculous to ask anyone but God to fundamentally change people or to untangle complicated situations.

But Jesus said:

> *And I will do whatever you ask in my name, so that the Son may bring glory to the Father. You may ask me for anything in my name, and I will do it.*
> John 14:13-14

No one but God in human flesh could make a promise like this. The New Testament doesn't suggest that praying in Jesus' name is some kind of abracadabra magic to get answers. It teaches that our prayers must be consistent with the character of the One who will answer them. When Jesus himself said, "You may ask for anything and *I* will do it," He personally promised that *He* will answer our prayers.

Obviously, praying in the name of Jesus does not mean that we'll get anything we ask for. Most of you would not think of saying, "Dad, please give me a million dollars," because most of your fathers do not have that kind of money. Neither do you ask, "Sara, will you help me throw stones at the neighbor's dog?" because you know Sara loves animals. Praying, "Jesus, help me make all the trees turn purple so I can get my name in the newspaper," would be unthinkable.

When you pray in the name of Jesus, remember that He has all power. Also, remember that you have to get to know Jesus well enough so that you know what to pray for. Read His Word and spend time with Him. You'll find out that He won't help you get straight A's without studying. But you'll discover that He wants to help you in many things—if you'll only *obey* Him.

> *I write these things to you who believe in the name of the Son of God so that you may know that you have eternal life. This is the confidence we have in approaching God: that if we ask anything according to his will, he hears us.*
> 1 John 5:13-14

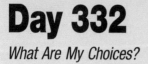

Day 332

What Are My Choices?

When you're deciding what to do with your life, the possibilities at first seem limitless. There are hundreds of occupations to choose from and probably thousands of people you could marry. You might want to live in sunny California, frigid Alaska, or maybe even settle in Paris or Rio.

But even when you're happily married, working at your occupation, and living in your dream home, you will still have to decide what to do with your life. There are only three real choices: (1) to live for yourself; (2) to live for other people—the ones you choose; and (3) to live for God.

When you think of all the mistakes you've made so far and contemplate all the errors you've watched others make, you should have a healthy fear of making your own decisions and doing your own thing. If there is a God who gave us the Bible and showed himself to the world through His Son Jesus, there is only *one* logical choice, and that is to live your life—all of it—for God.

Choose for yourselves this day whom you will serve. . . . But as for me and my household, we will serve the Lord. Joshua 24:15

This is what the Lord says: "Let not the wise man boast of his wisdom or the strong man boast of his strength or the rich man boast of his riches, but let him who boasts boast about this: that he understands and knows me, that I am the Lord, who exercises kindness, justice and righteousness on earth, for in these I delight," declares the Lord. Jeremiah 9:23–24

A guy named Skip loved animals and had a special interest in a pet monkey that was for sale in a local pet shop. He went to see the monkey often and enjoyed playing with it. Clerks who saw how much he liked the monkey kept hoping for a sale, but they always received the same answer. "I don't make a lot of money. If I bought a monkey I'd have to move because my neighbors think a monkey is a weird pet. Besides, I enjoy just coming here to see him because I get the benefit of enjoying him without the responsibility of caring for him and buying his food."

Skip was a confirmed window-shopper. He refused to get involved or make a firm decision. Skip couldn't honestly say, "I went shopping today for a pet monkey, but I couldn't find one."

A lot of people are window-shopping for Christianity. They are drawn by Jesus' love and the benefits of living for Christ. Because they may go to church and even read the Bible, they might be saying, "I'm seeking for God, but I just can't find Him." The truth is, if they didn't care what their friends thought, if they were willing to let God change their lives, if they would assume responsibility, and if they'd consider God more important than any possession or friendship, they would find Him.

You will seek me and find me when you seek me with all your heart.
Jeremiah 29:13

As Jesus started on his way, a man ran up to him and fell on his knees before him. "Good teacher," he asked, "what must I do to inherit eternal life?" . . . Jesus looked at him and loved him. "One thing you lack," he said. "Go, sell everything you have and give to the poor, and you will have treasure in heaven. Then come, follow me." At this the man's face fell. He went away sad, because he had great wealth. Mark 10:17, 21–22

Day 334
But What If I Find It?

What are you looking for? Be careful. You may say that you are looking for peace, happiness, or reality, but you have probably already decided what will give you this. You may have determined that enough money will give you peace of mind—you don't want to worry about finances the way your parents do. Marrying the right person should make you live "happily ever after." Or maybe you think you can find reality if you study all the great thinkers or take the right drugs to "expand" your mind and usher you into new experiences.

If you put all your energies into trying to accumulate money, you will probably succeed at just that. If you are determined to marry a certain person, you may reach your goal. You may also become very knowledgeable about philosophy or psychology. The problem is that all of us know of people who have gotten exactly what they wanted—only to be miserable. However, those who decide to get to know the real God who is revealed in the Bible are never disappointed.

Enough that God my Father knows,
Nothing this hope can dim;
He gives the very best to those
Who leave the choice with Him.
—Author unknown

Glory in his holy name; let the hearts of those who seek the Lord rejoice. Look to the Lord and his strength; seek his face always. 1 Chronicles 16:10–11

Blessed are those who hunger and thirst for righteousness, for they will be filled. Matthew 5:6

You've heard it and have maybe even said it yourself: "If that's Christianity, I don't want it." However, in many cases it's not *Christianity* that the person is rejecting but Pastor Law's eighty extra commandments or the stubbornness displayed by some church people or Hillary's hardhearted attitude toward the girl desperately needing help. Remember that *God* decides who the real Christians are, and many people who claim to be Christians really aren't. However, those who *are* real Christians don't always live their Christianity either.

It has been said that if there weren't any real dollar bills, there wouldn't be any counterfeits. Well, because there are real Christians, there are counterfeits. Don't reject Christianity because there are hypocrites in the church or because the German church didn't stand up against Hitler or because your uncle who reads the Bible all the time yells at you. If you do reject Christianity, first take time to read the New Testament for yourself so you know what you are rejecting. Then be honest enough to admit that you're rejecting *Jesus* because you're unwilling to make the changes He requires in your life. Jesus wants to be the Boss of your life.

> *On hearing it, many of his disciples said, "This is a hard teaching. Who can accept it?" . . . From this time many of his disciples turned back and no longer followed him. "You do not want to leave too, do you?" Jesus asked the Twelve. Simon Peter answered him, "Lord, to whom shall we go? You have the words of eternal life. We believe and know that you are the Holy One of God."*
> John 6:60, 66–69

Day 336

What Makes You a Christian?

Which of these would most certainly be a Christian?

(a) Charlene Church Attender

(b) Dudley Do-Gooder

(c) Baptized Benjamin

(d) Confirmed Connie

(e) None of the Above

You probably answered the question correctly because you realize that just doing something outward can't change you on the inside. Yet a lot of people think that believing the right things, using the right words, and running with the right crowd makes one a Christian. There is no magic in the words "Jesus, come into my life" if they're simply repeated because someone else thought it was a good idea.

Others think that being "born again" is just turning over a new leaf, a determination to be better. Your deciding to be different won't save you either. Of course, you have to believe that Jesus is God's Son who came to die for your sins. And after you become a Christian, you will want to do good deeds. Yet the missing ingredient here is *repentance*. Repentance means not only feeling sorry for your sin but also being willing to give it up and then turning around to face God honestly. If you admit your sin and are willing to let Jesus change you and run your life, then the words "Jesus, come into my life" have meaning, and the Spirit of Jesus miraculously enters you.

An early American evangelist was confronted on the street by a drunk. One of his critics turned to him and said, "There's one of your converts." The evangelist replied, "He must be one of mine. He certainly isn't one of God's." Are you God's convert or somebody else's?

In reply Jesus declared, "I tell you the truth, no one can see the kingdom of God unless he is born again." "How can a man be born when he is old?" Nicodemus asked. "Surely he cannot enter a second time into his mother's womb to be born!" Jesus answered, "I tell you the truth, no one can enter the kingdom of God unless he is born of water and the Spirit. Flesh gives birth to flesh, but the Spirit gives birth to spirit. You should not be surprised at my saying, 'You must be born again.'" John 3:3–7

When someone says, "Jesus is the Lord of my life," what picture do you conjure up in your mind—a person demanding things from Skyways Prayer Answering Service, Inc.; an employee who does the king's work when conditions are favorable; or a slave who bows before his master and calls him "Lord"? Because we don't have slaves and absolute rulers anymore, the word *Lord* doesn't mean much to us.

Back in Roman times, calling someone Lord meant that he, like Caesar, had absolute life-and-death power over you, that he had the right to this authority, and that you would obey him. In that context, can you really say that Jesus is the Lord of your life?

In our culture, no one wants to obey. A student once remarked, "I think too much of myself to do as you say." If we are so self-centered that we refuse to obey Jesus, we have no right to call ourselves Christians. We can think so much of ourselves that we'll miss heaven.

Not everyone who says to me, "Lord, Lord," will enter the kingdom of heaven, but only he who does the will of my Father who is in heaven. Matthew 7:21

But what does it say? "The word is near you; it is in your mouth and in your heart," that is, the word of faith we are proclaiming: That if you confess with your mouth, "Jesus is Lord," and believe in your heart that God raised him from the dead, you will be saved. For it is with your heart that you believe and are justified, and it is with your mouth that you confess and are saved. As the Scripture says, "Anyone who trusts in him will never be put to shame." For there is no difference between Jew and Gentile—the same Lord is Lord of all and richly blesses all who call on him, for, "Everyone who calls on the name of the Lord will be saved." Romans 10:8–13

Day 338

Till Death Do Us Part

If you've ever attended a traditional wedding ceremony, you've heard things like, "For better, for worse; for richer, for poorer; in sickness and in health . . . till death do us part." Taken seriously, that's a tremendous commitment to live up to. Would you describe *your* relationship with Jesus Christ as that kind of commitment, or do you think of it as "Try Jesus for ninety days; there's nothing to lose, and there's a money-back guarantee"?

Have you given yourself to Him because He is truth, because He made you, and because He, who is smarter than anyone else, has the right to run your life? Or do you just think it might be a good deal for you?

Do you think Jesus is pretty fortunate that you noticed Him, or do you realize that you in no way deserve His mercy and grace? The apostle Paul referred to himself as a "slave of Jesus Christ." Do you think of Him as the great genie in the sky who should consider your every wish as His command?

There are *facts* you base your life on—an operation will cure appendicitis, it's safer to slow down when driving around mountain curves, and jumping from a twelfth-story window is hazardous to your health. Whether or not you feel like acting in accordance with these facts, they are valid. They are true whether or not you understand the reasons behind them, and whether or not everyone else believes in them.

You must commit yourself to Jesus because of the facts—He is "the way, the truth, and the life"—and not because He'll give you a new high. Following Jesus and His truth has great end results, but it takes a *lifetime* commitment.

Anyone who does not take his cross and follow me is not worthy of me. Matthew 10:38

Suppose one of you wants to build a tower. Will he not first sit down and estimate the cost to see if he has enough money to complete it? For if he lays the foundation and is not able to finish it, everyone who sees it will ridicule him, saying, "This fellow began to build and was not able to finish." . . . In the same way, any of you who does not give up everything he has cannot be my disciple. Luke 14:28–30, 33

The great gift of God was His Son. The great response of humans is receiving Jesus. Repenting of sin and taking Jesus into your life made you a Christian. You believed God's Word, and as an act of faith, you accepted Jesus as your Savior. Because of this, God miraculously changed the direction of your life.

This is not the end of your responsibility, though. Study the Bible to find out how children of God are supposed to act and what characteristics they are to have. You will notice that we are to be totally *obedient* to our heavenly Father and totally *dependent* on Him. Even if this is not yet part of your experience, believe God's Word. Recognize that Jesus will work in you. Jesus lives within you to make you the kind of child that would bring honor to His name.

Know what God expects of you and don't try to live up to man-made rules. You don't always have to be serious, somber, and studious because Mrs. McFrown says you should be. You don't have to wear 1970 styles because Aunt Tillie thinks you'd look better if you did. But you do have to love your enemies because God says you must. How do you love your enemies when right now you hate them? This is just one of many situations in which you will have to receive Jesus' power in order to become God's obedient child.

Yet to all who received him, to those who believed in his name, he gave the right to become children of God. John 1:12

Here I am! I stand at the door and knock. If anyone hears my voice and opens the door, I will come in and eat with him, and he with me. Revelation 3:20

Day 340
But Don't Look in the Closet

Christ lives in your heart because you exercised faith—you let Him in. Someone has written a beautiful booklet that compares your heart to a huge house. Even after you let Jesus into your heart "house," you will discover that there are still more rooms to give to Him. Although becoming a Christian means giving Jesus your life, few people realize what that *means*. Jesus is usually invited into the "living room" and treated more like a guest than a landlord.

Little by little, Jesus shows us that He has a right to determine what goes on in the "recreation room," and He decides what is served in the "dining room." He even has the right to clean out the "closets"—to make you apologize for past words, to pay for things you've stolen, and to try to make things right with people you've wronged. He has glorious plans to remodel and redecorate your heart home—plans that are greater than you've ever dreamed of.

Most of all, Jesus wants to be your constant Companion, showing you His love continually. Let Jesus clean out your closets, make your plans, and share His life with you.

To them God has chosen to make known among the Gentiles the glorious riches of this mystery, which is Christ in you, the hope of glory. Colossians 1:27

I pray that out of [the Father's] glorious riches he may strengthen you with power through his Spirit in your inner being, so that Christ may dwell in your hearts through faith. And I pray that you, being rooted and established in love, may have power, together with all the saints, to grasp how wide and long and high and deep is the love of Christ, and to know this love that surpasses knowledge—that you may be filled to the measure of all the fullness of God. Ephesians 3:16–19

Day 341
Your Gift to God

Have you ever tried to "ungive" a present? You don't give your mother a beautiful plant for Mother's Day and then proceed to tell her, "I'll keep it up in my room because I'll take better care of it than you will." You've been taught from the first birthday party you attended that if you give something away, you don't take it back again.

This also holds true for your commitment to Jesus, and it's good to renew it each day, saying, "Jesus, I have given myself to you. I will follow you and serve you—I am totally yours." If you sin after making this surrender, don't think that your surrender was insincere. It's because you are still learning how to trust Jesus and give yourself to Him. Ask His forgiveness and reaffirm your surrender to Him.

Don't hold back anything. Confess every sin to Him. Give Him your mind and your thoughts, your mouth and the words you say, your heart and your love, as well as your job, your schoolwork, your stereo, your motorcycle, and even your hairdryer. He has a right to all you are, all you do, and all you own. If you give it, Jesus will take it; and what He takes, He will care for.

> I'd give you a rainbow
> If I had many colors,
> But alas my sky is gray.
> I'd give you a lark
> To greet your sunrise,
> But wings were made to be free.
> I'd give you a mountain,
> Blue and majestic,
> But all I have is one stone.
> I will give you my life, Lord.
> My gift to you is me.
> —Patrice Joncas

And they did not do as we expected, but they gave themselves first to the Lord and then to us in keeping with God's will. 2 Corinthians 8:5

Day 342
You Can Be Sure

Rachel was talking to her girl friend about heaven, but when she said that she knew she was going to heaven, her friend said, "That's presuming a lot; it sounds like a pretty proud attitude." If your status depended on your good works and flawless character, "proud" would be an understatement. But we are saved by faith and not by works. The Bible says:

Therefore no one will be declared righteous in his sight by observing the law; rather, through the law we become conscious of sin. But now a righteousness from God, apart from law, has been made known, to which the Law and the Prophets testify. This righteousness from God comes through faith in Jesus Christ to all who believe. There is no difference. Romans 3:20–22

God tells us in many places in the Bible that He will forgive us and make us His children if we confess our sins and make Him the Lord of our lives.

There is nothing humble about calling God a liar. You don't like it when someone doubts your word; you don't want people to think that you lie. Then how can we doubt God's Word? Unbelief in Jesus' power to save is nothing less than treating Him as a liar. Jesus commands us to be born again. He promised to give eternal life to anyone who believes in Him, and He means it. If you completely turned your life over to Jesus, He came into your heart because He said He would.

I tell you the truth, whoever hears my word and believes him who sent me has eternal life and will not be condemned; he has crossed over from death to life. John 5:24

Anyone who believes in the Son of God has this testimony in his heart. Anyone who does not believe God has made him out to be a liar, because he has not believed the testimony God has given about his Son. And this is the testimony: God has given us eternal life, and this life is in his Son. He who has the Son has life; he who does not have the Son of God does not have life. I write these things to you who believe in the name of the Son of God so that you may know that you have eternal life. 1 John 5:10–13

You may have seen the greeting card showing two contented children with the caption, "If you have Jesus, you have everything." Begin each new day with that thought. You may feel like a little lost lamb in a big bad world, but Jesus, your Shepherd, is with you whether you need forgiveness, help with a problem, or someone to love you. If you fall, He'll pick you up, and when danger is near, He'll protect you. He'll help you in temptation and guide you into His perfect will.

Let Jesus be your Shepherd. Let Him be everything to you.

In Him is all I need.
In Him is all I need.
His abundance for my emptiness,
And His life for my lifelessness.
His love for my coldness,
And His light for my darkness.
His truth for my deceit,
And His joy for my sadness.
His victory for my defeat,
And His rest for my restlessness.
—Translated from the German by Gerdi Sirtl

He who did not spare his own Son, but gave him up for us all—how will he not also, along with him, graciously give us all things? —Romans 8:32

Though I myself have reasons for such confidence. If anyone else thinks he has reasons to put confidence in the flesh, I have more: circumcised on the eighth day, of the people of Israel, of the tribe of Benjamin, a Hebrew of Hebrews; in regard to the law, a Pharisee; as for zeal, persecuting the church; as for legalistic righteousness, faultless. But whatever was to my profit I now consider loss for the sake of Christ. What is more, I consider everything a loss compared to the surpassing greatness of knowing Christ Jesus my Lord, for whose sake I have lost all things. I consider them rubbish, that I may gain Christ.
Philippians 3:4–8

Day 344

Green Pastures and Still Waters

Jesus promises to give us peace. Most of us think of peace as vacationing on a Caribbean island or being able to sleep until noon on Saturday. Yet if peace means escape, the only way to get it is to drop out of regular day-to-day living, with its overdue library books, traffic jams, and tight schedules. Fortunately Jesus offers peace that the world can't give—peace when your mother yells at you, peace when the car runs out of gas, and peace when the basketball bus leaves without you—peace in the middle of pressure.

An artist once portrayed "peace" as a little bird content in a nest on the end of an oak branch sticking out over roaring Niagara Falls. *That* is peace.

It's all too easy to adopt the world's mentality, assuming that peace is an impossibility at school and on the job in our stressful society—that only long vacations, lots of TV, and plenty of down can keep us from burning out completely.

But almost every New Testament epistle begins with the same kind of message:

Grace and peace to you . . . from the Lord Jesus Christ. Romans 1:7

It's our focus on Jesus and expectation of receiving His peace that can bring inner tranquility in the most trying of circumstances.

Paul commands us to "let the peace of Christ rule" in our hearts. If you keep your mind on Jesus and you look to Him in faith, you'll find green pastures and still waters, even in the middle of fifth-hour English class.

The Lord is my shepherd, I shall not be in want. He makes me lie down in green pastures, he leads me beside quiet waters, he restores my soul. He guides me in paths of righteousness for his name's sake. Even though I walk through the valley of the shadow of death, I will fear no evil, for you are with me; your rod and your staff, they comfort me. You prepare a table before me in the presence of my enemies. You anoint my head with oil; my cup overflows. Surely goodness and love will follow me all the days of my life, and I will dwell in the house of the Lord forever. Psalm 23

Do you ever feel like the little kid who sings, "Nobody loves me. Everybody hates me. I'm gonna go eat worms"? If you answered yes, join the human race. Loneliness and that "no one understands me" feeling are very common. Sometimes the people you think are your friends let you down. Other times they are too occupied with their own problems to notice that you need special help. Even if someone takes the time to try to help you, that person is often unable to understand your feelings.

Jesus wants to be your friend and constant companion, the One with whom you share your plans, your dreams, your failures, your sin, and your problems. Not only does He understand you perfectly, but He has all power, and He can direct you in the right way and show you how to get out of the mess you got yourself into.

Jesus will always be your friend—no matter what. He'll be the honest friend who lets you know when you're doing something wrong; the comforting friend to whom you can pour out your heart; and the counselor who will help you make your future plans.

Good friends spend a lot of time together. Jesus can't help you if you don't talk to Him, and He can't advise you if you don't listen to Him. You need a friend like Jesus. Take the time to get to know Him.

I no longer call you servants, because a servant does not know his master's business. Instead, I have called you friends, for everything that I learned from my Father I have made known to you. John 15:15

So do not fear, for I am with you; do not be dismayed, for I am your God. I will strengthen you and help you; I will uphold you with my righteous right hand. Isaiah 41:10

Day 346

I Am Weak But He Is Strong

Jesus wants to be your strength, but He can't be unless you let Him. In order to let Jesus be your strength, you must be weak—by God's definition; you must recognize that you are unable to live the Christian life—period. It is not a matter of desperately trying to be kind to a mean teacher and getting a little help from Jesus to push you over the top. It is not evangelizing like mad in your own strength and getting a snitch of God's power to keep going. No, it's recognizing that Jesus meant it when He said, "Apart from me you can do nothing" (John 15:5).

Sometimes we use the word *weakness* to cover up sins. A child who comes in from playing doesn't usually get by with saying, "I'm too weak to clean my room." Spending little time in Bible study and not helping others is not due to "weakness." It's more accurate to say, "I'm too lazy," or "I think other things are more important."

A child who struggles to put his shoe on the wrong foot, disregarding his mother's instruction, is not weak. He is *disobedient*. You may be trying to do something God doesn't want you to do; you can't expect His strength for that. If your mother baked a birthday cake for your younger sister and asked you not to touch it, your eating three pieces before the party is not weakness; it is pure selfishness.

If you want God's strength, you can have it. First of all, stop calling sin "inability to resist" and disobedience "weakness." Second, recognize that you don't just need *some* help from Jesus—you need Him to do the whole thing, from beginning to end. Now, this does not mean sitting in a chair for the next twenty years until a voice from heaven tells you to stand up. It does mean recognizing that you can't drive a car, work out at the gym, take a test, or go out for pizza *in such a way as to glorify and honor God* unless you admit your complete dependence on Him. Of course you can physically accomplish any of these things. It's *pleasing God* that you cannot do on your own. Just as you would constantly seek the guidance of your teacher while performing an experiment in chemistry class, so you should realize that the relationships and responsibilities of life require God's supervision if they are not to blow up in your face.

Once you acknowledge your weakness, by faith claim God's strength.

God promises strength for the weak. He has enough strength no matter what you're facing, as long as you don't rely on your own resources. Andrew Murray puts it this way, "The Christian is strong in His Lord—not sometimes strong and sometimes weak, but always weak and therefore always strong."

> Then Peter said, "Silver or gold I do not have, but what I have I give you. In the name of Jesus Christ of Nazareth, walk." Taking him by the right hand, he helped him up, and instantly the man's feet and ankles became strong. He jumped to his feet and began to walk. Then he went with them into the temple courts, walking and jumping, and praising God. Acts 3:6–8

Day 347

Righteousness—The Secret to Success

Tyne's father had been reassigned to a military base relatively near both sets of grandparents. First, Tyne and her sister, Lora, spent a week with her mother's parents. The modest house was so carefully decorated that it appeared elegant. Grandma and Grandpa Price had exciting things planned for the girls to do. An attitude of contentment, joy, and thankfulness pervaded the house. They shared answers to prayer and proudly displayed some gifts and pictures from missionaries they helped to support financially. The week went by all too fast.

Then Tyne and her sister packed up to visit Grandpa and Grandma Watson. After the first day, the girls realized that complaining would be on the menu for every meal. Their grandparents kept up a continual harangue about the fact that they had bought their home from a "crooked" real estate firm. Grandma Watson had an overwhelming fear of getting robbed, so each outside door had three locks. They had bars on the windows, a security system, and a German shepherd watchdog. They wouldn't allow the girls to leave the house for fear that something would happen.

After two days, Tyne was ready to tell her mother to come and get them. Then she realized that while Grandma and Grandpa Price knew Jesus and loved Him, Grandma and Grandpa Watson had no time for God. For the first time, Tyne realized the big difference that knowing Jesus could make in a life.

An evil man is snared by his own sin, but a righteous one can sing and be glad. Proverbs 29:6

The house of the righteous contains great treasure, but the income of the wicked brings them trouble. Proverbs 15:6

You get to choose between letting Jesus live His righteous life through you or falling for worldly ways of thinking and living. The older you become, the more your lifestyle will reflect the spiritual choices you've made. People without God have reason to fear the future. But with your hand in God's, you can walk into the unknown with the Architect of all your tomorrows by your side.

One morning before the eight-o'clock bell rang, a couple of guys from English class invited Jim to cut out with them and eat breakfast at McDonald's. English was the most boring class of the day. Jim felt a little guilty as he snuck out the side door with them, but he rationalized that he deserved a break. Besides—going out to eat wasn't exactly sin city.

What they didn't know was that in response to a PTA plea, the principal had initiated a new policy. Each student caught skipping would be suspended for one day. Jim was caught—and angry. Why should he get caught the very first time he broke a school rule when others seemed to get away with everything? Have you ever felt like Jim? Listen to the lesson Jim's friend taught him that day.

If being good is boring, there's a reason. Although you accepted the righteousness of Jesus by faith when you were saved, right now you're not walking by faith or relying on the strength of God. Instead, you're depending solely on human efforts rather than plugging into the Holy Spirit's power. Philippians 2:12–13 explains how you can cooperate with God in order to make right living a real adventure.

Continue to work out your salvation with fear and trembling, for it is God who works in you to will and to act according to his good purpose.

What a great privilege you have—to be able to draw upon the inexhaustible resources of the power of the Holy Spirit living in you. Then you'll be excited about cooperating with God's work in you to do what's right. And you'll resist evil because you love Jesus and want to please Him—not because it's expected of you.

The Lord detests the sacrifice of the wicked, but the prayer of the upright pleases him. The Lord detests the way of the wicked but he loves those who pursue righteousness. Proverbs 15:8–9

The Lord detests the thoughts of the wicked, but those of the pure are pleasing to him. Proverbs 15:26

Nothing is more pleasant than knowing you have the approval of the person you most love and admire. God has provided everything necessary for us to enjoy that kind of relationship with Him!

Day 349

The Gift of a Happy Heart

Jillian didn't like school and thought the teachers were out to get her. She resented the fact that she didn't receive any attention from guys, and she blamed God for creating her ugly. She was jealous of girls who were outgoing and likeable. The kids in the youth group tolerated her, but no one wanted to listen to her tales of woe. More and more, Jillian began to give up on life. She assumed that no one in her situation could ever be happy.

But that was before she met Candra. Candra had a terrible scar on her face. Closer observation revealed that she had an artificial leg and walked with difficulty. But her smile and resilience were disarming. She entered into activities with enthusiasm, and she was even a good volleyball player! She had a lot of friends. One day Jillian heard Candra's story. Her parents had died in a car accident—the same one that left her with a scar and an artificial leg. She lived with her grandparents and had to do most of the housework. Candra told Jillian, "God has used me to help other kids who feel that life has cheated them in some way."

A happy heart makes the face cheerful, but heartache crushes the spirit.
Proverbs 15:13

A cheerful heart is good medicine, but a crushed spirit dries up the bones.
Proverbs 17: 22

Where do happy hearts come from? When Jesus was praying for His disciples, He said:

I say these things while I am still in the world, so that they may have the full measure of my joy within them. John 17:13

By accepting the promises Jesus has given us, we can receive all His joy. Do you *really* believe that God has your best interests in mind?

Form the habit of constantly praising God and giving thanks in all things. When you face overwhelming problems, thank God that He's in control and will work out everything for your benefit. Praise God for the rain and the storm. A grateful heart is a happy heart.

Day 350

Who Put the Price Tag on You?

At school, Martina stuck to Becky like glue. Every day, she counted on her to listen to the unabridged version of her latest tragedy. Becky was usually very patient, but one morning she greeted Martina with a desperate look. "I can't listen to you today," she said abruptly. "I've got to spend every minute studying for a big Spanish test." And with that she rushed into the library.

Martina burst into tears. The fight she'd had with her mother last night was so terrible that she *had* to talk to someone. How could Becky be so rude? Martina started talking to Judy, the youth pastor's wife, every day after school. One afternoon, though, Judy answered the doorbell with a despairing plea, "Martina, please understand. I can't talk to you now. The baby's fussy, I haven't started dinner, and I have a meeting at church at seven."

Seldom set foot in your neighbor's house—too much of you, and he will hate you. Proverbs 25:17

All of you, clothe yourselves with humility toward one another. 1 Peter 5:5

As Christians, we are to think of others before ourselves, and we are to get rid of the pride that treats people as pawns to be used for our own convenience. Don't make yourself a nuisance. Don't pressure people. Don't be a leech. Visiting too often, staying too long, or coming just at mealtime is not only poor manners, it's a bad testimony.

If someone presents a good reason for not being able to help right when you ask, give that person the benefit of the doubt. Instead, learn to tell Jesus your problems. Don't be like Martina, who measures her self-worth by the reactions of others. Break your dependence on getting the right strokes from friends in order to have a good day. You're not an item whose price tag changes according to what other people think you're worth. Neither an insult nor a compliment can change the fact that you have intrinsic and immeasurable value because Jesus died for you. Whether you're being ignored or congratulated, Jesus views you as a great treasure.

Day 351

Act Like a Branch

Once upon a time there was a little branch named Twigger near the bottom of a large, beautiful apple tree. He envied the bigger branches and the ones at the top of the tree. He hated windstorms, winter snows, and kids climbing on him. Why couldn't he be one of those top branches?

Twigger became so worried that he prayed, "Please make me a branch. Please make me a branch that will bear fruit."

The branch next to him overheard his prayer and said, "That's a silly prayer. You *are* a branch, and the trunk has plenty of sap for you. If you'd stop making it impossible for yourself to receive the sap, things would change."

Twigger thought, *I may be brown and fruitless, but I am a branch. The trunk has the life-giving power I need. I must stop resisting this power and stop trying to run my own life and being dissatisfied with my position.*

Twigger soon realized the vast amount of power that the trunk had. All of a sudden, he was thankful to be just a little branch on the lowest part of the tree. He was thankful for harsh weather that made the whole tree grow stronger. He was thankful for the other branches too.

And do you know what? As Twigger concentrated on the trunk, stopped blocking the sap, and started believing in the power the trunk would give, he didn't have to try to bear fruit or blossoms. *It just happened.*

I am the vine; you are the branches. If a man remains in me and I in him, he will bear much fruit; apart from me you can do nothing. If anyone does not remain in me, he is like a branch that is thrown away and withers; such branches are picked up, thrown into the fire and burned. If you remain in me and my words remain in you, ask whatever you wish, and it will be given you. This is to my Father's glory, that you bear much fruit, showing yourselves to be my disciples. John 15:5–8

The world is filled with unfinished projects, broken diets, and uncompleted schemes. At first it seems simple or fun to do something new and different. But it's easy for all of us to fall back into old habits.

When we decide to accept Jesus, we are overjoyed by the new discovery that we can live by faith. After a while, though, it's easy to slip back into our old patterns of seeing everything from an earthly point of view. We try to cope with things through our own efforts. We sometimes call the attempt to live up to God's standards in our own strength "living under the law."

The problem is not God's sensible and necessary rules or the project we started or the healthy diet. It's just that we feel powerless to do what we should. Instead of living "under law," just thinking about the rules, God wants us to live "under grace," getting from Him the favor and strength God gives in response to our faith. We can receive from Him all the grace and power we need to live the Christian life. As we progress in faith, God gives us harder and harder tasks so our faith will grow.

Every situation we face and every command in the Bible is an opportunity to exercise our faith and receive God's grace. You need the faith that asks for and expects to receive God's grace. This faith is not an optional extra for daily Christian living; it's an essential.

See, he is puffed up; his desires are not upright—but the righteous will live by his faith. Habakkuk 2:4

When the servant of the man of God got up and went out early the next morning, an army with horses and chariots had surrounded the city. "Oh, my lord, what shall we do?" the servant asked. "Don't be afraid," the prophet answered. "Those who are with us are more than those who are with them." And Elisha prayed, "O Lord, open his eyes so he may see." Then the Lord opened the servant's eyes, and he looked and saw the hills full of horses and chariots of fire all around Elisha. 2 Kings 6:15–17

Day 353

Maybe You Need a Broken Leg!

A little lamb was always running away from the flock. Although the lamb loved the shepherd and was proud to belong to him, he had big ideas to explore the world, find better pasture, and make new friends.

One day the shepherd, because he loved the lamb, broke its leg. This required the lamb to stay close to the shepherd. The lamb developed a dependence on the shepherd. Even when the leg was completely healed, he stayed close to the shepherd and didn't wander away.

We're often like that lamb. Although we've supposedly surrendered everything to God, we can easily start doing our own thing.

You may give your good singing voice to God with the idea of becoming a great Christian singer, but God may have to shatter your dream of ever singing for Him until you learn to depend on Him. Many things we do for God with the best of intentions fail because God has to teach us to depend on Him. Otherwise we'll stray.

The important thing is not what you do but whether your attitude is one of total dependence on God. Jesus is the One who judges whether you are dependent on Him. Don't use "success" as the way of telling whether you've given yourself to Jesus. Don't depend on the feelings you have.

Don't be discouraged if all your plans for the youth retreat flop. God loves you so much that He wants you to learn absolute dependence on Him. The failure you experienced after you tried to do something for God may be His way of teaching you this all-important lesson.

Don't fall into discouragement. Fall into the arms of Jesus. As you learn to depend on Him, He can start using the things you give to Him—in ways more wonderful than you could ever have dreamed. Like the boy who gave his lunch to Jesus, give Him your smile, your concern for the poor, your athletic ability, and you'll be surprised what He will do.

So they sat down in groups of hundreds and fifties. Taking the five loaves and the two fish and looking up to heaven, he gave thanks and broke the loaves. Then he gave them to his disciples to set before the people. He also divided the two fish among them all. They all ate and were satisfied. Mark 6:40–42

If the Volume Is Up Too High, You Can't Hear the Still, Small Voice

If you and your boyfriend or girlfriend wish to clear up a misunderstanding, you don't do it during a time-out of the Super Bowl game! A marriage proposal is not generally made at a bustling railroad station when the young man must catch his train in five minutes.

Important discussions with other people need time and peaceful surroundings. Yet many of us approach our communication with God in the five minutes we have until the TV show comes back after commercial. Often we don't stay before God in prayer long enough for our minds to forget about the lost billfold or the last family quarrel.

Have you ever spent a half hour in absolute quietness before Jesus? Try it. It's wonderful. That unhurried quiet time is necessary if the Holy Spirit is to direct your everyday life. The busier you are, the more you need this quiet time before God.

Martin Luther reportedly remarked, "I have so much business, I cannot get on without spending three hours daily in prayer."

To hear the voice of God you must be deaf to other voices—the voices of your friends, the media, and your own desires. If you're so busy that there isn't quiet, unhurried time for prayer, the Holy Spirit can't speak to you.

Deciding to make quiet time with God a priority will be extremely difficult. Even other Christians might not understand. People will think it weird that a normal red-blooded teenager would give up something fun or profitable to spend time with God. But He has some very important things to say to you. You'll never hear them unless you turn down the volume and stop long enough to listen.

Be still, and know that I am God; I will be exalted among the nations, I will be exalted in the earth. Psalm 46:10

Day 355

His Sheep Am I

Shepherds in the Middle East still herd their sheep as their ancestors did centuries ago. A good shepherd loves each one of his sheep, giving protection, discipline, and direction. Sheep learn to follow their shepherd with an attitude of trust. To the extent that sheep are capable of it, there is a relationship of love and affection between the shepherd and his sheep.

The shepherd would do anything possible to protect and help the sheep. Recognizing this, the sheep obediently follow the shepherd.

However, there are things the shepherd must do that the sheep cannot comprehend. There are beautiful hills that the sheep are never allowed to graze on—the owners of those hills would rather have mutton than wool! Because there are many diseases that the sheep could catch, modern shepherds sometimes find it necessary to completely submerge each sheep in an antiseptic solution. This process, which must take place regularly, is something the sheep hate and fear. Yet it is impossible for the shepherd to explain to them why it is necessary.

Jesus, the Good Shepherd, also must take you through hard things that you, with your limited understanding, cannot figure out. However, if you take the time to get to know Jesus, you will have the certainty that He is the source of all good and all wisdom, and you'll want to follow Him anywhere. It's wonderful to follow Someone who knows in all cases what is best for you.

I am the good shepherd. The good shepherd lays down his life for the sheep. The hired hand is not the shepherd who owns the sheep. So when he sees the wolf coming, he abandons the sheep and runs away. Then the wolf attacks the flock and scatters it. The man runs away because he is a hired hand and cares nothing for the sheep. I am the good shepherd; I know my sheep and my sheep know me—just as the Father knows me and I know the Father—and I lay down my life for the sheep. John 10:11–15

Day 356
Are You a Rebekah?

Rebekah didn't like to wait. She and her husband, Isaac, had twin sons, Esau and Jacob. God had told her before the twins were born that Jacob, the younger son, would become greater and more important than his older brother, Esau. When it looked as if Isaac was going to give a special traditional blessing to Esau, Rebekah did not trust that God's promise would come true. She did not wait to see how the God who had made the universe would handle this apparent contradiction. She took things into her own hands. Rebekah tricked her husband by convincing Jacob to lie, so *he* could receive the blessing instead of Esau. The results were disastrous.

God has something very important to say about trusting Him when we don't see how things are going to turn out:

Who among you fears the Lord and obeys the word of his servant? Let him who walks in the dark, who has no light, trust in the name of the Lord and rely on his God. But now, all you who light fires and provide yourselves with flaming torches, go, walk in the light of your fires and of the torches you have set ablaze. This is what you shall receive from my hand: You will lie down in torment. Isaiah 50:10–11

We are always trying to light our paths with fires we start, but they rage out of control. You don't have to butter up the boss so that he'll give you the raise you need so badly. Just trust God. You don't have to drop your books in front of every member of the football team to try to land a date for Saturday night. God might just know what's best for your social life, so trust Him. You don't have to lie to your parents so you can go on the church retreat. God can even handle that situation. Trusting God takes the strain, pressure, and torment out of life.

Wait for the Lord; be strong and take heart and wait for the Lord. Psalm 27:14

Day 357

Walking on the Water

There's a book by John Ortberg called, *If You Want to Walk on Water, You've Got to Get Out of the Boat*. This title gets to the heart of a great spiritual truth: If we stay in safe territory all the time and never launch out in faith, we'll never experience all that God can do for us.

As a Christian teacher in a public school, I felt God wanted me to teach a lesson on true Christianity and the resurrection of Jesus. Since the unit was Roman history, I would not be breaking any law prohibiting religion in the classroom.

My fifth-hour class was filled with rowdy and sarcastic boys, not to mention the snotty girls. I was painfully aware of my inadequacies as a teacher, and my classroom control left something to be desired. Besides, if someone misunderstood, I could have gotten into problems with the administration. In spite of all this, I obeyed God.

When I started speaking, my voice was trembling and my hands were shaking. Yet immediately the students became quiet and listened intently. After class, I was shocked that I didn't receive any negative comments. I had just seen God work a miracle!

God doesn't always make it that easy once we start obeying Him, but as I've been told, "God doesn't give dying grace unless you're dying." He doesn't give us His miraculous power unless we are willing to put ourselves into a position where we need it. Do you intend to spend the rest of your life in the comfortable, boring boat, or do you plan to walk on the water?

> *"Lord, if it's you," Peter replied, "tell me to come to you on the water."* *"Come," he said. Then Peter got down out of the boat, walked on the water and came toward Jesus. But when he saw the wind, he was afraid and, beginning to sink, cried out, "Lord, save me!" Immediately Jesus reached out his hand and caught him. "You of little faith," he said, "why did you doubt?" And when they climbed into the boat, the wind died down. Then those who were in the boat worshiped him, saying, "Truly you are the Son of God."* Matthew 14:28–33

Day 358

Observing the "No Fishing" Sign

Dave had practically grown up in the church, and he'd heard a hundred Sunday school lessons entitled "Children, obey your parents." But when his parents said he could not go on a fishing trip with his buddies, Dave was determined to have his own way.

After all, wasn't God a pretty easygoing guy who would overlook Dave's breaking a few commandments? Weren't his parents too strict, and the people at church too concerned about *always* obeying God? Besides, he wasn't joining a motorcycle gang—he just wanted to go fishing!

So Dave concocted his scheme. With his parents' permission, he arranged to spend the weekend with Blake, a Christian friend. At school on Friday, Dave told Blake he couldn't come after all, and he sneaked off to go fishing with his friends.

How do you think the story ends?

(a) They get into a car accident and Dave tells his parents the truth from a hospital bed.

(b) Dave's best friend from Nevada comes for a visit, so Dave's parents call Blake's house.

(c) Dave gets by with lying and becomes a first-class hypocrite.

(d) Dave's parents are suspicious when he returns and aren't totally satisfied with his answers to their questions. They no longer assume that their son tells the truth, and that puts a lot of strain on their relationship.

When you face a similar temptation, remember that no lie has a good ending.

People with stubborn pride in their hearts cite biblical references to "prove" New Age doctrine, condone immorality, or consider their race superior—but mostly to justify the sin they wish to commit at the moment. If you're not *willing* to do God's will no matter what, then you will rationalize Scripture and imagine a God who doesn't mind if you break a few of His commandments. But if you submit to God's laws instead of using His words to justify what you want to do, you'll be able to say with the psalmist:

I run in the path of your commands, for you have set my heart free. Psalm 119:32

Day 359

Great Ideas—And Their Not-So-Great Results

The plant where Logan's father was supervisor was closing in two months, and he had to transfer or lose his retirement and all his benefits. When Logan registered at his new school, the counselor carefully looked at his school records. Because of his good grades and high test scores, she suggested he take "Great Ideas," an honors class for students whose grammar and writing skills were advanced.

Every book Logan read for "Great Ideas" contradicted what he believed. The teacher and his fellow class members brought up questions he'd never considered. How could he be positive that *everything* in the Bible was true? Was Jesus the *only* way to God? How could he *prove* God existed?

Instead of studying the Bible more and letting God give him answers, Logan decided to delve into every philosophy on his teacher's recommended-reading list. He made friends with some of the guys in his class and soon began to think a lot more like they did. In doing so, he defied the advice of the wisest guy to ever live:

> *My son, keep my words and store up my commands within you. Keep my commands and you will live; guard my teachings as the apple of your eye.*
> Proverbs 7:1–2

What should you do when you're surrounded by philosophies contrary to the Bible? You must constantly read, study, memorize, and meditate on God's Word or you won't be able to stand up against the bombardment of falsehood and error from media, textbooks, and casual conversation.

If doubts creep in, *don't panic*. The enemies of Christianity have been trying to destroy it for twenty centuries. Even if some new discovery seems to threaten your faith, remember that "science is a train that is always moving." Some of the things that were "scientific facts" a hundred years ago seem ridiculous today. Wait until all the evidence is in.

God's Word has always stood the test of time, and it always will. Jesus said it best: "Heaven and earth will pass away, but my words will never pass away" (Matthew 24:35).

Troy was the kind of guy Cherie had always dreamed of dating—intelligent, witty, handsome, always thoughtful, and sensitive. When she heard him drive up, her heart skipped a beat. After a couple minutes of casual conversation, Cherie asked, "How was the meeting you attended last night?"

Excitement danced in his eyes as he explained the Spirit/Mind Control seminar at the local community center. "I learned how to be controlled totally by the spirit. They taught me how to blank out my own thoughts, will, and emotions so that everything that passed through my mind would be from God. I never thought 'walking in the spirit' could be so easy."

"Wait a minute," Cherie interrupted. "The devil could also put thoughts into your mind. We need to check this out with the Word of God."

"Don't you trust my judgment?"

"We just have to be careful. A lot of cults can look pretty good at first."

"Well, next Thursday night I'm going again," Troy said firmly. "If you'd like to come, fine. I'm going anyway."

Something inside told Cherie that this new group was dangerous for her spiritual health.

Any group that claims to understand everything is dangerous. God is greater than we are, and certain things will always be a mystery. Deuteronomy 29:29 tells us:

> The secret things belong to the Lord our God, but the things revealed belong to us and to our children forever, that we may follow all the words of this law.

God in His knowledge has shown us the things we really need to know. Other things remain mysteries, perhaps so we will have to trust Him more. He gave us His written Word and commanded us to search the Scriptures for wisdom. Whenever anyone offers teaching that bypasses the serious study of the Bible, something is drastically wrong. It is *not* true that if your motives are pure, you'll never be deceived. Many people are sincerely wrong. Only the truth found in God's Word can guard us from error. The Bible tells us to review God's Word, constantly studying, understanding, and obeying it.

> *These commandments that I give you today are to be upon your hearts. Impress them on your children. Talk about them when you sit at home and when you walk along the road, when you lie down and when you get up. Tie them as symbols on your hands and bind them on your foreheads. Write them on the doorframes of your houses and on your gates.* Deuteronomy 6:6–9

"This exercise," explained Miss Kinoshita, Carrie's social studies teacher, "is designed to help you discover your own value system. Shakespeare said it hundreds of years ago: 'To thine own self be true.' Most of you have been squeezed into molds by your parents, your churches, and society at large. But *you* are important. You're the captain of your own soul. You have the ability to make your own decisions about what's right and wrong.

"For example, my parents taught me never to lie. But I can think of several situations in which lying would be the kindest and most humane thing to do. Some say that robbing is always bad, but stealing food makes a lot more sense than starving to death. People have such diverse personalities and needs that what's correct for one person might not suit the needs of another."

Carrie had never thought of things that way before. She'd always believed that some things were right and some things were wrong—*period.* But her teacher's philosophy did seem logical. Maybe it was true that she was the only one who could decide what was right for her. Carrie didn't realize that she was falling into a trap.

Don't equate your value with the "right" to decide what sin is "for you." You weren't created to decide right and wrong any more than you were created to fly. That in no way reflects on your worthwhile personality, your unique talents, or your intelligence. God built right and wrong into the universe, and you can't ignore that without paying the consequences.

If you want any machine or gadget to work well, you follow the manufacturer's instructions. The designer who made it knows what it can do and how it will work best. In the same way, your Creator knows how you will be happiest and most fulfilled. The Bible is full of promises for those who live by His rules.

All these blessings will come upon you and accompany you if you obey the Lord your God. Deuteronomy 28:2

"I don't want your girl in the house." LaTonya woke to hear her stepmother arguing with her father. "Send her to your mother. Now that we have our own baby, I don't want him to have to compete with his half sister for your attention."

"It's me *and* my daughter, or we're through," her father protested.

LaTonya's stepmother never mentioned the topic again, but when her father wasn't around, she took out her bitterness on LaTonya.

LaTonya began dating Tom, a much older man, even when her father forbade her to see him. LaTonya's friends warned her that Tom was bad news, but Tom treated LaTonya respectfully. For Valentine's Day, Tom gave LaTonya a dress. After their dinner, Tom reached into the glove compartment, took several small bags out, and laid them on her lap. "LaTonya," he said firmly, "your dress has secret pockets in the lining. Put these bags in the pockets and hide them in your room until I need them."

"What's in the bags?" LaTonya asked.

"Cocaine," answered Tom.

A fool finds no pleasure in understanding but delights in airing his own opinions. Proverbs 18:2

He who trusts in himself is a fool, but he who walks in wisdom is kept safe. Proverbs 28:26

A fool is so stubborn that he or she won't change, necessitating an elaborate self-defense system. A fool likes his or her ideas so much that he or she would rather repeat them over and over than hear anything new or wise. The parents of the fool suffer not only the disappointment of seeing a child make a bad decision, but the constant agony of watching a person who will not change repeat the same errors over and over.

The cure for refusing to change your mind is this: Line up your thoughts with God's, and you'll receive so much security from the fact that God loves you unconditionally that admitting you're wrong is no longer threatening. Whenever you don't agree with God, you're wrong. And He often uses other people to point out your faults.

Jed went on a weekend camping trip with a group of guys. On Saturday morning, everyone except Jed got up at 5:00 a.m. to go fishing. When Brandon tried to rouse him, he heard a grouchy, "This is vacation, man. And on vacation I sleep in."

By seven-thirty Jed could smell the frying fish, so he dressed for breakfast. When they passed the plate, he took the two biggest pieces and later took a generous helping of blueberries. Sleeping in the great outdoors really gave him an appetite!

Dan asked Jed to gather firewood. The trees in their autumn colors were spectacular, so Jed went exploring instead. On the way back he picked up a few dry sticks.

"Jed," Dan moaned, "what you've brought will keep the fire going for a full two minutes."

Later, the group decided to explore the caves by the lake. Jed decided to take a long afternoon nap. He woke up when he heard supper sizzling over the fire. Once again he helped himself to the biggest serving—and then dug into dessert. He kicked at the fire the others had stoked, stirring up sparks. When a spark caught in a patch of grass, Jed laughed while the others jumped to stomp out the flame.

Dan was struggling to control his anger. "You're too lazy to get up early in the morning, too lazy to gather firewood, and too lazy to help cook supper. You can't even get up when we might all burn to death!"

As vinegar to the teeth and smoke to the eyes, so is a sluggard to those who send him. Proverbs 10:26

The sluggard's craving will be the death of him, because his hands refuse to work. All day long he craves for more, but the righteous give without sparing. Proverbs 21:25–26

Laziness does not go the extra mile or give itself fully to the work of the Lord. If the habits of laziness are deeply enough ingrained, even a life-and-death situation won't change them.

Day 364

Better Than Cash and Comfort

It was Christmastime when Dionne met Dylan. He sold packaged chocolate candy to his friends to give as Christmas presents. Sales were great—until Vann opened the candy he bought and tasted it. Thanks to Vann's big mouth, it wasn't long before the whole school had heard that it was the worst chocolate ever and demanded their money back.

Dylan was mad at Vann and didn't try to hide his feelings. "If I were you," Dionne replied, "I'd be glad Vann ate the chocolates. I certainly wouldn't want to be responsible for disappointing so many people."

"Vann made me lose out on hundreds of dollars!" Dylan retorted.

When Dylan brought Dionne to visit his grandmother, Dylan mentioned, "It sure would be cool to have the new PlayStation."

On the way home, Dionne commented, "You sure sounded as if you were hinting to your grandmother for an expensive Christmas present."

"She's getting older and she needs a little guidance. I'd hate to get something I couldn't use," Dylan replied.

Dionne took a deep breath. "I sponsor a child in the Philippines. It's only twenty dollars a month. Wouldn't you like to do something like that?"

"I can't afford it," Dylan snapped.

Dionne didn't say anything, but she knew she wouldn't accept another date with someone as greedy as Dylan.

A greedy man stirs up dissension, but he who trusts in the Lord will prosper.
Proverbs 28:25

A stingy man is eager to get rich and is unaware that poverty awaits him.
Proverbs 28:22

Greed is like a fatal disease—more and more negative symptoms start to manifest themselves. David prayed for the only solution to greed and other nasty sins:

Create in me a pure heart, O God, and renew a steadfast spirit within me.
Psalm 51:10

Once your life is transformed by Jesus, He'll give you the power to break free from sinful patterns in order to follow Him. Don't repeat the story of the rich young man who was so tied to his cash and comfort that he couldn't part with it to serve Jesus. The words of Matthew 6:21—"where your treasure is, there your heart will be also"—suggest a great way to cure greed and selfishness. Winning the world for Christ is much more exciting than watching your bank account or quantity of possessions grow.

In Hillary's family, getting even was a game everybody played.

When her father lost a substantial amount of money playing poker, for instance, her mother went out and bought a lot of expensive clothes and charged them on his credit card. When Hillary borrowed her brother's car without asking and had an accident, he told her boyfriend that she was secretly dating another guy, and her boyfriend broke up with her. Hillary got so angry that she "accidentally" broke his CD player.

One night Hillary's parents entertained special company. She volunteered to clear the table, clean up the kitchen, and load the dishwasher. Without thinking, she put an antique porcelain plate made in 1869 in with the others. During the wash cycle, it broke into little pieces. Besides a fifteen-minute volcanic verbal explosion, Hillary's mother grounded her daughter for every Friday and Saturday night until the end of the semester. Hillary was furious. She hadn't done anything wrong on purpose.

Without thinking twice, Hillary drove over to her grandmother's house in tears. Explaining how unjust her mother's punishment was, she expected her grandmother to take her side.

But it backfired. Her grandmother flew into a rage. "*Just* a broken plate!" she screamed. "That plate was the only family heirloom we had from the old country. It was the only valuable thing I brought with me when I came to America. How could you be so thoughtless?" Hillary learned a lesson that day.

If a man digs a pit, he will fall into it; if a man rolls a stone, it will roll back on him. Proverbs 26:27

How do you handle injustice? When you've been wronged, the temptation to get even is strong. When you're unfairly treated, ask God to take up your case—and follow His command to love those who persecute you. Romans 12:19 is a strategy that has passed the test of centuries:

Do not take revenge, my friends, but leave room for God's wrath, for it is written: "It is mine to avenge; I will repay," says the Lord.